INSIDE OUT

INSIDE OUT

An Insider's Account of Wall Street

Dennis B. Levine

with William Hoffer

G. P. PUTNAM'S SONS
New York

G. P. Putnam's Sons
Publishers Since 1838
200 Madison Avenue
New York, NY 10016

Library of Congress Cataloging-in-Publication Data

Levine, Dennis B., date.
Inside out : an insider's account of Wall Street / Dennis B. Levine,
with William Hoffer
p.   cm.
Includes index.
ISBN 0-399-13655-X (alk. paper)
1. Levine, Dennis, date.   2. Insider trading of securities—
United States.   3. Investment banking—United States—Corrupt
practices.   I. Hoffer, William.   II. Title.
HG2463.L48A3   1991
364.1'68—dc20   91-3149 CIP
[B]

All photographs not otherwise credited are from Dennis B. Levine's
personal collection.
Printed in the United States of America
1 2 3 4 5 6 7 8 9 10

This book is printed on acid-free paper.
∞

This book is dedicated to:
Laurie
Adam
&
Sarah

This is a true story. The characters are authentic, the events real. Quotations have been re-created either from documented material or as accurately as long-term memory allows.

ACKNOWLEDGMENTS

I WISH TO THANK my wife, Laurie, for her support and devotion throughout our life together, especially during the last five difficult and uncertain years.

A special thanks to my children, Adam and Sarah, for their understanding and patience while I labored on this project for countless evenings and weekends which should have been spent with them.

I am blessed to have as my attorneys Arthur Liman, Martin Flumenbaum, Brad Karp and their colleagues at Paul, Weiss, Rifkind, Wharton & Garrison, whose continuing counsel and guidance have enabled me and my family to reassemble the pieces of our lives.

Numerous persons have contributed unselfishly to the production of this book, and several must be singled out for special mention. Thanks to:

Marilyn Hoffer, who was totally involved in every phase of the composition. Her sensitivity was appreciated.

Our agents, Robert Gottlieb and Mel Berger of the William Morris Agency, Inc., our publisher, Phyllis Grann, and our editor, George Coleman. Their professional advice was invaluable; their encouragement was essential.

My trusted and faithful friends, Irwin Kruger, Allan Miller and Stuart Sugarman, all of whom were there when I needed them.

The thousands of students and executives in my lecture audiences throughout the country, who inspired me, after years of reluctance, to write this book. I hope their questions are answered.

Finally, I wish to pay special tribute to my father and late mother for teaching me to believe in myself and overcome adversity.

—Dennis B. Levine
New York City
June 1991

AUTHOR'S NOTE

MUCH HAS BEEN WRITTEN about me in the past few years, but because I systematically declined TV interviews and refused to speak with journalists, the stories were necessarily pieced together with second- and third-hand information. The results were at best incomplete and often erroneous.

Now it is time for me to tell the story the way it really happened.

CONTENTS

13

PART ONE
PANIC ON PARK AVENUE

CHAPTER ONE

I WOKE WITH NUMBERS in my head, a one followed by seven zeros. That was ten million.

More precisely, it was ten million six hundred thousand.

As in *dollars.*

The nagging question was: Where was it?

If it had been transferred according to my instructions it was safely lodged in my new account at Morgan Grenfell Ltd., in the Cayman Islands, and everything was all right.

But if it was still at Bank Leu International Ltd., in Nassau, there was trouble ahead.

Laurie, waking slowly at my side, fought off a bout of morning sickness; we had just learned that she was pregnant with our second child. She knew nothing about the secret hoard, and thus could not realize my turmoil. Money was not a worry to Laurie. Long ago I had proclaimed to her, with youthful exuberance, that I would be a millionaire before I was thirty, and she had believed me. I had achieved that goal with room to spare, and if I had told her about the secret $10.6 million that preoccupied my thoughts this morning, she would have asked—after expressing her initial shock at learning of its existence— "Why in the world do we need it?"

I would have had no coherent answer.

Sometimes, in those scarce moments when I allowed myself time to reflect, it all sent me reeling. When I started in the business world in 1977, I earned $19,000 a year. Now, a mere, magical nine years later, as a managing director of the investment banking house of Drexel Burnham Lambert, my annual salary, bonus and investment income had skyrocketed to more than $2 million. Laurie and I had more than $1 million socked away in legitimate investments. We lived in a beautiful, freshly refurbished Park Avenue co-op. Parked in the garage nearby was a 1983 BMW 633CSI and a 1985 fire-engine red Ferrari Testarossa, my fantasy embodied in steel, so fresh that it still had only about 3,000 miles on it.

I had worked my way into a position of power within the firm now universally acknowledged as the hottest player in the most volatile game on Wall Street, the specialty known as mergers and acquisitions, or M&A, for short. Drexel was more than an investment banking house; it was an iconoclastic cult that attracted and held employees with an incredible sense of esprit de corps. Drexel people relished catchy slogans, and one of them was "one hundred percent market share." We wanted it all and, in the current milieu, that goal seemed altogether reasonable.

Working from his Beverly Hills office, super-financier Michael Milken had made Drexel famous for its ability to raise astonishing sums through the technique of issuing high-risk, high-interest financial instruments. Those who were jealous of Milken and Drexel referred to these derisively as "junk bonds," but those who were interested in becoming major players in the M&A field called them "high-yield securities" and lined up at Milken's door to join the network that bought and sold the bonds, passing billions of dollars back and forth.

Here in New York, I had moved into the role of one of Drexel's key dealmakers. I was one of the privileged few who put together the transactions that Milken financed. Only last month, I had been a featured speaker at Drexel's annual Bond Conference (aka the "Predators' Ball") in Beverly Hills.

Beyond all this, I was considering a new job offer, a sweetheart of a proposition from Wall Street's most famous risk arbitrageur (from the French word *arbitrer,* "to judge"), Ivan Boesky. Boesky's specialty was trading in the stocks of companies involved in takeover situations, playing the odds that the values of those companies would jump dramatically.

Boesky was acknowledged to be the best "arb" in the business, but he longed to take the next step up and become a corporate raider and bask in the public glory now enjoyed by Drexel's largest clients, men such as Carl Icahn, T. Boone Pickens and Ronald Perelman. To do that, he needed help, and he was determined to lure me away from Drexel. He had offered me a $5 million premium just for coming on board. On top of that he promised what he called a "seven-figure" salary, plus bonuses, that would bring my total annual income to more than $5 million. And on top of *that* he offered me a $20 million ownership position in a new company.

We had a phenomenal enterprise going on Wall Street, and it was easy to forget that the billions of dollars we threw around had a material impact upon the jobs and, thus, the daily lives of millions of Americans. All too often the Street seemed to be a giant Monopoly board, and this game-like attitude was clearly evident in our terminology. When a company was identified as an acquisition target we declared that it was "in play." We designated the playing pieces and strategies in whimsical terms: white knight, target, shark repellent, the Pac-Man defense, poison pill, greenmail, the golden parachute. Keeping a scorecard was easy—the winner was the one who finalized the most deals and took home the most money.

The principle players, men and women just like me, were the young superstars of the financial world. We were perhaps, a less patrician breed than Wall Street had ever seen before, but we were no less enthused and awed by the task of making money. It was the pace of our lives that differentiated us from the legendary dealmakers of the past. Ours was a Space Age world that brooked no waiting. We were young men and women in a hurry, because we had to be. If you did not rush to grab a deal, your competitor would take it from you. If you did not engineer a string of transactions that grew ever larger and showier, others would eclipse you. There was no time to think about all this; there was only time to do it. The sense of urgency, of lemmings plunging toward the sea, was epitomized by the frantic war cry of Drexel's chairman, Fred Joseph: "Ready, Fire, Aim!" Every waking moment, and many a sleeping hour, was devoted to *the deal.*

Thus, it was not unusual for me to awaken with money on my mind.

If I had been able, at the moment, to ponder the issue dispassionately, I would have realized that it was true: We did not need the money in my secret bank account.

But making money was my passion, more than ever, and the $10.6

million represented, not so much buying power, but points on the scoreboard. If it had arrived in the Cayman Islands, I was a winner. If it was still in Nassau, I was a loser.

That, in my naïveté, seemed to be the key issue.

Laurie and I were more in love than ever. Our son was the joy of our lives, and we had a new baby on the way. That was all I needed, but I was not yet sophisticated enough to realize such a basic truth. Only on this day, Monday, May 12, 1986, in the thirty-third year of this crazy life, would I begin to learn.

SUNLIGHT was beginning to filter in through the windows when I finished dressing in my basic investment banker's uniform: a navy blue suit, a white shirt and a yellow tie. I slipped into a pair of shiny black loafers. I kissed Laurie good-bye and patted her tummy. "I'll be home early," I said, and Laurie nodded. A "function" was on for the evening, a black-tie charity dinner at the Waldorf-Astoria for the benefit of Mount Sinai Hospital. It was the sort of gala where it was important to see and be seen. Although it was not the type of occasion that Laurie often relished, she was looking forward to this one. For the first time in her life she had gone to Givenchy's on Madison Avenue and ordered a beautiful evening gown with a long black bottom and a shimmering gold top. I knew she would look stunning in it.

I traded a few mock blows with our four-year-old son, Adam, then headed out the door and off to the job that consumed me.

A car and driver awaited me, provided by my employer. It was an acknowledged fact that those of us who had reached the high echelons of power at Drexel were far too busy to drive ourselves to and from work.

As the car headed down Park Avenue, I studied *The Wall Street Journal,* but the text blurred in front of my eyes. Where's the money? I wondered. Where's the money?

I arrived at the office at eight A.M. Before I could settle my mind for the upcoming meeting with my staff, I had to answer the burning question. Normally I shied away from using the office phones for clandestine calls, but the moment was too intense, the issue too extraordinary, for normalcy. I found an out-of-the-way telephone in the conference room—one that could not be traced directly to me—and called Bank Leu in Nassau.

It was early, but I reached a young bank executive named Andrew Sweeting, who knew me only by my code name. "Mr. Sweeting," I said, "this is Mr. Wheat. I'm calling to confirm the transfer of my money."

There was silence for a few moments. Where's the money? I asked myself in agony. Where's the money?

Sweeting announced, "Mr. Wheat, everything is taken care of pursuant to the instructions from your attorneys."

"The wire transfer has been made?"

"Everything is being taken care of, sir."

I hung up the phone and whistled a victory tune. The money was safe and so, I believed, was I.

I WAS in a bubbly mood when I met with my staff to review the day's agenda, which centered around a morning meeting at the Manhattan town house of Ronald Perelman. Only a few months ago I had been a driving force behind the deal that made Perelman famous, that transformed him from a somewhat obscure entrepreneur to the corporate raider who had wrested control of the giant cosmetics conglomerate, Revlon.

Perelman was already in the process of tightening his control on the Revlon ship. Under its former management, Revlon had gradually shifted its attention away from its traditional cosmetics business toward new subsidiaries that ran far afield. Perelman had seen the chance to use the value of these subsidiaries to pay for the cosmetics company. Already he had sold off two of the sideline businesses, recouping more than half of the money he had paid for the entire firm. Yet he still had the major prize in hand, as well as several other subsidiaries. His task now was to revitalize Revlon's flagging cosmetics business. He had chosen Susan Lucci, the star of "All My Children," to replace Joan Collins of "Dynasty" as the spokeswoman for Scoundrel perfume. He hired photographer Richard Avedon to upgrade Revlon's magazine ads.

He was also ready to consider an encore. This morning, we would discuss two possible deals. One was the multi-billion-dollar acquisition of a major consumer products company; the other was the buyout of a major entertainment corporation.

Something of note happened at that meeting. Perelman listened intently as I addressed my attention to the larger target, the consumer products company. After studying the projections carefully, on paper and in my head, I had come to believe that the risk level in the deal was too great. I showed Perelman the spread sheets that my staff had assembled. Sure, he could probably pull off the takeover, but the target company had plenty of resources and tough management; it would defend itself with vigor, meaning that the final price was likely to be stiff. Beyond that, there were complex regulatory issues involved that could add delays and legal costs. I pointed out to Perelman that he could probably afford the deal in the context of the present economy, but what if everything slowed? I argued that this was not a recession-proof buyout. If the cash flow stalled, the company might spin down the drain, sucking Perelman along with it.

It is always easy to say, "Let's do the deal." Wall Street lives on deals. Without a deal, you don't have anything. But it is incumbent upon an adviser to look at the whole picture, and when the circumstances demand it, say, as I did now to Perelman, "Don't do it. Just don't do it."

Perelman is a good listener, and unlike many corporate raiders, is not in the business of making critical decisions on an emotional basis. In terms of savvy, he is up there with the best of them, as evidenced by the fact that the Revlon deal vaulted him to the upper reaches of the *Forbes* 400 list of wealthiest Americans (as of this writing, he is third). He puffed on his cigar and stared at the smoke for a moment, watching it curl toward the ceiling. Then he announced that he agreed with my assessment. If I did not think that the deal was safe over the long term, he was not interested.

This was the sort of non-deal that generates no commissions and no publicity, but builds trust and respect. Amid the dealmaking insanity that raged on the Street, we had to maintain *some* perspective.

WHEN I returned to the office shortly after eleven A.M., my secretary, Marilyn Stewart, announced, "There were two gentlemen here looking for you."

"Yes?"

"They didn't look like clients."

Process servers again, I thought. It was routine for Drexel partners and associates to be ordered to give depositions regarding shareholders' suits; it was just as routine for us to try to avoid subpoenas. "Let me know if they return," I said.

On my desk was a message slip, noting that Ivan Boesky had called. Obviously he wanted to see if I had made a decision on his job offer. I called him back, but he was out.

Fifteen minutes passed. I was busy preparing for a meeting with Marty Davis, CEO of Gulf+Western, when Marilyn buzzed on the intercom and said, "The two gentlemen who were here earlier are back to see you."

"Tell them I'm not here. Refer them to Legal and Compliance." I thought, I don't have time to play around with these guys.

"Okay," Marilyn said. Then she added, "Oh, by the way, they're from the Department of Justice."

The Justice Department? Not the SEC? I saw my fist pound involuntarily upon my desk. For an instant it seemed as if my body ceased to concern itself with such mundane activities as breathing and blood circulation. My stomach cramped.

I've got to get the hell out of here, I said to myself. But somehow I found the composure to say to Marilyn, "No problem, I'll take care of this."

Grabbing my briefcase, I slipped out of my office from a side exit and edged toward the reception area to get a good look at these men. One of them was huge, perhaps 6'9" tall, with shoulders that seemed to span the width of the room. His partner was of average height, but the giant's commanding presence made the pair appear like Mutt and Jeff. They were incredibly out of place, their baggy, off-the-rack suits glaring in contrast to the tailored pin-stripes of the men who whirled about them.

Think, Dennis, I commanded myself. Do something. I ducked into the back stairwell. Holding my wire-rimmed glasses in place with one hand, I scurried down two flights of stairs to the sixth floor, scrambled into the hallway and punched the "down" button on the elevator. Nothing happened. No light illuminated. The elevators were not working, due to a fire alarm, but I was too upset to realize that. Paranoia grabbed hold of me. Instantly I conjectured that the feds had sealed off the building and probably had it surrounded. I was trapped!

I needed time to think. Get out of here, Dennis, I told myself. Call in. Get the facts. Assess the situation. Preserve your options. Get help.

I headed back down the staircase, the echo of my footsteps now competing for attention with the thud of my heartbeat. My mouth felt incredibly dry. My stomach burned. My muddled brain tried to formulate a plan. I knew that I could not exit the stairwell on the first floor, or I would trip the fire alarm.

When I reached the second floor, I decided that I had no choice but to try the elevator again. Emerging from the stairwell into the lobby of the Operations Department, I bumped into one of the women who worked there, nearly knocking her down.

"Mr. Levine, what are you doing here with the little people?" she asked good-naturedly.

I mumbled something about the elevators being out of order. But I jabbed at the button and, to my relief, it illuminated.

On the brief ride to the ground floor I donned sunglasses, the only disguise available to me at the moment. When the door opened, I glanced toward the front exit on my left. I saw nothing untoward, but I headed to my right, to the service exit.

Suddenly I was out on the street. I hailed a taxi and commanded, "Ninety-third Street and Park Avenue."

My mind now weaved in and out of a traffic jam of ideas with greater skill than the cabby. What is going on? I asked myself. It has to have something to do with the Bank Leu investigation. But what could it be? All the SEC had was a trail of suspicions. The feds were on a paper chase. I could only be one of hundreds of suspects who were privy to the inside information upon which the Swiss bankers had traded. At worst, I conjectured, the Justice Department men only wanted to question me.

But if that was the worst, why did they come looking for me at the office? The Justice Department never got involved in SEC investigations. The SEC concerned itself with civil violations. The Justice Department was a *criminal* unit!

The conclusion was inevitable: The worst-case scenario was worse than I thought.

CHAPTER TWO

LAURIE'S MORNING HAD BEEN comfortably routine. She had confirmed arrangements with the baby-sitter for this evening. Then she had tried on her Givenchy gown, thankful that she had told the saleswoman that she wanted something that was not too tight across her newly pregnant stomach. It fit comfortably and Laurie, pleased that she did not feel fat, could not wait to model it for me. After an early lunch, she had pampered herself with a nap.

Now she awoke to find me standing over her. It was only noon. I was *never* home during the day. She had known me since I was twenty years old, and I had always appeared to be in control. Until now. Her face paled.

"What's the matter?" she asked, visibly trying to shake the sleep from her head.

"I might be in a lot of trouble," I stammered. "I don't know. But if anybody comes here to see me, or calls for me, you don't know anything. You haven't seen me. Say nothing to anybody."

"Dennis, what are you talking about?" Her face registered total confusion. It was inconceivable to her that I had done anything wrong. She reached out toward me in a gesture that was both questioning and compassionate, but I squirmed away. "What's happening?" she asked. "What's wrong?"

"I can't tell you about it now," I said. "I have to get the car." My thoughts were jumbled, my words incoherent. I raced toward my desk and as Laurie followed, I issued directions. "Call for the car," I said. "No, I'm going to get it. Tell them . . . no, call for the car." I wanted the BMW because it had a cellular phone, and because it was far less conspicuous than the Ferrari.

I began stuffing papers into a large manila envelope. The more Laurie begged for an explanation, the more adamant I became. "I can't discuss it now," I said. "It would take too long. Just do as I ask, please!"

She called the garage. Then she asked, "Where are you going?"

"To Dad's. Just wait for me to call."

The car almost guided itself toward the FDR Drive, then north toward the Triborough Bridge and Queens, toward Dad's house, an instinctive haven.

I forced my mind to concentrate upon damage control. My family, my friends, my entire world would now learn about the double life I had led for these few, frantic years. What could I do? There was no time for self-pity or moralizing; that would come later. Now, somehow, I had to minimize the effects upon those I loved.

From the car I called my brother at his office. "Robert," I said, "I want you to meet me at Dad's house. I'm in serious trouble. I don't know what is going on yet, but we have to talk. Get hold of Daddy. He's probably playing racquetball."

"I'll be there before you," Robert pledged. He asked no questions. I was his brother and I was in trouble, and that was all he needed to know at the moment.

I called the office of Laurie's obstetrician, Dr. Joseph Finklestein, and badgered the nurse into putting the doctor on the line. I asked if a severe emotional trauma might jeopardize Laurie's pregnancy. The doctor said he did not think so. Laurie's first pregnancy had run a normal course. She was a strong, healthy woman, and he believed that even a severe stress would cause no overt problems. That calmed my worst fears.

Then I called my office. I could tell that Marilyn was crying as she asked, "Have you seen the Dow Jones tape?"

"No," I answered, "I really don't know what is happening."

Marilyn tried to tell me, but the words would not come. In frustration, she transferred my call to my old friend David Kay, head of Drexel's M&A Department. He asked, with genuine concern in his voice, "How are you?"

"I'm trying to find out what's going on here."

"Dennis, I don't think I should talk to you too much, but I can tell you that the SEC is after you. If I were you, I would get a lawyer quickly."

I heartily agreed.

Kay switched me to Cathy, a new arrival at Drexel, having come over from Kidder Peabody with Marty Siegel. I had given her my old job of Breaking News Coordinator. Part of that task was to monitor the heartbeat of Wall Street, the Dow Jones news ticker.

"Hi, Dennis," she said.

"I understand there is something on the tape regarding me," I said. "Marilyn is too choked up to read it. Could you please read it to me?"

Cathy intoned:

The SEC charged Dennis Levine, a managing director of Drexel Burnham Lambert, Inc., with insider trading in connection with an alleged scheme to buy and sell securities based on non-public information gained through his employment as an investment banker for a period of five years.

Drexel Burnham said it will "cooperate fully with the SEC" in the investigation.

"The SEC allegation, if true, would be a most serious breach of Drexel Burnham Lambert's standards," Drexel said. The company said this is the first such allegation made against a Drexel employee in its fifty-one-year history. The SEC's allegation covers the period of 1980 to the present. Levine joined Drexel in 1985.

The Commission charged that Levine did the illegal trading over a five-and-a-half-year period during which he worked for a total of four major Wall Street firms, none of which were named in the suit. In addition to Drexel Burnham, Levine worked for Shearson Lehman Brothers, Inc., a Shearson predecessor, Lehman Brothers Kuhn Loeb, Inc., and Smith Barney, Harris Upham & Co.

The Commission said it obtained a temporary restraining order and an order freezing Levine's assets in Federal District Court in New York . . .

The SEC alleges that Levine used non-public inside information to trade in the securities of "at least fifty-four companies since May 1980." The SEC also charged Levine's Bahamian broker, Bernhard Meier, in the insider-trading scheme. Also listed as defendants are two Panamanian companies allegedly controlled by Levine—International Gold Inc. and Diamond Holdings S.A.

The District Court ordered that a hearing on the SEC's request for a preliminary injunction be held May 22, the SEC said.

Investment bankers said the charges against Levine are potentially damaging to Drexel's reputation because the firm has been in the forefront of the merger and acquisition boom of the 1980s.

A source close to the SEC said that the agency also expects to file soon another major insider trading case.

Levine is widely known and well-liked in the closely knit fraternity of Wall Street lawyers and investment bankers who dominate the takeover business. Many said they were stunned by the SEC charges against him.

As he had promised, Robert was waiting for me when I reached Dad's home, but he had been unable to track down our father. I answered the questions in his eyes just as I had to Laurie. "I have no idea what is going on yet," I said. "I know I'm in very serious trouble. The government is after me for something. I don't want to tell you more."

From my father's house, I called Arthur Fleischer, Jr., the senior partner in the New York law office of Fried, Frank, Harris, Shriver & Jacobson. Fleischer was the firm's merger specialist; I had worked alongside him on many a deal and, only a few months ago, participated with him at an SEC roundtable discussion in Washington. I knew that Harvey Pitt of Fried, Frank's Washington, D.C., office, was representing Bank Leu, as a result of my referral. I wanted to see if the same law firm could take my case, or whether that would place it in an adversary position with Bank Leu. Fleischer was not available at the moment, so I spoke with another partner, Steve Fraidin. Only days earlier, Fraidin had initiated the job offer to me from his client Ivan Boesky.

"Dennis, I'm aware of what's going on," he said. "What can I do for you?"

"Steve, I need a lawyer. I'd like to hire Fried, Frank to represent me."

"Let me see if we have a conflict," he said. "If we don't, I'm sure we'd look forward to working with you."

"Okay, I'll hold."

Minutes passed before he returned to the phone to report, "Dennis, we have a very serious conflict. We can't represent you."

So there it was. Somehow, the SEC had cajoled or threatened or bludgeoned Bank Leu officials into giving me up. Somehow, the U.S. government had managed to circumvent the heretofore airtight Bahamian bank secrecy laws. This, and nothing else, was the logical conclusion.

Fraidin said, "I just want you to know I'm still your friend. I'd like to do whatever I can. I want to wish you the best of luck."

"Thank you, Steve. I appreciate it."

Next I called Joe Flom of Skadden, Arps, Slate, Meagher & Flom. He was an ally in numerous transactions, including Revlon. When I asked if he could help me, Flom replied, "That's not what we do. You need Arthur Liman."

I knew him also; this was an exclusive fraternity. Liman and I had labored together the previous year on Carl Icahn's successful proxy fight against Phillips Petroleum and, more recently, on Sam Heyman's attempted acquisition of Union Carbide. I had a great deal of respect for Liman; in my judgment, he was technically without peer as a securities attorney, and I knew that he had also achieved national renown as a trial lawyer.

Liman, a fifty-three-year-old senior partner of Paul, Weiss, Rifkind, Wharton & Garrison, had headed Governor Rockefeller's commission to investigate the Attica prison riot of 1971 as well as Mayor Koch's investigation of allegations against the city's medical examiner, Elliot Gross. His list of former clients included John Zaccaro, the real estate developer and husband of former vice presidential candidate Geraldine Ferraro; Steven J. Ross, chairman of Warner Communications; and fugitive financier Robert L. Vesco. "I have a call into him," Flom said. "We'll call you back."

The moments ticked away. I had to do something, but what? With shaking fingers I dialed my home number and asked, "Laurie, has anything happened?"

"Two people from the Justice Department were here looking for you," she reported.

Life had exploded upon her, yet she still had to take care of business. She told me that, after I ran off, she had consoled herself with the knowledge that I had always handled crises successfully in the past; surely I would take care of this, whatever it was.

Some time later, as she readied herself to pick up Adam at nursery school, the intercom buzzed. "Mrs. Levine," the receptionist said, "two men from the government are here to see your husband."

"Well, he's not here," Laurie replied. Despite the events of the past half hour, she could think of no possible reason why federal agents were looking for me. Suddenly an explanation dawned. "Wait a minute," she said. "There are two other Levines in the building. They must have us mixed up with someone else."

Within five minutes she was ready to leave. The doorbell rang just as she prepared to scurry out. She opened the door and found herself face-to-face with two serious-looking men.

"Are you Mrs. Dennis Levine?" one of them asked.

"Yes."

"Is your husband at home?"

"No," she said. "What is this all about?"

The reply was a curt and uninformative, "Obstruction of justice."

"Could you be more specific?"

"No. Is he here?"

It made no sense. Laurie asked to see the men's credentials and was satisfied that they were legitimate. But why would federal agents be looking for her husband? She gazed up at one of the men and was so taken aback by his size that she stammered, "How tall are you?"

"Six-foot-nine," he answered, his tone indicating that he was accustomed to the question.

Laurie repeated that I was not home and suggested that the men try to reach me at the office. "My son is expecting me at nursery school," she said. "I've really got to go."

"When will you be back?" one of the men asked.

"About an hour."

"Does it always take an hour to pick up a child at nursery school?"

These men are grilling me! Laurie realized. She replied, "Well, I do a little shopping." The men waited for her to continue, so she said, "If I speak to my husband, I'll tell him you were here. Just try reaching him at the office. That's where he should be. Maybe he's in a meeting. His secretary might be able to give you more information. Look, I've got to go now. My son is expecting me."

The agents left. Laurie shut the door behind them and took several deep breaths in an attempt to stop her body from shaking. Adam! she thought. I've got to get Adam.

She rushed downstairs and outside to Park Avenue, where she saw the government men speaking to one of the security guards at the gate. What the heck is going on? she asked herself.

The doorman flagged her a taxi. During the short ride she tried to reason out an explanation for this sudden attack of madness. But, of course, too many of the jigsaw pieces were missing. She worried, irrationally, about an expensive pair of earrings that she had charged on our American Express card, her private celebration present upon learning that she was pregnant. Did I put too much on the card? she wondered. Did Dennis forget to pay the bill?

She purposely took her time returning home with Adam, walking, stopping at several shops along the way. When she arrived back at our building, she stopped in at the security desk and questioned the guard: "Those two men who were here—what were they asking?"

"Oh," the guard replied, "they were asking how long you've lived here, what kind of people you and your husband are. I didn't give them too much information. I didn't think it was any of their business."

Back in our co-op, she sent Adam into his room to play a video game. Then she sat on the sofa, shaking.

She reported all of this to me in a tone that was a strange combination of panic, concern and icy aloofness. One of the men left his card, Laurie said, and she dictated the information to me. He was Thomas Doonan, a criminal investigator with the U.S. Attorney's Office for the Southern District of New York. "Dennis," Laurie demanded, "what is going on?"

What could I say? This was the woman whom I loved so dearly, and she was in agony. How could I soften the blow? How could I ease her pain when my own was so intense? "Don't worry, everything is under control," I said quickly, forcing a calm tone. "There is nothing to worry about. I'm dealing with this. Just don't talk to anybody."

"We're starting to get a lot of calls from the press—"

"Don't take any of those calls."

"Dennis, I—"

"Laurie, I have to go," I interrupted. "Try to stay calm." I hung up the phone, but my mind was making a thousand connections.

If the men had come looking for me at home, I reasoned, perhaps they would look for me here at Dad's house, too. I decided to get back into my car, to remain on the move. "Robert," I asked, "please just stay

available. I don't know what's going to happen, and I want you and
Daddy to come to the city tonight." Robert nodded, and I hopped into
the car.

A short time later, while driving toward the city, I was on a conference call with Joe Flom and Arthur Liman. Liman agreed to represent
me and asked what was happening at the moment.

"The Justice Department wants to serve me a subpoena. They are
looking all over the city for me."

"Okay. Where are you now?" Liman asked.

"I'm in my car."

"All right. Who is trying to serve you a subpoena?"

I relayed the information Laurie had given me. Liman asked, "Have
you ever been questioned by the government?"

"No."

"Here's what you do," Liman said. "First thing, you call this Doonan and arrange to meet him. Get the subpoena, and then we'll know
what we're dealing with."

That seemed reasonable. Until we saw the formal charges, we were
in the dark. We needed information.

"This is very important," he added. "Don't make any statements.
Don't talk about the case to anybody."

"Okay."

I dialed Doonan's number and said, "My name is Dennis Levine. I
understand you are looking for me."

"Yes, we are."

"I also understand you'd like to serve me with a subpoena. I am
prepared to meet with you and take care of that."

"Okay," Doonan replied. "When is a good time and place for us to
meet?"

"Why don't we meet at my apartment at seven-thirty this evening?
I'll be back in the city by then. I'm in my car right now, returning to
New York."

Doonan agreed to the plan, so I called Laurie back. I had to wait
frustrating seconds for the answering machine to play and beep. I knew
that she was screening what must be an onslaught of incoming messages, unwilling to answer the phone unless she knew that it was me
calling. Finally I heard the beep and I said, "It's me." She picked up
immediately. "I'm on my way back," I said. "I'm meeting Mr. Doonan
at the apartment at seven-thirty."

"I don't think you want to do that," Laurie replied.

"Why?"

"The building is surrounded by reporters. Channels two, four, five, seven, CNN, all the networks, all the newspapers. They have vans and cables all over the place. It's a zoo." She made no attempt to keep the fury out of her voice.

"Okay," I said. "I'll call Doonan back and meet him someplace else."

Doonan understood the situation and asked, "Would you like to come down here?"

"I have no problem with that. Where are you?"

"The U.S. Attorney's Office, right behind the federal courthouse." He gave me directions to 1 St. Andrew's Plaza.

DAD and Robert arrived at the co-op about six P.M., prepared to give support to Laurie and Adam. Robert had a cigarette in his mouth as he stepped inside.

A few weeks earlier Laurie had decided to give up smoking, at least for the duration of the pregnancy. But now she ripped the cigarette out of Robert's mouth, jammed it between her lips and took a deep draught.

Adam was still in his room, playing. As Dad, Robert and Laurie sat down to discuss the events of this unfathomable day, their thoughts were interrupted by a report on CNN, announcing that I had been accused of insider trading.

"This is a mistake," Laurie decreed. "Dennis never did anything wrong. What's insider trading?"

IT was seven-fifteen in the evening when I pulled up at the designated address, but there were no legal parking spaces available. Reasoning that it should take only a few minutes to have a subpoena slapped into my palm, I parked illegally on a side street. I passed through a metal detector, signed into the building and was directed to the sixth floor.

The elevator opened onto a deserted reception area. I pushed a buzzer and announced to the inquiring voice, "Dennis Levine to see Thomas Doonan." I glanced at my reflection in a glass partition. There I was, still dressed for my daytime role, briefcase in hand. I was the picture of a successful investment banker and the image, suddenly, brought a sense of calm. I remembered Ivan Boesky telling me about the dozens of times he had been questioned by SEC officials. Insider trading is a most difficult crime to prove. What could they do to me?

Relax, Dennis, I counseled myself. Tough it out.

A firm, well-modulated voice asked, "Are you Dennis Levine?" I turned to see a rugged, physically fit blond man who introduced himself as Thomas Doonan. "Please follow me," he said. He led me about thirty feet down a corridor to the corner office of Assistant U.S. Attorney Charles Carberry.

The room was hot and stuffy, and I was hit in the face by the overpowering odor of onions. On Carberry's battered desk, amid a clutter of paperwork, was an array of carry-out hamburgers, french fries and Cokes. Obviously, I had interrupted dinner.

Carberry was chief of the securities and fraud unit and a seven-year veteran of the federal prosecutor's office. He was also a former associate in the same law firm as Joe Flom. Pudgy and prematurely balding, wearing an ill-fitting but otherwise nondescript suit, Carberry introduced a third man in the room, a postal inspector, but I did not catch his name.

Doonan stood behind me as Carberry repeated the question for the record, "Are you Dennis Levine?"

"Yes, I am."

"Please have a seat."

I sat.

Then I heard unbelievable words: "Mr. Levine, we are placing you under arrest. I would like to inform you that you have the right to remain silent and if you give up that right, anything you say can and will be used against you. If you can't afford counsel, counsel will be appointed for you . . ."

I felt light-headed, barely hearing the words.

"Mr. Levine?" Carberry's voice broke into my thoughts. "Do you understand your rights?"

"Yes, I do."

"There is a fear that you will flee," Carberry explained. "So we are arresting you and we are going to place you in custody tonight."

Wall Street executives don't get placed in custody, I thought. They may be subpoenaed, indicted, even arrested, but they are not thrown into jail. Dennis, I lectured myself, you aren't as smart as you thought you were. Aloud I said, "You're going to put me in jail? I came in here on my own. If I had any intention of fleeing, why would I be here? Why would I voluntarily walk in the door?" Then I added, "Is this like the movies, where I only get one phone call?"

The meeting was interrupted by the sudden appearance of a man who introduced himself as Peter Sonnenthal, an attorney with the SEC. His eyes carried a look of disdain. "Are you Dennis Levine?" he asked.

"Yes." I was weary of the question.

He tossed a voluminous lawsuit onto my lap. Its cover declared that it was a civil complaint against me.

The weight of the papers informed me that I was the object of a double-pronged attack. There were both criminal and civil charges to deal with here.

Carberry said, "I would like to show you a piece of paper. We have a very strong case against you."

"Okay."

He slipped a sheet of paper across the desk. I picked it up and glanced at it. It was the form I used when I opened my account at Bank Leu, back in 1981. My signature was clearly legible. From some unknown reserve I mustered the ability to keep my face impassive. I handed the paper back without comment.

"Would you like to make a statement?" Carberry asked. "It will go a lot easier on you."

"No," I replied. "I'd like to call my attorney."

"Who is your lawyer?"

"Arthur Liman."

His reputation obviously preceded him for, behind my back, I heard Doonan mutter, "Oh, shit!"

I reached Liman at home. "Arthur," I said, "they're arresting me!"

"They are what?"

"They're arresting me. I'm going to jail. I'm going to spend a night in jail. I didn't think this was going to happen. Arthur, what is going on?"

Liman was in shock. I knew that he never would have advised me to meet Doonan if he thought I would be arrested. He asked, "Who is the assistant?"

"What is an assistant? What are you talking about?" I could feel myself losing composure.

"Who is arresting you?"

"Mr. Carberry."

"Okay. Let me speak with him."

The two men conversed for a few minutes, out of my earshot, before Carberry called me over and handed me the phone.

Liman said, "You're going to spend the night in jail. We can't find a magistrate tonight to bail you out. There's nothing we can do at this late hour because the courts are closed. I will talk to your wife. We will get you out first thing tomorrow. I'm sorry."

DOONAN said, "We're going to take your jewelry, your cuff links, your watch, your money, your briefcase, your wallet."

Suddenly I remembered the BMW. "I have another problem," I said. "My car is outside in a no-parking zone. Can I please move it?"

Doonan and the postal investigator shared a glance and a shrug. "Sure," Doonan said.

The three of us rode the elevator downstairs and stepped out onto the street. I indicated the spot around the block where I had parked the car.

A ticket decorated the windshield. "Sorry about that," Doonan said.

"That's the least of my problems right now," I pointed out.

When I pulled the car keys out of my pocket, Doonan extended his hand and declared, "I'll drive."

I sat in the back and watched him fumble with the keys. Obviously he had never driven a BMW before, and I had to tutor him. "This is a really nice car," the postal inspector said. "It must have cost a lot of money." There was nothing snide in his tone; it seemed a genuine compliment. Doonan babied the car into a multi-level municipal parking garage.

The two men took me back into the courthouse and led me across an enclosed walkway that connected this building to the federally operated Metropolitan Correctional Center. It seemed like the longest walk I had ever taken.

We rode an elevator to the bottom floor and stepped out to confront a barred door, surrounded by thick glass partitions. A guard sat behind a glass booth.

Doonan said, "Dennis Levine for processing."

The guard pressed a button. The barred door slid open, and we stepped into a small security area. The door behind us closed, and then another door in front of us opened.

Doonan handed over a batch of paperwork and left me in the custody of the jail guards.

"You're going to be processed," one of the guards said. He grasped my arm firmly and led me toward a waiting room, where a half dozen other men lingered. I was the only white man, and the only one dressed in a suit. "You have to stay here until we're ready for you," the guard said.

I was petrified. This was all so alien, something that never happened in real life. My head ached with worry: What would happen to my family, my career, my life? Everything was shattered.

A pay phone in the corner caught my eye immediately and I asked, "May I use that?"

"Yes."

Once more I had to wait for the answering machine to cycle before Laurie heard my voice and picked up the phone. "Where are you?" she cried. "What is happening?"

"Honey, I've been arrested. I'm going to be spending the night in jail. I can't talk." I assumed the phone was tapped. "I don't know what's going on myself," I continued. "Arthur will call you. He wants you to come to court tomorrow. He's arranging bail."

"He's already called," she said. It was obvious from the clipped, cool tone of her voice that Laurie, along with everyone else in my life, was operating on a crisis-footing. She was determined to keep her wits about her until we sorted through the details of this incomprehensible night. Later, when I was out of jail and back home, she knew there would be plenty of time to give in to hysteria. I winced when I realized the amount of explaining I had to do.

I offered a bald-faced lie: "Don't worry about me. This place is fine."

"Your name is all over the news," she reported. "You're a big story." There was quiet anger in those words. Laurie is a very private person. It was not on her wish list to be a media star. Nor did she appreciate learning the details of her husband's private life from a TV anchorman. "Your dad's here," she added. "Robert, too."

"Let me speak to Dad."

He reassured, "Everything is okay here. Laurie is fine. Adam is fine.

We'll be in court tomorrow. I'll bring Laurie down. There's nothing for you to worry about—on our end."

We said good-bye and I heard the phone line go dead. The silence reminded me of how totally removed I was, at the moment, from everyone and everything I loved. I turned away from the phone and idly ran my eyes over the men with whom I shared this new reality.

Each of the half dozen other prisoners held a copy of the charges against him, contained on a single sheet of paper. One towering, broad-shouldered man stared at the strange sight of a Wall Street investment banker, thrown into jail for the night, and demanded, "What the fuck did *you* do?"

"They charged me with obstruction," I mumbled.

"You a lawyer?"

"No."

His eye scanned the sheaf of papers in my hand. The official complaint was more than one hundred pages long. He said, "Shee-it, from the looks of that, you're in b-i-i-i-g trouble!"

I paced a few steps, moving toward solitude, wondering what I should do. The sudden weakness in my legs reminded me that it had been an incredibly long day and I had not bothered to interrupt it with food. I flagged the attention of one of my jailers and said, "I'd like to have something to eat. I haven't eaten anything all day." A few minutes later I was handed a tray of microwaved chicken that tasted as vapid and rubbery as my mood.

A guard led me to a corner office, where I stood in front of a desk and waited as a lieutenant reviewed my papers. He slid his chair back a few inches and stared at me, as if he was trying to see beyond my eyes.

"How're you feelin'?" he asked.

How do you answer such a question? Can you tell the lieutenant of the guard that you feel as if a brick wall has fallen on top of you? Dennis, I warned myself, you are probably under observation. Don't let them see that you are worried. Confidence! I commanded. Put on the veneer. I tried to answer in a firm voice, "Just fine," but the words sounded a bit shaky to my ears.

"You sure you're okay?" the lieutenant asked.

"Yes." Good, Dennis, I thought. That's better. More firmly I said, "I can't say I'm glad to be here, but I'm fine."

He squinted and continued to stare at me for several moments. His eyes flicked across the papers on his desk and then ran over me, from toe to head. I could read his thoughts: This is not the typical inmate. That could be good. Could be bad.

"I'm all right, really," I said.

He shrugged and dismissed me.

After I had filled out numerous registration forms and received a perfunctory physical examination, a guard brought me a fluorescent orange jumpsuit and demanded my street clothes in return. A few minutes later, when I was attired in prison garb, he announced, "We have no cells for now. We'll have to find a place for you in the holding tank."

Zzzzzzz . . . Clank! The electronic metal doors slammed shut behind me, locking me in with the rest of the night's haul. A toilet occupied one corner. The smell of urine and feces was overpowering. Somebody had taken wads of damp toilet paper and used them for target practice, throwing them against the walls, over the benches that lined the sides of the small room. The air was cold and, somehow, foreboding. Here I was, fallen to the very bottom of the heap.

I tried to lie down on a folding cot, but it was broken, and collapsed to the floor.

For many hours I sat alone on a bench in a corner of the room, trying to study the SEC complaint. My head pounded. My eyes blurred. It was nearly impossible to concentrate upon the words in front of me. I was ill with worry over Laurie and Adam.

IT was about three-thirty A.M. when a guard called me out of the holding tank. "We've got a cell for you," he said. He led me to an upstairs floor and opened the door to a tiny room. I stepped inside and again heard that horrible sound of a door being locked behind me.

A Hispanic man lay on the lower bunk, wideawake in the midst of the night, reading. He looked up from his book to study me. He nodded, and I said hello.

The upper bunk was a bare mattress, with a sheet, a blanket and a pillow arranged at the foot. I made the bed, then climbed in.

Sleep was out of the question. I returned my attention to the SEC complaint, despite the pounding in my head.

"What are you in for?" asked the man beneath me.

"Obstruction. How about you?"

"Drugs."

I said, "I'm leaving tomorrow."

A rueful laugh grated in my ears. "Yeah?" he said. "That's what I said eight months ago."

CHAPTER THREE

MY HEAD WAS SPLITTING from a migraine-type ache. I had not slept. Another prisoner arrived at my cell door, thrust a mop at me and commanded, "Mop the floor."

"I don't mop floors," I grumbled. "I'm out of here." I wandered off in search of food.

The man muttered at my back, "You'll learn."

I found a cafeteria and stood in line, selecting a small box of corn flakes, a half pint of milk, a cardboard bowl and a plastic spoon. I found a seat at a picnic-style table next to a motley group of other prisoners, my new peers. I had to stifle a wry laugh at the thought of how many times recently I had breakfasted with Perelman in his opulent town house. Morosely I mouthed a spoonful of corn flakes and glanced idly at the TV, elevated, in one corner of the room. The first thing I saw was my own picture. Somehow the news editors had obtained a copy of the photograph that Drexel used in its annual report; I was the lead news story on "Good Morning America," the principal in the largest insider-trading case in Wall Street history.

Someone pointed at me and shrieked with delight: "Hey, man, dat's you. We gots us a celebrity here!"

Oh, my God! I thought. This is bigger than I had imagined. I felt as though a knife was lodged in my stomach, and the blade was twisting. Quickly I returned to my cell.

I asked a guard for toothpaste and he handed out a jail-issue toiletry kit containing a disposable razor, a toothbrush and a can full of an unfamiliar substance labeled "tooth powder." My cellmate let me use his shaving cream.

It was about an hour later when I heard the delightful words, "Levine, come up front for release." I was escorted back to the processing area where I exchanged my orange jumpsuit for my business attire. Guards were not authorized to return my personal effects, so I was left without cuff links. The French cuffs protruded from the sleeves of my suit jacket as someone rolled my fingers in ink and then pressed them onto a sheet of cardboard. Someone else thrust a placard into my hands with my name on it, followed by a number. He told me to hold it beneath my chin. Then he took a photograph.

Doonan appeared, led me back through the long hallway to the courthouse and ushered me through a doorway. I had only taken about four steps outside when I saw Arthur Liman standing there, along with his partner Martin Flumenbaum, who had once worked in this very courthouse as an assistant U.S. attorney. Liman added Flumenbaum, one of Paul, Weiss's top young litigators, to the team the night before because of his experience in white-collar matters. Their gifted associate, Brad Karp, was with them.

Liman rushed over and embraced me. "How was your night?" he asked with concern.

"Terrible. But I'm happy to see you. Is everything taken care of?"

"We're in the process of negotiating your bail. You'll be going home today, don't worry. We're working a deal with Carberry. You'll have to post significant assets and forfeit your passport. Laurie brought it along. Brad's got it with him."

"Where is she?"

"She's right here. You'll get to see her soon."

Oh, I wanted to see her! I wanted to throw my arms around her and tell her I loved her. And yet I did not want to see her. I did not want to tell her what I had been doing all these years, behind her back.

Liman explained what would happen today: We would go into the courtroom. The prosecution would make a statement. We would make a statement. The magistrate would set bond, a prearranged figure negotiated by Carberry and my lawyers. "You'll sign some forms and then you'll be out of here," he promised.

Liman instructed Karp to stay with me as Doonan walked me through the necessary procedures.

I liked the young associate immediately. He sported a handsome tan on an athletic body. He fell in step next to me as Doonan led us away with the apologetic comment, "Paperwork."

In a third-floor office I filled out a biographical data sheet, listing the names, addresses and phone numbers of my relatives. When I finished, the clerk said, "Go to room three-oh-three."

When our convoy arrived at the designated office, I was given another form to complete. "Passport?" the clerk asked.

Karp handed it over.

The clerk said, "Go to room two-oh-seven."

A woman awaited me there, armed with yet another, larger form that demanded the details of my financial status. Under the heading "Annual Income" I wrote: "One million +."

After I completed the form, the clerk reviewed it. Suddenly her eyebrows shot skyward. Her finger pointed to the income figure and she asked, "Did you, uh, make a mistake here?"

"No."

Her face paled. Slowly she said, "Go to room two-nineteen."

As we neared the courtroom, we were subjected to a sudden deluge of reporters. I heard my name shouted out by dozens of people at the same time.

"No comment, no comment," I muttered, elbowing my way through the crowd, toward the corner of the courtroom where I saw Laurie and Dad waiting for me.

Laurie has always looked beautiful to me, but this morning she was especially so. She wore a stylish blue suit that set off her golden hair. She looked nervous and terribly concerned, but, somehow, she still glowed. As I hugged her she asked, "How are you? What was it like?"

"I'm fine," I said. I told her that everyone at the jail had treated me surprisingly well.

She snapped, "You were treated a lot better there than you would have been treated at home last night."

I should have expected the flash, but I had been too caught up in my own selfish thoughts. In less than twenty-four hours her confusion and fright had metastasized into justifiable anger. She must have felt as if she had spent the last fourteen years with a stranger. I suggested contritely, "Let's just get this over with. Once we're out of here, we'll figure out everything. I'll tell you what's going on."

We sat in the second row of the small courtroom. Off to one side a cluster of reporters crowded into a designated press area. "Try to look calm and confident," I whispered to Laurie.

She glared back at me as if I were a stranger. None of this seemed real.

Laurie noticed a man with a sketch pad on his lap. His fingers worked busily with a pencil. "Is he sketching us?" she asked.

"Yes," I acknowledged. "This will be in the newspapers."

Assistant U.S. Attorney Charles Carberry spoke to Magistrate Kathleen Roberts, announcing that he and the defense had agreed on the terms of the bail: $5 million. Liman's team had prepared the necessary papers, pledging our Park Avenue apartment and my Drexel shares as security, augmented by $100,000 in cash, which I had to deliver in the form of a certified check no later than five P.M. today. Magistrate Roberts gave her official approval to the arrangement and I signed the appropriate papers. It was all over in minutes.

Carberry asked us to come to his office to retrieve my valuables and my briefcase. Once we were there, Liman asked, "Can you please get him out of the building the back way, so that he doesn't have to deal with that whole mess of reporters out there?"

"Yes. Sure."

I was led downstairs and out to an expansive courtyard opening onto the back of the building. We found our way to the parking garage, where I retrieved my BMW.

Flumenbaum said, "Look, Brad's going with you to get the money. He'll get it back to the courthouse. I'm sure you're very tired and you want to get some sleep, so why don't we pick this up first thing tomorrow morning?"

"Bullshit," I replied quickly. "I'm going home to shower and I'll be in your office this afternoon. I want to get to the bottom of this."

I had at my service one of the most talented and aggressive lawyers in New York, and from the glint that suddenly appeared in his eye, it was obvious that he was pleased to realize that he had a fighting client. "Okay," he agreed. "Get to the office around three o'clock. We'll roll up our sleeves. In the meantime, don't discuss the case with anybody."

I was petrified with fear concerning the next few hours. Maybe Laurie and I could not discuss specifics, but we certainly had to talk about the broad picture. I had no idea how she would react to the story of my years of deceit.

A thousand times since that day I have been asked: "If you were making two million dollars a year, why did you risk everything by trading on inside information?"

There is no easy answer. To comprehend such a story, one must study its evolution.

PART TWO
MONEY IN THE BANK

CHAPTER FOUR

WE ASSUMED A COLLECTIVE AIR of reverence on that morning in early
March 1977 as we assembled in the Vice Presidents' Cafeteria in the
Citibank headquarters at 399 Park Avenue. There I was, one of scores
of young but otherwise nondescript management trainees, at once ex-
pectant and apprehensive over the prospect of rubbing elbows with the
elite. No one quite knew what to do. Should we disguise our anxiety
with the façade of normal conversation? Should we speak only in
hushed tones? Should we open our mouths at all?

The decision was made for most of my new associates when Walter
Wriston, the chairman of the board, strode in, accompanied by a reti-
nue of attendants. As if by signal, the other trainees sorted themselves
into a line that wound its way up to the eminent ruler of one of the
world's largest financial empires. I stood silently off to one side, observing. It was not that I was above kowtowing—it just seemed to me to
be a colossal waste of time. What did he care about us? Why would he
remember one name, one face, one handshake, offered from the bottom
of the corporate ladder?

I was twenty-three years old and in my first week on the job in
Citibank's Corporate Counseling Department. The salary was $19,000
a year, and it seemed like a great deal of money. It was enough of a start
to solidify my plans to marry my college sweetheart, Laurie Skolnik.
My task would be to help advise large U.S. firms on how to avoid

foreign currency losses, and I wondered whether I was equipped to handle it. What educational credentials I had came from the mass market of Queens public schools and tuition-free college classes. I possessed the obligatory MBA degree, but to obtain it I had commuted by bus and subway for three hours a day to attend the Baruch School of Business. I supposed that I knew as much as or more about the real world than many of the others in this room, but the inner workings of the corporate suites were a total mystery to me. Rather than a perfunctory handshake, what I needed from Wriston was the opportunity to pick his brain.

Suddenly a man approached and interrupted my thoughts with a disparaging remark about the gamesmanship being practiced by the other management trainees. He introduced himself as Robert Wilkis, a lending officer in the bank's Chemicals Division. He was somewhat balding, tall and slender, with a body kept physically fit by running.

There was something in his eyes, or perhaps in the tone of his voice, that communicated an affinity. It took only a few minutes of conversation to seed a friendship. We were both the products of middle-class families, and we both had an ardent desire to succeed in the business world, but Bob had a head start on me. He was four years older than I and boasted more impressive academic credentials. He had a degree from Harvard and an MBA from Stanford. Despite the educational pedigree, his job history was mottled. He had driven a truck in his hometown of Baltimore; he had worked on an archaeological dig in Israel; he had taught handicapped students in Boston; he had been a summer intern at the U.S. Treasury Department in Washington. He was fluent in five languages and had already developed contacts throughout the global investment community. I, on the other hand, was a raw beginner, a baby. What bound us to one another, almost immediately, was an intuitive realization that we were both mavericks.

We had only a few minutes to speak that day, but we knew that we were already on a common path.

SOME kids want to be pro football players or cowboys or soldiers of fortune; to me, all of those roles were encompassed by the field of investment banking. My father, Philip, had shown me how to read *The Wall Street Journal* at a young age, and it was love at first sight.

As a kid I always worked. I shoveled snow. I delivered newspapers. I mowed lawns. By my early teens I was making money playing keyboards in bands that performed at parties and school dances. Eventually one band achieved modest success; we opened local concerts for touring groups, including the Association, the Turtles, and Jay and the Americans. We even cut some records.

Dad had forged his own successful home improvement business, Armstrong Aluminum Company, in Queens, and during my high school and college years I worked for him, cold-canvassing door-to-door, trying to solicit business. It was exhausting work that taught me valuable lessons. I learned to overcome the rejection that so often arises in all phases of life. When a door slammed in my face, I had to move on to the next opportunity. Success was directly related to tenacity; the more neighborhoods I canvassed, the more doorbells I rang, the better were my chances of realizing a sale.

Dad made a good, solid, honest living at this business, and the key to his prosperity was the satisfied customer. He taught me early that a business is built upon referrals. Do one job well, and another will come your way.

But, of course, you have to get your foot in the door first, and this was the difficult part. Wall Street was an unlikely environment for a middle-class boy from Queens, but it was where I wanted to be, and I charted my course with care. I watched in fascination during the "go-go" 60s as American business entered the conglomerate age. Mega-firms such as Gulf+Western, ITT and LTV were fashioned by what was, to me, the creative use of paper. Repeatedly I saw money conjured from thin air. It was called "Chinese paper." A firm would authorize a new preferred stock issue and—as long as it could persuade investors that there was value behind it—simply swap the freshly printed paper for the stock of smaller companies.

To me, the geniuses in these transactions were the people behind the scenes, and I read whatever I could find about them. In a simplistic sense, the traditional role of an investment banker was to buy a new issue of corporate securities "wholesale," directly from the issuing company, and "retail" them to the public, taking its profit in the mark-up. But my perception grew that the investment banker was the one who quietly orchestrated complex transactions, performed important functions for the business community and, at the same time, earned significant amounts of money. What's more, the investment banker of the 70s was taking on a new role. No longer was he a mere purveyor of securities. Increasingly, he was the creator of new financial instruments and new tools for the wise use of business resources.

For me, there was a distinct downside. Investment banking was a remote environment. Jobs were often parceled out on the basis of social connections, old school ties and breeding. Some said that Morgan Stanley was a "Princeton firm" and First Boston was a "Yale firm." There seemed to be no place in the industry's higher echelons for a kid from Queens—there was no "Baruch firm." I reasoned that I could possibly find a spot somewhere on the fringes, but the top jobs in the prestigious companies were limited to those with impeccable academic and cultural credentials. Numbers alone dictated my chances. A large investment firm might receive 4,000 applications to fill a mere twenty positions a year. The rules of the day were nepotism and social pedigree.

It had loomed as an intriguing challenge. When I finally had my MBA in hand (my master's thesis dealt with the factors that influence underwriting profits), full of hope and ambition, I made the rounds of the major investment banking firms. In a few instances I managed to arrange an introductory interview, but no offers resulted.

All right, I thought, if an investment bank won't hire me, I'll start my own. I approached Professor Jack Francis at Baruch College. He was a well-known authority in the field who had previously taught at the Wharton School of Business and had authored several textbooks on corporate finance. Beyond that, he had inspired me through his teaching. He liked my idea: I would be the front man, selling our services more-or-less door-to-door, as I had done for Dad; he would be the behind-the-scenes technician.

I went to Richard Dorfman, husband of my cousin Lynn. He was an attorney, employed by a local savings and loan association. I asked him to draw up the necessary papers. In a matter of weeks, Levine, Francis & Co., Ltd., was born.

After considerable legwork and much study, we almost pulled off a small-scale leveraged buyout, but at the last moment, one of the principals backed off. And by then, I had landed my first job on the fringes of Wall Street.

*   *   *

THE Citibank job was a compromise, an entrée into the financial world where, from my small desk in the bullpen on the fourth floor, I could at least observe the Promised Land.

I plunged into the training program, learning what I could about foreign currency markets. Despite an "A" in my obligatory graduate school course on international finance, I was far from an expert. If you are a U.S. corporation and you sell your products for Swiss francs, what do you do with them? What are the tax considerations? What are the conversion restrictions? How and when do you want to move the francs into dollars or deutschmarks or yen or whatever? It was fascinating to realize the intricacies of the worldwide cash flow, and it was exhilarating to realize that I could play a role in these global economic transactions.

One day my cousin Stuart came into the city to meet me for lunch. I retained a very special, warm feeling for Stuart, for it was at his wedding reception a few years earlier that I had first set eyes on Laurie, who happened to be the cousin of the bride. Now we spoke of my upcoming wedding as we walked through the Citibank lobby. We were two young men, only a generation removed from immigration. Stuart was from Brooklyn and I grew up in Bayside, but either place might as well have been the wheat fields of Kansas. Stuart glanced about at the lunchtime mob of men in blue pinstripe suits and wingtip shoes, and commented, "Dennis, this is a strange world you're living in."

Strange and overwhelming.

Several times each business day I found myself wandering toward the Quotron at one end of the floor. Here, I could push a button and get up-to-the-moment information on world currency prices. This was good cover for my visits, but it was not my primary interest. As a would-be investment banker, I was fascinated by the manner in which stock price fluctuations mirrored real-world activities. For instance, the moment that a potential merger was announced, it was generally reflected by a spurt in the stock price of the target company. The rationale was simple. In order to acquire a company on the open market, in order to induce a sufficient number of shareholders to sell, you had to offer a price that was higher than the prevailing stock price. Therefore, the level of the offer set a new, higher market rate.

The stock ticker reflected the beginnings of the next major trend in American business: consolidation. History had seen three such waves already. The first came at the turn of the century and resulted in the formation of U.S. Steel, Standard Oil, General Electric and Eastman Kodak. The second wave, encompassing the latter half of the 1920s, brought giant banks and utilities into existence. The third wave of the late 1960s spawned the conglomerate age, largely accomplishing this through friendly acquisitions. And the signs were in place for the fourth wave to hit in the approaching 80s. There were now thousands of companies whose stock was undervalued, and that made them very good acquisition prospects.

It was almost routine for Bob Wilkis and me to encounter one another at the stock terminal. Unlike me, he was an active trader, and he always had a few particular stocks to check, to see how his portfolio was doing. My role was that of the interested spectator.

Before long Wilkis and I were frequent lunch partners. Sometimes, after work, we had a drink together. On one of these occasions, between puffs on his cigar, he mentioned in an offhand manner that he had recently earned an easy profit on a stock deal. By keeping his eyes and ears open on the job, he had learned the supposedly secret information that Airco, a New Jersey–based producer of gases and related products, was to be acquired by the B.O.C. Group, a British firm. Acting upon this news that was not available in the public arena, he had bought Airco stock. When the merger deal was announced, Airco's stock rose quickly in price and Wilkis sold out.

I knew without being told that this was a violation of both SEC regulations and Citibank rules. Profiting in the stock market as a result of "material information" unavailable to others has long been officially prohibited. The basis for prosecution of such an act is SEC rule 10b-5, which makes it a crime "to employ any device, scheme, or artifice to defraud . . . in connection with the purchase or sale of any security."

Wilkis contended that it was not only easy to deal in stocks this way, but also safe. Shortly after the transaction, Citibank investigated reports of insider-trading activity, but could prove nothing. Citibank, of course, had no way of knowing that Wilkis had traded in his mother's name through her brokerage account in Baltimore.

I listened to this story with interest. Wilkis's outlook on life was somewhat different than mine, and I sat across from him at the small cocktail table trying to determine whether he was more jaded, or more realistic. He had just confessed to me that he had shaded the rules. Did this make me feel uneasy? Or did I now view my friend as more sophisticated than I had realized? I was unsure.

LAURIE is slim and lithe, with long, dark-blonde hair that accentuates her blue-green eyes. She is the most exquisite and captivating woman I have ever known, but beneath the beauty is a warm, sensitive and highly intelligent individual. Her personality compliments my gregariousness.

Late on the night of our first date, when I took her back to her parents' home in Brooklyn, I had spotted a piano in the living room. "Do you play?" I asked.

She nodded, and I asked her to play something for me.

Soon the soft, familiar melody of "What Are You Doing the Rest of Your Life" filled the room. As I watched her play I knew exactly what I would be doing the rest of my life and with whom I would be doing it.

From the outset, we shared the same dreams: a successful business career for me and a family for both of us. Laurie has a degree in education from C. W. Post College. She worked for a time in advertising and then as a teacher, but her vision is inward. Her primary goals were and are to be the best wife and mother she can be. She has always desired a quiet, warm life, with family as the core.

We were married on December 17, 1977, at Congregation Beth Shalom in Lawrence, New York. We leased a $379-a-month apartment on Yellowstone Boulevard in Forest Hills.

Almost immediately, Bob and Elsa Wilkis became our close friends. They drew us into their world, introducing us to a wide range of new friends and business contacts. Elsa, an aristocratic Cuban-born immigrant, was an aspiring artist with fashionable tastes. We often went to dinner together, followed by a movie or a show. Laurie and I both delighted in the company of their young daughter, Alexandra.

Meanwhile, on the job, I watched. I learned. I grew uneasy. From my entry-level perspective I found myself amazed and concerned at the enormous inefficiency I witnessed. This isn't how Dad does it, I thought. He had the luxury of calling his own shots. There was not a committee in sight to gum up the works. When a decision needed to be made, he made it on the spot.

Such entrepreneurial spontaneity was totally lacking in corporate bureaucracy. Too many people at or near the top in big business seemed to be obsessed with a "cover-your-ass" mentality. All important decisions, both within Citibank and the corporations I served, were made by boards and committees; the results were predictably ponderous and bland: Write a memo, not to any person, but simply "to the files." It was the ultimate CYA defense.

This was distressing, for big business was where I wanted to be. Yet I had only placed my foot upon the bottom rung of the ladder, and here I was taking issue with the way big business attempted to get things done. Was I just being a smart-ass kid, I wondered? Did they know something I did not? Perhaps. I reminded myself to keep my mouth shut and study the available data. I had set a nearly impossible goal for myself, and I had to proceed with deliberateness.

I shared these thoughts with Wilkis, and he agreed. The fault of big business, he decreed, lay in the inertia created by its very bigness. He, too, appreciated the entrepreneurial spirit.

ONE day early in 1978, Wilkis drew me aside from the Quotron. Finding an island of quiet in a side conference room, he shared a stock tip with me. Citibank was involved in financing the takeover of a major U.S. chemical company. To protect the identity of the companies involved in any merger proposal, code names are assigned, accessible only to a few key individuals. But Wilkis had seen an overseas telex relating to the deal, and he had cracked the code.

Almost idly, he disclosed that he had bought a position in the company, as much as he could afford, once again trading through his mother's account. "It's easy," he said. "Everybody does it."

Only in retrospect would I realize that something snapped at this very moment, something that caused me to cross the clear lines of morality delineated by my father and my late mother, Selma. Ethical behavior was a routine component of my youth. I was a Cub Scout, then a Boy Scout. I went to religious school. Every Sunday was spent with grandparents, aunts, uncles and cousins. My schoolwork was adequate and otherwise unremarkable. I liked girls. My friends and I occasionally enmeshed ourselves in an exuberant prank, but there was nothing sinister about it. Dad taught me by example to conduct my affairs in an honorable manner. He performed his work well and on time, and he guaranteed its quality. He charged honest rates, and he serviced his customers. Quite apart from his sense of morality, Dad knew that this was the most effective way to build a business, and he drummed that concept into me throughout the years.

But somewhere between Queens and Wall Street I was losing track of those values. Throughout my college and graduate studies, I do not believe I even heard the word "ethics." In the big business environment of the late 70s, morality was not an issue. The liberal, radical, humanistic 60s were gone and society was veering toward materialism.

My response to Wilkis's words should have been: Trading on the basis of inside information is wrong. Instead I thought: Here's a way I can make some extra money.

I was a big boy. It was my decision. Wilkis did not twist my arm.

I thanked my friend for the tip and headed for the Citibank library to research the stock as completely as I could. I wanted to know the downside; if Wilkis's information happened to be wrong, I did not want to take a bath. The basic, public information paperwork—the fundamental research—convinced me that the company was sound and, therefore, there was no reason to believe that its stock would plunge too drastically in any eventuality.

Since my late teens I had maintained a minuscule account with the brokerage firm of Hertzfeld and Stern. My few, modest transactions over the years could only be described as amateurish and dabbling, with predictably mediocre results. Now, suddenly, I had a real basis for investing. I raided my savings account of its $2,000 balance and took a check over to Hertzfeld and Stern. Exploiting my margin privileges to the limit, I bought about $4,000 worth of shares in the chemical company.

Laurie did not know the reason for my investment, but she trusted my judgment. She knew that I took a conservative approach to the stock market, and she was pleased that I had found what I considered to be a safe, good investment.

What she did not know was that I, like Wilkis before me, had crossed the indefinite limits of a moral boundary. Wilkis and I had engaged in stock trading on the basis of what was then known as a "hot tip." It was easy to rationalize our actions. There was plenty of historical precedent. For example, there is a legend on Wall Street that the famed

London merchant bank of Rothschild cashed in big by receiving inside information, via carrier pigeon, of Wellington's victory over Napoleon. Rothschild, with great fanfare, began a selling spree of British government bonds. Others interpreted this as an indication of Wellington's defeat, and a panic ensued. As prices plunged, Rothschild quietly bought back huge positions in the bonds at bargain rates. In his autobiography Bernard Baruch admitted that, at the beginning of the century, he had profited on a tip from an insider concerning developments within Northern Pacific Railroad. In 1922, Joseph Kennedy, patriarch of the Kennedy clan, plunged into the market on the basis of a tip that Ford Motor Company was planning to acquire Pond Creek Coal. In a few months' time, Kennedy turned a profit of $650,000 on a $24,000 investment.

Such deals were not illegal at the time. But as speculation and abuses increased during the Roaring Twenties, Congress stepped in. The SEC was created in 1933 and President Franklin Roosevelt appointed Joseph Kennedy as its first commissioner. Its goal was to restore investor confidence after the great stock market crash, to create what came to be termed as a "level playing field" for all investors.

Over the years the SEC had very little success in stopping insider trading abuses. In the nearly half-century of its existence, the commission had brought only seventy-seven actions against inside traders, and the penalties, if any, were limited to fines and other civil sanctions. There had never been a single criminal prosecution for insider trading. In fact, there was (and is) no legal description of it in the securities statutes; it was an offense that was poorly defined by the courts.

In modern times, all you had to do was chart, in retrospect, the stock prices of companies that were involved in merger deals, and you would find, in nearly every case, mysterious price run-ups prior to any public announcement.

Clearly, trading on hot tips was a historical and cultural phenomenon. In trading the chemical company stock, Wilkis and I had committed what we believed to be no more than a minor civil infraction, if, indeed, it was a crime at all. It felt loosely analogous to jaywalking.

And, after all, it was the legendary economist John Maynard Keynes who wrote, "The game of professional investment is intolerably boring . . . to anyone who is entirely exempt from the gambling instinct."

CHAPTER FIVE

IN THE SPRING, a young man's fancy returns to investment banking. This is the time of year when the houses recruit, and in 1978, with a year at Citibank under my belt, I enhanced my résumé and tried my luck once more.

Smith Barney, Harris Upham & Co. responded quickly, with an invitation for a lunch meeting with Leslie Hannify and Norman Brown, associates in the M&A Department. Prior to the appointment, I researched Smith Barney in the Citibank library. One of the things I learned was that the principal force in the M&A Department was John Morgan, a Smith Barney vice chairman, no less a personage than the grandson of J. P. himself.

This was in character for, historically, Smith Barney was a conservative, old-line "white shoe" firm. By now Jewish-founded houses such as Salomon Brothers, Goldman Sachs & Co., Kuhn, Loeb & Co. and Lehman Brothers had assumed their own established positions in the business, but as best I could tell, Smith Barney had never hired a Jewish associate before (it was a well-kept secret that a past president of the firm, Nelson Schaenen, was Jewish). The lunch invitation was prima facie evidence of the fundamental, substantial changes taking place within the investment banking industry.

The upheaval had commenced in July 1974, when International Nickel Company of Canada (INCO) announced that one of its subsidiaries was issuing a $157 million tender offer for the stock of the Phila-delphia-based Electric Storage Battery Company (ESB). The price worked out to $28 per share, which was about 40 percent above the current market. Nonetheless, the ESB board of directors declared the offer to be too low. The board's recommendation that shareholders not tender their stock to INCO placed the proposed transaction into the hostile category and touched off a round of lawsuits and public relations ploys. A considerable number of attorneys, accountants and investment banking officials burned the midnight oil, attempting to strike a com-promise. By August INCO had raised its offer to $41 per share and corralled 95 percent of ESB's stock. The affair was little-noticed at the time, but was noteworthy in retrospect.

Prior to this, a hostile takeover was a relatively rare event, considered more-or-less unethical, and the large investment banking firms gener-ally did not lower themselves to become active participants, at least on the side of the offensive team. But this time the venerable firm of Morgan Stanley took the role of adviser to INCO, and when the hostile takeover succeeded, such activity was legitimatized.

This development took on greater significance after "May Day," May 1, 1975, when the SEC deregulated the heretofore fixed-rate com-missions on stock transactions. Suddenly scurrying for customers, brokers slashed their commission scales and basic revenues dropped accordingly, by about 40 percent. Numerous firms folded; others merged, and Smith Barney was one of them, joining forces with Harris, Upham & Co. in 1976. The investment banks suffered as well as the stockbrokers, for they had traditionally feasted upon revenues from large stock transactions consummated for their institutional clients.

Jacob Schiff, who headed Kuhn, Loeb & Company in the early part of the century, had once remarked that competition between invest-ment banking firms was "not good form." But suddenly it was the only form. Everyone on the Street was desperate for new business and natu-rally looked with favor upon the fertile field opened up by Morgan Stanley's participation in the INCO/ESB deal. As the decade of the 80s approached, it was obvious that American business was on the brink of a boom in mergers and acquisitions, whether friendly or hostile. The economy was emerging from a recessionary cycle that, coupled with high interest rates, high oil prices, high unemployment rates and low factory production figures, had kept stock prices depressed. The market was loaded with companies whose stock was trading significantly below book value; each was a bargain, ready to be snatched. Capital was available.

First Boston Corporation was one of the initial investment banking firms to formally acknowledge the trend. Joe Perella, a street-smart Harvard Business School grad of Italian immigrant stock, persuaded the partners that it was time to create an entire department devoted to mergers and acquisitions. He hired Bruce Wasserstein (brother of playwright Wendy), a creative lawyer from Cravath, Swaine & Moore and a former member of Nader's Raiders. Together, Perella and Wasserstein structured an M&A Department that set the standard for the industry.

Following the trend, Smith Barney, in its reincarnated form, expanded its M&A Department and set about to build an aggressive new image.

The personality of the Street changed radically in response to the more competitive environment. Genteel, patrician relationships gave way to more creative and aggressive dealmaking. Old school ties now mattered far less than the ability to get the job done. The question was not, who are you? It was, can you generate fees? In this environment, a boy from Bayside could make it, if he was willing to work hard.

I wanted in on this trend, and in the Citibank library, I made myself conversant with every large M&A deal in which Smith Barney was currently involved.

At lunch, Hannify and Brown seemed impressed with my knowledge of their firm and informed me on the spot that they were inviting me back to meet some of the senior people.

After a second round of interviews, one Smith Barney man reported in a memo that I was "pleasantly aggressive . . . I think he would be a good addition to the department." Another wrote: "Distinctive, vivacious. Appears to have accomplished a great deal at Citibank. A real driver." Still another concluded: ". . . think he is well worth going after."

When a job proposal materialized, I was ecstatic. I was ready to start before the ink was dry on my offer. Here was the culmination of a dream I had held for many years. I called Laurie and said, "We're going out to dinner." Wilkis joined us at the "21" Club and treated us to cocktails.

Before the change became official, I cleaned out my closet. I knew that one of the first things I would have to do is inform Smith Barney's Legal and Compliance Department of any and all stocks that I owned, and I did not want anyone to have a formal record of my chemical company transaction. By now I knew that Wilkis's tip had either been wrong, or the plans had stalled, for no merger announcement had been made. I sold the stock for about the same price I had paid and considered myself lucky that I had not lost my savings.

WHEN I joined Smith Barney I informed the Legal and Compliance Department, as required, that I had an open brokerage account, but I reported, quite truthfully, that I did not currently own any stocks.

Orientation sessions explained the security procedures that are basic to any brokerage firm or investment bank, designed to guard against the premature release of information: Transactions are given code names. Access to documents is restricted, and those documents are shredded, rather than trashed. Offices and telephones are swept routinely for "bugs." New employees are fingerprinted and checked for criminal backgrounds.

The first line of security is the very real existence of what is known as the "Chinese Wall," the veil of secrecy that prevents one department from sharing its knowledge with other departments. People in the Corporate Finance Department are not supposed to tell those in other departments what they are working on, and vice versa, unless and until they have a need to know. Once the M&A Department makes a decision to take a public stand on a deal, the Arbitrage Department freezes any pertinent transactions concerning the involved companies. There is a popular perception that the Chinese Wall is a myth, but I do not share that perception. There are tens of thousands of people on both sides of the wall, dealing in a legion of securities and, on balance, I believe, they keep their business to themselves. It is an inherent risk, however, that when the same company is buying and selling stocks through various departments, and when other departments are spinning out buy and sell recommendations to the public, and when still other departments are orchestrating deals that will impact stock prices, there will be an occasional appearance of impropriety.

However, none of these procedures can stop a determined insider from acting upon his private knowledge, or sharing his information with another party. As many as one hundred people, ranging from corporate executives to secretaries, may be privy to inside knowledge concerning a given deal; the very nature of the work requires that even the most junior people encounter non-public information; how can anyone prove who knew what?

Neither at Smith Barney nor anywhere else on the Street was there a sense of strict surveillance; rather, we worked on an honor system codified by means of the firm's restricted list, aka the "hot" list. Only the highest echelons of company officials, plus the compliance officers, were privy to that list. If I placed a buy or sell order for any stock on the list—and it could well be an innocent action—the burden of proof might be on me to show that I did so without having access to material, non-public information.

The message of my orientation was that if I wanted to trade stocks, I had two choices. I could open a Smith Barney account, which would be automatically monitored by the Legal and Compliance Department, or I could provide a compliance officer with confirmation of each transaction handled by an outside broker. On balance, I decided, it simply would be easier to remain out of the market altogether. My career dream was now assuming reality—my $23,000 annual salary felt like big-time—and there was no need for me to risk it by dabbling in stocks. I was glad I had sold my modest holdings in the chemical company.

MY new title was corporate finance associate, which, I discovered immediately, translated to "grunt." I was assigned to an open, hustling, humming bullpen area on the forty-eighth floor of the Corporate Finance Department in the headquarters building at 1345 Avenue of the Americas. More than thirty associates labored here in what seemed to be the modern-day equivalent of indentured slavery. An investment banking firm operates on the binary system; a partner is a "one" and everyone else is a "zero." A zero is expected to do whatever a one tells him to do, without question.

You never want to be the last associate to arrive at work in the morning or the first to leave in the evening. In this ultra-competitive environment, aware that you are constantly being watched, you search for some positive way to distinguish yourself, and you pray that you will not screw up.

I rolled up my sleeves. Most of the work involved rudimentary tasks such as comparisons of the values of common stocks, bonds and/or indentures of similar, but different, companies. For example, if I was given the task of analyzing the common stock of Ford Motor Company, I would compare it to the stocks of Chrysler and General Motors. I would hustle to the library and pull all the publicly available information concerning the three automakers, array the data and try to make some sense of it: What are the recent stock price ranges, what are the dividends, what are the performance ratios?

If the task was the analysis of a potential merger, I had to study all the recent acquisitions within the given industry, note the premiums that were paid above market, check the multiples of book value and earnings and identify specific elements, such as the types of compensation, that were critical to those past transactions.

I found work on a fairness opinion to be the most interesting. This is an analysis provided at the request of a company's board of directors regarding the specific financial nature of a given transaction. It was our job, as an independent, outside expert, to comment on the fairness of the transaction from the shareholder's point of view. Is the price too high or too low? What effect will the acquisition have on the stock price? Is the remuneration offered to corporate officials presented in the proper form? In sum, is this the right thing for the company to be doing? Our independent evaluation held great weight with the board of directors as it recommended a course of action to the shareholders.

This is all known as "crunching numbers," and it was the constant activity of the bullpen. In this pre-computer era, we pulled most of our recent stock performance information directly from old copies of *The Wall Street Journal.* Associates waited in the library with varying degrees of impatience for their chance at the stacks of newspapers. Often the lights of the library blazed throughout the night as we huddled over the pages, rubbing the sleep from our eyes with ink-stained hands. Those who attacked the job with resolution developed a genuine camaraderie. Even though we were killing ourselves with work, we felt like an elite breed, fortunate to have this opportunity to slave. We bitched about the so-called glamour of the investment banking industry, but it was good-natured grumbling.

There was art to this, as well as science. Our numbers were necessarily based on the publicly available data provided by the corporations and audited by independent accountants. In theory, the numbers all related to one another. In practice, there was considerable variability. Acting within the law, companies can play with the numbers by deciding, for example, when to credit certain revenues, when to take various deductions or how to treat tax considerations. As long as everything remains within the realm of "generally accepted accounting principles," it is all quite legal. Many corporations have a tendency to skew these numbers in such a way as to show consistent growth. That is what keeps shareholders happy and corporate officers employed. To an associate, it meant that one sometimes had to compare apples and oranges.

Whatever the task, it resulted in a potpourri of raw data that had to be organized into legible form. I would produce a large spread sheet that compared the figures in various categories. There was no margin for error; big decisions would be made on the basis of these numbers. Nor was there any margin for mediocrity. If you did your grunt work well, you knew that you would eventually be promoted to the next rung, second vice president. Just as assuredly, if you did your work haphazardly, you would be out on the street. The bullpen was clearly a winnowing area, and the winners and losers became obvious at end-of-the-year bonus time. If you received a good bonus, you could look forward to moving up in the investment banking world. If you received no bonus, you went job-hunting. It was extremely tedious work, but I did it because that was my task. What kept me going was the realization that it was the only way to advance. Every vice president and partner above me had crunched numbers at some stage of his career.

A simple mathematical slip could be equivalent to professional suicide, so I triple-checked the numbers before rushing my data to a statistical typist. When the typed version was ready, I triple-checked the numbers again, to make sure the typist got them right. The columns had to add properly. The percentages had to be correct.

With the final version of the spread sheet prepared, some associates considered the job finished. They passed the work on to the appropriate partner, sat back and sipped a cup of coffee.

But I wanted to produce more than numbers. I wanted to try to make some sense of all the data. What did the numbers really tell us? How does this company compare to its competitors? What happened in certain years to produce aberrations in performance that may have influenced the analysis? If the company is considering issuing a new debt instrument, how will it affect the company stocks and bonds that are already on the market? What will happen to its debt rating? How will it affect the industry in general?

Often, when I felt I had good answers to these questions, I included a bit of analysis along with my numbers. Some of the partners received such work with a cold "You're not paid to think" stare, but others appreciated it and took the time to show me where and why I might be mistaken. On occasion, some actually accepted my interpretations and acted upon them.

The reward for work well done was when an astute partner took an associate along to participate in a client meeting. The first time I was accorded such a privilege I came to understand that there was method to this madness. My numbers actually figured prominently into key decisions surrounding the deal. And it was fascinating to watch the partner work this particular client. There was art to this, too. The more you understood about a client's personality and motivations, the better your chance of bringing him around to your point of view.

I was thinking about this when the partner put me to the test. His voice suddenly broke into my consciousness: "Dennis, you did all the numbers, why don't you answer that?" I reached for my briefcase and breathed a sigh of relief that I had thought to bring the raw data with me. The client leaned close as I reviewed the numbers with him, and when I was finished, he accepted the package we were presenting. It was an exhilarating feeling, and I believed that I had found my future niche in the business. Crunching numbers was fine for the time being, but I was an outside man, a contact man. I could sell, and I knew it.

The workweek required of the associate was obscene. But if you wanted to stick around, you sometimes stayed at your tasks for as much as 100 hours in a single week. Pulling an "all-nighter" was a common phenomenon. Laurie, Dad and Robert jokingly referred to me as a "wage slave."

But I thought: I'm doing what I always wanted to do, and I'm doing it well.

WILKIS was a genuine friend who was delighted that I had landed my fantasy job. Beyond that, slowly, quietly, we started to explore the avenues of opportunity opened by my new position. Whenever we spoke one of us asked, "What are you working on? What's going on?" and I responded by sharing with him stories of the incredible amounts of information that now flowed through my daily life. I understood, without his directly admitting it, that he was trading on the basis of my news. It produced a delicious tingling sensation to realize that Bob was beating the system, but it was not for me.

"I can't trade securities," I said matter-of-factly one day. "At least not in companies I'm working with."

"I could do it for you," he responded. "Through my mother's account."

I declined. Although I had participated in the fruitless chemical company transaction while I was still at Citibank, I was not motivated to do any more secret deals. I was where I wanted to be, in the thick of the investment banking business, and I saw no reason to jeopardize my good fortune. I wished Wilkis luck with his investments, and I freely shared office gossip with him, but I left it at that.

TWO months after joining Smith Barney, I was laboring over a spread sheet at eight-thirty P.M. on a Friday night. The bullpen was empty, save for me, when David Faber, the man charged with the special responsibility of supervising the associates, approached. In a southern drawl he asked, "How ya doin', Dennis?"

"Fine."

"Dennis, do y'all speak French?"

"No," I replied, unable to hide the curiosity in my voice.

Without explanation, he walked away. But a short time later he returned and asked, "What about your wife? Does she work?"

I explained that Laurie was a teacher, but that her career goal was to be a housewife and mother. He seemed to approve, but he walked away again.

Curiosity got the better of me. I set down my spread sheet and walked over to his office. "Dave," I asked, "what's going on?"

Each year, he explained, Smith Barney sent one of its associates to its Paris office to crunch the numbers for a multinational group of partners who worked the European markets. "Based on the fine work you've been doin', and your international experience at Citibank, you'd probably be a natural," Faber said. I would be the only associate there, so I would be involved in every aspect of the business. When I returned after a year, I would have a unique experience on my résumé and I could choose my next assignment.

"M&A Department," I said without hesitation.

He nodded.

I was flabbergasted. I called Laurie and said, "I'm coming home."

"What's the matter?" she asked. It was not even nine P.M. yet, far too early for me to leave the office, even on a Friday night.

"You're not going to believe this," I said. "I'll tell you when I get home. I've got a great proposition for you."

I cleaned up my paperwork and hopped a subway train for Forest Hills. When I arrived, Laurie met me at the door with the question, "Where are we moving to? California? England?"

"Who told you we're moving?"

"Nobody. I just guessed."

"I was asked to move to Paris for a year. I don't know how you feel about just picking up and—"

"Let's go," Laurie interrupted.

CHAPTER SIX

WE TOOK A CRASH BERLITZ COURSE in French. Smith Barney reimbursed me for the $2,544.40 it cost us to break the lease on our apartment in Forest Hills. Before we realized what was happening, we found ourselves off the North American continent for the first time, living in a spacious, two-bedroom penthouse on Avenue Foch. The terrace offered a distant view of the Eiffel Tower. Unable to secure a work permit, Laurie busied herself with activities conducted by the American Women's Group. She immersed herself in French culture as I, at the tender age of twenty-five, sat at an antique desk in an office on the Place Vendôme and studied market data by the light of a Louis XVI chandelier. In New York I was accustomed to working through lunch and after dinner, grabbing sandwiches on the run. But in Paris, Laurie and I slipped immediately into the Continental habit of the two-hour lunch, using this time to explore the local restaurants. I realized an immediate affinity for French cooking, and my waistline began to show it. When I was not working late, we spent time in Left Bank clubs, listening to jazz.

At my new office, the partners offered a study in cosmopolitan personalities. The office was headed by an American, Ed Miller. The others were a French banker, Jean-Pierre Pinaton; Mark de Frishing, who held dual citizenship in Great Britain and Switzerland; Hansgeorg Hoffmann, our German trader; and Richard Janiack, a knowledgeable, patient man who taught me much about the European markets in general and the Scandinavian markets in particular.

I plunged into the task of preparing a $25 million Eurobond Convertible Issue for Texas International Air Corporation, Frank Lorenzo's holding company. The son of a Spanish immigrant (his given name was Francisco), Lorenzo and his partner Robert Carney had purchased Texas International in 1972 and turned it around with an innovative offering of off-time, cut-rate fares. Now they had their sights on other acquisitions, and they planned to use European money in their attempts to strengthen their hold on the airline business.

Smith Barney was co-manager of the issue with Kidder Peabody. My job was to make the numbers meaningful from a European perspective, prepare a prospectus and arrange for the "road show" so that Miller could shepherd Lorenzo to London, Zurich, Frankfurt and elsewhere in Europe to familiarize analysts and institutional purchasers with the details concerning the bond issue.

Our Paris luncheon, held at the Hotel Ritz, featured Norwegian salmon, accompanied by Chablis-Abbage 1976 and Château-Giscours 1969. This, I realized, is the civilized way to sell convertible debentures.

I was low man, but here in Paris the totem pole was not that tall, so I had a chance to observe closely. I was amazed at Lorenzo's energy, vitality and grasp of the human elements of business. He had a little-boy look about him and a zeal in his eyes. He was a crusader against the wastefulness of corporate bureaucracy, one of the first to raise publicly the themes that would fuel the fires of a coming business revolution: Big business had grown fat and lazy; overpaid executives act as if they, and not the shareholders, own the corporations; an isolated management is insensitive to employers; productivity is sacrificed in favor of policy; mountains of paperwork stifle efficiency; long-term planning is lost in the rush for short-term results; creativity is dead. These were to become rallying cries of a new populist movement in the American business world. The "have-nots" looked at the "haves" and declared: We can do a better job.

Change could not occur, of course, as long as the "haves" controlled the purse strings, and this was why Lorenzo was in Europe seeking $25 million.

With the money we helped raise for him, Lorenzo set about implementing his own lean management style. He was virulently anti-union, even though, as a Coca-Cola truck driver working his way through Columbia University, he had been a Teamster. Eventually when he acquired first Continental Airlines and then Eastern Airlines he attempted to cut costs by busting their unions.

SOON I was regularly analyzing world capital markets, arranging financing deals and advising on acquisitions. Here was a small merger; there was a Yankee bond offering (a European issue to be offered on the U.S. capital markets). On occasion a partner in New York would call to order a rush job on the analysis of some exotic company.

As the only associate in the office, I had to practice my own form of *détente*. Once, for example, I was laboring diligently on a task for the Frenchman Pinaton when Hoffman threw a job onto my desk. I explained politely, "I'll get to that as soon as I can, as soon as I finish this."

"Who are you doing this for?" he asked.

"Jean-Pierre."

Hoffman puffed out his shoulders, doing his best Prussian officer impression. "Fuck that frog!" he railed. "Do my work first."

LAURIE relished the role of playing hostess to a continual stream of family members and friends who took advantage of our temporary address as a jumping-off spot for seeing the Continent.

One of these was Bob Wilkis. From time to time during this busy year, he phoned from New York, to ask how things were going. Once, he called with the news that he had landed a position as an investment banker for Blyth Eastman Dillon & Co. I was as pleased for him as he had been for me.

During our conversation I casually passed on the news that a British packaging company, Metalbox PLC, was planning to acquire a small U.S. company, Risdon Corporation, a producer of cosmetics and specialty packaging. I knew that Wilkis would trade on the information, and I hoped he made money.

I had been in Paris for nearly a year when Wilkis called to announce that he was coming over on a business trip, and we would have a chance for a lengthy visit.

It was a warm feeling to see him. He came to our apartment for dinner, and I had the opportunity to see him several other times during his stay. We brought each other up to speed on the events of our lives. Smith Barney had offered me the chance to move on to its Japanese office for a two-year stint, but Laurie and I were ready to return home, and I was eager to cash in on the promised job in the M&A Department. Opportunities awaited me back in New York.

Quite naturally and easily, we spoke about private stock trading. Wilkis said, "We have all this information that we could trade on. We could make a lot of money."

Almost immediately I realized that I had changed. Life in France and, indeed, all of Europe, opened my eyes. The value system was completely different. Here was laissez-faire practiced to the extreme. I knew now that it was the norm, not the exception, for European executives to maintain bank accounts in Switzerland, Liechtenstein and/or Luxembourg. Americans often grumbled about their tax burden, but the rates in Britain, France, Sweden and other European countries were particularly punitive to the upper income echelons. Thus, international bank accounts were often perceived as necessary tax havens. As a side benefit, some of these men found secret accounts a convenient way to hide their assets from their wives and other family members. It was the Continental way of life, and many times the sophisticates shrugged at my naïveté and commented, "You Americans and your tax laws . . ."

In the U.S., where about half of all common stock is owned by the individual investor, market manipulations are perceived, rightly or wrongly, as attacks upon people. But in other industrialized nations the major shareholders are institutions. Everyone assumes that these organizations are privy to non-public information, but there is no private investor to cry "foul." Therefore, insider trading is not seen as an abuse; it is, rather, a part of the normal course of business. I discovered that in countries such as West Germany, Switzerland and Japan, insider trading was legal, considered to be one of the privileges associated with high corporate rank. No one chose to broadcast this fact, lest it disrupt the game. Thus, private accounts are useful and almost necessary for conducting quiet stock trades.

Viewed from my office on the Place Vendôme, trading on non-public information seemed, somehow, to be a way of life, and it was the most natural thing in the world for me to respond to Wilkis's words with the acknowledgment, "Everybody's doing it," followed by the question: "Why not us?"

We spoke at length about how best to proceed. Wilkis said that it was ridiculous for him to continue using his mother's brokerage account in Baltimore, when we—or anyone else—had easy access to foreign banks that routinely veiled customer data behind strict secrecy laws.

"How do you open a secret account?" I asked.

"I don't know," he admitted, "but it can't be that difficult."

I trudged off to the American Book Store and bought copies of *How to Open a Swiss Bank Account* and *Everything You Wanted to Know About Swiss Banking.*

Wilkis and I studied carefully; it did seem easy.

"But if we are serious about doing this," I declared, "we have to set careful ground rules, and we have to follow them." We hammered out a strategy that, if we had dared commit it to paper, would have looked like this:

1. *Each of us will only trade on the other's information.* Wilkis would trade on the basis of my tips and I would trade on his. Since neither of us would exploit our own information, how could anyone prove inside knowledge?

2. *We will never share tips with other members of our family or with friends, and we will keep our activities secret even from our wives.* In what we considered to be the most unlikely event that we ever got into trouble, our wives would know nothing, and thus be protected. Beyond that, of course, I knew that Laurie would disapprove strongly. This new, secret side of my life would be in character, I rationalized. Laurie knew that I was not allowed to talk about deals in progress until they were publicly disclosed, so I rarely brought the business home with me. It would be simple, I concluded, to compartmentalize this aspect of my life.

3. *We will trade stocks only through secret foreign accounts.*

4. *We will share information only in person, and when we speak to each other by phone, we will refer to one another by a code name so that no one will notice our association.* We chose "Alan Darby." If either of us had to leave a telephone message for the other, that is the name we would dictate to the receptionist.

The final rule was encompassing: 5. *We will use common sense.*

*   *   *

"DENNIS," Laurie said. "You've been tossing and turning in your sleep. What's wrong?"

"Nothing," I replied. "Everything's great."

"Something's bothering you," she continued. "Is the job that stressful?"

"No, I love my job."

"What's wrong?" she asked again.

"Nothing," I repeated.

EARLY in July I bought an airline ticket—paying cash so as not to leave a paper trail—and flew to Geneva. Somewhere in the back of my brain I knew that what I was about to do was wrong, but it simply did not feel that way. No one would get hurt. I did not believe that I would, in any way, undermine the ability of my clients to do business. As a mere associate, I had little influence over big decisions. All I would do was take advantage of my position on the inside of the industry and this, by now, appeared to be a normal course of action. I weighed the risks, just as I would analyze any other potential investment, and I concluded that the benefits outweighed what I perceived to be a minuscule chance of getting caught.

In Geneva, I made my way to the financial district and stepped inside the first large bank I found. I declared to an officer that I wanted to open a private account and he, in turn, explained that, because I was an American citizen, his bank would ask me to sign a waiver of secrecy so that, in the event of an inquiry, it could divulge details to proper authorities. "No thanks," I said.

Next I tried Pictet et Cie, one of Switzerland's most prestigious financial houses. Promotional material declared: "Private Bankers since 1805 . . . Investment Management Services." An account officer said that he did not require a waiver of secrecy, but he did need a reference.

"I work for Smith Barney in the Paris office," I said.

"You must know Mark de Frishing," the banker exclaimed.

De Frishing, I remembered, was a Swiss citizen as well as an Englishman. I replied, "I work very closely with Mark."

The banker said, "There will be no problem in opening your account."

He was very pleased with the prospect of my business and openly discussed my special requirements. I explained that I would be returning to the U.S. soon, and I wanted to be able to handle long-distance transactions with ease and discretion. Secrecy was my top priority.

To maintain secrecy, the banker suggested that I utilize a code name.

"How about Mr. Gold?" I asked. That seemed in character with my fantasies.

He furrowed his brow and replied, "No, we already have a Mr. Gold."

I chuckled at this confirmation of my suspicions that others were doing this, too.

After a moment the banker suggested the alias "Milky Way." "When you call," he said, "why don't you just say it's Mr. Way?"

"Fine. I'm Mr. Way. Now there's another thing. I only want to make my deposits in cash, because I don't want any instrument being traced back to me, but I don't want to come all the way over here every time. What do you suggest?"

Without any sign of reticence, the banker declared that I might find it convenient to deal through Pictet Bank & Trust, Ltd., the firm's subsidiary in the Bahamas. This sounded like the perfect solution. Nassau is less than a three-hour flight from New York, close enough for me to visit and return in a single day, without anyone, particularly Laurie, knowing that I had been out of the country. I could come and go between the two nations without the necessity of a visa and its telltale trail. Since Nassau is in the same time zone as New York, telephone communications would be easy.

Beyond that, this Swiss banker explained, the Bahamas are blessed with banking secrecy laws that are, if anything, more stringent than the Swiss codes. My Bahamian bank would be prohibited from disclosing any account information without my prior written consent.

I told the banker that within a matter of weeks, shortly after I returned to the U.S., I would visit the Bahamian branch and make an earnest deposit.

We shook hands.

It was as easy as the books said it would be, so easy that the full import of what I had just done did not hit me until I was in a cab headed back to the airport.

I had flown to Geneva to open a secret bank account.

I was positioned to cash in on whatever information Wilkis could supply concerning deals at Blyth Eastman.

Who knew how much money I could make? What were the limits?

Suddenly I felt like a character in a James Bond novel.

CHAPTER SEVEN

LATE IN THE SUMMER of 1979, Laurie and I returned to New York. After a three-week stay at the Plaza Hotel, we moved into a one-bedroom apartment in Manhattan, at 225 East 57th Street.

As soon as I checked in at Smith Barney, I reminded my superiors that they had promised me an opportunity to join the M&A Department, and they set a meeting for me with the new department head, J. Tomilson Hill III. Until recently he had called himself Jim, but, having lost a power struggle with Bruce Wasserstein of First Boston's pioneering M&A Department, he had joined our firm and introduced himself to everyone as Tom Hill. We could only suppose that he had decided it was time to change his image.

He was the quintessential WASP, having attended the Buckley School here in New York, Harvard University and Harvard Business School. The first-class education had produced a rigid, methodical, often humorless, supremely organized individual who kept his shirt-collar buttoned and his tie knotted during even the warmest summer's day. "Structure" was the operative word for his approach to life.

Hill did not know me, so he took me out to lunch to find out why I was so interested in his line of business. He seemed suitably impressed with my enthusiasm and my basic knowledge and agreed to take me on, at an increased salary of $31,000 per year.

He decreed that my time would be divided between two specific tasks.

The first was to assist on any and all tender offers: crunch the numbers, deal with the lawyers and company officials, run to the printer, proofread the documents. I knew instantly that this would be far more interesting than anything I had yet done. Most of the people in Smith Barney's Corporate Finance Division were client service personnel. There, if you found yourself assigned to the Dow Chemical account, you worked with that one company for the rest of your Smith Barney life, handling little more than routine business and financing tasks. But the M&A boys were the hired guns, brought in for specific transactions. They hit, then ran on to the next deal. It promised to be fast, furious and fun. Within the firm, M&A business was beginning to bring high fees and, it followed, high recognition. It was a unique opportunity for a young associate.

My second task was even more intriguing. The best way for an investment banking firm to land a hot client, Hill lectured over lunch, is to identify it before it is publicly "in play." "At first Boston," he said, "we had a function called 'Breaking News Coordinator.' I'd like you to handle that here. One of the things you'll have to do is watch the tape throughout the day to see what companies suddenly become active. You've got to study the news of the entire business world and bring important events to our attention."

This was fascinating. Hill wanted me to train myself to ferret out the evidence of aberrant trading! Sudden action in stock sales is a signal that somebody knows something—or thinks he knows something—and is rushing to act upon that knowledge—or hunch—before the rest of the world learns of it.

Hill also wanted me to stay in close contact with the new in-house rumor mill, otherwise known as Smith Barney's Arbitrage Department. Arbs had become critical players in M&A transactions, and more and more investment banking firms sought to institutionalize the species. Hill spelled it out for me: Suppose a company announces that it is involved in merger discussions, and the announced or rumored price that it will offer for the stock of the target company is $50 per share, perhaps $20 higher than the current market price. Typically, the price of the target company stock will jump up almost immediately to a level slightly below that speculative price, say, $47 per share. There are likely to be thousands of investors who have held that stock for years. Perhaps they bought it at $20 or $30. They could hold out to see if the final price is, indeed, $50, but they may be quite happy to sell immediately for $47.

In such a market environment, an arb will buy a significant position in the stock at $47 if he believes in the likelihood that the deal will close at $50, or if he suspects that another bid will surface at an even higher level. As the process continues, more players may enter the game, stimulating news or rumors of still higher prices, bringing fresh waves of buying. At each stage, the arbs will calculate whether or not to plunge more deeply.

Performed skillfully, risk arbitrage is lucrative, but the necessary tasks entail ferreting out information in any manner possible. There are some who refer to risk arbitrage as "the second-oldest profession."

Hill had convinced the Smith Barney hierarchy that it could not run a good M&A Department without an equally sharp Arbitrage Department, and he had lured Brian McVey to the job. The two men knew one another from their days at First Boston, but McVey had left there sometime earlier to work for Ivan Boesky, the most famous independent arb in the business. Now McVey was with us, and it was his job to keep abreast of the latest M&A developments. He had to be prepared, almost at a moment's notice, to decide whether to jump into a deal or refrain. He and his people had to look at proposed merger deals instantly, assess the track records of the buyers and sellers, determine the capitalization, psychoanalyze the personalities of the principals and phone everyone involved, searching for clues. If the deal was hostile, was there the potential for the emergence of a white knight, a more friendly would-be acquirer whose presence was likely to raise the offering price further? Was there a potential antitrust problem that might kill the deal and depress the stock price? What were the thousands of other subtleties that might make or break this merger? McVey's young department had its own network of researchers, so I would need to speak with him frequently if I was to gain a handle on the breaking news.

In sum, Hill said, it would be my job as Breaking News Coordinator to listen to the distant tom-toms of the trading world and report the messages to the partners.

"Would you like to do that?" Hill asked.

"Yes," I responded immediately. "I'll need a Quotron." No one in the M&A Department had one of these little screens on his desk. But how else could you follow the pulse of the market unless you had instant access to information concerning individual stock prices as well as fluctuations in the more general market indices?

"You'll have one," Hill promised.

* * *

EVEN as I settled into my new tasks on the job, I hustled about to plan
my financial future. Wilkis and I had a good system outlined, but I
needed to fund it.

I approached family members with a quiet request to borrow whatever cash I could in order to finance a nebulous business proposition.
To them, I was the sophisticated banker, just back from Europe. They
trusted me, asked no questions and, to my surprise, handed over the
money.

In addition, I took my credit cards to the limits of their generosity.
It all added up to a $40,000 fund. Seed money, I thought. The start of
my fortune.

One Friday I found a pay phone and placed a collect call to Pictet
Bank & Trust, Ltd., identified myself as Mr. Way and arranged an
appointment for the following day.

That evening I told Laurie in a nonchalant voice, "I'm going on a
business trip tomorrow."

"Oh, where?"

"Florida." This did not really feel like a lie. It *was* business. And
Nassau was close to Florida. The sudden trip did not surprise Laurie
at all, for such journeys were now a fact of my life as an investment
banker.

I had the entire $40,000 on me—stashed neatly in a briefcase under
a pile of official-looking papers—when I arrived at LaGuardia Airport
for my flight. Once more I purchased my ticket in cash, so that there
would be no paperwork trail. But I had some moments to wait before
boarding and, as I sat in the terminal, sudden dark thoughts gnawed
at me. What was I doing? I had put Laurie and myself into debt to our
family, as well as the credit card companies. It was not scruples that
bothered me, but a pragmatic question. What if the plane went down
in flames, incinerating not only me, but the money as well? Forgetting
my precaution concerning paperwork, I rushed to the flight insurance
counter and bought $40,000 worth of coverage.

NASSAU'S business district centers on Bay Street, a picturesque, palm-
lined avenue where cars zip by on the left-hand, British, side of the

road, dodging quaint horse-drawn carriages full of tourists. On the side streets, venders hawk their wares and seem disappointed if you agree to their first price and refuse to make the effort to bargain. Gorgeous ebony-faced children hover around any obvious tourist, ready to smile broadly at evidence of a camera.

Bay Street is a boulevard of banks. The names read like a roll call of financial giants: the Bank of America, Citibank, Chase Manhattan, Bankers Trust, Barclays, Crédit Suisse. Banking is second only to tourism as the nation's largest industry.

"I have been expecting you," the Pictet manager said as he pumped my hand. "I received a telex from Geneva regarding your account. We are happy to accommodate your business."

There are scores of important reasons for American businesses and American citizens to have accounts here, and two of them attracted me especially. First, there is no Bahamian income tax and, second, account records are protected by strict laws, which my new business associate detailed. Chapter 96 of the Banks Act mandated:

> Except for the purpose of the performance of his duties or the exercise of his functions under this Act or when lawfully required to do so by any Court of competent jurisdiction within the Colony or under the provisions of any law, no person shall disclose any information relating to the affairs of a bank or of the customer of a bank which he has acquired in the performance of his duties or the exercise of his functions under this Act.

The penalties for violating that secrecy provision were a 1,000-pound fine and/or one year in prison on each count.

This was augmented by the Banks and Trust Companies Regulations Act 1965, which declared (as amended):

> No person who has acquired information in his capacity as director, officer, employee or agent of any licensee or former licensee . . . shall without the express or implied consent of the customer concerned, disclose to any person any such information relating to the identity, assets, liabilities, transactions, accounts of a customer . . .

Under this new law, the maximum penalties for each offense were a $15,000 fine and/or two years in prison.

The conversation satisfied me completely. In a half hour I was on a return flight to New York, muttering to myself, I can't believe I did this. It was so easy.

When I arrived home, I called Wilkis and told him that everything was in place. Soon thereafter, he announced that he was ready, too, with his own account at the Nassau branch of Crédit Suisse.

IN the office, at a desk near the back of the M&A bullpen on the forty-eighth floor of Smith Barney's headquarters building, my days took on a dual personality. I conducted a pro forma analysis on one proposed merger after another. This latter task was the M&A version of number-crunching. If a merger was proposed or even fantasized, we needed a statistical picture of the ultimate results. I analyzed the two companies separately and then attempted to forecast what would happen if they merged into a single entity. How much capitalization would they have? What were the tax considerations? Would we have possible problems with antitrust regulations? What would the combined earnings ratio be? What would be the best form of financing to consummate the deal? Bonds? A new stock offering? A stock swap? Straight cash? A combination of such instruments and, if so, in what proportions? One plus one rarely equaled an even two. The bottom-line question to all this was: What is the proper price to offer for the target stock, the price that will persuade shareholders to sell and yet will still make the deal profitable for the acquirer?

Meanwhile, I kept one eye on the Quotron, watching zillions of numbers fly by, quantifying the machinations of the investment world. The market tells us on a second-by-second basis what is going on out there in the real world, but it is sometimes very difficult to interpret the messages. A stock shoots up three points in the space of a week on twenty-five times its normal volume. Why? The answer is obvious in its broad parameters: somebody is accumulating it because he knows something—or thinks he knows something—that others do not.

If I spotted anything of interest concerning a specific company, I ran for the brokerage library. One of the first things to check was who, if anyone, had filed a Schedule 13D. SEC rules dictated that when any single investor achieved a 5 percent ownership position in the stock of a given company, he had to file notice declaring the size of his ownership position, via Schedule 13D, within ten days, and he also had to disclose whether or not he was planning to attempt a takeover. It might be a corporate raider, trying to amass stock quietly before announcing a tender offer. Or perhaps it was an arb, gambling a fortune on the chance that the company was about to come into play. Whatever was going on, I could be certain that it would come to a head quickly. Everything in the M&A field seemed to be gaining momentum.

One day I participated in a lunch discussion with Bill Ziff and his associate Marty Pompadour about the possible sale of Ziff's specialty magazine publishing company, Ziff-Davis. CBS was a potential buyer and the deal looked as if it could have about a $600 million price tag. During lunch we treated the two men to a preview of Smith Barney's ambitious new ad campaign. The TV screens in the private lunch room showed the sagacious, no-nonsense face of actor John Houseman proclaiming, "Smith Barney makes money the old fashioned way. They *earn* it!"

That was the hallmark of the firm, one that was traditionally oriented toward long-term relationships. Of course, we all realized that the message was aimed at the retail market. In investment banking, the old-fashioned ways appeared to be dying.

Undervalued corporations were running scared and increasingly exhibited an acquire-or-be-acquired mentality. They were creating their own Strategic Development Departments to consider their proper roles: what companies to buy and what divisions to sell in order to make themselves less desirable targets. They now had men and women whose sole jobs were to ponder defensive strategies to take in the event of unfriendly attack. Armies of private advisers were kept on retainer, so as to be ready to swing into action at a moment's notice.

Investment banks had beefed up their own intelligence-gathering capabilities. We all maintained extensive files on corporate America— who owned what? who owed what? what was the corporate history? what was the stock performance history?

Whenever an official Offer to Purchase and a Letter of Transmittal were sent out to the shareholders of a target company, my phone rang off the hook. In its simplest form the offer detailed: If you, the shareholder, tender your stock by such-and-such a date, you will receive X number of dollars per share. But there were always far more intricate conditions involved, many of which were naturally confusing to the layman, so that, following fifty or more pages of small print, the offer always included the names of the information agent and the dealer-manager, plus phone numbers to call. Because I was the grunt working behind the scenes, those calls were routed to me. I spent a great deal of my time explaining the details of a sophisticated merger to neophytes. And to arbs.

As part of their nonstop information-gathering task, arbs spoke to investor relations personnel, corporate officers, law firms and anyone else they could find who had some knowledge of a pending deal. That included me, and they, in turn, developed into natural resources of information for a Breaking News Coordinator. Soon I had built contacts with various men in numerous arbitrage firms, and we shared public information with one another freely. If, in the course of general conversation, one arb referred to a deal that neither I nor anyone else at Smith Barney was working on, it was quite ethical for me to pass that rumor along to others.

The smart arbs never tried to put me into a compromising position, but they could impart great knowledge, and they were eager to help, aware that information flows in two directions. One might say, "Dennis, I like your deal. But I think you might have a problem here, because I have knowledge that Morgan Stanley is developing a white knight. You're going to have to bump your price up to $80 a share."

They would do anything to stimulate the market, to drive up the price of the target stock. "Dennis, you're not involved in this deal," one might say. "But have you thought about 1-2-3 Corporation. They'd be an ideal white knight. Why don't you call them, see if they'd be interested?"

The bigger the deal, the greater the barrage of information and innuendo that came my way. It was a constant task to separate the real information from the self-serving gossip.

Success at this task proved to be more hard work than genius. I kept a logbook of information, a sort of scorecard to track the players. By comparing various bits of input, I achieved a better understanding of what was really happening.

To my delight, the effort translated into visible fees. One day, for example, I heard a rumor that a large block of stock in Koehring Company, a heavy machinery manufacturer, might be up for sale by its owner, U.S. Filter. I knew that if a new buyer gained control of that key block, he would be positioned to initiate a takeover action. I rushed to the Smith Barney library and pulled whatever information I could on Koehring. Then I identified several companies that might be interested in acquiring it. Koehring appeared to be an appealing target, indeed.

I delivered this information to Hill, and he passed it on to officials at Koehring. For weeks I watched the Koehring stock carefully. Its price rise, unaccounted for by any news, seemed to indicate that the rumor had substance. Finally the public announcement came: A Canadian firm, Dominion Bridge, had bought the block and would initiate merger discussions with Koehring. Because we had exhibited such foreknowledge of the deal, Koehring hired us to render a fairness opinion for a $250,000 fee.

It was found money. Hill and I shared a knowledgeable grin and basked in the compliments of those about us. We had generated significant revenues and that, in the current environment of the investment banking world, was becoming the principal reason you came to work in the morning.

Here was a paradox: Information was the lifeblood of my job; using it within the confines of my office resulted in millions of dollars in gains and losses for various players; using it outside of the office could be illegal.

WORD of this early success, and a few other similar coups, filtered out beyond Smith Barney. One day I received a call from a partner in the executive recruiting firm of Hadley Lockwood. "We've heard some good things about you," he said. "We wondered if we could get together and learn a little more about you, complete a résumé, that sort of thing."

We met for breakfast.

The approach was flattering, and Hadley Lockwood opened a file on me. But I was nowhere near ready to make a move, and beyond that, I was dubious about going to work for their major client, the upstart firm of Drexel Burnham Lambert. Everyone knew that Drexel was strictly minor league.

*   *   *

As cogs in our respective investment banking machines, Wilkis and I were now both perfectly positioned to benefit from each other's information. One day I arrived at my desk to find a message that "Alan Darby" had called. I called Wilkis back immediately, and he suggested that we meet.

Between the Smith Barney office in the Burlington building at 53rd and Sixth, and Blyth's offices two blocks south, lay the labyrinth of pedestrian tunnels beneath Rockefeller Center. Amidst the bustle of the lunch traffic, Wilkis and I met there. As we munched on slices of pizza, he told me that one of Blyth's new clients was ERC, a reinsurance company that was about to become the target of a takeover bid by Connecticut General. I thanked him for this news, wiped the tomato sauce from my face and ran back to the Smith Barney library to do some quick research to allay my fears about the downside possibility of this investment. Had the news spread too far already, or did I still have a chance to get in on the early action? What if the merger did not materialize? If nothing happened could I be reasonably sure that the bottom would not drop out of the stock? How much stock could I buy without attracting undue attention?

Having reassured myself that ERC was a basically sound company, I returned to the underground maze, found a bank of pay telephones and, as Mr. Way, placed a collect call to Pictet. I instructed my Nassau banker to purchase stock in ERC, as much as I could afford.

Only a few days later, when the merger announcement was made, the stock shot up and I sold out quickly, realizing my first tangible insider profit. I grew uneasy when I learned that Smith Barney had represented the acquirer, since this was contrary to the guidelines Wilkis and I had established, but there were no repercussions.

On another occasion, as Wilkis and I spent our lunch break punching the flipper buttons on pinball machines, he disclosed that Blyth was working on an acquisition of Furr's Cafeteria. "It's a done deal," he assured me. I headed to the bank of pay phones and made my second profitable deal.

This was almost too easy to believe.

GIFFORD Hill, a Dallas-based cement manufacturing firm, wanted to acquire a similar company in California, known as Amcord, and hired

Smith Barney to represent its interests in the friendly deal. This was the typical, business-driven deal, involving two firms within the same industry. I mentioned it to Wilkis and, interestingly enough, he told me that Ed Stanton at his own firm was handling the Amcord side of the negotiations. Wilkis bought a position in Amcord, but I decided to pass up the opportunity. I was actively involved in the deal; it was too close to home.

One October day Tom Hill and I, with a briefcase full of documents, walked a few blocks to 48th Street and Park Avenue, to the offices of the powerhouse law firm of Wachtell, Lipton, Rosen & Katz, the legal reps for Gifford Hill. Our task was to review the batch of paperwork with a team headed by Marty Lipton, the patriarch of the firm and (along with Joe Flom of Skadden, Arps) one of the two foremost legal experts in the M&A world. On the thirty-sixth floor, Hill and I were ushered into Conference Room 1, where more than twenty men were already assembled. There were representatives here from both Gifford Hill and Amcord, as well as investment bankers and attorneys on both sides of the equation. The meeting began at ten A.M., but soon Lipton drew the principals off to a side room for private talks.

Those of us who remained behind stood, stretched, ambled over to the coffee pot and gravitated into those small cliques where so much real business is done. After a time I approached a tall, slender, good-looking and somewhat timid-appearing young man. He was young, but a bit of premature gray was mixed in with his dark hair.

"Hi," I said, offering my hand. "I'm Dennis Levine from Smith Barney."

"I'm Ilan Reich," he replied. He was twenty-five years old and had graduated from Columbia Law School less than six months earlier. Now he was working as Marty Lipton's associate on only his second tender offer. There was a quickness in his eyes that broadcast enormous intelligence. We shared a common bond as neophytes.

WILKIS moved to Lazard Frères, taking a job in the International Department, where he worked under Frank Zarb, the former U.S. energy czar. This was an exciting development for both of us. In the "go-go" era of the 60s, Lazard had been known as "the merger house," the first investment banking firm to downplay the traditional role of underwriting securities in favor of acting as an agent in reorganizations, mergers, acquisitions and the forming of new corporate entities. Its abrasive but venerable patriarch Andre Meyer was recognized by his peers for instituting this change of direction. Meyer's most notable deal, perhaps, was the 1970 merger of International Telephone and Telegraph and the Hartford Insurance Company. David Rockefeller had called him "the most creative financial genius in our time in the investment banking field." *Fortune* magazine named him "the most important investment banker in the Western world." Meyer was dead now, and Lazard's reputation as "the merger house" had waned, but its new, French-born leader, Michel David-Weill, and Meyer's protégé, Felix Rohatyn, seemed eager to follow the trail that Meyer had blazed.

Wilkis's move meant that more information would come our way.

As the Gifford Hill deal progressed over the course of several weeks, Reich and I spent long, late hours together, preparing documents, proofreading them and even hand-carrying them to the printer. Reich was less gregarious than I, but affable and extremely capable. The more I got to know him, the more my sixth sense told me that he might be willing to bend the rules. This could be important, I thought. It would be nice to have another source of information.

"I met a guy at Wachtell," I said to Wilkis one day. "He's about our age, very capable. He doesn't appear to have the typical corporate-soldier mentality."

We both knew that a contact at Wachtell would give us a line on perhaps half of all pending merger deals. If we could establish a new source, it would further cover our tracks. Our trading would have a much less discernible pattern if some of the leads came from outside either of our firms. Wilkis readily agreed that I should try a discreet approach. There was no need for Wilkis to know the other man's name, so we decided to refer to him as "Wally," a term loosely derived from Wachtell, Lipton.

Reich and I met for lunch in early March, and after we shared small talk about our families and our jobs, I carefully brought up the subject of trading on non-public information. In the proper quiet tone, I said, "You know, a lot of people do this."

"I know," he replied.

"We're the guys at the bottom. We kill ourselves so that our clients and our partners can make a lot of money. Everybody's getting rich but us."

Reich acknowledged the truth of my words with a nod, but we were both aware of a significant event that had occurred only a few days before, involving a printer named Vincent Chiarella who worked for Pandick Press, a firm that printed stock prospecti and tender offer materials. SEC investigators charged that Chiarella had studied these classified documents and used this knowledge to trade stocks. What made the case noteworthy was that the Justice Department jumped in. Previous cases of insider trading had been punished with a civil slap on the wrist from the SEC, which had no criminal jurisdiction. But Chiarella was prosecuted as a felon, convicted on seventeen counts of securities law violations and sentenced to a year in prison![1]

Chiarella, I pointed out, had made no effort to camouflage his actions. He traded openly, through a local brokerage account in his own name. It was almost as if he wished to get caught.

"How stupid can you be?" I asked. "If you do things right, it's pretty foolproof. There is virtually no chance of getting caught."

Reich was cautious, but interested. "What do you mean?" he asked. "Go on."

I told him about some of the executives I had met in Europe who maintained hidden trading accounts. It was a simple matter, I said, to set up a foreign bank account and handle transactions over the phone, anonymously. Reich's silence was tacit agreement, and it emboldened me. By using plural pronouns, I let him know that this was a multi-player game. "We already have a lot of sources on the Street," I said. "If you would work with us, we can come to an arrangement. Nobody has to know your name. If you decide to do this, you would only have to talk to me. I would trade securities for you, and even give you a nest egg to start. Nothing would be listed in your name. You could make a lot of money."

---

[1] In 1980, the U.S. Supreme Court vacated the conviction on the grounds that Chiarella, since he was not a corporate officer, had no fiduciary duty to the shareholders of the companies in which he invested; however, a dissenting opinion authored by Chief Justice Warren Burger opened the door for the SEC to apply a broader theory of "misappropriation" of information that could well be applied to a non-employee of a corporation who was, nonetheless, in a "position of trust."

He asked, "Well, how much of a nest egg?"

"Twenty-five thousand. On a margin account you'd be able to buy $50,000 worth of securities, just by talking to me. If you want to, we could set up an overseas company without using your name."

Reich was now clearly intrigued. It appeared to be a no-lose proposition. He was fully insulated against discovery, and he did not even have to put up any money. But he was not yet convinced. He thought about all this for a few moments, then replied warily, "Maybe. But you have to prove to me that you have other sources."

"Fair enough."

I reported this conversation to Wilkis, who scurried about his office to see what he could learn.

A deal came up shortly. Wilkis learned that the big French energy company, Elf Aquitaine, was planning a hostile takeover attempt of Kerr-McGee Corporation, a major oil and gas producer based in Oklahoma City. It was possible that this would be the first hostile takeover in history with a pricetag of more than $1 billion. It was a *big* secret.

As it happened, Wachtell, Lipton was handling the legal end. Wilkis managed to copy drafts of working documents composed by Marty Lipton himself, complete with a key to the confidential code names of the principal companies. He supplied the package of information to me and I called Reich immediately, announcing, "I think we should meet."

Our rendezvous took place in front of the Plaza Hotel on Saturday morning, March 22. It was the first day of spring and the weather was satisfyingly mild. Both of us were dressed in blue jeans. We strolled into Central Park and found a large rock to sit on. Reich glanced around nervously. "How safe are we?" he asked. "Are you sure we weren't followed?"

I told him not to worry, but I thought a bit of paranoia was a healthy defense mechanism. Then I disclosed that I was aware that his firm was working on a deal for Elf Aquitaine to acquire Kerr-McGee.

"You're unbelievable!" he exclaimed.

"Here are the documents," I added, handing over the packet of information that Wilkis had purloined.

Reich's eyes grew wide as he studied the secret file. He was both flabbergasted and convinced, and he was in, enthusiastically.

We planned to do as much of our business as possible in person, but in case we had to transmit information over the phone, we set up a code, using various editions of the *Standard & Poor Stock Guide*. Reich could phone me, identify himself as "Mr. Davis," and say, simply, "One, one hundred ten, fourteen." I would grab the first edition of the stock guide, turn to page 110, count down to line fourteen—and know that this company was about to come into play.

ON Monday I was ready to plunge headfirst into the market. This latest deal, with its potential to reach historic proportions, was a grand temptation, and I threw caution to the winds, multiplying the power of my money by purchasing call options on Kerr-McGee, rather than settling for a mere stock position. In my mind I earmarked a portion of the transaction for our new partner, Ilan Reich.

The deal proved to be volatile, and I was able to play it both on the upside and the downside. Before long, Kerr-McGee became a rumored target of Elf Aquitaine and, when the stock rose in price, I sold out. Then, when Reich informed me that the deal was about to fizzle, I sold Kerr-McGee short and profited from the drop in price when the merger failure became public information.

LATE one night, when Laurie was asleep, I sat at my desk and pondered the delicious feeling of success. Through only a few transactions, I had managed to triple the balance in my secret account. I calculated that I now had more than four times my annual salary stashed secretly in the Bahamian office of Pictet Bank & Trust, Ltd. It was a comforting, secure, intoxicating feeling . . .

CHAPTER EIGHT

WHEN I PHONED PICTET to verify my account balance, I was surprised to receive a lecture. My account manager said that his boss in Geneva was concerned about the timing of my Kerr-McGee trades. I had bought options only days before merger talks were announced, then sold short only days before the announcement that the talks had collapsed. The transactions were too suspicious, and he suggested that I might do well to modify my trading tactics, dealing in basic stock purchases rather than the more volatile and aggressive options and short-selling strategies.

This was more confusing than disturbing. Why, I wondered, should the bank care what I did, so long as it reaped lucrative commissions in the process?

I called the man's superior in Geneva and discussed the situation more thoroughly. The Swiss banker acknowledged that there were two schools of thought in such matters. Yes, it was true that both Swiss and Bahamian law guarded the secrecy of my transactions, but some banks were more cautious than others. Pictet, he said, tended toward the conservative view. He intimated that if I did not wish to pursue the course suggested by my account manager, it might be best for me to take my business elsewhere.

"Get another account," Wilkis agreed, when I reported this to him.

* * *

UNBEKNOWNST to my father or my brother, I sneaked their passports out of their desk drawers and made photocopies.

Then I took advantage of the Memorial Day holiday to fly to Nassau on May 27, 1980. When I arrived, dressed like a tourist in blue jeans and a sport shirt, I flagged a cab and headed for Bay Street. I simply stopped at a phone booth and looked up banks in the local version of the Yellow Pages. The first ad to catch my eye was that of Bank Leu International Ltd. It was described as a "wholly owned subsidiary of Bank Leu Ltd. Zurich (Switzerland). The oldest private Swiss bank. Founded 1755." Among its listing of services offered was "International Portfolio Management." I located the office in the Bernard Sunley Building in Rosen Square and walked in.

The bank occupied the second and third floors of the small office building. I liked the fact that there was no need for ground-floor space. Clearly, this bank was not interested in consumer operations.

I did not know how to pronounce the name of this institution. "Loy" the receptionist said. "Like toy." She directed me to the third-floor desk of general manager Jean-Pierre Fraysse. He appeared to be in his mid-forties and carried himself with a Continental air.

I announced, "I'm interested in opening an account to trade U.S. securities."

"Yes," he replied. He explained in educated but accented English that one had to be a foreigner to open an account here. Fraysse said that he had only recently joined the firm. His background was in the investment business, and he had been sent to the Bahamas with the specific mandate to improve the bank's trading activities.

"I am currently dealing with another major institution, another Swiss bank," I said. "But I'm not pleased with the way it is handling my affairs, and I am seeking an alternative. My first requirement is absolute security."

"Yes."

"You never call me; I call you, collect."

"Yes."

"I need to have my transactions executed promptly, immediately."

"Yes."

I asked Fraysse what U.S. brokerage houses he utilized to handle his buy and sell orders. He replied that he used Europartners Securities Corporation on an exclusive basis, because it was associated with Bank

Leu's home office in Zurich. "I want you to deal through different brokers," I said. "Break up the transactions, so that no large deals are going through any one broker."

"Yes."

"You have someone who understands U.S. markets."

"Yes." He brought in Bruno Pletscher, assistant vice president. The man was unassuming and surprisingly young, thirty-one, for a man with such a pronounced beer belly. All business, Pletscher explained that Bank Leu handled many trusts and "discretionary" accounts for U.S.-based clients. He would set up my account on the bank's computer system, so that everything could be accomplished with efficiency.

I asked, "What do you require from me?"

Fraysse answered, "A letter of reference from your existing institution. Can you tell us who that is?"

"I am currently banking with Pictet."

Fraysse said, "If you are banking with Pictet, you will have no problem with us."

That very day my banker at Pictet provided the necessary recommendation. Pletscher processed the paperwork for my interest-bearing account #777,470,11/10. I filled in my name and address on the signature card. I provided a power of attorney, which could be used either by my father or my brother, and I also handed over signature samples as well as photocopies of their passport pictures, so that, if necessary, they could verify identities. All of the background paperwork was placed into a special vault. Fraysse and Pletscher pledged that my identity would be known only to them.

Since most of our business would be conducted by phone, we needed a code name. I settled upon the designation "Mr. Diamond."

Fraysse recommended that I establish a Bahamian-based company with nominee directors appointed by the bank. This would be an added level of insulation to shield my activities but, I also realized, would provide another means for the bank to earn fees. I declined.

To these sophisticated, international financiers, it was all business as usual. They implied that they were happy to accept deposits from virtually anyone, with no questions asked. From time to time, one of these bankers told me, they accepted huge deposits of cash brought to them in bags. When I suggested that this might be drug money, they shrugged. They told me they never questioned the source of their clients' money. They were happy to accept the transfer of my account balance of $128,900.

Fraysse told Pletscher that my account was good for the bank and told him to do everything possible to provide outstanding service.

When I returned home I entrusted my father with a sealed envelope containing a copy of the power of attorney and instructions on how to deal with Bank Leu. "In case something ever happens to me," I said, "open this." Dad looked perplexed. I had a fleeting vision of him, grieving for me, opening the envelope and pondering its curious contents.

ON Thursday, June 5, only days after my money was deposited at Bank Leu, Ilan Reich disclosed that Wachtell, Lipton was representing Kraft Foods in a deal to acquire Dart Industries, a consumer products manufacturer, whose brands included West Bend and Tupperware.

That same day, during my lunch hour, I called Bank Leu collect. Bruno Pletscher accepted the call from "Mr. Diamond" and took my order to invest half the account balance in shares of Dart Industries. He executed the transaction immediately, purchasing 1,500 shares at a cost of about $61,000. The following day, just after the market closed for the weekend, Kraft, Inc., announced that it was planning to merge with Dart. When trading opened on Monday, the stock immediately rose about three points. Quickly I phoned in a sell order, bagging a modest profit, after Bank Leu deducted its rather high commissions, of $4,093.

The remainder of the month did not go so well. On June 9, acting on a tip from Wilkis, I purchased a position in Biscayne Federal S&L and nervously watched the stock drop steadily for a week before I could stand it no longer. I sold out for a loss of $11,480. I made two other small-scale trades that month and, at the end, I figured my balance sheet. Three of the four transactions were profitable, but the losses on the Biscayne Federal deal outweighed them. For June, I showed a loss of about $1,000.

That made me edgy. The loss of a thousand dollars was bitter—and it sensitized me to the greater risks. What if I plunged too heavily on the wrong deal and lost tens of thousands? I pondered and concluded that part of the problem was that, unfortunately, Wilkis was in a rather low level position at Lazard, and he was cloistered in the International Department, removed from the hot, domestic action. His intentions were good, but I just could not be sure that he was privy to reliable information.

Furthermore, I realized that the Biscayne Federal loss had caused me to panic. I jumped at the next few deals that came along without stopping to catch my breath, or research the stocks. I had been indiscreet, and that was dangerous.

What I needed, I knew, was better information concerning fewer, but bigger, deals.

IN a speech to the National Investor Relations Institute, SEC Commissioner Joseph A. Grundfest addressed the issue of insider trading and gave some insights as to the difficulties of proving and prosecuting abuses. When the SEC demands an explanation as to why an arb or other trader plunged into a particular stock prior to a public announcement, Grundfest said the typical response is something like this: "I'm in an airport waiting lounge, or bar, or elevator of an office building, and overhear these two guys talking about the big deal they're going to announce on Friday."

Such a story, Grundfest declared, "is up there with 'The dog ate my homework' as a credible explanation . . ." But although the SEC investigators might not believe such a cover story, Grundfest admitted that proving anything to the contrary is often difficult, or impossible.

THROUGHOUT the course of the summer I developed a friendship with Ira Sokolow, a husky, mustachioed six-footer, who, like Wilkis, was addicted to cigars. At twenty-six, Sokolow came with the proper credentials appended to his résumé: He had an undergraduate degree from the Wharton School of Business and a master's degree in taxation from Bentley College; he was a CPA, who had previously worked for the respected accounting firm of Arthur Anderson; he had completed the first of his two years of MBA studies at Harvard and was interning at Smith Barney before going back to school. He was on the fast track, and Smith Barney wanted to hire him full time after he completed his coursework.

Since Sokolow was such a good catch, I was assigned the task of wooing him. As part of that process, Laurie and I socialized with him and his wife, Judy, on several occasions, taking them out to dinners and a Broadway show.

Sokolow was a hard-working man, a good numbers cruncher and analyst. Beyond these basic skills, he possessed what I considered to be the proper personality for the Street. He was efficient at employing the social graces, but he was not overly effusive. There was a chemistry between us, the same spark of irreverence that earlier had passed between Ilan Reich and me.

"I have this kid working for me this summer," I said to Wilkis. "He's very discreet. He's going back to Harvard this fall, and then he's coming back to the Street. I think he wants to play."

"Okay," Wilkis said.

At what I felt was an appropriate moment, I broached the subject of insider trading to Sokolow, making the same offer to him that I had made to Reich, a $25,000 stake in my secret account.

"I would love to do it," he responded without hesitation. He was willing and able, but not ready. We reached the clear understanding that after he finished his MBA studies at Harvard, wherever he went to work, he would join our growing network.

ON September 24, I was sitting at my desk in the back of the M&A bullpen when the phone rang.

"This is Mr. Davis," said a curt voice, which I recognized immediately as belonging to Ilan Reich. "I'm out of town."

Referring to my stock guide, I replied, "Give me the number."

"I don't have one." He paused to think, then suggested, "Get *The Wall Street Journal*. Turn to the OTC page . . . okay, look in the fourth column, count ten down."

My finger rested on the name of Jefferson National Insurance.

"Buy it," Reich said. "Now."

I glanced at the clock. It was almost three P.M., one hour before the market closed. "Okay," I said. " 'Bye."

I hustled down to the first floor of the building, found a pay phone, called Nassau and ordered Pletscher to sink the entire balance of my account into shares of Jefferson National. Then, as "Alan Darby," I called Wilkis and advised, "Shoot the load."

One hour later I was back at my desk when Reich called again.

"What's going on?" I asked excitedly. "Did it—"

"The deal's dead," he interrupted.

My body went limp. I felt my pulse flutter. I had my *entire* account riding on this one deal. My eyes shot to the clock and I grimaced with the realization that the market had just closed.

"Got to go," Reich said.

I rushed back downstairs to grab a phone and report to Wilkis. He was as stunned as I was, but there was nothing we could do until the market opened in the morning. Nothing but hope. I had no idea where Reich was, what he was doing, what went wrong.

After a sleepless night I was at my desk early in the morning, as usual, trying to concentrate upon my work, waiting for the market to open so that I could sell out and eat whatever loss I had to digest.

But Reich called again, from wherever he was, with a short, sweet message: "Everything is okay. The deal is all right." With a lightened heart I relayed the news to Wilkis.

That morning trading in Jefferson National was suspended pending an announcement, and later, Zurich Insurance Company disclosed that it was buying Jefferson National. The target's stock soared.

Reich and I talked it over when he came back to town. "There was a breakdown in the discussions," he explained. "The deal died and then it came back." Then he asked, "How did we do?"

I reported that we had sold our 8,000 shares for a whopping profit of $155,734. Reich's share of that was about $20,000.

Jefferson National was the first big hit, and it changed the parameters of the game. Now we would be able to take larger positions, just as the M&A boom was picking up steam. It was a time of unprecedented opportunity for profitable speculation. Who knew what would come of it all?

THE winter months were a blur of activity.

Reich ran at full speed, throwing deals my way. Once he even took the initiative to photocopy Marty Lipton's personal work sheet, handwritten on a yellow legal pad, detailing every client that his firm was involved with at the time, as well as the status of each transaction.

This appeared to be a gold mine, but I tried to learn a lesson. On the Jefferson National deal, and in several others, Reich had been, perhaps, too hasty. I did not want to risk a big loss if a deal fell through. So I took my time, reverting to my old habit of researching the stocks thoroughly, to assure myself that there was a sound fundamental basis for the investment even if the takeover deal did not materialize. On balance, I only made about one investment a month. Now, most of my business was handled by Assistant Vice President Christian Schlatter, Bank Leu's new securities trader.

Life screamed along at an incredible pace, and there was no time for reflection, no time to worry about where all this might lead. If I had stopped to analyze it, I would have seen that there were now two Dennis Levines. One was a conservative investment banker, busier than ever at his office, working his way up the ladder as quickly as he could. Laurie was very proud of this persona, but she knew nothing of the ethereal Dennis Levine, who had hundreds of thousands of dollars stashed in a secret bank account.

In March 1981, Wilkis identified St. Joseph Minerals Corporation as a takeover target of Joseph E. Seagram & Company, the giant liquor distillery owned by the Bronfman family. It was late one afternoon when I placed a buy order for an enormous amount of options on St. Joseph Minerals. The next morning, after the deal was announced, I called the Bahamas and asked, "How did we do?"

"The market was closed," Schlatter said. "It was too late to place your order."

You win some, you lose some, I thought. I was disappointed, but I knew all along that this would require delicate timing.

John R. Shad, a balding, bespectacled gentleman of mild-mannered appearance, had recently left his post as vice chairman and head of corporate finance at E. F. Hutton to become chairman of the SEC. Upon taking the post, he announced that policing the crime of insider trading would be his top priority. In fact, he declared to one reporter that the SEC was going to come down on insider trading "with hobnail boots." Rallying to his cry for justice, SEC staffers bought him an actual pair of hobnail boots, which he displayed in his office.

Now those boots trod upon what the SEC described as "certain unknown purchasers" of stock and options in St. Joseph Minerals, who had bought immediately prior to the public announcement of the Sea-gram takeover bid. Federal Judge Milton Pollack froze certain sus-pected insider trading profits that resided in the New York branch of Banca della Svizzera Italiana. Then he upped the ante, threatening to slap the Swiss bank with a $50,000-per-day fine until it identified the "certain unknown purchasers." The government soon learned the iden-tities of a principal trader and three off-shore corporations affiliated with them.

By sheer luck, I had missed on the deal. The close call scared the daylights out of me, and I resolved to follow the advice of my old Pictet banker and curtail my trading in options. It was too obvious. From now on, I decided, if a deal was not yet publicly announced, I would trade only in standard stock shares. I would only consider options if the deal was already in the public's eye.

What I did not know at the time was that Fraysse was also very concerned. He wrote a memorandum to Schlatter (with a copy to Pletscher), dated April 10, 1981, noting that the SEC was cracking down on inside traders. "We have one," Fraysse said.

As a precaution, he said, the bank might want to spread its business among several brokers. In any event, he said, "such transactions" must be watched and new orders "should be immediately reported to me."

But, in fact, approval of my trades came from the highest level of the bank's hierarchy. Hans Knopfli, chairman of Bank Leu's Zurich man-agement committee and CEO of the Nassau subsidiary, personally approved my request to trade on a margin account.

Bank Leu continued to process my trades willingly, and only much later would I learn how much attention Fraysse and the others were paying to my business.

My brothers and I booked a banquet room at the Waldorf-Astoria, hired a band and threw a surprise, black-tie, sixtieth birthday party for Dad. Larry and his wife flew in from California as a special surprise.

Dad was overwhelmed by emotion and the grin on his face was ample evidence of the pride he felt for his sons. Robert was moving the family contracting business into bigger and better things. Larry was successful in the tough world of California real estate. And, although I was a very small cog in the financial markets, my proud father was convinced that I had taken Wall Street by storm.

Laurie was especially radiant that night. Family was, is and always will be the most important thing in the world to all of us. At the moment, however, neither Laurie nor I realized that our lives were about to change radically.

One evening, not long after the party, Laurie informed me that she suspected she was pregnant.

This was long-term good news and short-term disaster. We both very much wanted to start a family, but, as far as Laurie knew, we were still living from paycheck to paycheck. I was accustomed to methodical, strategic planning, to researching everything before I moved ahead, and I did not feel prepared for the unexpected onset of fatherhood.

On the afternoon of Laurie's pregnancy test, I phoned her at home and asked. "What did they say?" The eyes of my co-workers showed interest. Several of them grinned. I felt my face redden.

Laurie had not yet heard the results. "Give me the number of the lab," I suggested. "I'll set up a conference call and we can hear the news together."

Within a few minutes we were on the line with a receptionist at the medical laboratory, who announced, "Mrs. Levine, your test results are positive."

What did that mean? I asked, "Positive she is pregnant, or positive she is not pregnant?"

"Mr. Levine, your wife is pregnant."

It was one of the few moments in my life when I could think of nothing to say.

I caught the eye of a colleague, working at the desk next to mine. He grinned and waved his checkbook at me.

Incredible, conflicting emotions ran through my heart. I loved the idea of being a father, and I shuddered at the responsibility. My mind boggled at blurred visions of baby food, diapers, school clothes, a car on his sixteenth birthday—it would be a boy, wouldn't it?—and at the far end of my fantasies loomed the prospect of college tuition. I had to pay for all this. That was a father's job, wasn't it? But how could I be a good father when I was working eighty hours a week?

When the shock wore off, I found myself enchanted by the growing bulge in Laurie's tummy. She was determined to deliver naturally, so we enrolled in a six-session course of Lamaze classes, but my attention was diverted, of course, by yet another business deal. Amfac Corporation, based in Honolulu, was contemplating a major investment in the Fairmont Hotel Corporation, and I found myself traveling for extended periods of time.

My three-man team was asked to make a presentation to the Amfac board, and we flew out to Hawaii to do so. As it happened, Amfac was opening a new hotel on the small island of Kauai, and the board would be present for the occasion. So we hopped a puddle-jumper aircraft to Kauai.

Henry Walker, the CEO of Amfac, liked to brag that he was the only fellow in Hawaii other than actor Tom Selleck who owned a Ferrari. When he saw the three of us from Smith Barney, he made a wry face and said, "I would appreciate it if you would not wear your pinstripe suits for the board meeting tomorrow."

"Well," I said, "all we brought with us is our business clothes."

"You're in Hawaii now," Walker responded. "You have to wear aloha attire—flowered shirts and the like." He sent us off to Liberty House, Hawaii's largest department store, which was also owned by Amfac.

Suffering the effects of jet lag and wishing to be fresh for the presentation, I went to bed early that evening. The next morning, bright and early, I learned that one of our team members, having had too much to drink last night, had committed the cardinal sin of making a pass at one of the director's wives. I roused him from bed and packed him onto the next flight out.

With that embarrassing situation settled, we made our presentation and secured the business.

THE pace of life escalated steadily. I was only able to attend the first Lamaze class—and I even arrived late for that.

Many of Laurie's fellow students were convinced that she was a single mother.

CHAPTER NINE

THERE IT WAS in front of me. Tyler Corporation, a manufacturer of explosives and cast-iron pipes, was in the process of acquiring the specialty chemical manufacturer Reliance Universal. Smith Barney represented Tyler and it was my job to coordinate the preparation of the tender offer. It was only a small $72 million deal and the companies involved were decidedly boring, but it was business. I shared the information with Wilkis and I knew that he would profit from it, but why, I wondered, shouldn't I go ahead and do the same thing?

The ground rules that we had sketched during our meetings in Paris—it seemed like a century ago—prohibited this. To cover our tracks, we had agreed not to invest in deals in which we were involved as principals. But I had developed enormous confidence in the veils that I had set in place. My bankers assured me that everything was safe, and I even made sure that I switched the locations of the pay phones that I used whenever I called the Bahamas, on the off-chance that the bank's line was tapped. There was not a piece of paper anywhere in the U.S. that could link me with the trades and, by law, Bank Leu could not provide any outsider with information regarding my account. What could be more safe?

Our machine was humming. Wilkis and Reich were enthusiastic. Ira Sokolow, finished with his Harvard studies, had joined Lehman Brothers Kuhn Loeb and was ready to play.

My God, this is so easy, I said to myself, and I ran for a pay phone to call in a buy order for Reliance Universal.

DUE to the cost of new aircraft purchases from Lockheed and Boeing, as well as problems with its acquisition of National Airlines, international price wars and falling domestic traffic, Pan American World Airways was staring in the face of a $400 million loss, the largest one-year deficit in the history of its industry. Its long-term debt and lease obligations were perilously close to the limits of its debt-to-equity ratio, as dictated by its bank loan agreements. In search of cash, William Waltrip, president of the Airline Division, attempted to talk the unions into accepting an across-the-board 10 percent wage reduction but met understandable resistance. A group of lenders led by Citibank offered $200 million in temporary credit, but the interest rate was a whopping 21.375 percent, and the banks made the loan conditional upon four of Pan Am's five U.S. unions accepting the wage reduction package.

In desperation Pan Am decided to divest itself of its major profit-making division, Intercontinental Hotels Corporation, which owned eighty-three facilities in forty-eight countries. Pan Am, of course, needed an investment banking firm to attend to the details, and its traditional house, Lehman Brothers, assumed that it would get the job. But thanks in part to my work as Breaking News Coordinator, Smith Barney received the business and Lehman Brothers was forced to assume a subordinate role.

There was no shortage of potential buyers. An executive from Hilton Hotels Corporation called our office on Monday and was told that Intercontinental might be for sale. Westin Hotels, a subsidiary of United Air Lines, was so interested that, when he heard of the possible acquisition, the company chairman rushed from his fishing boat to attempt to telephone an offer. Another group of investors from Abu Dhabi discussed a bid of $450 million.

This deal moved along like lightning. When the Hilton executive called back on Tuesday, we told him that Intercontinental was already sold. We had found a willing buyer in Grand Metropolitan Ltd., an acquisition-minded British hotel and liquor firm, which agreed to pay about $500 million. There were two forces at work here. First, Pan Am needed the money fast, and Grand Metropolitan was willing to expedite the sale on a handshake basis. Second, Pan Am loathed the thought of selling to Westin, owned by a competitor airline.

When the Pan Am deal closed, those of us who worked on it were invited into the inner sanctum, the office of Smith Barney Vice Chairman John Morgan himself, grandson of J. P. After we had assembled and offered bits of hesitant small talk to the prim and proper gentleman, he rose from his over-sized desk and reached behind him to the bookshelves that held bound volumes of the business documents from past deals. He took down three or four of these tomes and set them on his desk. Then he reached into the cavity on the bookshelf and produced a bottle of vintage white wine.

"Let us celebrate," he said.

Realizing that he was sans corkscrew, he reached into his pocket and extracted a dime. He pulled a screwdriver from his desk drawer. With deliberate movements he positioned the dime flat on top of the cork, then applied pressure with the screwdriver until the cork, and the dime, popped into the bottle.

"Let us celebrate," he repeated, as he poured out the wine.

SEVERAL transactions competed for my time. I was performing advisory tasks for Penn Central Corporation and also doing work for J. Ray McDermott, a New Orleans based offshore drilling platform manufacturer; John Morgan was a director of that company. In the meantime I helped service Smith Barney's largest account, Dow Chemical.

On top of all this, I got my first chance to work on a leveraged buyout (LBO) when I helped Olin Corporation divest itself of its subsidiary, Winchester Firearms Company.

The LBO was an old idea that was back in vogue, a fiendishly simple device that paid off handsomely. The word "leveraged" is a euphemism for OPM, or "other people's money"; the term "buyout" is self-explanatory. On a relatively small scale, those concepts are the basis for the spate of get-rich-quick investment strategies proposed by real estate gurus, and when considered on that level, they are easy to understand. The ideal is for an investor to purchase a home or apartment building or office complex for little or no money down. The purchase price, or the bulk of it, is financed by one or more mortgages. If the deal is a good one, the monthly rents generated by the tenants will be enough to cover the mortgage payments and the investor will eventually reap his profit from the appreciation of the property—all without putting up a cent of his or her own money.

Multiply that concept by a hundred million dollars, add a variety of refinements tailored to the specific deal, and you have an LBO as it applies to the world of corporate business. The LBO specialist sniffs out a company that he can buy with borrowed money secured, not by his own assets, but by those of the target company. Once he acquires the target, he will seek to repay that money in one of two ways. Perhaps the company will generate enough cash through its normal operations to service the debt, or perhaps the entrepreneur can sell off enough assets to pay his creditors. The goal is to wind up with at least a portion of a viable, ongoing business, unencumbered by significant debt, which costs nothing.

As the M&A boom picked up steam, more and more astute corporate managers used this technique to acquire their very own companies. Many on Wall Street were quick to praise the trend, pointing out that when the top management team of a public corporation became the ownership team of a suddenly private corporation, it naturally assumed a greater interest in the efficiency of the enterprise.

But to me, a management-sponsored LBO almost seemed to be a legalized insider trade; I had crunched enough numbers to know that the CEO and senior executives of a public company have a far better handle on the true value than the horde of anonymous shareholders. Not only is management positioned to better know the facts, but also to manipulate them. Every corporation has hidden assets, very often in the form of real estate that may have been on the books for decades and is carried at its acquisition value rather than its present market value. Real estate holdings were always one of the first assets we looked at when we attempted to assess the value of a company from the outside. Real estate was a vibrant market, and it was *common* to find a parcel of land, or a building, carried on the books for perhaps $25 million, when it's fair market value was tenfold that. We already knew that one of the best ways to leverage a transaction was to sell off the under-valued real estate to pay off the cost of the acquisition. If the company needed the facility, it could negotiate a lease-back provision into the sales contract.

The power of management to fudge the figures was pointed out by SEC Commissioner Bevis Longstreth in a monogram. An annual report, he noted, could consist of multiple pages of rosy predictions or a single page of dour forecasts. Assets can be bought or sold, opportunities can be accelerated or deferred, dividends slashed, debts paid, advertising budgets juggled, all for the purpose of affecting the stock price. Longstreth argued that management could thus induce shareholders to sell their stock back to the management cartel at a relatively low price. Not all LBOs were conducted in such a manner, but the temptation was inherent, and Longstreth asked rhetorically whether it was fair for management to "arrange things" so that it is "the only bidder, and then bless its own offer?"

I came to characterize some of these transactions as crimes that aren't crimes.

Fair or foul, the LBO was becoming a major feature of the business landscape. Before the 80s, most LBOs had been small potatoes, generally involving less than $100,000. They began to gain momentum, however, as corporate executives watched the success of a few pioneering deals. The archetypical example occurred during this year, 1981, when a group called Wesray, headed by former U.S. Secretary of the Treasury William E. Simon and his partner, Ray Chambers, pulled off an LBO of Gibson Greeting Cards, purchasing it from RCA in a transaction that appeared to hold lucrative potential for the principals.[1]

By now there were investment firms, such as Henry Kravis's Kohlberg Kravis Roberts & Company and Theodore Forstmann's Forstmann Little & Company, formed specifically to pull off LBOs, hold the companies private for a time, and then take them public or sell them. The average profit on such a deal was reported to be about 40 percent, but was often much higher. Ultimately, one of the SEC commissioners would characterize an LBO as "little more than a charade" and a financial officer of Goodyear Tire & Rubber would call it "an idea that was created in hell by the devil himself." It was, nonetheless, effective and lucrative.

*   *   *

---

[1] A mere year and a half later, Wesray took the company public, reaping an incredible hundredfold profit on its investment.

IN the past, the path to success in investment banking was slow and steady. If you managed to land an entry-level job with a respected firm, you stayed put for the rest of your working life, climbing slowly up the ladder. Today's world was different. Du Pont Corporation had just spent $9 billion to take control of Conoco, and the transaction was a clear indication that absolutely no company was immune. The M&A business was on the move and so, in turn, were its practitioners. John Morgan and two of Smith Barney's most senior partners were leaving to launch their own M&A "boutique," a specialty firm to handle the high-level details of major transactions. I knew the volume of our business would drop dramatically. It was time to hunt for a better paycheck.

Sokolow was not the only person I knew at Lehman Brothers. Another friend had moved there recently, and I reasoned that this gave me a foot in the door. That venerable firm, launched as a cotton brokerage in the mid-nineteenth century by Henry, Emanuel and Mayer Lehman, had passed through several incarnations and nearly went bankrupt in 1968. But now, under the management of Peter G. Peterson, who at age thirty-four had been president of Bell & Howell and then served as U.S. Secretary of Commerce under President Richard Nixon, Lehman Brothers was challenging First Boston for the role of the most active and respected M&A dealmaker on Wall Street. Peterson traded freely on his contacts in social circles; along with his wife, Joan Ganz Cooney, president and founder of the Children's Television Workshop, he was a fixture on the New York artistic scene. Lehman Brothers seemed to have more clients, more talented dealmakers and, thus, more clout than anyone else. For the past three years it had earned ever higher record profits.

I asked my friend if he could arrange an introduction for me with Eric Gleacher, the head of Lehman Brothers' M&A Department. That feeler resulted in an appointment for a breakfast meeting with Gleacher, to be held downtown, in the firm's private dining room at 55 Water Street.

In my usual manner, I studied everything I could find concerning Lehman Brothers and Gleacher. He was a former Marine who had reached a status in business where he was frequently quoted in newspaper reports concerning various high-level transactions.

One day when business took me to Marty Lipton's office, it was my good fortune to catch his ear. I said quietly, "I'm thinking of joining Lehman Brothers. Could I use you as a reference?"

"Absolutely," Lipton replied. "It would be a great move for you."

On the appointed morning, I stepped off the elevator into the Lehman Brothers' offices and gaped. The Lehman family members were world-class art collectors. Original works of impressionist painters graced the deep-grained wood-paneled walls. Here and there a sculpture stood on a pedestal over the marble floor.

Gleacher greeted me warmly and took me to one of the firm's exclusive dining rooms. The chefs here were renowned for their cuisine. This was only breakfast, but we feasted on exquisitely prepared omelets and fresh croissants.

Gleacher and I got along well. He was suitably impressed by my work on Pan Am's divestiture of Intercontinental Hotels, wherein Smith Barney had lured away the lion's share of the business from Lehman Brothers. He was aware that Smith Barney, despite its ad campaign, was not doing things "the old-fashioned way" and he was interested in bringing fresh enthusiasm to his own firm. During one point in the conversation he cast a conspiratorial glance about the opulent dining room and declared that he had always viewed himself as a maverick, not one of the typical Ivy League kids, but a scrapper.

"A Marine," I pronounced.

"Yes." He laughed.

During the conversation I quoted several of the statements he had made recently to various financial reporters.

"You've done your homework," he acknowledged. Like me, Gleacher believed that the successful dealmaker transcended number-crunching. He knew that a client would pay for shrewdness, for instinct, for a carefully timed smile. "I want you to see some of my partners today," he said. "Do you have the time?"

"Absolutely."

"Do you have references?"

"Call Marty Lipton," I replied.

Within days Lehman Brothers made me an offer that, as a prospective father, I could not refuse. On November 3, 1981, I would join the firm as a vice president at a base salary of $50,000 per year plus, of course, an annual bonus that would be a multiple of my salary.

* * *

ON the heels of the St. Joseph Minerals investigation, the SEC alleged that several Middle Eastern investors had earned $7.8 million by trading options involving Santa Fe International Corporation, shortly before a takeover attempt. Those profits were divvied up in four accounts: in one Swiss bank, in the Swiss offices of Citibank and Chase Manhattan and in a deposit account in the New York office of a firm owned by Crédit Suisse. On October 26, 1981, U.S. District Court Judge William Conner ordered the monies frozen until the case was resolved.

In an effort to codify procedures, SEC enforcement officer John Fedders hammered out a Memorandum of Understanding, whereby Swiss bankers pledged to breach their traditional wall of secrecy in certain cases of insider trading—if those activities violated the less-exacting Swiss laws as well as U.S. laws.

Wilkis and I both said, "Uh-oh," when we heard this news, and we were thankful that we had shunned the Swiss banks for the more convenient offshore locations in the Caribbean.

As the starting date of my new job neared, Wilkis, knowing that my position would bring me more prominence on the Street, and concerned over the SEC's increased vigilance, suggested that I take further steps to shield my other life. He explained that he had already insulated his position by setting up a dummy corporation to stand between him and his account. He gave me the name of his Bahamian lawyer, Hartis Pinder, and urged me to set up the same sort of arrangement.

I arrived in Nassau the day before Halloween with a mission to fulfill. First, I met with Pinder and explained my situation: I wanted to establish a corporation and transfer the assets of my personal account at Bank Leu to the new business entity. Pinder suggested, since I was especially concerned with secrecy, that I base the corporation in Panama, rather than the Bahamas, because Panamanian law would not require that my name be disclosed on any documents. For appropriate fees, certain individuals in Pinder's law firm would act as directors and handle all the necessary paperwork. All I had to do was arrange for Bank Leu to transfer the fees to the law firm, Pinder said, and he would take care of everything else.

When I explained the corporate arrangement to Bank Leu officials, they jumped onto the bandwagon. There were fees to be earned here, and everyone wanted them. You don't have to bother with the law firm, they said, we will be the directors.

Fraysse introduced me to a new player, fifty-year-old Richard Coulson. He was a graduate of Yale University Law School and a former investment banker in New York. He was an established member of the Bahamian business community and was one of the bank's legal consultants. Coulson suggested an innovative strategy. Bank Leu could establish a mutual fund to shield the source of the investment activities. Bank officers would be named as directors of the fund but they would, in fact, act only upon my orders, since all of the money in the fund would be mine. This way, Coulson said, my investments would appear to be managed by others, should anyone ever nose about.

But I declined all of the bankers' suggestions. In truth, I wanted to spread the business around, but I offered the reasoning, "I don't want to put you in a difficult position. In the event of an inquiry, I would rather not have a corporation affiliated with you."

"Well," Fraysse said, "an inquiry would be irrelevant. We couldn't, under Bahamian law, respond in any way, shape or form."

"No," I repeated, "I want it separate, distinct. I never complained about your commissions, which are outrageous . . ."

Fraysse stiffened at my blunt words.

". . . because you're in business to make money, and I understand that. I want everybody to make money."

"You're a valued customer," Fraysse acknowledged quietly. In fact, I was, by now, Bank Leu's *most* valued customer.

BACK home, I retrieved from Dad the envelope, still unopened, containing the power of attorney that would have allowed him access to my personal account at Bank Leu. I replaced it with an envelope containing new instructions and bearer shares of Diamond Holdings. Whoever walked into the bank with those shares in hand controlled the company and its account.

Thus was born Diamond Holdings, consisting of a few legal papers in a file folder. Pinder was listed as the president. His law partner Richard Lightbourn was vice president, and one of his employees, Maris Taylor, was secretary.

* * *

ON Saturday, December 5, not long after I joined Lehman Brothers, Laurie went into labor. I rushed her to New York Hospital and, with my mind in a fog, arranged the details.

I heard a clerk's voice emanate from some distant planet, "Would you like Mrs. Levine to have a semi-private room or a private room?"

"Uh, private."

"Would you like a water view, or a non-water view?"

This is like checking into a hotel, I thought. I stammered, "Well, if the water view is available, I guess we'll take it."

My child was in no hurry to be born. For twelve hours Laurie did the hard work, as I held her hand, tried to do what I could to help and, paradoxically, tried to stay out of the way. I had missed the tour of the maternity ward that is part of the Lamaze classes, and everything amazed me. I heard what sounded like horrible screams emanating from a delivery room down the hall, and I wondered if Dr. Marquis de Sade was on duty.

Lamaze or not, Laurie finally had enough. She had been in labor for eighteen hours when she begged for an epidural anesthetic and the doctor complied. He moved her into a delivery room, and I donned a gown and mask to accompany her. By now it was Sunday morning.

"What are you doing?" the doctor asked when I entered.

I was laden with a camera and a tape recorder. "Taking pictures," I replied. "Recording the sound."

The doctor shook his head, but he was not about to tangle with me. I scrambled around documenting the moment. Under the effects of the anesthesia, Laurie fared better. "Push!" I heard. "Push! Push!!!"

All of a sudden, the baby was *there*.

A nurse squealed, "It's a . . . a . . . a boy."

The doctor said, "You have a son."

Laurie shrieked, "I can't believe it." Tears poured from her eyes. Pain and anxiety drained away in an instant, replaced by pure joy.

"Is he healthy?" I asked.

A nurse reported, "He's got all his toes and fingers. He looks wonderful."

Now we heard from the principal character. He emitted a wondrous, joyful, incredible cry.

Scrubbed and polished, wrapped in white linen, the boy was placed in Laurie's arms. She clutched him eagerly and cried out with joy, "It's a baby!"

I laughed and asked, "You expected a watermelon?"

"Mr. Levine," said a voice behind me.

I jumped, startled, and turned to see the doctor. "Yes?"

"Would you like to hold your son?"

"Yes, yes," I said. I found my hands quivering as I reached for him. A nurse approached. Laurie held the bundle up and the nurse passed him to me. He felt so fragile in my arms. I could barely see his tiny features through my own tears. I leaned close and said, "Hello, Adam. I'm your daddy."

Through fuzzy eyes he tried to gaze back. At that instant I knew that Laurie and I were partners in a deal that made anything on the Street fade into insignificance. If I had been able to hold that concept in the forefront of my mind, perhaps everything would have been so different.

But I was a baby myself in so many ways. By eight A.M. Monday, I was at the office with a box of rare, Cuban-made Monte Cristo cigars in hand. I made the rounds to all the senior partners and announced that, yesterday, my son, Adam, had arrived on this crazy earth.

Bill Morris, then head of Corporate Finance, sniffed appreciatively at the cigar I offered and asked, "How did you get these?"

"I got them," I replied enigmatically.

"Well, keep doing things like this, and you're gonna be a partner in this firm, young man."

Ira Sokolow accepted my cigar with pleasure.

But when I offered one to my new boss, Eric Gleacher, he snapped, "What are you doing here, schmuck? Get to the hospital. Spend some time with your wife and son. I don't want to see you back here for a few days."

I arrived at the hospital to find Laurie enjoying the sight of a huge bouquet of flowers, sent by Gleacher.

He was, of course, attempting to teach me an invaluable truth. But I was, unknowingly, already too addicted to the elixir of success.

CHAPTER TEN

IN THE PAST, deals simply came to Lehman Brothers, but now the partners sensed that some business was passing them by, corralled by more aggressive firms.

I brought them an innovation, suggesting the position of Breaking News Coordinator. "I can't believe you guys don't do this," I said to Gleacher. The competition had grown too fierce to be passive, I argued. First Boston had named Bill Lambert as its "creative director," a euphemism for the job of aggressively seeking out target companies and just as aggressively finding potential acquirers willing to put the targets into play. Morgan Stanley had established a group whose job was to study every announced merger and search for a white knight that it could persuade to come in with a better offer. We could not afford to sit back and wait for merger business to come to us. We had to seek out targets and then propose them to other companies. I explained how the job of Breaking News Coordinator had paid off for us at Smith Barney, and I volunteered for the task. "I'll need a Quotron on my desk," I said.

Lehman Brothers was in the process of computerizing its operations, and I spent considerable time establishing an ambitious electronic spread sheet file containing data of major U.S. and multinational corporations. I categorized them by industry, size and location. I recorded whatever I could find concerning their financial status and cross-referenced to compare them to their competitors. Special files showed me, at a glance, a company's M&A history, whether as an acquirer or target.

The setup procedures were ponderous, but after a time, I had at my fingertips the basic data necessary for evaluating almost any deal.

ONE day Ira Sokolow came over to my office in the M&A Department. He mentioned that Motorola was preparing to acquire Four Phase Systems and he was working on the target's end of the deal. He asked quietly, "Are we doing this?"

"I don't know anything about it," I replied. "Tell me."

He explained what was afoot and declared, "It's one we should be doing."

I relayed the information to Wilkis and we plunged ahead, making more than $60,000.

Deals came and went. On July 13, 1982, I bought 12,000 shares of Thiokol Corporation, an electronics company. Six days later the announcement of an acquisition proposal netted me $116,205.

A month later, Reich passed on a tip that Dyson-Kissner-Moran Corporation was considering an offer for Criton Corporation, an aerospace firm near Seattle. I bought a position in the company and, at the same time, saw a chance to demonstrate to Gleacher the value of a Breaking News Coordinator. I told him that I had picked up rumors that Criton might become a target. Gleacher called a Criton official, who claimed no knowledge of the rumor and expressed the opinion that we were out of our minds. After the deal was announced, he called back and asked us to huddle with him to map out defensive strategies. Sokolow and I flew to Criton's headquarters in Bellevue, Washington.

While we were there, it became obvious that the price was going up. Over lunch at a Mexican restaurant, Sokolow and I quietly debated what we should do with our knowledge.

"I really don't want to make a collect call from here," I said. "How many people are in Bellevue, Washington? I just don't know if it's traceable."

But it seemed like very easy money—after all, the deal was already announced—and we could not resist the temptation. We finished our lunch and, before returning to our afternoon meetings with Criton, I called Nassau and increased my position to 27,000 shares of the company's stock. I sold within a week, after Dyson-Kissner-Moran announced its increased tender price, for a profit of $212,628. The money was nice but, in addition, Gleacher's confidence in me increased; obviously, I had impeccable sources of information.

ON a July trip to Nassau, I traveled light, carrying only a garment bag and a tennis bag. I met a new employee of the Nassau office, Bernhard Meier, an investment expert transferred from Zurich to replace Chris Schlatter. His job as assistant vice president was to help Bank Leu handle its increasing volume of stock transactions. He was a small, sophisticated man, about my age, outgoing and gregarious. His wife Helene was a member of one of Switzerland's most prominent banking families, the Sarasins, one of whom sat on the board of Bank Leu, Zurich. Meier himself had studied at the Wharton School of Business. He chain-smoked throughout our conversation.

TRUE to Shad's vow, the SEC appeared to be taking more vigorous action against inside traders. Wilkis and I paid careful attention whenever anything hit the press and compared the details to our own situation. There was, for instance, the case of Carlo Florentino, a young partner at Wachtell, Lipton. He was an associate of Ilan Reich's and I had worked with him on a couple of deals, but no hint of impropriety had passed between us. When he was arrested for insider trading, I was amazed to learn that he had the audacity to conduct his activities through his personal brokerage account at E. F. Hutton, where he traded in the securities of companies that he was personally advising.

Wilkis and I said to one another, "Can you believe how stupid he was?"

Florentino's lawyer characterized his client's actions as "more neurotic than criminal," and managed to get him off with a sentence of two years' probation. His career, of course, was finished. In my Rolodex, I searched through the "W" listings for my contacts at Wachtell and drew a line through Florentino's name.

The incident stunned Reich into caution. By now, in the autumn of 1982, his share of my account was more than $100,000. I asked him if he wanted any money, but he declined. In fact, he said, he wanted to stop.

"Fine," I told him. "No problem. But your money is there, anytime you want it."

IN the latter months of 1982 the SEC had made inquiries through Europartners Securities, the New York brokerage through which Bank Leu dealt, concerning transactions in shares of XOG International, Inc. Dr. John Lademann, who was a board member of Europartners as well as a director of Bank Leu International in Nassau and a member of the executive board of the parent company in Zurich, sent a telex to the Nassau office on September 14, 1982. The text was in German, so Bruno Pletscher translated it into English for his colleagues. Although I had not traded XOG, Lademann indicated that he knew the details of my transactions.

Two days later Pletscher, in a telephone call with Lademann, concluded that there was no problem with my trading, even if it was based upon inside information, because it was not a violation of Bahamian law. Nonetheless, Lademann advised caution.

Following this, Fraysse ordered that several new brokerage accounts be opened at various offices in the U.S. This was a defensive measure to spread my transactions around among other brokers and was a clear indication that Bank Leu valued my business and wanted to assure its continuity.

Shortly thereafter, Fraysse wrote a review of the new man's performance, describing Meier as "intelligent, methodical, with a good feeling for business and markets." Fraysse recommended a promotion and a pay raise for Meier and concluded, "He should do well for BLI and its clients."

Only much later would I learn that Meier, after viewing the success of my market activities, had concluded that I was onto something big. "Mr. Diamond" was making big bucks with his fast turnaround buying and selling, and Meier decided that he, too, could participate in what seemed to be as close as possible to a sure thing. He determined to copy at least some of my trades.

This is a tactic known as "piggybacking." It is not illegal in the Bahamas, nor is it illegal under U.S. law, per se, unless the piggybacker has knowledge (or ignores strong evidence) that the trader he is copying is acting upon illegal information. However, piggybacking was very much contrary to the rules that governed the actions of officers and employees of Bank Leu and any of its branches. To cover his tracks, Meier set up a private account for himself at Bank Leu, code-named "Ascona."

THE clandestine portion of my life took relatively little time and energy. What really preoccupied me was legitimate endeavors. I was at my desk one day in May 1983 when word came over the wire that Maryland Cup Corporation was in merger discussions with an undisclosed acquirer. Scuttlebutt held that the potential buyer was a European firm. My fingers spun across the computer keyboard and my eyes scanned the CRT to discern what our data bank could tell me.

Based in Owings Mills, Maryland, just outside Baltimore, the target company was an important manufacturer of disposable paper and plastic products for industrial food service companies, and it happened to be the single largest producer of ice cream cones. Its most recognizable brand names were "Sweetheart" paper plates and "Eat-it-All" ice cream cones. It had $400 million in assets.

The most interesting tidbit I learned was that Maryland Cup was a previous client of Lehman Brothers. Back in the latter part of 1980 and the first half of 1981, we had represented the company in merger discussions with Fort Howard Paper Company, based in Green Bay, Wisconsin, a major manufacturer of industrial paper products, with a balance sheet showing $650 million in assets. No deal was consummated at the time, but I wondered, was Fort Howard still interested? Were they interested enough to assume the role of a white knight? I ran to the appropriate partner and asked, "Are we doing the Maryland Cup deal?"

He replied, "What are you talking about?"

Within a half hour we had tracked down Merrill L. Bank, Chairman of the Board and CEO of Maryland Cup. We spoke to him via a golf course telephone and persuaded him to give us a chance to find another buyer, a higher bidder. Through Fort Howard's investment banker, Morgan Stanley, we opened negotiations. Fort Howard was a natural buyer, for its business meshed well with the target. Both were successful at selling their paper products to food service companies, but Fort Howard appeared to have superior production expertise that could be brought to bear upon Maryland Cup's facilities. The deal made sense.

Early in June, I phoned Meier in Nassau and ordered him to purchase about $600,000 worth of Maryland Cup shares for my account. What I did not know at the time was that, after buying 15,200 shares for me, at an average price of $39.25, Meier then bought 300 shares for his own coded account.

After a furious few weeks of activity, featuring a series of clandestine meetings at airport hotels, where we brought together the principals, we cut a deal between the two firms on June 27. Maryland Cup shareholders were given the option of receiving either $52 in cash ($3 higher than the current market price) for each share they held, or swapping each share for .85 percent of one share of Fort Howard (currently trading at about $55 per share). The shareholders voted their approval and Maryland Cup became a wholly owned subsidiary of Fort Howard Paper. We kept the business under U.S. ownership and generated a commission of $2,732,000 that otherwise would have gone elsewhere!

I sold out my private holdings of Maryland Cup on July 7, for a profit of $121,807. Meier earned $1,769.

WITH an ever-growing network of contacts and a track record of successful transactions, I gained the reputation of a "rainmaker," someone who could bring in new clients. My career was on the move, and for the first time I really began to believe that I could make it to the big time, legitimately. This realization helped Laurie and me decide that it was time to go house-hunting. Adam had reached the toddling stage and we felt cramped in our one-bedroom Manhattan apartment.

A broker showed us a top-floor unit at 1199 Park Avenue, an attractive post-war building. Laurie loved the fact that Carnegie Hill was a clean, safe, family-oriented neighborhood. The co-op was within our price range, but before we agreed to buy it, I wanted my Dad to look at it through his contractor's eyes.

"The roof of the building has problems," Dad pronounced. "And this is a top-floor apartment, so you'll have problems. Don't buy it." He found several other flaws.

As we left the building we walked south, past a magnificent structure, dripping with Old World charm. "Boy, I'd like to live in that building," I said to Dad. "But I can't afford it."

A short time later a six-room apartment became available in that very building, through an estate sale. If we financed to the hilt, we could afford it, so we took a look. Laurie admired the ornate entrance gate and the vaulted ceilings in the hallways, but the unit itself was a disaster. It had been built in 1929 and showed its age. The original, inadequate plumbing was still in place. Shreds of old wallpaper hung from some of the walls. There was not a modern convenience in sight. We found a clothesline stretched across the kitchen, attached to squeaky pulleys. Nevertheless, it was spacious, with 2,200 square feet to work with, and we saw potential. Because of its condition, it was priced well below market. We made an offer, putting down 10 percent in earnest money, which was accepted pending approval by the co-op board.

We submitted our application, along with a letter of reference from Lehman Brothers Chairman Pete Peterson, who declared that I was "extremely well regarded" and respected within business circles. My integrity, he said, was "of the highest order."

Laurie and I had to appear in person before the board, which ultimately granted its approval. Then we contracted to have the apartment gutted and remodeled before we moved in. The entire process would encompass more than a year.

THE Lehman Brothers' hierarchy succumbed to infighting, erupting into a bitter feud between Peterson and his counterpart in the Trading Division, Lewis Glucksman. Glucksman, whom Peterson had elevated only a few months earlier to the post of co-chief executive, had tired of being viewed as a second-class citizen, a mere "trader." This was a classic confrontation between the urbane Peterson—who referred to former U.S. Secretary of State Kissinger as "Henry," to Federal Reserve Board Chairman Volcker as "Paul" and to his tennis-playing buddy Buchwald as "Art"—and the cigar-chomping Glucksman, a plump, disheveled, demonstrative and highly talented scrapper, who peered over the top of half-frame glasses to view Peterson's airs with disdain.

By now, many a Wall Street firm had been swallowed by the merger environment and Glucksman was worried that the fifty-seven-year-old Peterson had plans to sell out to the highest bidder, before he was required to sell his stock back to the company when he reached age sixty.

Glucksman blatantly announced to Peterson that he wanted to take over total management of the company and Peterson, after deep consideration, decided that a battle would be too divisive. At a special board meeting on July 26, Peterson resigned and the outcome of that war was further evidence that the power structure of the Street was changing.

The boardroom infighting debilitated the company and Glucksman made some swift moves that caused further disruption. He increased the annual bonuses for himself and certain of his cronies and slashed them for others. He shuffled job positions around, making as many enemies as friends in the process. In short order six partners announced plans to leave; the most prominent among them was Gleacher, who accepted a partnership at Morgan Stanley and was replaced as head of the M&A Department at Lehman Brothers by the fiery, egotistical Peter Solomon.

The mass exodus caused Lehman Brothers more than personnel problems; it precipitated a cash crisis. Under the firm's bylaws, a departing partner was required to sell his stock back to the company, and Lehman had to cough up some $30 million to pay off the six men who bolted. This depleted its capital base by about 17 percent.

Some of us wondered how long Lehman would be able to retain its classy, old-line image.

EVER since the February death of Gulf+Western's chairman, Charles Bluhdorn, the conglomerate had been liquidating its holdings in subsidiary companies such as J. P. Stevens, Brunswick, Hammermill Paper and the Bank of New York. One of its last remaining holdings was the educational book publisher Esquire, Inc., and rather than sell its 30 percent interest, Gulf+Western decided to buy a majority share. In October, Esquire engaged Lehman Brothers to work on its end of the transaction, and I was assigned to the task. Peter Solomon, my boss, was an Esquire director. In the process, I bought and sold 15,200 shares of Esquire's stock, netting a profit of $121,728. Once again without my knowledge, Meier piggybacked 300 shares for his own account.

Sometime after that, Ira Sokolow informed me that he had recruited an associate at Goldman Sachs, who had agreed to pass on information. He did not want to tell me the man's name, and I did not want to know. We referred to him merely as "Goldie."

Sokolow's share of my account was now worth several hundred thousand dollars. He asked for some of it in cash, and I made plans to have Bank Leu supply it.

IT was about this time that Meier, in Bank Leu's continuing quest to diffuse my business among numerous brokers, opened a trading account with Brian S. Campbell, a broker in the New York office of Merrill Lynch, Pierce, Fenner & Smith.

Rather quickly, Campbell and Meier developed a working friendship. Meier realized that Campbell exhibited a good sense of timing. He knew how to buy or sell expeditiously, but he also knew when to exercise caution, lest he arouse the suspicions of the SEC. Beyond that, Campbell was able to offer the bank a generous break on commissions. Since I was unaware of this at the time, it was not necessary for Bank Leu to pass those savings on to me.

ILAN Reich, who had continued to let his money sit in Nassau, collecting interest, suddenly reappeared. In November 1983, he and I were both present at a "21" Club lunch celebrating the closing of a deal between Clabir, Inc. and HMW (formerly Hamilton Watch) in which both of our firms had participated. This renewed our friendship and, once more, we began to meet for occasional lunches. He did not provide any additional tips, but I sensed that he was merely biding his time.

How, I wondered, could he afford to ignore the opportunities? The M&A boom had accelerated beyond anyone's wildest predictions. Prior to 1980, U.S. business history recorded only seven acquisitions capitalized at $1 billion or more. Already, little more than three years into the decade, there had been more than thirty such deals. Not only were these transactions bigger and more numerous than before, but they were also tougher. Having gained a foothold of respectability, hostile deals now accounted for about one-third of all mergers and acquisitions.

I was promoted to senior vice president. I scrambled toward a future that seemed rosy indeed, although there was never any time to stop and think about it.

These days, I never saw a product. If I was in a supermarket or a shopping store and I saw a brand-name of anything for sale, I thought of the company behind it. I saw a balance sheet, a takeover candidate, a possible acquirer. I saw a deal.

Sometimes Laurie would interrupt herself in mid-sentence to ask, "Are you with me, Dennis? Am I talking to the wall?"

CHAPTER ELEVEN

SEC CHAIRMAN JOHN SHAD kept his "hobnail boots" promise. In three years' time, he brought more than forty cases of insider trading to the courts. Shad was joined in his crusade by Representative Timothy Wirth (D-CO), who chaired hearings of the House Subcommittee on Telecommunications, Consumer Protection and Finance and sponsored the Insider Trading Sanctions Act, enabling the SEC not only to demand that an inside trader return his profits, but that he pay treble damages as well. And on top of *that,* Shad developed good relations with the U.S. Attorney's Office in Manhattan, paving the way for more vigorous prosecution on criminal charges such as securities fraud, tax evasion, obstruction of justice and perjury. All of this seemed a bit watered down to President Reagan, who, when he signed Wirth's bill into law, commented that there was still no definition of insider trading and that such a definition "might be appropriate."

But in truth, the definition was evolving right under the president's eye. On January 4, 1984, Deputy Secretary of Defense Paul Thayer, the second-ranking official in the Pentagon, resigned his post in the aftermath of SEC and Justice Department charges that he had illegally provided confidential stock information to acquaintances. The accusations covered the years 1981 and 1982, when Thayer was chairman of LTV Corporation and a director of Anheuser-Busch Companies, Inc., and Allied Corporation, and alleged that he tipped eight associates to

inside information that resulted in stock trading profits, for them, totaling $1.9 million. One of the alleged recipients of the sixty-four-year-old
Thayer's tips was a thirty-seven-year-old former receptionist at LTV
with whom Thayer maintained a "private, personal relationship."
Other alleged beneficiaries of Thayer's information were former New
York Jets running back William H. Mathis, now an Atlanta stockbroker, and Billy Bob Harris, a Dallas-based stockbroker who broadcast
his own market predictions on local television. Thayer vowed to fight
the charges.

On the heels of this came the story of dapper, bearded, quick-witted,
avowedly gay R. Foster Winans, one of the two authors of *The Wall
Street Journal*'s "Heard on the Street" column. The column published
market news obtained, ostensibly, from legitimate sources. Winans had
once declared, "The only reason to invest in the market is because you
think you know something others don't." The wide readership of the
column meant that if a rumored deal appeared there, the publicity alone
might be enough to move the market. In March 1984, knowing that he
was the subject of an extended investigation, Winans admitted to SEC
officials that he had accepted, in concert with his roommate David
Carpenter, $31,000 for providing advance notice of the news contained
in his upcoming columns to Kidder Peabody stockbrokers Kenneth P.
Felis and Peter N. Brant. Over a period of about four months, the
stockbrokers were reported to have gained more than $600,000 in
trading profits as a result. Winans did not deny the charge, but he
contended that the activity did not fall into the poorly defined category
of insider trading. Nevertheless, he was convicted and sentenced to
eighteen months in prison, but he remained free pending appeal.[1]

These were highly publicized cases and, perhaps, they should have
caused Wilkis and me to temper our activities. Instead, we scoffed,
noting with disdain that Winans and his buddies had made no attempt
to hide their transactions. We agreed with the conclusion reached in the
March 12 issue of *Forbes* magazine, which declared, "Most people who
get caught are dumb or naive or careless." The magazine openly offered
this advice: "It helps to hide your trail if you deal only with foreign

---

[1]The sentence was later reduced to one year in prison, plus five years' probation, 500 hours of
community service and a $5,000 fine; in November 1987 the U.S. Supreme Court upheld the
conviction.

banks that have no presence in the U.S., which leaves the U.S. courts with little leverage to break the secrecy laws of other countries."

Wilkis, having experienced a falling-out with his Crédit Suisse bankers, had moved his business to the Bank of Nova Scotia Trust Company in the Cayman Islands, and my private Panamanian corporation traded under the veil of Bahamian secrecy laws. We saw no reason to stop.

VICTOR Posner, a Miami-based power broker who operated through Chesapeake Financial Corporation, Southeastern Public Service Co. and other subsidiaries, held approximately 24 percent of the stock of Peabody International, a pollution control equipment manufacturer located in Stamford, Connecticut. He was obviously in a strong negotiating position to block anyone else from attempting an attack, and he wanted Peabody for himself. He announced plans to parlay his investment into an acquisition.

Peabody retained Lehman Brothers to render a fairness opinion on Posner's proposal, and I headed the team assigned to the task. Very quickly we were put off by the dual nature of Posner's offer, which entailed two different types of securities and which would result in some shareholders receiving unfair treatment. Despite pressure tactics emanating from Posner's camp, we decided to advise Peabody's board against recommending the offer to its shareholders. We knew that this would suit Peabody's management, for it wished to remain independent, if possible, and beyond that had no desire to be associated with Posner, whose reputation for "rape and pillage"—stripping an acquisition of its assets—was widely known.

We presented our findings to the Peabody board, but one of the members, former President Gerald Ford, had a scheduling conflict, so we had to arrange for an additional, private presentation. Ten days prior to the meeting, we supplied our Social Security numbers to the Secret Service, to arrange for security clearances.

The meeting took place in a private suite at the Waldorf-Astoria Towers. I had heard rumors that President Ford was not an astute businessman, but he proved otherwise during the forty-minute meeting. He knew his subject matter and he asked sensible questions. With his support, we succeeded in keeping Peabody out of Posner's grasp.

*   *   *

Avon Products announced plans to sell off its subsidiary, Tiffany & Co. One of the potential buyers was Donald Trump, who already had dealings with Tiffany. Trump Tower is adjacent to the Tiffany Building at 57th Street and Fifth Avenue, and Trump had previously purchased the air rights to assure himself that no one would obstruct his view from the top. My associates and I considered Trump to be a negative in any deal; he insisted on tying up too much of his money in the volatile casino business, and he exhibited a tendency to act with his heart rather than his mind. There was no question that Trump liked to go for glory, and the Tiffany name certainly held the kind of allure that would tempt him.

I knew that Tiffany's CEO, William Chaney, would be concerned over the prospect of working for Trump, and moments after the Avon announcement came over the newswire I managed to get Chaney on the phone. He did not know me, but he listened to my suggestion that his own management team structure an LBO to purchase itself from the parent. Indeed, he was already considering this option but was unsure of how to proceed.

At first I brought in Ray Chambers of Wesray, to see if their LBO group could team up with Chaney, but the negotiations fell apart rather quickly.

Still, Chaney liked the concept of being at least a partial owner of the company he managed, and he believed he could repay the borrowed cash out of company profits so long as the business climate remained good, but he worried that the economy might move into a down cycle, putting him into a bind. It was a valid worry, I said, and I complimented him on his caution. But I pointed out that he had numerous safety valves. For one thing, he had the famed Tiffany diamond, which could bring the company a quick $12 million almost on a moment's notice. Then there was the value of the name. Over the years Tiffany's had guarded its reputation carefully, refusing to sign any lucrative licensing agreements. Fine, I said, hold to that. But remember that if you get into a cash flow problem, you can raise a great deal of fast money by licensing the name. That escape valve was the final point that sold him on the $135.5 million deal.

Chaney's main financial backer was Investcorp, a subsidiary of Arabian Investment Banking Corporation, based in Bahrain, run by Iraqi-born, Fordham-educated Nemir Kirdar. Investcorp, which was backed in part by money from the Saudi royal family, put up $95.5 million in loans and paid an additional $48 million to buy Tiffany's building on Fifth Avenue, which it leased back.

The convoluted nature of the financial chain fascinated me. It typified the intricate nature of the modern business deal. Our market was the world.

IN late March, Wilkis told me that Lazard had been hired by The Limited, Inc., the Columbus, Ohio–based retail clothing store chain, to represent it in a takeover attempt aimed at Carter Hawley Hale Stores, a California department store chain that owned, among other subsidiaries, John Wanamaker, Neiman-Marcus, Bergdorf Goodman and Waldenbooks. The target company's assets were six times greater than the potential acquirer, which meant that the financing was a critical component. Leslie Wexner, The Limited's chairman, managed to construct a web of loan commitments from a consortium of foreign banks, as well as Security Pacific Bank. Bank of America was originally involved, but dropped out. This was all done, ostensibly, without revealing the name of the target company. Wilkis bought 20,000 shares of Carter, and I bought 33,000 shares.

Without telling me, Meier bought shares for his own account and, furthermore, approached his colleague Bruno Pletscher and suggested that he, too, buy the stock. Meier reminded Pletscher that I had "an excellent track record" and asked, "Why should not you also benefit from such trades?"

Pletscher had little money to invest. He passed on the deal, but he said, "Let me know if you have the next deal coming up. Mention only situations to me in which you feel comfortable and you expect a nice profit, because I cannot afford to lose money."

Wilkis and I watched the market developments with great interest and noted that, despite The Limited's security precautions, the word seemed to have leaked. In a six-day period, the volume in Carter trading increased dramatically, much of it coming from purchases through brokers based in Panama and Liberia; in all, thirty-three banks located in ten different countries were known to have speculated, trading a total of 265,900 shares, running the price of the stock from $22 to $26. Responding to this unwelcome activity, The Limited rushed out its tender announcement on the evening of Monday, April 2, offering $30 per share for more than 20 million shares.

The usual run of lawsuits and countersuits followed. The Limited raised its bid to $35 per share and threatened to dismiss Carter's entire board of directors once it gained control. Carter, in response, announced that it had put together a defensive financial package that included considerable support from Bank of America, one of The Limited's original financiers. Ultimately, The Limited was forced to back off.[1]

Wilkis sold out for a profit of $95,000 and I made $222,000. What neither of us knew was that Meier made a profit of $6,729.

MY 1984 base salary at Lehman Brothers was $75,000 and I was guaranteed a minimum annual bonus of $100,000. The senior management of the firm made me a "profit participant," a designation given to only about one hundred of the 3,500 employees. As one deal after another flew across my desk, as I saw my efforts turn into mountains of cash for my clients and the firm, it became obvious that I was positioned to earn more, through my profit participation, than some of the partners. Indeed, I believed that this was the year that I was going to become a partner myself.

But suddenly I became a victim of the M&A trend. For 134 years Lehman Brothers had been a privately owned firm, its stock held by the partners. Thus, it was invulnerable to a hostile takeover bid; it could be acquired only if enough of the partners chose to sell. But the resolve of those partners had been sapped by last year's bitter battle between Peterson and Glucksman.

Rumors flew about the financial press that Lehman Brothers was on the auction block, and these gained credibility when the seventy-two partners held a series of secret meetings. Some said that European investors were interested. Crédit Suisse already owned a sizable share of First Boston, and there was a considerable amount of Continental money and Japanese money that wanted to get a toehold on Wall Street. It was difficult to concentrate on work.

In May, Shearson/American Express acquired Lehman Brothers at a cost of $360 million (of the total, $325 million went directly to the

---

[1]In February 1991, Carter Hawley Hale announced that it was filing for bankruptcy due to decreased sales and, according to some analysts, its inability to meet interest payments on the debt incurred in fighting the takeover attempt by The Limited.

partners) and immediately set about putting its imprint on the Lehman mystique. The new entity was called Shearson Lehman/American Express (later shortened to Shearson/Lehman Brothers). Fifteen of the partners disappeared from the premises.

Wall Street's oldest investment banking partnership was gone. The unique flavor of the small firm disappeared overnight. Now, I was a cog in the machine of a financial conglomerate. *Business Week* quoted me as saying, "A lot of the spirit, a lot of the drive was gone."

I searched for a new position but decided to take my time.

ALTHOUGH Ilan Reich still refused to accept any of his profits, he was back in the game. Only later would I learn that he was worried that his marriage might be in trouble, and he thought he might need an infusion of cash to handle alimony and child support payments. Beyond that, he had received a "mixed report" in his annual review at Wachtell, Lipton and worried that it might damage his future. There was no question that Reich was brilliant and creative, but some of his associates wondered whether he was a "team player."

Whatever his motivation, Reich quickly gave evidence that he was back on our team. On May 3 he tipped me to the fact that his law firm had been hired by Warburg, Pincus & Company to handle the legal end of a possible acquisition of SFN Companies, an encyclopedia publisher. Throughout the summer, as Reich reported to me on the progress of the complex negotiations, I acquired 20,000 shares of SFN.

UPDATING my résumé, I was able to report that I had generated $10 million in fees for Lehman Brothers in 1982 and $15 million in 1983. My projection for the current year was $20 million.

It was gratifying to realize that the headhunters were after me, trying to lure me to any of several firms. I was wooed by Merrill Lynch, Pierce, Fenner & Smith, which had greatly increased its investment banking activities under the management of Donald Regan, before he moved into the Reagan cabinet, but I did not like the idea of trying to fit into such a huge bureaucracy. One executive recruiter asked if I would like to run the M&A Department at E. F. Hutton, but this was unappealing, for the firm had never been a powerhouse in investment banking. I had several promising interviews with Kidder Peabody, raising the possibility of working side by side with Marty Siegel, and an overture from Morgan Stanley. The New York offices of several foreign banks were after me. And Hadley Lockwood was still trying to persuade me to join Drexel Burnham Lambert.

A preliminary report to Drexel declared that I enjoyed two things: doing deals and making money. The report characterized me as "something of a workaholic," who was so busy that it was difficult to pin me down for an interview, except on short notice. It declared that I needed to be convinced "that the opportunity represented by Drexel Burnham is significantly superior" to my job at Lehman Brothers.

I took a hard look at Drexel. It was an amalgam of the old firm of Drexel Harriman Ripley, I. W. Burnham and Company (founded in 1936 by "Tubby" Burnham, former chairman of the Securities Industry Association) and the Belgian firm Group Bruxelle Lambert, controlled by Baron Léon Lambert.

Long entrenched in the second tier of investment banking firms, Drexel finally seemed to be on the move. During the past year Drexel had drawn the Street's attention with its role in a pair of high-profile dramas. Early in 1984, Texas financier T. Boone Pickens, Jr., through his company, Mesa Petroleum, set his sights on the acquisition of Gulf Oil. Pickens came to us at Lehman Brothers for tactical advice, but he went to Drexel for financing. In short order, Drexel obtained commitments to raise a whopping $1.7 billion for Pickens's war chest. He bought up more than 13 percent of Gulf's stock but lost a proxy fight that would have given him the authority to restructure the company. The ultimate winner was Standard Oil of California (later Chevron), which paid $13.2 billion for Gulf. When Pickens sold out, Mesa Petroleum earned a pre-tax profit of about $500 million, but Drexel had missed out on financing the largest takeover deal in history.

The second notable event occurred in midyear when Saul P. Steinberg, through his Reliance Group Holdings, Inc., launched an attempt to take over Walt Disney Productions Corporation. Steinberg, a baby-faced, roly-poly fellow who favored bright red bow ties, was the founder and CEO of Leasco Data Processing Company and had made his first significant fortune by leasing IBM computers to the business community. He displayed that fortune by purchasing a twenty-eight-room, 35,000-square-foot triplex apartment at 740 Park Avenue, previously owned by the Rockefeller family. He had been regarded as the enfant terrible of the takeover world ever since he had launched a hostile takeover bid for the giant Chemical Bank. The traditional business powers ganged up on him, dumping Leasco stock by the truckload, sending its price into a downward spiral and causing him to abort his attack on Chemical. The highly publicized affair placed Steinberg, for many years, firmly into the anti-Establishment camp.

Now the Disney episode brought a resurgence of those feelings. Here again was the swashbuckling Steinberg, attempting to take control of something that was far more than a company. Never mind the fact that Disney carried vast Florida and California real estate holdings on its books at values substantially lower than fair market price—Disney was an American institution. Such entrenched corporate giants were supposed to be invulnerable to a raid from a smaller entity, but Drexel amazed the investment banking community with its ability to finance the attack.

Steinberg was the principal in an investment team that included financier Kirk Kerkorian, the majority shareholder of MGM/UA Entertainment Company, and Fisher Financial & Development Company. Steinberg reportedly paid his partners a total of $1.5 million in return for loan commitments of $150 million. He then set up a new corporate shell to handle the Disney bid, dubbed MM Acquisition Corporation, unabashedly named after Mickey Mouse. Some suspected, however, that the name was a tip of the hat to Michael Milken, Drexel's by-now legendary financial wizard, who arranged $1.5 billion worth of financing for the proposed transaction. MM purchased 11.1 percent of Disney's stock and announced a $970 million tender offer for an additional 37.9 percent of the shares.

Disney squirmed out of the tight corner by agreeing to buy back the stock that the Steinberg group had acquired, paying a premium over the market price that resulted in a profit for Steinberg in excess of $30 million. Disney also agreed to reimburse MM for some $28 million in what were described as "out-of-pocket" expenses incurred in the bid; the money was, in fact, out of Disney's pocket and mainly into Drexel's as payment of loan commitment fees.

It was a classic example of what had come to be known as "greenmail," a practice criticized by many, but successful in this case, both from the perspective of Disney and Steinberg. The incident demonstrated the muscle that Drexel could flex and the fees it could generate, but it also exhibited a lack of finesse. Observers wondered, could Drexel ever finish what it had started?

In sum, I knew that Drexel had Pickens, Steinberg and a horde of other wheeling, dealing entrepreneurs ready to become major figures on the American business scene, but it still lacked that final touch of deal-closing ability.

Drexel's mistake in both the Gulf Oil and Disney deals, I thought, was that it insisted on offering shareholders a mixed bag, proposing to pay them off approximately half in cash and half in equity and/or debt instruments that were difficult to evaluate. The target company, in its defense, could argue that such a proposition was, in the words of Marty Lipton, a "coercive, two-tiered deal," muddle the issues and persuade a majority of shareholders to retain their stock. To my way of thinking it would be better to offer all cash—then the shareholder would know with certainty what he was getting and would be more likely to surrender his stock. I wondered how long it might take Drexel to figure this out. I said to myself, if these guys at Drexel ever get their act together, they will be unbeatable.

A major appealing factor was Drexel's growing image as a company not hung-up on the issues of social pedigree and Ivy League education. *Money* magazine called Drexel "an unpretentious, eclectic bunch."

I checked with my acquaintance Jay Bloom, who had recently left Lehman Brothers to join Drexel as a vice president. "It's the greatest place to be," he enthused. "We need people like you. You should definitely come on board. It's unbelievable how much business these guys have, and they really don't know what to do with it all. They need to get organized. They need someone who will come in and say, 'This is how we're going to do it.' "

Finally I agreed to an initial round of interviews.

THROUGHOUT the summer of 1984 a series of intriguing events occurred. Rumors hit the street that Carnation Corporation was about to become a takeover target, and the price of the stock shot from just above $50 per share to about $66 per share on August 7, at which point a Carnation official publicly declared that there were "no corporate developments" to account for the sudden action. The company re-

peated the announcement two weeks later, when the stock was selling
at $72 per share. Finally, on September 4, Nestlé, S.A., announced an
agreement to acquire Carnation at $83 per share. It was an obvious
example of insider trading (in which Wilkis and I had no part) that was
certain to promote the concept that "everybody does it" and just as
certain to prompt SEC Chairman Shad to polish his hobnail boots.

ILAN Reich's tip on Warburg, Pincus & Company paid off on August
23, when the firm announced its plan to acquire SFN Companies. The
SFN stock shot up, and I sold out the following day for a profit of
$129,316.

Reich came right back at me with another deal, disclosing that
Wachtell, Lipton was representing the Searle family, owners of G. D.
Searle & Company, the maker of NutraSweet. The family had decided
to sell much of its closely held stock, and Reich and I both knew that
once those huge blocks of stock arrived on the market, Searle would
be an appealing takeover target. I shared the tip with Wilkis, bought
60,000 shares for my own account and waited for something to happen.
For a time, nothing did.

Searle is based in Chicago. Near the end of September, Wilkis and
I, our patience growing thin, placed a call to Herb Greenberg of the
Chicago Tribune. Wilkis had spoken with this reporter previously,
using the alias "Mr. Freeze." On that occasion, Wilkis had provided
a news tip that ultimately proved correct, so that, once he identified
himself as "Mr. Freeze," Greenberg expressed immediate interest. Wilkis reported, "The Searle family is selling its stock. The company will
be a target."

"How do you know?" Greenberg asked.

"Because we're in the business of knowing," Wilkis replied. "I was
right before, and I'm right about this situation, too."

Greenberg had no reason to worry about how the caller got his
information, only that it was correct. He checked around, verified the
tip and published his latest scoop.

When the story broke, I netted $834,743. I was thrilled to hear Meier
report the results. The high was still there, but it was not as tingly as
before, and I wondered if I was growing jaded. By now, taking down
nearly a million dollars almost seemed routine and, in the day-to-day

context of my business life, where I dealt routinely with billions of dollars, rather remote from my perception of reality.

OFTEN I groaned when I realized that I had to blow an evening at a "function." Sometimes these obligatory social occasions led to important contacts, but often they were a waste of time. However, I was excited about attending the 1984 Annual Dinner of the United Jewish Appeal, for it would provide an opportunity to meet the UJA's Man of the Year, who also happened to be Wall Street's most renowned arb. He was the son of a Russian-born Detroit delicatessen owner known, by some in the business, as "Ivan the Terrible." Some others called him "Piggy."

An attorney by training, Ivan Boesky had become a Wall Street legend during the past decade by building a personal fortune of about $200 million, qualifying him for a spot on *Forbes*'s list of the 400 richest Americans. For a minimum of $10 million you could buy a piece of the action of his Ivan F. Boesky Corporation, which now had nearly $1 billion at its disposal for use in arbitrage deals; through a subsidiary, Seemala Corporation (named after his wife, Seema), Boesky owned a seat on the New York Stock Exchange. He also controlled Cambrian & General Securities PLC, a British investment trust, in which he had holdings of about $50 million. He and his wife owned 53 percent of the Beverly Hills Hotel, valued at more than $100 million.

Boesky was so successful that Wall Street flattered him by emulating him. If word leaked out that Boesky had plunged into a stock position, that alone was enough to bring a horde of copycat investors in after him. He could move the market all by himself. His reputation was so secure that an investor who wanted to jump on the Boesky bandwagon and pour money into his arbitrage fund had to agree to give him 40 percent of all profits, while absorbing 90 percent of all losses.

One of my investment banking colleagues once remarked, "Ivan has the ability to coin money." Another said, "Boesky's up to his ass in inside information."

Over the years he had used some of his fortune, rather overtly I thought, in an attempt to buy respect. After he contributed hundreds of thousands of dollars to Harvard University, he was appointed to an advisory panel at the school, and thus qualified for membership at New

York's Harvard Club, a location he preferred for business meetings as well as squash matches. After he donated $2 million to the Jewish Theological Seminary of America, the school named a library for him and his wife. Over the previous five years he was reported to have contributed more than $100,000 to the campaign coffers of national political candidates; in turn, he was appointed an adviser on Jewish affairs to the chairman of the Republican National Committee. Now he was the UJA's Man of the Year, which implied another large contribution.

I wondered if he ran his business endeavors on a similar theory of quid pro quo.

Photos I had seen showed a handsome, polished man, and I had a mind-picture of him as tall and stately, a person with presence. "He's not at all what I pictured," I said to Laurie, as we inched along in a receiving line, awaiting the "privilege" of shaking his hand. He was lean and athletically trim; however, he stood only about 5'6" tall. To be sure, he was handsomely attired in a dark, tailored suit with a gold watch chain looping across the vest, but the face was a conglomeration of unflattering features. The eyes were dark and seedy. The nose was far too big. A crooked and somewhat sardonic grin played upon his forty-seven-year-old face. His hair was dishpan gray. The man was a giant in business but, in person, resembled a gnome. As we moved closer, I thought, it may be unkind, but he's just plain unimpressive.

He was glib as he pumped the congratulatory hands. His tongue was fast in finding a smooth comment for just about everyone. He did not know me, but as our eyes met briefly his seemed to say, "What can I do for you and what can you do for me?"

CHAPTER TWELVE

I MET WITH DAVID KAY, the debonair, extroverted head of the M&A Department at Drexel Burnham Lambert, to discuss finally the possibility of coming on board. He began with the brash proclamation that Drexel was about to revolutionize the industry. Drexel and Drexel alone, he said, could now provide enormous amounts of financing to companies that normally would not qualify. This activity emanated, not from New York, but from California, from the High-Yield and Convertible Bond Department, known informally as "the Drexel Bank."

The Beverly Hills office was run by Michael Milken, whose title as a mere senior vice president obscured his importance to the firm; in fact, he owned 8 percent of the company, making him the largest individual shareholder. Milken had maneuvered Drexel into a position unique in the history of investment banking. For the first time, he could offer gargantuan sums of fast cash to medium-sized and even smaller companies and to individual entrepreneurs. All told, the Drexel Bank had as much as $200 billion at its disposal.

But there was a hitch. Kay bemoaned the fact that Drexel had not yet found the means to harness that power. The firm, as yet, had very little effective senior dealmaking ability. Because it was historically viewed as a second-tier investment bank, many of the industry's established dealmakers had consistently refused to come on board. Drexel's goal was to couple tactical expertise with Milken's financial muscle.

Then, Kay proclaimed, Drexel would have a balanced weapon that would vault it to the forefront of the takeover arena.

Yes, he admitted, they had failed to close Pickens v. Gulf Oil and Steinberg v. Disney, but my job would be to help change that pattern. I would be the strategist and tactician, the man whose assignment was to figure out how best to bring a deal to completion.

There was more. In the past, the investment banker had served as an aide to the acquisitor. In the present market, the investment banker had become a creative supplier, initiating many of the deals that had a trickle-down effect upon the entire U.S. economy. Kay was aware of my rainmaker reputation, and he proclaimed that Drexel needed me to help create deals as well as to close them.

It sounded appealing, but I wondered if this new kid on the block could realize his ambitious dreams. Drexel was poised to leap over the old-line companies and become the new power in investment banking, but would it succeed? Should I cast my lot with the upstart, or with the venerable powers-that-be? It was a tough call, and I wavered.

Kay introduced me to Frederick H. Joseph, Drexel's head of corporate finance. He was the son of a cab driver from the tough Roxbury section of Boston, who had risen from those humble beginnings to study Shakespeare at Harvard (on a partial scholarship), where he also won three collegiate boxing championships. At the age of forty-seven, he kept himself in shape through hunting and other outdoor activities on his upstate farm. His first boss in investment banking, at E. F. Hutton, was none other than John Shad, now the SEC chairman. In fact, Joseph had served for a time as special adviser to the SEC.

He was a sandy-haired man with a straightforward, self-assured style, polished to a high sheen. Despite his high-level position, he maintained his desk in the middle of the Corporate Finance Department bullpen, a large, open area populated by about fifty professionals. He wanted to be out with the troops. Joseph casually propped one leg over an arm of his chair and told me that his slogan was "Ready, Fire, Aim!" I liked him immediately.

Joseph's long-standing mission was to develop what he called an "edge" for Drexel, and he had a two-pronged approach to the task. When he had joined Drexel a decade ago he had systematically raided his most recent employer, Shearson, for the best and brightest of its talent. At Drexel, these individuals were known as the "Shearson

Mafia" (Kay was one of them). Accepting the fact that the firm did not have the clout to lure the most elite clients, he had set his people to work to establish Drexel as an investment banker that would give the highest-quality service to small- and medium-sized corporations. Coupled with Milken's growing abilities to generate capital, Joseph's efforts were succeeding. He took me to a small, glass-walled conference room containing a sofa, two chairs and a cocktail table.

"Excuse me," Joseph said, responding to a buzz from his phone only a few minutes into our discussion, "Michael's on the phone."

I backed off, idly watching the activity in the bullpen as Joseph conversed with Milken in California. A deal was obviously pending, but Joseph kept his end of the discussion discreet.

When we resumed our talk, Joseph reached into the pocket of his suit jacket and pulled out his wallet. He extricated a page of paper and unfolded it meticulously, displaying it for me. It was a typed summary of Drexel's revenues and profits for the past five years, and it revealed exponential growth. The M&A craze continued to accelerate: Standard Oil of California paid $13.4 billion for Gulf; Texaco acquired Getty Oil for $10.1 billion. In both instances, the government failed to raise antitrust objections. The appetite was there and the political climate was right. The numbers were growing ever larger and who, Joseph asked rhetorically, had the money? Drexel was increasing its market share by dramatic proportions each year, cutting into the profits of the old-line firms. The bare numbers proved that this was an awesome financial machine, fueled by Milken's fund-raising abilities. Milken, Joseph said, was the smartest man he had ever met and understood the philosophies of credit better than anyone else in the world.

Both Joseph and Milken shared a common philosophy: The scarce resource was not money, but people.

"With people like you coming in," Joseph declared, "we're going to be able to continue this trend."

Joseph's phone buzzed once more. "Excuse me, again, please," he said. "If it was anyone but Michael . . ."

By the time Joseph had finished with Milken, I was ready with a specific condition. "If I do come on board, Fred," I said, "I'll never work on the Posner account." I knew that Posner, the man whose acquisition attempt we had fought off for Peabody International, was a Drexel client. Earlier this year, Milken had also worked with Posner in the latter's attempt to acquire Fischbach, a large electrical and mechanical construction company. "I want no part of him," I asserted.

"Okay," Joseph agreed, and I sensed that my antipathy toward Posner was a strong point in my favor. At the moment, Posner was involved in a flap with Milken. With his sights set on an acquisition of National Can, Posner had approached Milken for financing, but at the same time made overtures to E. F. Hutton and Bear Stearns. Milken, who expected loyalty, was reportedly infuriated.

After Joseph and I concluded our conversation, I met several other senior bankers in the firm, men such as Steve Weinroth, Chris Anderson and Herb Bachelor. I found myself impressed, both with their knowledge and their ambition. One of the men in the M&A Department had a poster on his wall, a mock advertisement, showing a Drexel man as GI Joe, leading a platoon into battle, his machine gun blazing. The atmosphere here was supercharged, vastly different from anything I had ever experienced.

We had several additional meetings. After a time, I was close to making a decision, but I wanted to wait until the end of the year, when I received my annual bonus from Lehman Brothers. I explained that, although Lehman's fiscal year ended September 30, I had arranged for a deferred payment, for tax-planning purposes. The men at Drexel understood this completely, and expected it. Absolutely no one on the Street pays his taxes a day earlier than necessary, or announces a career move until his bonus check has cleared the bank.

BOB Wilkis told me that he had cultivated a new source, "a kid," working as an M&A analyst at Lazard Frères. Wilkis had seen hunger in the young man's eyes and quietly and carefully offered him the same sort of deal that I had previously struck with Ilan Reich and Ira Sokolow. All that the "kid" had to do was provide information; Wilkis would stake him to a share in his own private account.

In September, Wilkis relayed a report from his kid: Chicago Pacific Corporation had hired Lazard to manage a hostile takeover attempt of Textron, Inc., a Rhode Island–based conglomerate whose products ranged from Bell Helicopters to Bostitch staplers. The Textron board had authorized the repurchase of 2 million of its 34 million shares of outstanding stock in an attempt to protect itself from just such an attack, but Chicago Pacific was ready to move anyway. The deal was in its earliest, most secret stages. Lazard's task at the moment was to buy up Textron stock as quietly as possible, until it reached the critical threshold of 5 percent ownership, at which point it would have to file the required public statement acknowledging its position. Until that required announcement was made, Textron's depressed stock price was a rare bargain.

Wilkis had already purchased 29,000 shares of Textron. With full confidence in our system, I decided to use this information doubly. I quietly bought up a block of 51,500 shares for my Bahamian portfolio. Then I put the information to work at the office.

I knew that Lehman Brothers had handled deals for Textron before, and, on October 9, I went to see Steve Waters, the managing director who handled the account. He was one of the Lehman Brothers partners whom I most respected, a steady, soft-spoken straight-shooter. We were an effective team, for his laid-back style complemented my innate aggressiveness. I reported, "Steve, I've heard a rumor that Textron may be susceptible to a takeover."

"How good is your information?" Waters asked.

"It's good. I've been watching the stock for the past few days, since I heard the rumor. It's trading up in a down market, on more than average volume." This conversation, of course, was perfectly reasonable in the light of my job as Breaking News Coordinator.

Waters said, "Let's call the company." Within minutes he had Bev Dolan, CEO of Textron, on the phone to report that his colleague, me, had picked up a rumor that Textron might be the subject of an unsolicited offer. "We thought it would be wise to bring this to your attention," Waters said. He added that we had been watching the stock. This very day it was trading up in a down market. He emphasized that we were reporting a rumor, not hard news. Then he added the sales pitch. If anything developed, he said, Lehman Brothers would like a role in helping Textron fashion a defense.

Dolan indicated that this was the first he had heard of the rumor. He thanked Waters for the information and said he would keep us in mind if, indeed, the need arose.

After the call, I asked Waters for his assessment. What was the likelihood that we would get the business, if it developed.

"Dolan is a very straight guy," Waters responded. "We've worked with him in the past. The chances are very good."

THE Lehman Brothers powers-that-be were especially impressed with the string of successful transactions that I had closed. I wondered also whether they had gained inside information concerning my round of job interviews. Whatever the reasons, someone had realized that the firm was going to have to resort to extraordinary means to stem an exodus of key personnel. At any rate, the day after I told Waters about Textron, Lehman Brothers informed me that my annual bonus check would be in excess of $500,000. This was more than five times the amount they had guaranteed me. It resulted from my enhanced status as a "profit participant," and it was clear evidence that my value to the firm was recognized. Along with this news came the long-awaited promise to promote me from senior vice president to managing director.

But it was not enough; I had seen the future, and it was Drexel.

FOR several weeks Waters and I kept our senses alert for further signals on the Textron deal. Wilkis informed me on the progress that Chicago Pacific was making in lining up financing. Meanwhile, the stock price edged upward as the rumor spread, providing further evidence that our own little group was merely one small booth at the insider trading bazaar.

Anticipating that Lehman Brothers would get the account, I worked up a standard presentation for a defensive strategy.

The $1.5 billion hostile takeover attempt was formally announced on October 24, and Waters called Dolan in an attempt to nail down a contract with Textron.

Thanks, Dolan said, but he had already hired Morgan Stanley.

"Let's find a white knight," I suggested. It was clear that Dolan and Textron were going to fight the takeover attempt, and that opened up the possibility that we could produce a more friendly acquirer. If Textron came to believe that acquisition was inevitable, it would, of course, seek to cut the best possible deal, and it might be willing to crawl into bed with a white knight. There were all sorts of tactics it could utilize to make the new acquirer willing to offer the shareholders a higher bid

and, not coincidentally, offer the current officers better severance benefits, if necessary.

I always thought it was better to represent the target company, rather
than the acquisitor since, if a deal is consummated, any one of several
potential buyers might be involved, but the target company would
certainly be involved. The target side of the deal was sure to result in
fees. But Textron had cut us out and so I headed for my computer.
Moving swiftly, I called up data on companies that shared the same
Standard Industrial Codes (SICs) as Textron. These were the firms
whose lines of business overlapped with the target and were most likely
to see the wisdom of an industry-driven acquisition. I grabbed a half
dozen associates and set them to work assembling information packages
on Textron.

Waters and I grabbed the phones. This was the part of the business
that resembled Dialing for Dollars. We knew that all the major firms
were soliciting customers just as we were, so we worked with a sense
of urgency. Several potential buyers expressed early interest. We rushed
our research package to them and tried to hammer out a deal, but
nothing came about. Textron stood firm, announcing that it believed it
could defend itself against all offers.

Ultimately, Chicago Pacific's bid failed when Citibank withdrew as
a lender, but I still netted $200,000 from a temporary rise in the stock
price of Textron, caused by the sudden flood of rumors that hit the
Street. Wilkis made a profit of more than $137,000.

OVER lunch the mercurial Ilan Reich told me that he had corrected the
difficulties raised by his annual review and was now in line to become
a partner—and I, in turn, told him that I was seriously considering
moving over to Drexel. After lunch, as we walked along the sidewalk,
Reich announced that he was once again going to withdraw from
participation in our clandestine activities.

"Okay," I said. "Do what you want to do. Do what you have to do.
You've got about four hundred thousand dollars in the account now.
Do you want any of it?"

"No," Reich said.

I repeated what I had said the first time he pulled back: "Anytime
you want it, it's yours."

I was now sure that Reich was out for good, but that was all right. Somewhere in the back of my mind I believed that I would stop some-day also. I considered Reich to be a superb corporate attorney, and, even if he did not want to continue to supply stock tips, I still wanted to work with him on legitimate deals.

I wished him well.

FINALLY the work was completed on our new home. Contractors had smashed down the old walls and restructured the rooms to our specifi-cations; some of the walls included decorative archways. A glass-block wall separated the dining room from a bedroom. The ancient plumbing was redone, of course, and the marble-walled master bath included a Jacuzzi and a steam shower. The living room and dining room were covered with bleached-oak flooring.

We moved into our Park Avenue apartment during the month of December.

LEHMAN Brothers and the other old-line firms still held the undeniable lure of respectability. For example, Waters was hard at work on a possible deal wherein Occidental Petroleum would acquire Diamond Shamrock Corporation, a Dallas-based oil, gas and chemical firm. Dia-mond Shamrock was our client, and Waters had hopes of engineering a friendly deal. If all went as planned, Occidental would issue 130 million new shares of common stock and swap them one-for-one for Diamond Shamrock shares. Both companies would benefit. For Dia-mond Shamrock, the price of $3.27 billion was right. For Occidental, the new issue would more than double its outstanding stock and thus vastly improve its debt-to-equity ratio, which was currently weak. This, in turn, would make Occidental a far less likely takeover target.

It was both fun and enlightening to watch Waters work on the transaction. Anytime you dealt with Occidental's eighty-six-year-old chairman and CEO, the world-famed philanthropist Armand Hammer, it was big-time stuff, and I knew that if I stayed here at Lehman, I would find myself in more and more transactions such as this. My thoughts on this subject stopped short when I remembered that Ham-mer was a Drexel client!

When Hammer had taken over Occidental Petroleum in 1956, it had a net worth of $34,000. By 1980 that figure had grown to $3 billion, but Hammer was not about to stop. In 1981 and 1982 Occidental acquired Iowa Beef Processors and Cities Service Corporation with debt financing arranged by Drexel.

Before making a final decision on whether or not to jump to Drexel, there was one more thing I had to do. I said to Fred Joseph, "I'm very interested, and I might come on board very soon. After all, I already have a wardrobe full of shirts monogrammed D-B-L."

It took a moment for him to make the connection between Drexel Burnham Lambert and Dennis B. Levine. He chuckled, but his eyes gave a hint of a scowl when I added: "But first I want to meet Milken."

"Well, that's a little unusual," Joseph replied.

"Unusual or not, I don't come to Drexel until I talk to him."

"He's very busy," Joseph said. "Maybe we can get you fifteen minutes with him."

"Okay," I agreed. "I'll go out to Beverly Hills to meet him, and while I'm there, I'd like to meet the corporate finance people who work from that end."

Laurie and I flew to California for an extended New Year's weekend, coupling my Drexel interview with a visit to my brother Larry in Orange County and a brief vacation at La Costa spa. When we arrived in Beverly Hills, we checked into the Bel Air Hotel and rented a car.

Drexel's office was located at the corner of Rodeo Drive and Wilshire Boulevard, which is about as good an address as you can get. I knew that Milken himself owned the four-story glass-and-polished-granite office building and leased most of it back to Drexel. A Gumps Department Store took up the lower level. A second-story suite held a branch office of Columbia Savings, one of Milken's best junk-bond customers; in fact, Milken was a partial owner of the S&L. Drexel's business was expanding so rapidly that the firm was building a second office structure next door that would feature a pedestrian bridge between the two.

Here, in the pre-dawn hours of Friday, January 4, after I checked in with the ground-floor security guards, I met with John Kissick, who headed corporate finance from the California end. "We need people like you," he said. "We have this financing capability on the one side, but we have limited experience on the other side. We haven't done a lot of transactions, and we don't have the experience we need in M&A. We want to get up the curve quickly, so we have to bring in people who do have the experience."

Kissick took me around to shake the hands of various individuals, who greeted me effusively, with comments such as "What can we do for you?" and "Is everything okay?" All were bent on selling Drexel to me and I was pleased and flattered by the attention, but I still wanted to see the heart of Drexel, the trading floor, and meet the man who really *was* Drexel.

Kissick ushered me into an elevator and we rode down. When the door opened, we stepped into a foyer and faced a tough-looking security guard, who resembled a New York Giants linebacker. He nodded when he saw Kissick and passed us through into the inner sanctum of the trading area. Kissick explained that, over the years, Milken had grown ever more security conscious. He was making waves in the business world, fighting the establishment, facing down the big boys. Who knew what measures a desperate foe might take? During business hours, Milken never went anywhere, Kissick said, without his guards.

He took me to a small conference room located behind Drexel's trading floor and told me that Milken would meet with me within a few minutes. There was an air of anticipation.

CHAPTER THIRTEEN

MANY PEOPLE IN THE BUSINESS referred to him simply as "The King." No one had ever seen anybody like him.

Michael Robert Milken was a curious and unique combination of a 60s flower child and a modern-day business hotshot—with a dash of good old-fashioned values thrown in. He was politically and financially liberal, yet conservative in his personal life. Rumor held that Milken's income was the highest on Wall Street. He lived in what everyone liked to describe as a relatively modest home in Encino, ten blocks from his mother's home. In truth, although the secluded, multi-level house was not pretentious, it had a glorious history; it had been the guest house on the Clark Gable–Carole Lombard estate, which had long since been subdivided. Milken paid $700,000 for it in 1978, which was big money at the time, even for him.

He had been married for seventeen years to his wife, Lori, whom he had met back in the seventh grade; images of his children, twelve-year-old Gregory, nine-year-old Lance and four-year-old Bari, decorated his desk and sparkled from his eyes when he spoke of them. Despite the press of business, he managed to coach his boys' basketball teams. It was said that, following the birth of his children, despite Milken's incredible work schedule, he took the one A.M. feedings to share the parenting experience with Lori. He disdained alcohol, tobacco, caffeine, carbonated beverages and profanity.

147

Milken had enrolled at the University of California at Berkeley in 1964, when that school was the philosophical launch pad of the anti-Establishment generation. While there, he declared that he had chosen Wall Street as "my battleground" for improving society. His theories of finance were particularly influenced by an esoteric, multi-volume study of bond performance from 1900 to 1943, W. Braddock Hickman's *Corporate Bond Quality and Investor Experience.* Hickman concluded that a portfolio of low-rated, high-yield bonds, if held over a long period of time, generated greater revenues than a comparable portfolio of highly rated bonds; although the low-rated bonds did, indeed, exhibit a greater default rate, the percentage of realized returns outperformed the blue-chip bonds.

After graduation from Berkeley in 1968 (where he was elected to Phi Beta Kappa), Milken married Lori and headed for Philadelphia to attend the Wharton School of Business. It was here that he began his own analysis of low-rated bonds and concluded, contrary to the traditional wisdom of Wall Street, that many of the issuing corporations were better credit risks than the marketplace perceived them to be.

He joined the Philadelphia office of Drexel in 1970, after having worked there part time while completing his studies. At the age of twenty-four he was transferred to the New York office as the chief researcher for fixed-income securities.

In 1973 Milken was assigned to head the department that specialized in "non-investment-grade" securities, also known as "high-yield" bonds, or "junk" bonds. His compensation agreement provided that as much as 35 percent of the department's annual profits would be placed into a year-end bonus pool, to be distributed to departmental employees based upon Milken's allocations. That compensation formula remained in force over the years as Milken turned the High-Yield and Convertible Bond Department into a booming concern. The ever-growing bonuses tied employees to Drexel and Milken cemented the relationships further by bringing many of his employees in as partners in a convoluted string of lucrative sideline investments and partnership arrangements, known as "golden handcuffs."

Through the early years of the 70s, stock prices had been in an extended slide; all told, the equity value of American corporations was eroded by about 40 percent. Concerned that many companies would be forced into bankruptcy, banks became ever more selective in their lending practices. Only a handful of America's elite companies had access to large-scale financing on the most favorable terms, and this ruffled Milken's innate sense of fair play. A simple geographical study showed him that larger corporations based in New York, Illinois, California and Texas had their own special "ins" with the financial markets; firms in the other forty-six states, as well as smaller firms in general, had a much tougher time raising capital. Milken counted less than 800 U.S. corporations that received an investment-grade rating for their bonds, and more than 20,000 which did not.

One of Milken's first areas of concentration was on the market value of convertible debentures (bonds that can be swapped for common stock). He concluded that institutional investors who had originally bought these debentures had, amid the current gloom, panicked and oversold them back into the market, which meant that they were now available at bargain-basement prices. He followed this with his own study of non-investment-grade bonds, updating Hickman's work, and decided that many of them, since they were sold at what was called a "deep discount" below face value, were far better investments than the blue-chip bonds.

More and more, Milken came to believe that the bond-rating companies tended to lump high-risk bond issuers into too broad a category. Standard & Poor's rating system encompassed a scale from AAA at the top to D at the bottom. The other rating system, Moody's, assigned similar letter grades. Bonds in the higher categories were known as "investment-grade" and considered to be "well assured." But any bond classified lower than BBB by Standard & Poor or Ba by Moody was lumped into a category known as "speculative grade," and the issuers of these bonds had to pay a premium rate of interest in order to get investors to buy.

Milken saw basic inequities. It was the old binary concept. A bond was good or bad and there was no gray area in between. What's more, he realized, both S&P and Moody factored a company's size into the equation, as if "big" meant "good" and "small" meant "bad." They also considered historical stability, as if "old" meant "good" and "new" meant "bad." The predictable result was that only the largest and oldest firms, more-or-less those listed on the *Fortune* 500, qualified for an "investment-grade" rating, and were "allowed" by the system to raise billions of dollars via the sale of new bonds. Numerous institutional portfolio managers were prohibited by their own criteria from investing in "speculative-grade" bonds.

Where did that leave the well-run, but smaller companies? Milken asked himself. What about new companies? What about larger companies that experienced temporary difficulties? What about the 22,000 U.S. corporations that did not belong to the club?

Milken concentrated his attention on selling bonds that paid 3 percent to 5 percent above the prevailing U.S. Treasury bond rate. Over time his customers came to the happy realization that these high-yield bonds exhibited a surprisingly low default ratio. These were not junk bonds, Milken argued, but bargain bonds. He could point out intriguing statistics: high-yield bonds brought a return in excess of 13 percent, about twice the profits available from AAA corporate bonds, and yet the default rate was less than 2 percent.

In the past, no bond began life with a low rating. New bonds were issued almost exclusively by the elite companies and became "speculative grade" only when those companies ran into financial difficulty and found themselves regarded as "fallen angels." But by 1977 Milken had hopped onto the coattails of a simple idea. That was the year that Lehman Brothers and Goldman Sachs underwrote the first new bond issue *conceived* as junk; it produced $75 million for LTV Corporation. Lehman followed up with new issues for Zapata Corporation, Fuqua Industries and Pan American World Airways.

Now the way was clear for an investment banking firm to underwrite issues of high-risk, high-yield bonds. If a medium-sized firm, or even a new venture, was confident enough in its business projections, it would be willing to offer investors a premium rate of interest, if it had to, in order to gain access to the lifeblood of the business world, capital. In many cases, the borrower did not even have to begin making good on the interest payments until a decade had passed. What's more, it was all subordinated debt, meaning that, depending upon the covenants, companies might well be able to continue to negotiate conventional loans that would take precedence over interest payments on the bonds.

Thousands of companies were so eager for cash that they readily agreed to pay a premium not only to investors, but to the investment banker. The sale of investment-grade bonds generally brought a commission of 0.875 percent of face value. But when Milken discovered that he could get 2 percent, 3 percent, or even 4 percent commission on junk bonds, the onslaught began. He plunged into the market and did not even bother to submit new bond issues to the traditional ratings makers, because he did not care what rating they received.

Sales grew slowly at first. Some institutional investors relaxed their rules in order to reap greater profits, but many others remained wary. What if they purchased a multi-million-dollar position in a new junk bond issue, and later wanted out? Investment-grade bonds could be resold immediately on the major exchange, but there was no public, centralized exchange for the new securities. Milken's response was to make a market in junk. He established a trading floor where anyone could buy or sell high-yield bonds via a quick phone call or telex. He promoted the establishment of mutual funds dedicated to these new investment vehicles, to tap into the money of the masses.

The high-yield bond, a Drexel publication proclaimed, was "a financial instrument whose time has come."

It was soon apparent that Milken had met a vital need. Drexel became known as the place where a trader could deal in any number of bonds, convertible debentures, preferred stocks, bankrupt securities, sinking fund securities, private placements and real estate investment trusts. The client list included corporate names associated with fiscal integrity: Prudential, Equitable, Fidelity, Kemper.

In the summer of 1978, when Milken learned that his father had been stricken with terminal cancer, he persuaded Drexel to allow him to move the entire department to California, so that he could be close to his family. It was an unprecedented decision to forsake Wall Street, and Drexel's approval of the plan was a clear measure of Milken's value to the firm; about twenty of the department's professional staff members relocated with him. Milken hired his younger brother Lowell, an attorney, to manage corporate and personal assets with an eye toward tax savings. Reportedly, the brothers helped to finance Dino De Laurentiis's movies. Some said that Lowell Milken functioned as the hatchet man, and that he enjoyed the role of the heavy in a good guy/bad guy routine with his brother.

In 1978 a total of $1.5 billion worth of junk bonds were issued, and the beginnings of a trend were apparent.

The next ingredient was supplied in 1981 by Leon Black of Drexel's Corporate Finance Department, who hit upon the idea of using junk-bond issues to finance LBOs and other acquisitions. It was surgically simple. Thus emerged the corporate raider, who no longer had to wrestle with the often slow, always finicky bankers. If he needed big cash fast, he could come to the "Drexel Bank." Following this development, Fred Joseph launched a campaign to beef up Drexel's M&A capabilities.

In 1982 the U.S. Congress passed the Garn–St. Germain Depository Institutions Act, which provided Milken and Drexel with additional sources of capital. The act essentially deregulated the Savings & Loan Industry, and, among other provisions, it allowed thrifts to invest in corporate-debt securities. Suddenly there was $1 trillion worth of S&L money ripe for the picking.

During a three-day brainstorming session, held in Beverly Hills in November 1983, the Drexel hierarchy determined to escalate its promotion of the marriage between high-yield bonds and the M&A business. The idea flew beyond anyone's dreams. By the end of 1983 the total sale of new junk bond issues had risen to $7.3 billion, and Drexel was responsible for nearly 65 percent of it. Drexel's July offering of $1 billion worth of high-yield bonds for MCI Communications enabled the upstart firm to carry on its epic struggle with AT&T for control of the nation's long distance telephone lines.

By now, Milken had cultivated a network of eager investors willing to commit many millions of dollars in an instant response to a phone call from the dynamic guru. He was able, like no one before him, to arm David for a battle with Goliath. The Beverly Hills group had developed tremendous sources of cash within pension funds, mutual funds and insurance companies. California-chartered S&Ls were big customers, thanks to the state's liberal rules regarding their investments in debt securities.

The junk-bond investor could expect to receive a net profit about 4 percent higher than investment-grade bonds would pay and, for spice, might even be able to cash in on one of Drexel's special deals, such as the $1,000 bond from Sunshine Mining, redeemable in 1995 for its face value or 50 ounces of silver—take your choice—or the Texas International bond redeemable for $1,000 or 29 barrels of oil.

In fact, the term "junk" was not always coupled with "bond." A close look at Drexel's activities revealed the presence of junk debentures, junk notes and junk preferred stocks. Nevertheless, critics lumped them all together, and the most severe referred to Milken's junk as "atomic bonds." The implication was obvious: Sooner or later they would explode in the faces of their investors.

But Milken was confident that the default rates would remain within the realm of acceptability. Thus far they had, partly because Drexel had established a Special Planning Committee that helped troubled companies work out their difficulties. Of some 200 issues, only six had fallen on hard times and, in one of these cases, Drexel itself picked up the tab, offering investors a bail-out price of 95¢ on the dollar.

Milken disdained titles and had no desire for a private office; he refused press interviews, eschewed social functions, attempted to buy the rights to any photograph of himself and absolutely demanded that the company keep his picture and even his name out of its annual report. Any listing of departmental personnel was always presented in alphabetical order.

All the clocks in the West Coast office were set on New York time, so that the staff could stay in tune with the market. Those clocks declared that it was seven-thirty A.M. in New York when Milken started his workday. Throughout the long day he was on the phone constantly either trading securities or embroiled in conversations with the heaviest hitters of the business world; these were generally one-sided, with Milken doing the talking. Breakfast, lunch and dinner were provided by Drexel's food service department and delivered to the jobsite—Milken's desk and the desk of anyone else who wanted to succeed there. The day's schedule was jammed by meetings with corporate executives who wanted to speak to him, and they often had to wait for an hour after the appointed time. Following his last meeting—and never before seven-thirty P.M. California time—Milken headed home, carrying two battered canvas bags stuffed with paperwork. He claimed to need only three or four hours of sleep each night. Theoretically, Drexel operated on "Milken Time," but the boss was smart enough to know that few could keep up with him, so three personal assistants were assigned to work in rotating shifts.

Milken's success had snowballed to the point where he was not only the greatest marketer of junk bonds, he was also one of the largest customers. His personal trading account held more than $100 million and he had woven a complex web of partnerships, not only with his key associates, but also with outside entrepreneurs such as the Bass brothers of Texas and Saul Steinberg. His various networks controlled billions of dollars in capital through scores of accounts. He was also the third largest shareholder in Drexel's own $3 billion bond portfolio.

He and his brother Lowell had established the Milken Family Foundation, which had grown into a cluster of charitable organizations. He was reported to have donated more than $350 million to these foundations, which, in turn, passed the money on to worldwide social service agencies, with particular emphasis on programs in the fields of education, health, medical research, human welfare and community services. One of his favorite charities was the Los Angeles–based Simon Wiesenthal Center.

His friends came not only from the business world, but through his charity-work contacts. I learned, for example, that he was very close to singer Michael Jackson, who on occasion baby-sat the Milken children. He had also maintained close ties with some of his old school buddies.

But it was business for which he was known, and he had transformed Drexel into something special. The conventional investment bank is driven by the corporate finance people, who look to the trading department as a corollary and most definitely inferior operation. This dominant attitude had been the cause of the rift between Pete Peterson and Lew Glucksman that led to the sale of Lehman Brothers. But things were different at Drexel, and the only other comparable firm was Salomon Brothers, whose trading department was also dynamic and powerful. At Drexel, Milken's High-Yield and Convertible Bond Department was the engine that drove the train.

The growth of the department's power could easily be measured in one simple statistic. In 1978 there were twenty-five employees in Drexel's Beverly Hills office. Now there were more than two hundred.

SHORTLY before seven A.M. Milken strode into the conference room and greeted me cordially. He was jacketless and, thus, appeared to be in an all-business mode, which was a true picture. He was just shy of his fortieth birthday, slim-built, and the sharp features of his elongated, steel-jawed face were reminiscent of actor Ted Danson's.

He made direct eye contact as he pumped my hand.

Milken knew what I, and any other job candidate, would want to see first, so he drew me forward, toward the trading floor, and waved his hand to display the setup. It was critical to the success of the sale of new junk-bond issues that there be an active secondary market, and this was the major business of the trading room. Computer screens, keyboards and phone lines littered the floor space. Market makers sat at small stations along four long rows of desks shaped into a huge letter "x." They held phones in either hand, shouting out buy and sell orders, quoting prices, tossing wads of paper or other available projectiles at other traders in order to get their attention. In the midst of this barely controlled mayhem—at the hub of the x-shaped line of desks—was Milken's chair, offering a view of everyone. This was a war room. Every trader here would be judged at the end of each day on the basis of his or her sales figures. There was no room here for the laid-back, easy sell.

Milken introduced me to Jim Dahl, one of his top salesmen, but there was no time for anything but a brief amenity. In an instant Dahl was back on the phone dealing, dealing, dealing!

At one end of the room was a conference table, situated at a window overlooking a Japanese garden. It was a relatively small trading floor compared to those I had seen in New York, but it was abuzz with activity even now, as most other Californians were sipping their first cups of coffee. Traders were here, ready to make a market in any of more than 7,000 securities; on any given day, the department's trading position approached $4 billion. The markets were open in New York; thus, Drexel was open.

Someone ran up, chattering, "Michael, what do I do about this . . .?"

He turned from me and devoted his full attention to the task of the instant. Do this, do this, do *that,* he commanded with cool confidence.

Then he glanced briefly at his desk and surveyed a gargantuan sheaf of telephone messages (he took more than 200 calls every day) before he returned his attention to me. Despite the sense of urgency that enveloped us, he took a few moments to straighten the stack of message slips and otherwise place his desk in order.

After he ushered me back into the conference room, Milken said earnestly, "I have spoken with Fred about you. He wants you at Drexel. We've heard wonderful things—"

Suddenly, the conference room door flew open and a young, wild-eyed man screamed, "Michael, Occidental just announced!"

"Get me bodies!" Milken shouted, and, through the open door in front of me, I could see the electricity level of the trading room sky-rocket.

Milken turned back to me. He was obviously stunned and trying to think of a thousand strategies at once. He said quickly, but quietly, "Excuse me. I have to get on top of this."

"I fully understand," I replied, and I did. The Dow Jones tape had just broken the news that Diamond Shamrock was in merger discussions with Occidental Petroleum; a $3 billion deal was in the offing, and it naturally followed that teams from First Boston, Morgan Stanley, Kidder Peabody, Salomon Brothers and other investment banking houses were marshaling their forces, just like Milken. Everyone wanted in on the deal, and it did not really matter which side. Of course, I already knew that Lehman Brothers had the Diamond Shamrock account.

"I hope we can have a few minutes to speak later this afternoon," Milken said.

"It would be my pleasure," I replied.

Then he was gone. I knew that he was a close friend of Armand Hammer. If *any* company was in play, Milken wanted the business. But if Occidental was in play, he wanted it even more. Within minutes, he had Hammer on the phone (*nobody* refused to take a call from Milken), and within a few more minutes, he had piled his "bodies" into a special chauffeured van loaded with dealmaker's paraphernalia. Normally Michael Brown, Drexel's West Coast M&A director, used the van so that he could conduct business as he commuted to and from his home in Newport Beach. It was the perfect vehicle for emergencies such as this.

As the van headed for Hammer's office at Occidental, Peter Ackerman, executive vice president of the division, resumed the task of selling Drexel to me. In a smooth, confident, articulate presentation, he explained that Drexel was a cult of relative youngsters with an Avis-like "we try harder" attitude. I simply would not find a higher level of esprit de corps anywhere in the business, he proclaimed. The firm had assembled a cadre of talented, aggressive individuals and kept them loyal by paying them well and treating them as important parts of a whole. This was a firm of rebels, Ackerman said, determined to shake Drexel's "second-tier" image. In the process, they were shaking Wall Street and all of corporate America.

Others spoke with me, and the conversation invariably centered upon

Milken. This was a California guru, a man who had been able to instill his associates with an incredible sense of loyalty. I heard countless stories concerning Milken's acts of generosity: He loaned an employee money to cover an emergency operation; he and his wife frequently cared for the young son of a man stricken with multiple sclerosis; when a member of Drexel's support staff was diagnosed with leukemia, Milken hugged him and promised to take care of any "financial responsibilities"; he took an active role in the rehabilitation of a friend's daughter, seriously injured in a traffic accident.

Several people preached to me that the offer of a high-level Drexel job was akin to stumbling upon a pot of gold. Quite apart from the salary and the annual bonus, they said, was the opportunity offered by the matrix of private investment partnerships that would be offered along the way.

"Within two or three years," Kissick predicted, "you will have personal investments worth at least $10 million."

I was totally consumed by the mystique. In my mind I coined a term: "DrexelWorld."

IT was two P.M. when Milken reappeared and declared that he had about fifteen minutes for me.

"I was very impressed by the way you brought your troops into action this morning," I said. I flashed a half-grin and added, "As you probably know by now, Lehman Brothers is on the other side of the deal."

"Yes," he acknowledged. "And we've got Occidental."

"I'm impressed," I repeated. Just like that, Milken had nailed down the opportunity to participate in a $3 billion transaction.[1]

The promised quarter-hour turned into a three-hour discussion, beginning in the conference room and continuing as we walked through the various offices and ultimately focused our attention back upon the trading floor.

Milken spoke to me about the rosy future of the takeover business, tossing out one rhetorical question after another and answering each

---

[1] By Monday the deal had fallen through, due to the objections of several Occidental board members.

with the fervor of an evangelist. We discussed the Pickens v. Gulf deal, of how he had raised nearly $2 billion to enable his company, Mesa Petroleum, to set his sights on raiding the giant oil company and had thereby changed the rules of the M&A game. The junk-bond juggernaut was on, and its power was awesome. Suddenly, no company could consider itself immune to a hostile takeover attempt. David did not have to slay Goliath; he could buy him out.

One moment Milken was introspective and cerebral, discussing his dreams with me with the fervor of a visionary. The next he was a screaming dynamo as his attention was momentarily diverted by market developments. He flashed evidence of an incredible memory for detail concerning thousands of transactions. He possessed an almost clairvoyant grasp of the broad strokes of the business. His comprehension of the intricacies and possibilities of financing was on an intellectually higher plane—far higher—than anyone I had ever met. Even so, I could see that he did not possess a strong sense of the technical and political aspects of handling a merger. That was not his field; he needed me—or others like me—for that. There were calm, quiet moments as we discussed our families. At such moments, the tone of his voice grew exceedingly warm.

As we stood on the trading floor, his secretary interrupted constantly with announcements such as, "Icahn on three," "Steinberg on six" or "Boesky on four." The stack of telephone messages on his desk grew larger every hour, by an order of magnitude. Occasionally he broke from our discussion to take calls, sometimes speaking into two phones simultaneously.

After a time I pointed out that, despite his success in securing money for Pickens, the deal fizzled.

"It's your type of skill we need," Milken acknowledged. "Now, companies go to the Kidders and the Lehmans for advice and they come to us for the financing. We want to do it all. We need people who know how to do good deals, and how to close them."

I spoke at length about my own developing philosophies. The ability to close deals, I said, is the essence of modern high-level investment banking.

Milken nodded.

Making a deal happen, I declared, requires equal doses of financial acumen and psychoanalytic finesse. The other players in these high-stakes games have *enormous* egos, and it is the investment banker's job to subordinate his own feelings, to retain objectivity when no one else can. Only then can you balance the interests of the managers, the directors, the shareholders, the banks, the lawyers and the other investment bankers—and still manage to stay three jumps ahead of them all.

I wanted to understand the corporate personalities with whom I dealt. When a deal appeared on the horizon, my first step was to plunge into a research mode, studying the backgrounds of the officers and directors, analyzing how and why corporate decisions were made in the past. Is the board conservative or liberal in its approach to problems? How long has the CEO been there? Does he have stock options? Is he due to retire soon? If he has $30 million in severance pay, a so-called "golden parachute," will he float off quietly into the sunset? What other boards do the directors sit on, and how will those business relationships affect their votes on this issue? Who, among the directors and officers, are the key decision-makers, the swing votes?

There is exciting art to this, I said. The more successfully you can peer into the heads of the corporate managers and directors, the better your chances of either winning them over or simply outmaneuvering them.

"That's what clients pay for," I said. "They pay for negotiating skill and judgment that transcends anything that the business schools teach. They pay for instinct."

Milken grinned and nodded in agreement when I confessed that at night, visions of white knights rode through my brain, often precluding sleep.

"If I come on board," I said, "I'm going to take a firm position. Drexel should not be in the business of starting mergers that it cannot complete. We should be in the business of *closing* deals. If we are going to be a presence in the M&A business, we've got to make sure that our clients actually merge and acquire."

Milken again nodded his agreement, and then he spoke, with fire in his eyes, of the larger picture, of how Drexel had already transformed the world of finance and how it would, in the future, alter the existence of, perhaps, every man, woman and child on the face of the earth. Already, today, he proclaimed, if you held a few mutual fund shares, if you worked on the assembly line in a factory owned by several layers of corporate management, if you had any cash socked away in an S&L,

if you were a taxpayer, then Drexel—and, by extension, anyone in the freewheeling investment banking world of the mid-80s—had an impact upon your life. That was a truism that was going to expand and enlarge, exponentially, during the next few years.

Beyond that, he said, gesturing widely, was a world that needed capital. Money could feed the hungry, clothe the naked, house the homeless. Drexel was already beginning to work its magic in the world at large, Milken said, and he was determined to carry his gospel to Japan, Germany, the other industrialized nations and, ultimately, to where it was needed most, the Third World.

It could happen, he said. It will happen.

When I left that day, I knew I was going to move to Drexel.

I *had* to.

CHAPTER FOURTEEN

On February 4, 1985, at the age of thirty-two, I joined Drexel Burnham Lambert as a managing director—the position was the equivalent of partner. Drexel paid Hadley Lockwood a placement fee of $267,000. My annual salary was $140,000 per year, but that was only the tip of the iceberg. Almost immediately Drexel authorized a $200,000 payment to me, an advance from the current year's Corporate Finance bonus pool. I was, in fact, guaranteed a minimum annual bonus of $750,000. Drexel operated on the assumption that owner-employees were the most loyal, and they issued me 1,000 shares of Drexel common stock, worth about $100,000. I purchased an additional 2,000 shares, with 100 percent financing arranged by Drexel.

In addition, Joseph told me that I would be invited and encouraged to participate in various co-investment programs made available to Drexel senior executives; they were putting on "golden handcuffs" right from the start. The boys on the West Coast had a myriad of such deals going. The reported genius behind these transactions was Lowell Milken, who structured partnerships so that Drexel could gain a slice of ownership in a variety of deals. For example, if you wanted Drexel to raise $500 million for you, part of the price might be that you are required to allocate warrants to one or another of the Drexel partnerships. These warrants could be exercised in the event that a deal turned out to be lucrative for the principals. Lowell, it was said, had the Midas touch, for it was he who dictated who would be allowed to participate in a given deal, and at what level.

Joseph did not say so, but it was obvious that, in an attempt to placate the second-class Drexelites in the Corporate Finance Division, Milken was beginning to throw a few bones their way. A few partnership positions were available to us and the amount of participation was dictated precisely. These deals operated as a sort of mutual fund specializing in unique investment opportunities, and while all of us in New York knew that they would probably be profitable, we also knew that the biggest plums remained in the hands of the Beverly Hills crew.

There was a curious anomaly here. Of the powers in Corporate Finance, Joseph was supreme. But he was the one who never took advantage of the partnership investments, concerned that they might put him in a compromising position. This stance, however, did not stop him from presenting the propositions to his colleagues.

This all went far beyond my early fantasies of a career on Wall Street, and it sent my head spinning.

On that first day, Joseph lectured me. "We all know what kind of place Lehman Brothers is," he said. "There are a lot of political battles there, a lot of infighting. We don't have that here. We don't need that here. We make so much money that it's not necessary."

MY new office was in the Corporate Finance Department on the eighth floor of 55 Broad Street, across from company headquarters and a mere football field away from the New York Stock Exchange.

I was thrown into the fray immediately. That first evening one of my partners invited me to his home for dinner with Sam Belzberg. The dinner was elegant, the wine lavish. On this first evening I learned that a Drexel expense account is an open invitation to enjoy the good life. Unlike the other firms I knew, Drexel rarely questioned an item on an expense account. In fact, the more lavish the expenditures, the more they assumed that you were doing your job properly.

This evening, my partner introduced me as Drexel's "new M&A guy." The Belzberg family, Sam and his brothers William and Hyman, were widely regarded as Canada's most aggressive business partnership, plugged into Milken's network of junk-bond issuer/buyers. It was the Belzbergs who had introduced Pickens to Milken, prior to the assault on Gulf Oil. Belzberg spent the evening discussing his ambitious plans for the coming year.

Later my new partner surprised me with a "Welcome Aboard" present contained in a long, slim, gift-wrapped box. I opened it, laughed and displayed it for Belzberg. It was a dark blue silk tie, covered with a pattern of tiny, bright red letters: DBL.

THERE was little time to acclimate myself to new surroundings, for the action at Drexel was as frantic as I had fantasized. On my second morning Joseph said to me, "I'd like you to get involved in this deal—see how we operate." It was Carl Icahn's attempt to take control of Phillips Petroleum Company. I had to pick up the history of the deal very quickly, and there was much to learn.

The drama had begun the previous year. Having failed to acquire Gulf Oil, T. Boone Pickens had trained his attention upon Phillips and its $13 billion in corporate assets. When word of the possible assault hit the Street, speculators naturally plunged, buying up Phillips stock in enormous chunks. The arb who accumulated the strongest position was Ivan Boesky.

Boesky once defined risk arbitrage with the bland statement: "The arbitrageur bids for announced takeover targets." He admitted, however, that in "special situations" he plunged headlong into the market prior to any public announcement, speculating on the basis of rumor and innuendo. Clearly there were two paths to success in the business. One method was to outperform one's competitors in research activities, taking more sensible, better-calculated risks. The other method was to assemble a reliable web of market informants, which is not necessarily illegal, but inevitably brings one close to the limits. Indeed, a critic of the profession called risk arbitrage "organized espionage." And, like the CIA, Boesky seemed to have sources everywhere.

Over the past few years, the arb had developed a working relationship with Drexel and Milken. In September 1983 Drexel, through Milken's office, underwrote a $100 million public offering of high-yield debt to capitalize Boesky's subsidiary, Vagabond Hotels. In January 1984, as a partner, along with his brother Lowell and other investors, Milken had purchased a block of non-voting shares in Boesky's Seemala Corporation. Three months later Drexel underwrote a $109 million offering of subordinated notes issued by the Ivan F. Boesky Corporation. In December, Drexel underwrote a $67 million offering of high-yield debt for Farnsworth and Hastings, another Boesky subsidiary.

The latest deal between Boesky and Milken had run into snags. Boesky wanted to arrange a financial restructuring of his company that would provide him with $660 million worth of fresh capital. The closing had been set for this past January, but was many times delayed, partly because of objections from Drexel's Underwriting Assistance Committee, which almost always rubber-stamped Milken's deals, but uncharacteristically balked at the idea of putting fresh capital into the hands of the notorious arb. Some raised a conflict-of-interest objection; as part of its fee for conjuring the capital, Drexel was to receive an equity interest in Boesky's arbitrage firm. In the normal course of events, Boesky would, in turn, use that capital to bet on the outcome of Drexel's deals. If he guessed correctly, Drexel would gain a percentage of the profits. It was incestuous, at best.

Boesky's business represented less than 1 percent of the action at the Drexel bank and, on the surface, there was little reason for the two men to become business allies. On the whole, Boesky traded stocks; Milken traded bonds. But each was the major player in his field. It was undoubtedly galling to Milken and his competitive drive that Boesky took much of his business elsewhere. Milken wanted it all, and that included the significant chunk in Boesky's pocket. Therefore, Milken was currently at odds with some of the members of the Underwriting Assistance Committee for blocking his plans.

Having accumulated 3.7 million shares of Phillips for an average price of about $49 per share, Boesky was one of the most interested spectators in the Pickens/Phillips negotiations. Everything looked good for him when Pickens's firm, Mesa Petroleum, commenced a tender offer for Phillips on December 4 of the previous year. The price of $60 per share, to be paid in a combination of cash and securities, would allow Boesky to turn a profit of more than $40 million. Feeling confident, he increased his holdings to a total of 5.87 million shares, paying ever higher prices.

Boesky, I learned, happened to be vacationing in Barbados on the evening of December 23 when an aide informed him by phone that Pickens had reached an agreement with the Phillips board and its chairman, William C. Douce, turning a potentially hostile takeover into a friendly restructuring. Phillips proposed a recapitalization plan and Pickens agreed to call off his tender offer. If the plan was approved at an upcoming special shareholders' meeting, Pickens would receive a minimum of $53 per share for his holdings in Phillips, reaping a pre-tax profit of just under $90 million. It was not a classic case of greenmail wherein only the raider reaped the rewards. Pickens had previously vowed never to accept such money, but he agreed to this plan because all the shareholders would benefit. On the other hand, arbs such as Boesky who had continued to buy near the $60 level were understandably upset.

Determined to salvage his position, Boesky hopped aboard the earliest available flight to New York, but the market was already open by the time he arrived, and Phillips stock was down ten points. The open-market price was lower than the value of the proposed restructuring plan. If Boesky sold now he stood to realize a loss of about $25 million. Instead, he decided to hang tough. He descended upon his friends at Drexel, raging that the price was too low, demanding that they hunt for another buyer who would pay more.

Drexel obligingly hounded its list of clients and found one who was willing to play. He was Icahn, who, through his Icahn Group, Inc., authorized Drexel to buy blocks of Phillips stock at the current, somewhat depressed price. Milken worked to get the financing ducks in order for a possible tender offer, persuading Icahn to agree to pay enormous commitment fees if and when he had to solidify the arrangements.

When he learned of this development, Boesky called Icahn directly and said, "I hear you are involved with Phillips." Boesky went on to rage at Pickens for accepting the restructuring deal, and he suggested that Icahn join forces with him to wage a proxy battle to put their own "people" on the Phillips board. Icahn responded that he was not interested in a joint venture. Whatever he would do with his Phillips holdings, he would do alone.

Nevertheless, in early January the two men met at Boesky's 163-acre estate in upper Westchester County (which was conveniently close to Icahn's home) to discuss what Icahn characterized as "different strategies" they could use to increase the value of their holdings. One possibility was a joint takeover bid, for which, Icahn said, Boesky would have to put up between $100 million and $150 million in cash.

They could reach no accord during that discussion, but throughout the remainder of the month Boesky continued to call Icahn, trying to find out what the raider planned to do.

Late in the month Icahn made his decision. He alone would make a takeover bid for Phillips. To strengthen his position, on January 28 he bought 2.74 million shares from Boesky at a price of about $47 per share. It may have been an interesting gambit on Boesky's part; he sold a portion of his stock low, hoping to aid a takeover bid that would enable him to sell the remainder of his position high.

The very day I came on board at Drexel, Icahn wrote to Phillips, announcing his interest in acquiring 100 percent of the company's stock at a cost of $55 per share, payable half in cash and half in the form of a subordinated note. It was my job to help follow through on the details.

Immediately I teamed with my new colleagues Leon Black, head of the Leveraged Buyout Department, the man who had conceived the idea of the junk bond–financed takeover, and John Sorte, another managing director who headed the Petroleum Department. They introduced me to the incredibly intense Icahn, a former philosophy student at Princeton whose eyes broadcast an evangelistic fervor as he likened the modern corporate manager to a hired gardener who had come to believe he owned the estate. Icahn liked to refer to himself as the "Lone Ranger" and, in years past, had functioned without the services of an investment bank. Now, he was firmly in the Drexel camp, with about $155 million worth of Milken-raised money sitting unused, in a "war chest."

Icahn was a former options trader whose private passion was gambling; it was said that he enjoyed playing Monopoly for real money. But it was also said that he was tight-fisted with his cash, to the point of being cheap, and he was known for a hot temper, although his rages tended to center upon business, rather than personal, issues.

When I looked at what Drexel was prepared to do, I swallowed hard. It was indeed evident that this crew, while it had the money, did not have the level of M&A experience that I had seen at Lehman Brothers. One of my colleagues had come up with a fanciful plan to take care of Icahn's $7.5 million in loan commitment fees. He wanted to "dump" these fees onto the arbs, assuming that they would be happy to pick up the tab in exchange for the profits they would reap as a result of a successful takeover.

This is stupid, I said to myself. First, the plan would alert everybody to what was happening. Second, the tight-fisted arbs would never agree to it, particularly Boesky, who had already made a concession,. And finally, the SEC would probably rule against the procedure anyway.

Here was a delicate problem. The "genius" of this idea had been with Drexel for some time. How could I, the new kid on the block, blow him out of the water?

I took him aside quietly and said, "Listen, about this idea to get the arbs to pick up the commitment fees. You have to consider that three things will happen." I listed the snags.

To my relief my new colleague saw the wisdom of my arguments and voluntarily pulled back from his plan, saving me the agony of having to confront him during a meeting with Icahn and the other members of the team.

That part was settled, but almost before I could take a breath, things turned ugly between Icahn and his target. The Phillips board issued a public statement on February 6, rejecting Icahn's friendly proposal. "With the present uncertainties in the world oil market," the press release stated, "the Board believes that this is not the time to obtain the best acquisition price for a major integrated oil company. Nor in its view should Phillips and other major oil companies be liquidated or busted-up for the benefit of speculators and corporate raiders. . . . The Phillips Board intends to take all appropriate action to protect Phillips shareholders from abusive takeover tactics and being forced to accept questionable securities for their Phillips shares." Following this rhetoric, the board declared that Icahn's price was too low; it would not budge for less than $62 per share.

So, it was to be war.

Both Black and Sorte were good men, but they reflected Drexel's lack of experience in how to put a merger together in the most effective manner. They were superb advisers in financial matters, but lacked some of the political and M&A skills. The language of the legal papers was not precise. The timing was off. Most of all, I was concerned that shareholders would be deterred by the two-tiered (part cash, part securities) nature of the offer. I argued that we had to persuade Icahn to shift his thinking toward an all-cash offer. To my relief, Icahn understood how important this would be to shareholders. He exhibited a pillow inscribed with the motto: "Happiness is a positive cash flow."

All of us were willing learners. Black and Sorte had much to teach me about raising capital at Drexel, and I, making delicate suggestions, showed them how to handle a thousand details, how to work with Icahn's staff, how to draft the language of press releases, how to coordinate with Icahn's special counsel, Arthur Liman, and his brilliant protégé, Mark Belnick.

Despite Joseph's initial counsel, it was obvious from the start that enormous egos and just as enormous jealousies were at work here at Drexel, where the traditional relationship between the Corporate Finance Department and the traders was inverted. A certain amount of tension pervaded the air whenever my colleagues in New York discussed affairs out at the "Drexel Bank." The way to success in this firm, it appeared, was to be one of Milken's friends. There were grumbles concerning nepotism whenever Lowell Milken was mentioned, and there were cutting remarks about men such as Harry Horowitz, who had been Milken's friend since grade school and who had been brought in to organize Drexel's lobbying efforts as well as to help plan and execute the annual Bond Conference. Horowitz, it was said, was now worth tens of millions of dollars, thanks to Milken's benevolence.

Scuttlebutt held that some of the higher-ups in Beverly Hills were earning $10 million, $15 million, $20 million or more per year—and one had to assume that Milken's salary was a multiple of those grand figures.

Right from the beginning, I resolved to rise above these jealousies. One day, someone grumbled, "Those goddamn guys on the West Coast are making so much money it's obscene."

I responded, "But look how much money they are making for the firm." It was the way of the Street in the 80s. If you can generate hundreds of millions of dollars for the firm, you deserve to earn tens of millions for yourself. Why work hard if you can't make a lot of money?

I quickly learned, however, that the finance men in California exhibited a rather pushy air that contributed to the hard feelings. Many of them lacked a good formal education, but they were street-smart and they quite obviously enjoyed flaunting their success in front of their better-educated, patrician rivals on the East Coast.

Having come from Lehman Brothers, where the M&A people almost never spoke with the traders, I was taken aback by the volume of calls

I got from various people in Beverly Hills seeking details on the progress of the deal. These were people who had no "need to know," and whether or not their inquiries breached the "Chinese Wall," they certainly gave the appearance of impropriety. I tried to give them only routine information.

My concerns were compounded as I received a growing volume of calls from arbs and other information-seekers who often prefaced their comments with, "I heard this from your Beverly Hills office."

I was embroiled in my studies of the Phillips deal when my secretary buzzed and announced that Ivan Boesky was on the phone. I picked up and heard a voice say, "Mr. Levine, this is Ivan Boesky calling. I understand from one of your partners that you are handling the Phillips thing for Carl."

"Yes."

"What can you tell me?"

Wall Street's most famous arb, I knew, still held a huge position in Phillips and was extremely nervous. I provided him with routine, public-record details.

Boesky thanked me for this news and hung up. I knew that he would immediately dial another number, seeking yet more data.

In fact, Boesky went right back to the primary source. On Saturday evening, February 9, he was a dinner guest at the Icahn residence. Boesky disclosed that he had bought "quite a bit of stock again . . . four to five million shares." That night, and in another meeting the following day, the two men again spoke of a joint tender offer. Once more they could not agree on the terms, and once more Icahn resolved to go it alone.

On February 13 we commenced the tender offer to buy 70 million shares (about 45 percent) of Phillips common stock at $60 per share, to be paid in cash. It was conditional upon the shareholders, at their special February 22 meeting, rejecting the recapitalization program already proposed, and Icahn was confident that the shareholders would see things his way, since they stood to gain about $7 per share. Icahn immediately set us to the task of contacting the larger shareholders; seeking to gain enough proxy votes to defeat the recapitalization plan. He declared brashly that Phillips "can't stop me."

To cover the costs of buying the stock, plus the expenses associated with the deal, Icahn estimated that he needed to raise $4.05 billion.

Now Drexel unleashed its secret weapon, an idea that evolved from the collective consciousness of all of us who were involved in the planning. It was a revolutionary method of assembling financial backing with a minimum outlay of front money, and it carried the side benefit of promoting secrecy. Over the past two years, Drexel had polished its abilities to obtain blind financing commitments. A borrower would agree to purchase perhaps $10 million worth of an upcoming junk-bond issue simply because Milken advised that it would be a good investment. Drexel supplied the lender with a sealed envelope containing details of the contemplated deal, most important, the name of the target. The envelope was not supposed to be opened until the deal was announced, and an accompanying letter declared: "You are obligated not to trade in securities of the subject company while you are in possession of material non-public information about the tender offer described within."

This was akin to telling a five-year-old to keep his hand out of the cookie jar. Early in 1984, when Pickens made his run at Gulf Oil, and later in the year when Steinberg stalked Disney, the Street witnessed dramatic run-ups of the stock prices prior to any public announcement. Disney stock rose from about $50 per share to nearly $69 per share in a three-month period. Milken knew that it was imperative for Drexel to learn how to raise money without alerting the entire Street.

In the traditional deal, a corporate raider had to have his money in hand before he could initiate a tender offer, but Milken realized that it did not have to be so. If the deal fell through, the raider did not need the money, so why not make the financing contingent upon the consummation of the deal? All the would-be borrower had to do was pay a commitment fee, assuring that the financing was there if and when it was needed. There was no law that said the money had to be assembled; the only issue was whether or not the shareholders believed that the money could and would be there. And in the current market, the words "money" and "Milken" were becoming synonymous.

Why, then, did Icahn or anyone else have to pay enormous loan commitment fees in advance? Why did Drexel have to worry itself over the prospect of raising money? The Beverly Hills traders were known here, in the New York office, as "unguided missiles" and once unleashed, they could probably sell oil to the Arabs. Over the years they had developed a variety of hardball tactics, and their aggressive style made it easy to apply the pressure. The message was clear: Buy these junk bonds or we won't be so anxious to sell your next issue.

There seemed to be a general impression, both among my Drexel associates and the clientele, that the "unguided missiles" did not worry overly much about some of their trading practices. No one expressed alarm over this, but no one wanted to know the details either. We were seduced by the simple fact that we were all making a great deal of money.

These days, when Milken's salesmen spread the word that a new, unnamed deal was in the offing, Drexel's telex machines were jammed with an influx of acceptance messages. Clerical personnel were drafted and thrown into limos to help deliver the necessary reams of paperwork. The money could be there at the wave of Milken's hand.

Realizing this, Drexel now unilaterally made a fundamental change in the procedures of the M&A business. Milken devised a simple letter, which he unveiled in the Phillips tender offer. "Based on current conditions," Milken wrote, "[Drexel] . . . is highly confident that it can arrange the necessary . . . financing commitments . . ." That was it, a simple pledge offered by the wizard of Beverly Hills. It was the first-ever tender offer for which the financing was not yet in place.

When Phillips management questioned this unheard-of tactic, Icahn responded, "Drexel's ability to raise financing is well-established. The relationship between Drexel and its financing sources is proprietary information. But as you know . . . Drexel has stated that it is highly confident that it can raise the requisite financing."

It was true. If Milken was highly confident, so was everyone else on the Street.

Nobody could quite believe the simple, clever solution. In all, we proposed to raise $2 billion in floating-rate senior notes, $2 billion in senior subordinated debentures and $600 million in preferred stock—and everyone was willing to take Milken at his word that he could do it. We did not even have to enlist the aid of a bank to swing the senior financing. For starters, Icahn paid Drexel a $1 million fee. He further agreed to pay a 2 percent commission on the financing package of $4.6 billion.

The "highly confident" letter set Wall Street on its ear.

*   *   *

IN the days prior to the Phillips shareholders' meeting, Milken wanted to nail down the loan commitments that he was so confident he could get. But Icahn balked, because he would have to pay a fee for those commitments, whether or not they were ultimately used. He authorized Milken to raise $1.5 billion worth of commitments now, but deferred the remainder until he knew the outcome of the proxy fight. In forty-eight hours, Milken had the $1.5 billion pledged, drawing upon such reliable sources as the Belzberg brothers and Saul Steinberg.

The Phillips board launched a desperate media campaign prophesying that if Icahn gained control he would move Phillips headquarters out of Bartlesville, Oklahoma, and thereby destroy the capital base of the small town. The Phillips logo was displayed throughout Bartlesville almost as reverently as the American flag, and it had significant impact upon the myriad of company employees who also happened to be shareholders. The company made public references to the "bust-up and liquidation" of Phillips, "and the resultant hardship to the thousands of employees who would be thrown out of work . . . ." Local newspaper ads asked, "Is Icahn for Real?"

Indeed, he was, and the Phillips media campaign did not fly with the vast majority of shareholders who lived outside of Bartlesville. We won the proxy battle, and Phillips came up 9 million votes short of the 77 million it needed to authorize its recapitalization plan. Its board had no choice but to meet us at the negotiating table.

On March 4, with the company's investment bankers from Morgan Stanley and a bevy of lawyers, we hammered out a revised plan. Icahn agreed to withdraw his tender offer and Phillips agreed to pay him $25 million to "cover his expenses." The company further agreed to offer all shareholders the chance to redeem their stock for a package of securities worth $62 per share. Icahn had succeeded in raising the value of the stock by $9 per share, assuring himself and Boesky of an astronomical profit.

Other winners were those investors upon whom Milken was "highly confident," to whom Icahn paid a total of $5,625,000 in commitment fees.

The newsletter *Corporate Control Alert* watched it all from the sidelines and concluded that Drexel's performance for Icahn "has given credibility to its claims that it can finance almost anything."

CHAPTER FIFTEEN

ANOTHER BIG DEAL occurred simultaneously.

One week after I joined Drexel, I was in John Sorte's office when he took a phone call from David Arledge, senior vice president for finance of Coastal Corporation, a major oil and gas exploration company based in Houston. Arledge confirmed to Sorte that Coastal was ready to go ahead with plans for what we code-named "Operation Gull," a tender offer for American Natural Resources Company. In the old days, this would have been a ridiculous proposition. Coastal had a market value of about $450 million, whereas ANR's market value was four times larger. In today's environment, thanks to Drexel, it was quite possible to consider such a transaction.

The pipeline industry was generally on the sidelines during past periods of business consolidation. The companies were heavily regulated, subject to extreme scrutiny by the federal government, which historically looked somewhat askance at monopolistic mergers. But this was the era of Reaganomics, when antitrust considerations were pretty much tossed out the window, and the oil and gas pipeline industry was ripe for a major deal.

Arledge wanted Drexel to arrange as much as $600 million of mezzanine financing to support the senior, or bank, financing, and Sorte, picking up quickly on Milken's new catchphrase, responded that he was "highly confident" that the Beverly Hills boys could raise the money both quickly and, just as important, quietly. He added that Drexel had a new man on board who was a specialist in handling the dealmaking details. Me.

After the call, Sorte briefed me. If the deal flew, it would exceed $2 billion and would bring us much attention.

I studied carefully and was pleased to realize that the numbers "crunched" in Coastal's favor. This was clearly an industry-driven deal between two firms with common interests and abilities. There were economies of scale available to Coastal that would benefit no other buyer. Both Coastal and ANR were pipeline companies, and when I mapped out the geographical patterns of their current pipeline operations, it was obvious that the two systems would mesh perfectly into one larger, far more efficient system. Coastal's pipeline system stretched from Wyoming to the Texas panhandle. ANR's system lay generally east of this, with little duplication. The merged company would have access to major energy-producing areas from Canada to Mexico, from the Midwest to the Rockies, and would bring in combined annual revenues of about $9 billion. All of this meant that Coastal could afford to offer more for ANR than any other possible buyer.

A successful takeover bid would balloon Coastal's debt to about $3.5 billion, but I calculated that the company could reduce that rather quickly by selling off a couple of ANR subsidiaries, such as its trucking unit and its coal properties.

My guess was that ANR would resist fiercely, and I believed that management's best chance at fending off Coastal would be to attempt an LBO to buy the company from the stockholders and take it private. I called Beverly Hills and asked, "Mike, if you were to do an LBO of American Natural Resources under the most aggressive financing techniques available, what would the price be?"

Together, Milken and I decided that $60 per share was the critical point. If the price approached that level, we believed that the ANR directors would be unable to defend. If we had to, Milken said, we could go $5 per share higher.

It was important, I pointed out, for Drexel to do a better job of security. The "highly confident" letter would be a great help in preventing the premature spread of information. Michael said he would implement yet another new strategy. For the first time, the "Drexel Bank" would put together an anonymous prospectus of the deal, identifying both the potential acquirer and the target company only in generic terms. The prospectus would describe the credit position and financial terms of the deal without identifying the principals by name. It was an important step forward in holding down the pre-announcement speculation.

Once I had satisfied myself that the deal was viable, I arranged a meeting with Bob Wilkis, at lunchtime on a Thursday. Often, I now felt sad when I saw Wilkis. As my career had skyrocketed, his had languished, and I thought I knew why. He was an urbane, capable man in many areas, but he just did not seem to have a grasp of some of the intricacies of the M&A business. He was not a dealmaker. I had tried to teach him, to help him along, but it just was not working. He felt he needed a change, and he began to shop around for a new position on the Street. I had introduced him to Dave Hart at Hadley Lockwood, the recruiting firm that brought me to Drexel, but he reported no progress, as yet.

After lunch, as we stood out on the sidewalk, not far from the New York Stock Exchange, I disclosed, "We're working on a deal for ANR. It looks like it's gonna go."

We parted and I sought out a pay phone, placed a collect call to Bernhard Meier at Bank Leu and instructed him to begin buying stock in ANR, as much as he could without moving the market. I reminded him that I wanted him to spread the purchases among several brokers.

Meier set about executing the trades for me. In the meantime, without telling me, he bought 2,000 shares for his own account and persuaded the previously skittish Pletscher to join him. Pletscher was in for 500 shares.

TWENTY-FOUR hours later I was even more confident of the deal. I called Meier again and told him to sink the entire balance of my account, now more than $7 million, into ANR stock.

Only later would I learn that Meier, after he hung up the phone, ran to Pletscher and said, "Bruno, you should increase your ANR. Why do you not buy another thousand?"

Pletscher moaned, "That is too much for me. I have already invested a lot of money."

Meier suggested that Pletscher buy on a margin account, so that he only had to put up half the cash. Pletscher, still very skeptical, agreed to purchase another 500 shares.

ON Sunday night I met with Arledge and two other senior management officials, Coastal's president, James Whalen, and executive vice president, Austin O'Toole. Coastal maintained a suite on the thirty-eighth floor of the United Nations Plaza Towers and it was here, overlooking the U.N. building and the East River, that we prepared for war. We discussed the possibility of floating the senior financing for the acquisition through a consortium of Arab, Swiss and Canadian banks.

The chairman and CEO of Coastal was Oscar S. Wyatt, Jr., a Texas rancher and oilman who had parlayed his early successes into a big-time regional business. He was one of the more feared takeover artists in the business, but he had compiled a less-than-distinguished track record. For the past two years he had been trying to buy a major pipeline company, but his attempts had failed. His "wildcatter" reputation generated a great deal of static and stirred up much trouble but, thus far, brought poor results. When Arledge told me that Wyatt's plan was to announce a tender offer in the mid-50s, I protested that this would be a critical mistake.

"If you want to win, you don't lowball," I argued. "You go in with a winning bid. You go in in the fifties and you're going to get overbid at sixty—either by a white knight or in an LBO attempt led by management—and then you're going to have trouble because that overbid is likely to be a friendly deal and it will have lockups. Certain divisions are going to be sold out from under you. Stock options are going to cut into your numbers—not to mention the fact that you'll pay enormous legal fees.

"I've already talked to people on the Street," I added. "I have a sense of what's happening." I disclosed that I had learned that arbs were already buying up ANR stock. Somehow, they had learned of the deal, perhaps when we made our initial contact with the commercial bankers. In one sense this was good for us, I pointed out, because the arbs were in the market for the short term. No one would ever have to twist Boesky's arm to get him to sell, if the price was right. On the other hand, he was shrewd. If he felt the price was too low, he would pull whatever strings he could to get another bidder involved. And that, of course, was something we hoped to avoid.

I concluded, "We strongly recommend that you go in at sixty dollars per share. What that tells the world is: You can go higher. My sense is that, if you go in at sixty, you're going to keep all the corporate players on the sidelines and the only thing you'll have to contend with is a potential LBO. The ANR board will bring in its people from Goldman Sachs and try to engineer a deal. But I've talked with our West Coast people, and they don't believe that ANR can put together an LBO at the sixty-dollar level—not one that's viable—without Drexel to finance it."

I also pointed out the need to make the offer an all-cash deal. A cash tender offer could be completed in thirty to sixty days' time. If ANR management tried to put together an LBO, they were looking at six months of work. Our job was to give Boesky and the other arbs the chance to opt for a quick buck. To them, that's no choice.

Figuratively, I kept my fingers crossed throughout this entire lecture. I knew that it was going to take considerable persuasion to get Wyatt to budge from his lowball offer.

I phoned Nassau and Meier reported to me that he had acquired a total of 145,000 shares of ANR for my account at an average price of just under $50. All told, I had a whopping $7.2 million at risk. It was virtually my entire portfolio, but it was more than money that I gambled. Now, for the first time, I had made an insider trade based on a deal where I was the senior banker, intimately involved in the transaction.

In my consciousness, everything was nicely compartmentalized. I saw no conflict between my $60 per share recommendation and my $50 per share purchases. My advice to Coastal, I rationalized, was based upon sound business reasoning and would have been the same, whether or not I had a personal stake in the matter.

Nonetheless, I was ecstatic when Wyatt finally agreed to my pricing structure. On Friday, March 1, after the market closed, we announced the offer at $60 per share, all cash. On Monday morning, ANR stock opened near that price and I sold out for a profit of $1,370,610. Wilkis, playing more conservatively, made $300,000. Unbeknownst to me, Meier profited nearly $25,000.

The news brought a delicious sense of giddiness, of invulnerability, despite reports emanating from Washington, where, the day after I instructed Bank Leu to sell my ANR stock, former Deputy U.S. Defense Secretary Paul Thayer, along with Dallas stockbroker Billy Bob Harris, pled guilty to charges of giving false testimony and obstructing justice in connection with insider trading activities.

ANR's management fought back even harder than I had anticipated. Chairman and CEO Arthur R. Seder, Jr., termed Wyatt's bid of $60 per share "entirely inadequate" and rushed to set up inducements for its traditional investment banker, Goldman Sachs, and the boys from First Boston. Goldman stood to make a $6 million commission when the deal went through. But if it could find a higher bidder, or if it could persuade Coastal to raise its bid, it would receive a premium amounting to one-third of 1 percent of the purchase price. First Boston was guaranteed a $3 million fee, but could double that if it arranged a workable LBO that included the employees as equity partners.

In short order ANR announced a defensive move to sell some of its assets in order to buy back two million shares of its own stock. In the meantime, First Boston tried to fashion a modified LBO, under which the company would be purchased by its employees in partnership with a consortium of three Texas-based firms, Transco Energy Company, Houston Natural Gas Corporation and Texas Oil & Gas Corporation.

Both sides, of course, filed lawsuits, charging numerous violations of securities laws.

The battle raged fiercely, but briefly. Various members of Coastal's management team called me throughout the day to ask, "What have you heard?" As I had predicted, the numbers did not crunch well for ANR. Coastal's bid was just high enough to discourage serious competition. I watched in amusement as the Texas-based white knights pulled back almost without a whimper of protest, leaving the clear impression that others in the industry really wanted Wyatt to win this one, so that, perhaps, he would remain quiet for a while. ANR's only viable choice was to get the most it could out of Coastal's offer.

Realizing this, my counterpart at Goldman Sachs reached me by phone and asked, "What's your number?"

"I think the principals should negotiate," I replied.

Much happened within a matter of days. On March 13, Boesky disclosed to the SEC that he owned 3.74 million shares of ANR, about

9.9 percent of the company. He had purchased these during a month-long buying spree, and I found it interesting to learn that he had begun his buying on February 14, two weeks prior to the public announcement of our offer. Obviously he made a lucky guess, or he had very good sources of information. He had spoken with me about the deal, but only after the announcement. Who, I wondered, might have tipped him?

That same day Wyatt and Coastal's president, James R. Paul, met in Detroit with Seder and ANR's president, William T. McCormick, Jr., for what the companies described as "serious negotiations."

Also on March 13, the SEC opened an inquiry into the possibility of insider trading on ANR stock. The NYSE's computerized monitoring equipment had picked up a pattern of heavy trading that preceded the official announcement. ANR's stock jumped from $46.50 per share on February 22 to $49.75 per share on February 27, two days before our tender offer was disclosed. I was not concerned about the SEC scrutiny, for I knew that my activity paled in comparison to that of Boesky and the other arbs.

AFTER a late night of negotiations that Wyatt termed "sincere and friendly, straightforward and businesslike," he announced that Coastal and ANR had hammered out a compromise. By raising his price to $65 per share, Wyatt turned the hostile tender offer into a friendly deal and saved himself considerable headaches, not to mention legal expenses.

At $2.46 billion, it now stood as the largest successful unsolicited takeover in history, wherein the initial bidder prevailed. It was a coup for Wyatt; for Goldman Sachs, which realized an additional $2.2 million in commissions as a result of the raised bid; for First Boston, which received a $3 million commission for very little work on its LBO proposal; for the banks that wrote $1.6 billion in conventional loans; for Milken, who placed $600 million worth of high-yield debt; for Wilkis; and for me, both on a professional and personal level. I calculated Boesky's profit at about $15 million.

Drexel earned a $20 million commission and enhanced its growing reputation. One takeover attorney told a financial reporter that Drexel could "raise the money to put any company into play, and I mean *any* company."

*   *   *

SEC investigators made initial checks but soon discovered insufficient evidence to pursue charges of insider trading in ANR stock. How can you prove a contention based upon rumor and innuendo? The incident escalated my confidence in the safeguards that Wilkis and I had in place.

In fact, I was so smug about the strength of our defenses that I acted upon a tip from Ira Sokolow (relayed from his contact "Goldie") the day after the SEC announced its inquiry. Sokolow informed me that Goldman Sachs had been retained by McGraw-Edison to advise it in connection with a proposed LBO by Forstmann Little & Company. I bought 79,500 shares of McGraw-Edison for about $3.4 million. Only a few days after the deal was announced, I sold my stock for a profit of $906,836. If I had waited another day or two I would have made even more, because Cooper Industries came into the arena with a higher bid, but I was more than satisfied.

I would have been incensed had I known that Meier made a profit of $12,750 by piggybacking the trade and, what's more, had persuaded Pletscher to do likewise by reporting, "This is a sure winner."

THE M&A trend had advanced to the point where it was now the focus of debate on Capitol Hill. Professor F. M. Scherer of Swarthmore College presented to a congressional hearing the findings of his study of nearly 4,000 businesses involved in takeover transactions during the past twenty-seven years. He concluded that the key attraction of a target, contrary to the raiders' rhetoric, was undervalued assets, rather than inept management; in fact, he argued, most of the targets were already well managed. He declared that takeovers encouraged a short-term dash for quick profits at the expense of long-term modernization and research and development activities.

This position was in direct conflict with the President's Council of Economic Advisers, which declared that mergers and acquisitions "improve efficiency, transfer scarce resources to higher valued uses, and stimulate effective corporate management."

At Drexel, we tended to side with the latter view.

*   *   *

ON Monday, March 18, I met with Sir James M. Goldsmith in his New York office in the Piaget Building at Fifth Avenue and 52nd Street. His 6'4" frame carried considerable bulk on it, creating an imposing air. Now in his early fifties, Goldsmith exhibited a snow-white ring of hair around a bald pate. A deep dimple was tucked into the centerpoint of his chin. His eyes seemed to smile in concert with the lips. He had reason to be happy. Goldsmith was emerging as one of the major corporate raiders on the U.S. scene.

He was an Anglo-French financier, a wealthy, polished, highly articulate, anti-Establishment type who was well known in European circles for his flamboyant life-style as well as for his business endeavors. He owned *L'Express,* the largest newsweekly in France, as well as a weekly newspaper in Belgium, and he had waged journalistic war on what he perceived as the KGB's systematic "disinformation" campaign to subvert the Western press. His other businesses in Europe and the U.S. marketed diet foods, chocolate and snuff. His holding company, Générale Occidentale, managed the Grand Union chain of supermarkets and Diamond International Corporation, a timber harvesting firm.

One year earlier Goldsmith had launched an attempt to take over the timber company St. Regis Corporation. When he announced that he already held 8.6 percent of the corporate stock, purchased at about $35 per share, the news sent the speculators into action. Their buying spree pushed the market price up to $42. The St. Regis board of directors quickly struck a deal to buy Goldsmith's stock back from him at $52 per share, netting Sir James a cool $51 million profit. He had pulled off a similar greenmail deal with another timber company, the Continental Group.

Since the previous December, Goldsmith had been acquiring a large position in the stock of Crown Zellerbach, a Nevada corporation with its headquarters in San Francisco. Among Crown's $2.5 billion in assets, those that Goldsmith particularly coveted were its 2 million acres of timber. Buying quietly, he had accumulated a significant position at a cost of about $30 per share. In December he had filed Schedule 13D with the SEC and simultaneously notified the management of Crown Zellerbach by letter that he had reached a position of 5 percent ownership. By now, three months later, his holdings had grown to 8.6 percent. He had sunk $78 million into the market, and he was ready to make his move. At Drexel, we stood to earn flat fees totaling

$750,000, plus a substantial commission on the price of securities we sold to finance the acquisition.

Together with Goldsmith and my colleagues, we debated the formidable defense that was set in place. The previous year, the Crown Zellerbach board had adopted a so-called "poison pill" defense; this is the strategy whereby a company sets into place any of numerous procedures to dilute the value of its stock. Those procedures kick in if and when a would-be acquirer appears on the horizon. Crown Zellerbach had declared that if one entity acquired 20 percent of its stock, shareholders would receive the right to purchase—at half price!—stock in any company that emerged as a survivor from a merger with Crown Zellerbach. Obviously this lucrative right would make it prohibitively expensive to acquire the company.

Goldsmith believed that Crown Zellerbach's poison pill could be voided in the courts on the basis that, by making a takeover unlikely, it violated the shareholders' right to obtain the best value for their property, and I agreed.

The day after our meeting, Goldsmith confronted William T. Creson, chairman, president and CEO of Crown, and informed him that his intentions were not "passive," and that he was not interested in being bought off in a greenmail transaction. He declared that Crown had four alternatives: 1) do nothing; 2) merge with a third party; 3) negotiate a sellout to Goldsmith; 4) negotiate an agreement giving Goldsmith status as a minority shareholder, including representation on the board of directors.

Creson responded that he thought Crown should remain independent.

No one knew what would happen next. Meanwhile, Goldsmith—and everyone else who mattered in the M&A business—hopped a plane for Beverly Hills.

CHAPTER SIXTEEN

THE REGENT AIR JET, a customized Boeing 727, carried me and an army of Drexel operatives to California in high style. During the flight I had an opportunity to chat with a Drexel client, Charles Hurwitz, CEO of the holding company of Maxxam Group.

Our destination was the seventh incarnation of what was officially called Drexel's annual Institutional Research Conference, known informally as "the Bond Conference" or "the Predators' Ball." The stated purpose of the gathering was for bond buyers to mingle with bond issuers. Attendance was by invitation only (Drexel spouses were conspicuously excluded), and if you were there, you knew that you had achieved status in the M&A world.

The four-day affair was timed to occur the week following the Academy Awards. Drexel had booked virtually every room in the pink-and-green Beverly Hills Hotel. When I checked in, along with David Kay and Chris Anderson, one of the clerks remarked, "Gee, we thought the movie people put on a show, but you guys take the cake!" It was an exciting, ironic moment, for I knew that our host, the man who owned 53 percent of this hotel, was none other than Ivan Boesky.

By five-thirty the next morning, what seemed like an endless loop of stretch limos (each with a well-stocked bar) began shuttling the movers and shakers of the business world—some 2,000 in all—from our hotel, the Beverly Wilshire, the Century Plaza and the Bel Air, bringing us all to a ballroom at the Beverly Hilton Hotel, only a few blocks distant from Milken's office.

I found myself fascinated by the business across the street from the host hotel. It was a Budget Rent a Car office that specialized in exotic automobiles. You could rent a Rolls-Royce, a Lamborghini, a 12-cylinder Jaguar convertible or whatever other fantasy automobile you might want to take for a spin. Only in Beverly Hills, I thought.

About 2,000 people awaited the opening session of the conference with a high sense of expectation. Here were the money managers of the world's largest life insurance portfolios, S&Ls, college endowment accounts, mutual funds, offshore banks and financial syndicates. Here were the world's best-known corporate raiders. I kept my eyes open for Goldsmith, so that we could resume our discussions concerning Crown Zellerbach.

At about six-thirty A.M., the lights dimmed and Milken walked on stage. He greeted everyone effusively and presented the first of countless Drexel sales pitches, augmented by slick videos shown on floor-to-ceiling screens. He then presented Dr. Armand Hammer, who responded with brief remarks extolling the virtues of Drexel in general and Milken in particular.

The keynote speaker was Oscar Wyatt, who detailed the intricacies of the Coastal/ANR deal to an audience that had envy dripping from its collective eye. Every real and potential corporate raider in attendance wanted to pull off such a coup, and we all wondered who would be standing up there next year, as the man who had just concluded a deal of historic size and significance.

Following Wyatt's speech, the real work began as the participants took a break from formal proceedings and clustered in the hallways and reception rooms, forming into power blocs. I was chatting with a few new acquaintances when Milken's voice penetrated my consciousness: "Dennis, come over here." I turned to see him wave. "Come over here," he repeated.

I joined Milken, who was surrounded by an assortment of businessmen as well as groupies and a handful of security guards. "I'd like you to meet Dennis Levine," he said to the crowd. "Dennis just joined us from Lehman Brothers and he was the man who orchestrated the Coastal/ANR deal."

I shook hands with T. Boone Pickens, whose slim, deep-lined face had only recently graced the cover of *Time;* Carl Lindner of Cincinnati, one of the richest men in America, a tithe-paying Baptist whose American Financial Corporation was among Drexel's biggest purchasers of junk bonds; Saul Steinberg, who, with Disney's greenmail cash in his pockets, was an ever more highly valued Drexel client; Nelson Peltz, relatively unknown until the previous week, when his tiny Triangle Industries, a vending machine company, bid $456 million for National Can, backed by Drexel-issued junk bonds; Irwin Jacobs, the tall, dark, broadly built Minneapolis-based raider known as "The Liquidator"; and Dort Cameron, a former Milken assistant who managed the Bass Investment Limited Partnership for the Bass brothers of Fort Worth. The partnership held $1.2 billion worth of capital to be used for investing in junk bonds and LBOs; Milken and other Drexel personnel held a 45 percent minority ownership position.

"How do you do? How do you do?" I said, as I pumped the offered hands. It was heady wine. Here was Milken, certifying to the other members of the club that I was "good people." In this milieu, Milken was clearly the king of finance, indicating to the other members of the club that I was to be trusted.

THE sleeves were rolled up in the hospitality suites funded by the world's leading corporate raiders, who orchestrated graphic, peripatetic sales pitches. The entrepreneurs may have been the flashy front men, but we Drexel insiders were the ones who had the power to make or break them. We could put every facet of the deal together. Sometimes, as long as a deal made good business sense, it almost seemed as if it did not matter who was the target and who was the titular principal. Certain corporate raiders were referred to as "Drexel inventions."

Discussions ran into enormous numbers. One topic under consideration was whether or not some of the more well-known raiders launched their hostile tender offers with expectations of winning, or whether they were really in search of greenmail. Icahn had pocketed numerous lucrative payoffs—$6.6 million from American Can, $9.7 million from Owens Illinois, $8.5 million from Dan River Mills—just to back off. Irwin Jacobs was bought off by Pabst Brewing for $20 million; Kaiser Steel paid him $30 million to walk away. Rumor held that the Bass brothers made a profit ranging from $300 to $400 million the previous year when they accumulated 9.9 percent of Texaco's stock and sold it back to the company at more than $1.50 per share above the prevailing market price. In 1984 alone, Pickens was believed to have profited as much as $1 billion without really pulling off a substantial acquisition.

Almost at every turn I was confronted by Nelson Peltz, relentlessly seeking details about his run at National Can. "Did you hear anything? Did you hear anything?" was his constant, plaintive question to me, and to other Drexel execs.

An interested spectator in all this was U.S. Representative Timothy Wirth, who had sponsored legislation against insider trading and repeatedly expressed his concern over the M&A trend. Drexel had taken him on as an evangelistic target and invited him to the Bond Conference to see for himself what it was all about. Wirth was clearly interested.

ONE afternoon, along with my Drexel colleagues Chris Anderson and Doug McClure, I met with Goldsmith in his suite at the Bel Air Hotel. We were joined by Goldsmith's principal legal adviser, Joe Flom. While sipping champagne, Goldsmith brought us up to date on his unsatisfactory meeting with Creson of Crown Zellerbach and disclosed to us that he was willing to go higher than $40 per share with a hostile bid. Crown was trading now in the low 30s.

The next morning, from a pay phone, I placed a collect call to Bank Leu. Meier was away on vacation, so Pletscher handled my business, which was to buy $4 million worth of stock in Crown Zellerbach. I was just in time, for that same day, Thursday, Creson formalized his response to Goldsmith's initial approach, declaring in a press release that he believed that Crown should remain independent. The announcement had the opposite of a calming effect. The word was out officially now; Crown was in play and arbs jammed the phones in Beverly Hills. The stock soared.

THURSDAY night found me at a champagne function in a pink, three-bedroom cottage at the Beverly Hills Hotel. By now this was a famous—or infamous—annual event, the Bungalow 8 party. The rank and file among the conference attendees had been shuttled off to a special show at a movie lot; this party at a remote, private corner of the hotel grounds was reserved for the one hundred heaviest hitters among

Drexel's clientele. Some brought their spouses; others preferred to tap the resources of the multitude of social climbers, parasites and beautiful, elegant young women who seemed to make themselves visibly available.

After drinking themselves into a festive mood, the party-goers hopped into limos for dinner in a private room at Chasen's. Many then returned to Bungalow 8, but several of us opted to visit the Polo Lounge instead.

The moment I stepped into the lounge I heard someone call, "Dennis!"

I glanced up to see one of the conference attendees struggling to approach me. His steps were impaired by significant amounts of alcohol, and by the three women who clutched at his arms. They were young, gorgeous and attired in the latest Rodeo Drive evening fashions. One of them smiled at me in a manner that was suggestive, and yet somehow innocent.

The man nearly stumbled as he reached toward me. He grabbed my arm for support. For a moment he looked around, as if trying to remember where he was.

"Dennish," he said, "Dennish . . ." He tossed an arm around one of the women, a platinum blonde, and announced, "This one's mine." With his other arm he gestured toward his two other companions. He lowered his voice and asked in a serious tone, "Which one ya want?"

What was I supposed to say? I was the new man at Drexel. This conference, this night, this world was unlike anything I had ever witnessed at Smith Barney or Lehman Brothers. Did I dare risk alienating a man with whom I was likely to be involved in billion-dollar deals? Finally I said the only thing I could say: "Thanks, but no thanks."

He traipsed off, unoffended. And I felt better when I realized that he probably would have no memory of the incident.

I accepted some of these excesses as a necessary evil of the business world. I enjoyed swigging a drink with the best of them, but the overt philandering disgusted, and even bored, me. If Drexel was going to gain respect as a first-tier firm, I thought, it was going to have to clean up the environment.

THE next morning, shortly before the Corporate Finance Breakfast before a standing-room-only crowd in the Beverly Hills Hotel, I stood in the back of the room, surveying the scene. Suddenly I recognized the man standing next to me. The dreariness of his appearance startled me once more, as it had during our brief introduction the previous year. Although we had spoken by phone several times, this was only our second personal encounter.

I offered my hand and said, "Hi, Ivan, I'm Dennis Levine."

"Ahhh, how are you?" Boesky asked, pumping my hand effusively, flashing a toothy, Cheshire-cat grin.

"Good," I said. "I've enjoyed the meeting." I waved my hand at our elegant surroundings and added, "And I've enjoyed your hotel."

"Let's chat," he suggested. He drew me behind a curtain in the back of the room and congratulated me on both the Phillips Petroleum deal and the Coastal/ANR deal. "I'd like to get together again with you in New York," he said. "We've got a lot of things to discuss."

"I'll look forward to it," I replied.

His eyes brightened with a sudden thought. "Can I fly you back to New York on my jet?" he asked. "We could talk then."

"That won't be necessary," I demurred. "I'm going to stay out here for the weekend, to visit my brother and his family." I had to hide my amusement, for this was the fifth or sixth such offer I had received. It was fun working for Drexel. These men, whom the world viewed as so successful and powerful, knew that *they* needed *us*.

THE bond conference traditionally culminated on Friday night, when Drexel booked a major entertainer into the ballroom of the Century Plaza, and the identity of the star was guarded more closely than any stock market secret. Last year the surprise guest was Frank Sinatra.

Outside, a line of limos disgorged the wealthiest and most powerful businessmen and women in the world, attired in their finest regalia. They passed through entranceways manned by grim-faced security guards who checked name tags with care. Inside was an atmosphere of tension, as everyone tried not to show what was, in his mind, the primary concern of the evening: Where am I sitting? America's most powerful business tycoons, as evaluated by Milken, sat at the center tables on the ballroom floor, with a close-up view of the stage. Those of lesser rank were scattered throughout the remainder of the available space.

On either side of the stage were enormous screens telecasting advertisements extolling the virtues of Drexel. Piped-in music approached the decibel level of a rock concert.

Los Angeles Mayor Tom Bradley welcomed everyone and said, "Please leave a lot of cash in our city." Milken followed this with his own greeting.

Most of the revelers awaited the appearance of the surprise guest, but I found the real entertainment occurring during dinner. I watched in fascination as the dealmakers worked the room. I had never witnessed anything quite like the Drexel cult in action. This was a carefully orchestrated spectacle of monumental proportions, costing millions of dollars, and all designed to sell you on Milken's way of doing business. Champagne flowed freely.

We were in the midst of dinner when the general din suddenly subsided; Milken had taken the stage to introduce a video prepared by Lorimar Productions.

Following that, without any introduction, the band struck up a fanfare. Artificial fog billowed across the platform. A slim woman in a glittery evening gown appeared in the midst of the haze, microphone in hand, and began to sing "Ain't No Mountain High Enough." The room burst into applause as an unmistakable voice filled the air.

Eli Broad, chairman and CEO of Kaufman & Broad, tapped me on the shoulder and asked, "Dennis, who is that?"

"Diana Ross," I replied.

He shrugged his shoulders.

She sang for about forty minutes, interrupting her performance with occasional patter, keyed to this unique audience. At one point she exclaimed, "I can't believe how much money is in this room, how much power is here." The audience erupted with self-congratulatory applause. With the exception of Broad, the performer held her audience in a spell, woven with a mixture of oldies from "The Supremes" as well as new material and a few standards. Then she brought her act into the audience, singing as she walked about. Finally she settled onto the lap of Carl Lindner and sang to him.

I was one of the last to leave that evening, consciously lingering to prolong the euphoria. The ballroom was nearly deserted by the time Diana Ross emerged from the wings. She was flanked by a bodyguard, and by Milken himself. At the moment, it was difficult to decide who

190 DENNIS B. LEVINE

was the bigger star. Milken escorted her into a limo and they rode off, probably to one or more of the very exclusive parties that were still on the night's schedule.

THE following morning I checked out of the Beverly Hills Hotel and headed for the Budget Rent a Car office, where I rented a fire-engine red Ferrari convertible. With the top down, I set off along the San Diego Freeway in the warm glow of the California sun.

When I arrived at my brother's home in Orange County, he whistled at the car and exclaimed, "Geesh, you must be doing very well!"

CHAPTER SEVENTEEN

IVAN BOESKY DEMONSTRATED his muscle. Ever since a conservative lobby group called Fairness in Media—whose national spokesperson was Senator Jesse Helms (R-NC)—had issued a preposterous threat to launch a takeover attempt against CBS, Inc., in order to eliminate what it called the network's "liberal bias," Boesky had been quietly buying CBS stock. Not for a moment did he believe that the pressure group could mount a serious challenge (although he and his wife had both contributed the legal maximum of $2,000 to Senator Helms's re-election campaign the previous year); rather, he liked any talk that might put a company into play.

He already owned a sizable position in CBS when Capital Cities Communications, Inc., announced an agreement to acquire the ABC broadcasting network. Now Boesky assumed that a copycat would be inspired to act, so he beefed up his ownership position to 8.7 percent and filed the required Schedule 13D. Once the Street learned this, it assumed that Boesky knew something. Just like that, CBS was a target, and strengthened its defensive arsenal by arranging a $1.5 billion line of credit.

Boesky asked to meet with CBS executives in an attempt to get them to buy back his position at the new, inflated market price of about $105 per share. But a CBS spokesman responded, "We see no reason to meet."

Several possible buyers emerged, including Denver oilman Marvin Davis, the former owner of 20th Century-Fox Film Corporation, publisher Rupert Murdoch, the Bass brothers and General Electric Co. But the one who rose to the bait most eagerly was cable TV mogul Ted Turner, who came to Drexel for financing. Fred Joseph took a team to Beverly Hills to discuss the situation with Milken. I remained behind in New York to handle other matters, but I contributed my input via telephone.

"No way," I argued in a strategy session. "CBS is a very public company, a *news* company. If we take it on, we will be under scrutiny every step of the way. It's a suicide deal. There is only a small chance of winning and it's not worth it."

Milken shared my concern about the potential for negative publicity. Recently, some of our takeover targets had scored points by criticizing the use of junk bonds. Marty Lipton's catchphrase was that such-and-such a deal was another "coercive, two-tiered, junk-bond, bust-up take-over." This type of public relations campaign is known as a "scorched earth" defense and it tarnished our image. We had no desire to see Drexel and its junk bonds featured in a "60 Minutes" segment.

Beyond that, someone else pointed out, there were regulatory issues. This would be a battle between cable television and network television and although other government agencies in the Reagan Administration appeared to have grown blind to antitrust issues, the Federal Communications Commission was sure to raise a myriad of sticky issues. Whether or not we could resolve them, the hassles were sure to delay things and give CBS valuable defensive time.

Finally we looked at the cash problem. Turner Broadcasting had about $50 million in cash, plus a $190 million line of credit. The pricetag for CBS would probably be higher than $4 billion. This was by no means an insurmountable obstacle for Drexel, but when placed alongside our other objections, it gave us a convenient "out."

We turned thumbs down on the deal, and Turner sought another investment banker.

OVER a period of two weeks the stock of Crown Zellerbach rose on the open market from the low 30s to $41.625 per share. On April 1 Goldsmith sent a letter to Creson announcing that he was prepared to effect a transaction in which Crown's shareholders would receive "in excess of" $41.625 per share—if the Crown board took action to remove the poison pill within one week's time. Crown quickly set a board meeting for April 10 to discuss Goldsmith's proposal.

My partners and I held a series of frenetic meetings with Goldsmith, whose holdings in Crown Zellerbach had reached 9.36 percent. Via conference calls, we spoke to Milken about the financing arrangements for the final push.

By now the arbs had accumulated massive blocks of Crown Zeller-bach stock, guessing at the highest price Goldsmith would be willing to pay. Rumor held that Boesky had plunged the deepest, and this was confirmed when he filed his own Schedule 13D. Whatever we did, we knew now that we would have to fit Boesky into the equation.

I visited Boesky to get a feel for his intentions. His opulent offices were situated on the top floor of the Piaget Building at 650 Fifth Avenue, the same address where, by coincidence, Goldsmith maintained his offices.

I had never been here before, and Boesky enjoyed showing me around. With a chuckle, he declared that this suite was once occupied by Marc Rich, the commodities trader who had fled to the Alpine village of Zug, Switzerland, in 1983 to avoid trial on dozens of criminal counts. Boesky showed off a desk that included a bank of video screens hooked up to closed-circuit cameras that allowed him to keep an omniscient eye on his associates in the trading rooms. His phone system was incredible; it had 160 direct lines and a surveillance system that allowed him to monitor his employees' calls.

From this office Boesky had helped to change the business. In the "old days" of a few years ago, arbs were not very important in takeover deals. But Boesky invested so heavily in the stocks of takeover candidates that his participation altered the parameters of any transaction. He was so successful at this that others had followed suit. Today, if you wanted to be successful in the M&A business, you had to know how to deal with arbs.

What's more, the participation of these arbs accelerated the pace of everything. Not too many years ago, once a merger proposal was announced, an investor had at least several hours, or perhaps a full day, to decide upon a course of action. Typically, someone like me at an investment banking house would call the appropriate stock exchange and declare, "We have a pending announcement regarding XYZ Corporation, and we'd like you to halt trading." Trading in the stock of XYZ Corporation would be suspended and, once the market closed, we would announce our news. That procedure gave the arbs and everyone else a long night of work to plan their strategies. By the time the market opened in the morning, brokers would have fistfuls of orders regarding the stock, and it was likely to open at a radically adjusted price.

But now, responding to the escalating action, Jefferies & Company, a large, independent, Los Angeles–based broker, had developed and exploited the third market concept. The "primary" market is the first, direct sale of stock between the issuing corporation and the buyer. The "secondary" is a brokered market, such as the New York Stock Exchange, the American Stock Exchange, or the Over-the-Counter market, where stocks are resold among buyers. Boyd Jefferies explored and expanded the third market, offering large investors the opportunity to barter huge chunks of hot issues twenty-four hours a day, particularly during times when trading was suspended on the major exchanges. Suddenly, arbs could move into the market instantly, no matter the day or the time.

The third market was now a powerful force, so much so that, during the height of the Steinberg-fueled Disney buying, the New York Stock Exchange, after suspending trading pending an announcement, reopened Disney due to what it called "significant trading" off the floor.

Time was, more than ever, money, and Boesky husbanded the resource. He told me that he usually arrived at the office between four A.M. and five A.M., took a midmorning breakfast break across the street at the Pastrami 'n' Things coffee shop, and worked until late in the evening. He said he only slept two or three hours a night.

Only later would I realize what Boesky was up to on this very day. Now that his accumulation efforts had helped put CBS in play, he was ready to cash in. Whether he knew that Ted Turner was about to launch a shaky bid, or whether he merely made an uncanny guess, I could not know. But for whatever reason, he began selling off 1.3 million shares of CBS. When other investors heard that Boesky was selling, they bailed out also. CBS stock fell $9 per share in a single day.

AT Drexel, I was in a far better spot than ever to know what was going on inside Wall Street, and the same was more true of Wilkis, who landed a job as a first vice president in the M&A Department of E. F. Hutton. When Hutton spoke, Wilkis listened, and passed the news on to me.

ON April 9, Crown Zellerbach stock closed on the NYSE at $41.875. The following day we announced a tender offer, proposing to buy 14 million to 19 million shares at $42.50 per share, to be paid in cash.

Reading through the convoluted list of Goldsmith's business structures brought a chuckle to my throat, for it was reminiscent of the operations of the other European businessmen I knew and, indeed, of the manner in which Wilkis and I operated secretly. The official purchaser making the tender offer was CZC Acquisition Corporation, established in the state of Delaware only one week earlier for the specific purpose of consummating this deal. It was a wholly owned subsidiary of GOSL Acquisition Corporation, also established in Delaware the previous week. GOSL Acquisition, in turn, was a wholly owned subsidiary of General Oriental Securities Limited Partnership, organized six days ago in Hamilton, Bermuda. The general partner of the limited partnership, known as General Oriental Investments Limited (GOIL), was the old man of the group, having been organized six months earlier in the Cayman Islands; GOIL now owned more than 2.5 million shares of Crown stock, having purchased the bulk of it from Dia Investment Antilles N. V., a Netherlands Antilles corporation, which had been Goldsmith's major open-market purchasing vehicle; GOIL had acquired another large block of shares from Cavenham Holdings, Inc., a Delaware subsidiary of Goldsmith's French-based Générale Occidentale holding company. A majority of the voting stock of GOIL was owned by Compania Financiera Lido, a Panamanian holding company. Sixty percent of Lido's stock was owned by Enderbury Financial, Inc., another Panamanian company operating out of the same office. All of Enderbury's stock was owned by the Brunneria Foundation, headquartered in Liechtenstein; Brunneria was described as a charitable organization. The tender offer noted dryly that, since Sir James Goldsmith was chairman of most of these various entities, he "might be deemed" to be the principal in all of this.

CZC Acquisitions, the official purchaser, had assets of $200 million, making it less than one-tenth as large as its target, but it had arranged $845 million in financing: $95 million of its own cash; $350 million in loans from commercial banks, obtained at an interest rate of one per-

cent over prime, plus considerable commitment and facility fees; and
$400 million to be raised by Drexel through the placement of debt and
equity securities of one or more of the companies in the long string of
CZC's parent companies. The tender offer included a letter, signed by
me, declaring that Drexel "is highly confident that it can obtain such
commitments."

In our tender offer we noted brashly that we had not been informed
what measures, if any, the Crown Zellerbach board planned to take to
detoxify its poison pill, and thus were disregarding it and commencing
lawsuits seeking to void the target's defensive measures. Goldsmith also
declared that he intended to seek proxy votes to be exercised at the
company's upcoming annual meeting, with the purpose of gaining seats
on the board and, via that route, rescinding the poison pill provisions.

Goldsmith sent Crown Zellerbach CEO Creson a letter concurrent
with the tender offer, stating that he would be pleased to meet and
negotiate on any and all points. But the target company's board issued
a statement the following day, declaring that the offer was not in the
best interests of the company or its shareholders and recommending,
in effect, that shareholders toss it into the trash can. The board announced that it would proceed with the previously announced restructuring program, but was "prepared to work with any responsible
person" who was willing to offer what it considered to be a fair price.

Goldsmith and Crown Zellerbach immediately followed what was
becoming a customary procedure; they filed lawsuits against one another, charging all sorts of unfair business practices. Goldsmith also
began actively soliciting proxy votes for Crown Zellerbach's annual
shareholders' meeting, with the express purpose of electing three of his
own people to the board.

AFTER we turned down Ted Turner on his plan to raid CBS, he scurried
to E. F. Hutton, which was desperate for any kind of business.

In the meantime, CBS hired Drexel to look at possible defenses in
conjunction with Morgan Stanley, its traditional investment banker.
The motive seemed clear: CBS wanted Drexel "on the bench," so that
we could not represent Turner or any other potential buyer.

For a time I was, perhaps, the best-informed spectator on the Street.
On the one hand, CBS Chief Financial Officer Fred Meyer called me

every day to ask, "What do you hear?" On the other hand, Wilkis was now our resident spy at Hutton, and he kept me apprised of developments at that end.

The campaign went public on April 19 when Turner commenced an offer for all CBS shares. Turner offered no cash. Instead, he proposed to redeem each share of CBS for a package of securities that included a seven-year senior note, a fifteen-year senior debenture, four zero-coupon notes, a twenty-year subordinated debenture, one share of preferred stock and one share of Class B common stock. Turner's analysts proclaimed that the package was worth about $175 per share, which was about 60 percent higher than CBS's current market value.

One outside analyst called this "the most audacious takeover bid ever." Another declared, "It's paper, nothing but paper. There's not a dime of cash in it."

The day the offer was announced, the market price of CBS stock fell from $109.75 per share to $106.25 per share, providing a clear message of investor reaction.

The CBS board of directors rejected the bid out-of-hand and released an auditors' report declaring that a combined entity of CBS and Turner Broadcasting could not service the resultant debt and could be bankrupt within two years. This was accompanied by a Morgan Stanley letter declaring Turner's offer "financially imprudent."

CBS fought off the bid with comparative ease, but nonetheless its defensive measures forced it to incur $954.1 million in new debt.[1]

A white knight emerged on April 24, seeking to save Crown Zellerbach from Goldsmith. Burnell R. Roberts, chairman of the Mead Corporation, the giant paper products company, sent a letter to Crown Zellerbach proposing an offer of $50 per share ($35 in cash plus Mead common and convertible preferred stock valued at $15). The offer was contingent upon approval by Mead's board, which would consider the matter the following day.

Upon learning all this, I phoned Nassau. Meier was still on vacation,

[1]Late in 1986, encumbered by a weakened balance sheet, CBS succumbed to the cumulative stock purchases of Loews Corporation, which became the largest minority stockholder and succeeded in installing its chairman, Laurence A. Tisch, as the new CEO of CBS.

so I spoke with Pletscher and instructed him to buy additional shares of Crown Zellerbach stock for my account. Since this was an announced tender offer, I could now purchase a larger position without attracting undue attention. "Buy as quickly as possible," I said.

Pletscher did. Then he phoned Switzerland and discussed the transaction with Meier before he bought 300 shares for his own account.

I had an eight A.M. meeting scheduled with Goldsmith for the next day. It was an alluring spring morning and I decided to walk the thirteen blocks from my co-op to his town house on 80th Street, just off Park Avenue. I was still super-charged from the Bond Conference, flooded with adrenaline. I arrived a few minutes early and found Sir Jimmy on the pavement out front, coming toward me. "I'm taking a walk," he said. "Join me?"

I turned and strode alongside him, counterclockwise around the block.

As we walked, Goldsmith told me of the strategy he was ready to adopt regarding the Mead proposal. He had devised numerous preconditions in his mind that Mead would have to fulfill before he would sell them his block of stock.

His mood this morning surprised me. I had found Goldsmith to be a cut above the other entrepreneurs I had met. He was a man of enormous vision and sensitivity, and corporate raiding was not his reason for living. He was involved in politics, concerned with global issues. Normally he thought well beyond the task of the moment, and I was taken aback by his shortsighted view of this transaction.

"Jimmy," I advised, "I think you're moving in the wrong direction."

He raised an eyebrow, somehow fashioning it into a question mark.

"Let's look at it from another perspective," I suggested. I stopped walking and turned around. "Let's walk this way."

As we retraced our steps, moving clockwise around the block, I endorsed a more reasonable approach. "Keep an open mind," I said. "See how things develop."

Calmer now, Goldsmith nodded his agreement.

We spent the remainder of the morning in meetings with Goldsmith's other advisers, including Joe Flom and his partner, Finn Fogg. George Lowy of the New York law firm of Cravath Swaine & Moore, representing Mead, joined us for an elegant lunch. Our best guess was that Mead's $50 per share offer was likely to succeed. One of the key beneficiaries would be Boesky, who by now had acquired 7.4 percent ownership at a considerably lower price; he would be ecstatic to sell to Mead at $50 per share.

Goldsmith had just decided that he, too, would sell to Mead and be satisfied with his own quick profit when Lowy excused himself to take a phone call from one of his partners, who was attending the meeting in Dayton. Lowy reported back to us that the Mead board had nixed the deal, without providing any explanation.

This threw me into turmoil. I knew that the word would spread quickly, and that the price of Crown Zellerbach stock, which had been soaring toward the magical $50 mark, would suddenly head south. As soon as I could get away, I found a pay phone, called Pletscher and ordered, "Sell the Crown Zellerbach!" I managed to squeeze out a profit of $82,334 on the deal, and it was just in time, for the following day, the cagey Goldsmith, realizing that the white knight had ridden off into the sunset, announced that he was terminating his tender offer. Now, even Goldsmith's $42.50 benchmark price had disappeared.

Suddenly, everyone who owned Crown Zellerbach stock was close to panic. No one knew what would happen, and uncertainty sends stock prices down.

In the ensuing days, Creson proposed a compromise. He offered Goldsmith two seats on the Crown Zellerbach board in return for a "standstill" agreement, limiting Goldsmith's purchases of company stock for the next three years. Goldsmith declined and directed us to orchestrate a fresh counterattack to Crown Zellerbach's poison pill. Now, he declared, we could move back into the market and buy still more Crown Zellerbach stock at depressed prices. Unencumbered by the tender offer, we could "sweep the Street" for the best deals.

THE April 29 issue of *Business Week* carried a cover story entitled, "The Epidemic of Insider Trading: The SEC Is Fighting a Losing Battle to Halt Stock-Market Abuses." The magazine reported the results of a commissioned study of fluctuations in stock prices prior to public notice of a takeover attempt. It discovered that, in the month before an announcement, 72 percent of the target stocks rose in price. The magazine declared: "Insider trading is running rampant, despite a major law enforcement crackdown and toughened penalties."

On the day after that article was published, Wilkis reported to me that his "kid" at Lazard Frères had tipped him that InterNorth, Inc., had set a board meeting at Manhattan's prestigious Lynx Club to approve an offer to acquire Houston Natural Gas. "My kid is working on the deal," Wilkis said. "They're meeting tonight."

I phoned the Bahamas and made my buy quickly, routinely. Meier bought 74,800 shares for my account.

By now, Boesky was after me relentlessly, pressing for information. If I gave him the information he craved—brought him in on the deal of the day—his trades would make mine seem comparatively modest. As soon as I found an appropriate moment in the conversation, I dropped the tip. "I hear good things about Houston Natural Gas," I said. "If I were you, I'd own that stock."

"How did you get your information?" Boesky asked.

I did not respond to the question. I merely repeated, "I would own the stock."

In the six trading days prior to the public announcement of the deal, the price of Houston Natural Gas rose by $13.25 per share. I profited $907,655 on that deal. Boesky, who bought more than 300,000 shares, made more than $4 million.

When I reported this development to Wilkis, he suggested that I should continue to share tips with Boesky, after we had established our own stock positions. It seemed likely that our trading was going to become ever more active, ever larger, and we needed to bolster our defenses. "If a question ever comes up," Wilkis said, "you can just say you heard a rumor that Ivan Boesky owned the stock."

ON May 6, Ira Sokolow phoned me, said he had some news and suggested lunch. We met at the Palm Too restaurant at 45th Street and Second Avenue. Over sirloin steak, he alerted me to a big one: RJR, the tobacco company, was in friendly but secret negotiations with Nabisco Brands, Inc. Nabisco had hired Sokolow's firm, Shearson Lehman, as its financial adviser and, he said, it looked like a good deal, one that was destined to close. That same afternoon I bought small holdings in Nabisco and alerted Wilkis.

*   *   *

EARLY the next morning, Chris Anderson and I met with Boesky in his office. If Goldsmith was "sweeping the Street," Boesky was in the catbird seat, and he knew it. Goldsmith was determined to buy enough stock to bring his ownership up to 19.9 percent of the company, stopping just short of the point that would trigger Crown Zellerbach's poison pill provisions. This would make him by far the largest single shareholder, and he could harass the Crown Zellerbach board until it found some way to appease him. The most efficient manner in which to accomplish this was not to buy the stock on the open market, but to negotiate with the largest shareholders. It was my task to help accomplish this.

"Ivan," I said, "you know we terminated our public offer, but we're still in the market privately. There are several blocks of stock we're interested in, and we know you have one of them. But you have to act quickly."

Boesky was smug. His 2.5 million shares constituted the single largest block of stock, save for Goldsmith himself, and he relished the position of power. He brought in one of his top analysts, Lance Lessman, to present a detailed analysis of what, in his opinion, Crown Zellerbach stock was currently worth. Not surprisingly, Lessman concluded that the proper price was significantly above the current market price and even higher than the now-dead tender price of $42.50 per share. It was also a good deal higher than the top-line price of $43 per share that Goldsmith had authorized us to offer.

I responded, "I don't really care what your analysis says. You either take our offer or you don't."

Lessman protested, "But we've done all this analysis and—"

"You don't seem to understand," I interrupted. "The stock—any stock—is only worth what somebody is willing to pay for it. And this is what we're willing to pay. If you think it is worth more, go get more from somebody else."

Negotiations dragged throughout the day. Whenever we needed information from Goldsmith's office, all we had to do was ride the elevator downstairs.

We were still at it late that night. With us in Boesky's office was Roland Franklin, Goldsmith's principal lieutenant for U.S. business matters, and Steve Fraidin, Boesky's corporate attorney.

Boesky held firm on his price demand, dropping quiet comments such as "I hear there's another bidder out there about to come into the action. I might get ten dollars a share more."

"Ivan," I advised, "you really better cut this deal, because, as a matter of fact, we're in negotiation with other arbs, some of them who are priced lower than you."

"Nobody else has a block as large as mine," he said.

"Don't be so sure," I cautioned.

Our offer had reached the $43 limit. Boesky wanted another 12.5¢ per share. It was a mere eighth of a point, amounting to a total differential of $312,500. To both Goldsmith and Boesky this was pocket change, but neither camp would surrender.

In the wee hours of the morning I excused myself to take a phone call. It was my turn to be smug when I returned to the meeting and advised Boesky, "Well, we just bought a block from Sandy Lewis, trading through our brokers in London." Boesky's face turned white at the mention of the rival arb. "Now," I announced, "we can only buy a smaller portion of your shares."

He appeared to have a difficult time retaining his composure, but a few minutes later, after he agreed to sell us 1.75 million shares at $43, for a total of slightly more than $75 million, he said in a subdued voice, "Very well done, gentlemen." Then he turned to me and added, "Why don't we let the lawyers finish this. May I please drive you home?"

"Thank you," I said. "I accept."

We made our way downstairs, where an obsequious driver waited with Boesky's obnoxious silver stretch-limousine, embellished with the predictable vanity license plate, "IFB." I crawled inside and sat on the plush white upholstery, bolstering my aching back against a gauche, tiger-skin pillow. The car phone had three separate lines.

The driver headed up Park Avenue, to the 90s, and pulled into the courtyard of my building. "You live here?" Boesky asked, clearly impressed.

"Yes."

"Well, I look forward to doing more business with you in the future. Perhaps we should have lunch."

"I look forward to it," I echoed.

We shook hands, and then he was gone.

CHAPTER EIGHTEEN

EVEN AS I LABORED at my desk the next day, bleary-eyed from the long night of negotiations, former Deputy U.S. Defense Secretary Paul Thayer was sentenced to four years in prison. The term was only one year shy of the maximum possible sentence and was the most severe punishment ever meted out to an inside trader. Federal District Judge Charles R. Richey declared that the severe sentence was necessary in order to deter others.

LATE one afternoon, Boesky and I met for cocktails at the Harvard Club. He had just finished a game of squash and was fresh from the showers. We sat at a corner table in the dimly lit lounge. He took the chair next to the wall, so that he could see who else was there. We both ordered Perrier.

During an otherwise forgettable conversation, he dropped a bombshell. He said, "You have excellent information, Dennis. You always seem to know what's going on. You are also very discreet. This could all be very useful to me, very helpful, and I feel that you should be compensated for this information."

His words seemed to come at me from a distance, hazy, but unmistakable in their intent. It was difficult to maintain the veneer of gentility that had characterized our previous conversations. Inside I was flabbergasted that he would expose himself so blatantly, and to such a relative stranger.

I already had one secret life going, and I did not need another. The purpose of my relationship with Boesky was information and not money. "That's completely unnecessary," I replied, "and I'm shocked that you would make such an offer. We have a wonderful relationship. There's no need for you to compensate me. I'm already well paid. I'm just not interested."

"Well, I want you to think about it."

"What's to think about? I'm just not interested."

For a few moments we stared into one another's eyes, and I wondered how many of my secrets he could discern. He suggested, "Let's think about it logically."

"First of all," I countered, "I would never want any record of you paying me any money for anything. Second, I would never give you information about Drexel deals, any deals that I'm involved with."

"Yes," Boesky said, "but you have knowledge about many things beyond Drexel deals, and I'd be willing to pay you for that other knowledge. As to *how* I could pay you, well, that could be done through foreign bank accounts or through the transfer of shares in foreign companies. It could be done outside of the United States. It could be done in cash. That is not a problem."

I asked an obvious question: "You've done this sort of thing before?"

"I can't talk about what I do and don't do. Ours would be a very special relationship that no one else would know about. We could work out a formula for me to pay you."

It was clear that Boesky had thought through this entire proposal, but I wanted no part of it. I waved my hand and said, "Ivan, I don't think this is worth exploring."

He changed the subject, and within a few moments it was as if the conversation had never occurred. We finished our Perrier and adjourned to the Algonquin Hotel for a bite to eat. Then, accompanied by his bodyguard, we climbed into his limo. Boesky ordered the chauffeur to drive me home.

My head pounded, forcing sleep away for many hours that night. With his proposal, Boesky had bared himself to me. He had crossed the line.

*   *   *

MY brain was bombarded with stimuli. I spent considerable time working for Allied Corporation on its proposed purchase of Hughes Aircraft Corporation. It was a potentially important deal, for Allied was the sort of blue-chip firm we were trying to lure to Drexel. In the end I recommended against the purchase, due to the negative effect it would have on Allied's credit rating; the Allied board seemed to respect this view, and Joseph and I believed we had laid the groundwork for a more long-term relationship.

I also labored diligently trying to arrange an LBO of Multimedia, a South Carolina–based communications company. We brought in three separate groups of potential buyers: William Simon and Ray Chambers of Wesray; Merv Adelson, CEO of Lorimar Productions; and Jack Kent Cooke, the feisty owner of the Washington Redskins football team. Although nothing came of the Multimedia negotiations, they illustrated an interesting phenomenon. In the past, three separate buyers would probably have been represented by three different investment banking firms. Each one, wary of potential conflicts of interest, would have wanted its own representation. But Wesray, Adelson and Cooke all chose to work through Drexel, and the reason was simple: That's where the money was.

The Goldsmith/Crown Zellerbach deal was at a critical stage and Jimmy was both excited and edgy. He wanted me with him frequently to help plot our next moves. At the office, deals and potential deals flew about at the speed of light. If I dared arrive at my desk a few minutes past eight A.M., there was likely to be a small stack of phone messages from Milken and his Beverly Hills crew. Throughout each crazy day my attention was diverted by one or another of my associates with questions that ran the gamut from the picayune to the sublime:

"Dennis, can you check the wording in this paragraph? . . ."

"Dennis, what do you think Wasserstein will do on this? . . ."

"Dennis, can you be in Fred's office at two-forty-five? Peltz is coming in. . . ."

Often I had to field these questions as I attempted to carry on a phone conversation.

I loved it. This is where I had always wanted to be. This is what I had always wanted to do.

Two, three or four times a day, Boesky called. On each occasion he had a specific query, but the larger question remained unspoken.

It was difficult to find even bits of time to slip away. But when I could,

I checked with Wilkis and Sokolow, and they checked with me. Drexel accorded me the privilege of a private phone line in my office and I gave the number to Wilkis and Sokolow, but not to Boesky—not even to Milken—not even to Laurie. When I heard that phone ring, it sounded like the *ding* of a cash register.

Throughout the month, as Sokolow briefed me on progress in the Nabisco negotiations, I called the Bahamas to increase my position. By mid-May I owned 150,000 shares of Nabisco, purchased for an average price of $61.30. I had a whopping $9.2 million tied up.

By now it was routine for Meier and Pletscher to piggyback my trades without my knowledge; they both took a position in what Pletscher referred to as the "cookie business."

THE more I pondered, the more I wondered why I had been so reluctant to accept Boesky's offer. If he was going to make a fortune off my information, why shouldn't I enjoy a slice of his pie? After all, I would never disclose Drexel deals to him.

I was more receptive when, during a private meeting in his office, he once again raised the subject.

Smiling knowingly, displaying confidence that I would come to my senses, he described his formula: "If the information you give me is new, I will pay you five percent of any profits from the transaction. If I make a hundred million dollars on the deal, you make five million dollars. No risk to you. No questions asked." If I gave him information that merely elaborated upon a deal where he was already involved, simply corroborating his previous knowledge, he would pay me 1 percent. On the scale on which he dealt, that could still be considerable money.

The plan did not seem to entail any additional exposure on my part, but I laid down a specific set of ground rules. We would use foreign bank accounts to exchange money, and no third party was to be involved, ever. He readily agreed to this, and he also said that he would provide me with access to his trading records, whenever I wanted to see them. This was acceptable. I knew that, because Boesky used other investors' money in his arbitrage deals, his books were audited regularly by an outside accounting firm; he could not skim profits on me.

His grin broadened. He offered his hand and said, "We have a deal."

* * *

IT was only a few days later that we put the new arrangement to its
first test. I called Boesky to arrange a meeting, and he suggested that
we rendezvous in the lobby of the Waldorf-Astoria.

There, as we walked a plush-carpeted hallway, away from prying
ears, I disclosed, "Nabisco would be an interesting stock to start accumulating a position in." His eyes lit up. I did not reveal the source
of my information, nor did he bother to ask. That afternoon he began
to buy Nabisco.

On May 23, Laurie and I took off for a five-day stay at the Sandy
Lane Hotel in Barbados. It was supposed to be a vacation, but Boesky
managed to track down my phone number. Throughout the week he
harassed me with calls, asking nervously, "How are foods doing? How
are the foods?"

I checked as best I could under the circumstances and reported,
"Fine. Nothing to worry about."

As Laurie and I basked in the Caribbean sun, Goldsmith announced
that he had acquired 19.6 percent of Crown Zellerbach's stock. Taken
by surprise, Crown's board of directors entered into earnest negotiations. The parties announced an agreement on May 26. Both sides
agreed to drop their lawsuits against each other and to cooperate on a
financial restructuring program that would prove of maximum benefit
to all shareholders.

Two days later, Crown Zellerbach announced that Sir James Goldsmith had been appointed to its board of directors.

AT the end of a week-long buying spree, Boesky had amassed 377,000
shares of Nabisco at a cost of more than $25 million. But he went
beyond that, employing a crafty strategy, purchasing positions in General Foods and Kraft as well. In the first place, it was smart from a
business point of view. When one company is targeted, the stocks of
others in the same industry group tend to rise also, on the theory that
a copycat deal is likely to surface. In addition, this was insurance;
Boesky explained to me that if he was ever questioned as to why he had

bought Nabisco before the deal was announced, he could simply say that it was one of many food company acquisitions he made, because he believed in foods as a group.

On May 29, the day after Laurie and I returned to New York, RJR and Nabisco announced exploratory merger talks. Throughout the morning, as I attempted to concentrate on other business, I kept one eye glued to the Quotron. Trading in Nabisco was suspended until brokers could sort through the phenomenal imbalance of orders. Then, suddenly, the stock popped. Nabisco opened a full $18 per share higher than its previous close. My pulse surged.

Within seconds Boesky was on the phone with me. He was laughing as he said, "We did very well." He saw the potential for a third-party bidder and an even greater run-up, and he announced that he was going to buy more.

I had just hung up when my private line rang. It was Wilkis, exhibiting the same exultant glee.

Sokolow called, too, barely able, in his excitement, to speak.

Keep the grin off your face, Dennis, I said. Anybody might pop into your office.

What should I do now? I wondered. Should I hold the stock and bank on Boesky being right? Or should I take my profits and be satisfied?

This was a bit of a dilemma, for it is difficult to dump 150,000 shares without disrupting the market. Suddenly I slapped myself on the brow. Boesky and the other arbs were buying. It was the perfect time to sell!

"Back in a few minutes," I said to Marilyn.

My secretary showed no surprise. I could be off on any one of dozens of legitimate errands.

I raced onto the street, hunted up a phone booth, called Meier and sold out for a profit of $2,694,421—my largest trading profit ever. I knew that I was on an adrenaline high. This is beautiful, I thought. This could go on forever.

But this incredible episode was not yet over. No sooner had I returned to my desk than I realized: *Nabisco is in play.* My fingers raced across the computer keyboard, searching for potential white knights. Within minutes I had rounded up a team of associates and we started "Dialing for Dollars."

*   *   *

NOT long thereafter, Boesky presented the commencement address to the School of Business Administration of the University of California at Berkeley, Milken's alma mater. Here, where two decades earlier, the social protest movement was nourished, Boesky told the graduating class of would-be Yuppies, "Greed is all right, by the way. I want you to know that. I think greed is healthy."

The audience responded with appreciative applause.

TROUBLE suddenly erupted in my private life. Laurie's mother called from Miami with the news that her dad, Leonard Skolnik, had been diagnosed with cancer of the esophagus. Doctors gave him six months to live.

I was crushed. Laurie's dad and I had grown very close. He was a man of tremendous energy and a ribald sense of humor that frequently sent me into spasms of laughter.

Laurie sobbed, "Dad always promised me he would live to be a hundred."

I sprang into action. I called my in-laws back and said, "Come up here and see some real doctors. I'll get you set up with the best in New York. We'll get other opinions. Don't give up."

Laurie and I scurried about, getting her father to the top specialists. Ultimately we heard the bittersweet prognosis that a team of surgeons at Mount Sinai Hospital believed they could extend his life with radical surgery. In a complex procedure they removed half of his esophagus and portions of his stomach. He remained in intensive care for a prolonged period of time as, at our insistence, Laurie's mother boarded with us. We all pulled for Dad, but it was a difficult, wrenching time, a time when my business activities should have paled in importance. Still, if I worked less than eighty hours a week, I felt as if I was stealing time.

The drama with Laurie's dad made me think of my own father more and appreciate all that he had done for me. As Father's Day approached, I decided that it was time to do something special for him. I asked him what his fantasy car was. Without hesitation, he replied, "A Jaguar XJ6." I bought him a spanking-new one, shiny black, with a tan leather interior and polished wood trim.

*   *   *

It became more and more apparent that Drexel was hitting the target with its attempt to become a major player in the takeover business. We could now boast that on a number of occasions we had placed more than $500 million worth of securities in a matter of days. Not only was the amount significant, but so was the speed. Today's takeover artist needed to work fast to avoid complications, such as the emergence of a white knight, or the adoption of a poison pill defense.

Whether or not the blue-chip companies now saw Drexel as a first-tier firm, they clearly regarded us as a powerhouse with which they had to reckon. Following the lead of CBS, other companies such as Gulf+Western and Burroughs retained Drexel just to get us on their side, to create a conflict of interest in the event someone tried to hire us to launch an attack against them.

The burgeoning activity brought personnel changes. Robert Linton stayed on as chairman of the board, but Fred Joseph was promoted to Linton's other post, CEO, and Herb Bachelor took over as head of Corporate Finance.

We chipped in $500 apiece and threw Joseph a party at an elegant Italian restaurant, where we presented him with a bulldozer and a shotgun, just the sort of items he could use during weekends at his farm. But there were no illusions as to who remained in control. That night, Joseph joked that he was now the highest titled employee of Michael Milken. On another occasion, making an obvious reference to Milken, Joseph described his job as "handling the heavyweight champion of the world."

THE half-decade-long boom in M&A activity had resulted in a predictable spate of criticism and a just as predictable plethora of proposed laws to fine-tune the process. After conducting a lengthy study that included considerable input from the two acknowledged legal pundits of the industry, Marty Lipton and Joe Flom, as well as Bruce Wasserstein of First Boston Corporation, the SEC considered some key amendments to its already complex encyclopedia of regulations. In particular, the commissioners debated the wisdom of speeding up the disclosure process. Under current rules, once an investor had acquired 5 percent of a company's stock, he had ten days before he was required to file Schedule 13D. That was a window of opportunity, during which he could continue, quietly, to increase his holdings. Now, the SEC considered narrowing the deadline to forty-eight hours. It also debated provisions that would prohibit, or at least restrict, such tactics as golden parachutes and greenmail, which seemed obviously detrimental to the interests of public shareholders. Some industry observers attacked the use of junk bonds to finance takeovers.

The SEC was joined in its assault by numerous legislators and, as 1985 sped forward, it seemed likely that some changes were about to occur. Representative Timothy Wirth, who had attended the 1985 Bond Conference, appeared ready to sponsor "corrective" legislation. I was worried that Congress was going to act, but when I expressed this fear to Joseph, he commented in a cavalier tone, "Don't worry about it."

I was assigned to a Drexel committee whose task was to get our message across in Washington. To this end, we sponsored a congressional breakfast. Joseph, others from Drexel and I prepared presentations, and Milken's group compiled a booklet analyzing the effect of high-yield bonds on American companies. The key selling point to most legislators was our contention, supported by statistical evidence, that traditional financing through investment-grade bonds was reserved almost exclusively for blue-chip corporations based in the industrialized states. We could make a logical case that the new spirit of competition fostered by Drexel's infusion of money was a major reason for the current health of the economy, especially for high employment rates. Congressmen and senators from the less industrialized states were clearly interested in our picture of junk bonds as a weapon whereby the little guy could join the battle against entrenched corporate bureaucracy. It made for good press.

It soon became obvious that the Reagan Administration had communicated to the SEC that it wished to continue its laissez-faire policy. The commissioners voted unanimously not to seek any major changes in the laws regarding mergers and acquisitions. Chairman Shad called all such proposals "obsolete."

WE labored diligently to produce innovative tools, such as the Off Balance Sheet Leverage Transaction. The goals of this particular plan of action were to allow one company to take control of another with a minimum—or even no—adverse impact upon its own credit rating. As a side benefit, the plan allowed the acquirer to shore up its own defenses. The genius of the plan was was that it called for one company to acquire 49 percent of another company's stock. While it was a percentage point shy of absolute voting control, the practical results were the same, for it would require an unbending coalition of virtually all other shareholders to block any action. Yet, because 49 percent is technically a minority ownership position, the acquiring company would not be required to consolidate its financial data with that of the target company. The debt incurred as a result of the buyout would be carried on the books of the target company, but would not affect the cash flow, debt position and earnings figures of the acquirer.

Once the deal was in place, the acquirer could then set up certain safeguards—known as "shark repellents"—to protect itself against a hostile bid. For example, if Alpha Corporation owned 49 percent of Beta Corporation, the board of the former could issue a large block of its voting stock to the latter. Because Beta was not a majority-owned subsidiary, it would be permitted to vote its stock and thus counter any action on the part of other shareholders. The two boards could also structure an agreement declaring that if a triggering event occurred, such as a hostile bid, then Alpha Corporation would automatically guarantee the debt of Beta Corporation, forcing a consolidation of the two companies, watering down the balance sheet and making an acquisition less attractive. A matrix of put and call options could also be set up between the two companies, so that at any given time they could alter their respective financial standings.

Meanwhile, of course, the two companies would be likely to operate almost as blood brothers, cooperating on various manufacturing and distributing ventures.

It was also a simple matter to invert the plan. One company could divest itself of a majority position in a subsidiary, retain 49 percent ownership and reap the same benefits.

It was the type of financial engineering for which we were becoming renowned. It was beautiful.

Thus, the game continued, and its pace accelerated.

OFTEN, now, our home phone rang before six A.M. Laurie, rubbing sleep from her eyes, would answer, hand me the receiver and grimace as she said, "It's Ivan." At least she was glad that it was not someone calling with bad news about her father.

More and more, Boesky became an unrelenting intruder, calling me a dozen times a day, from his office, from his home, from one of the three phones in his limo, from a private, rented plane, tracking me down almost every place I went—although, despite his efficient detective abilities, he never followed my trail to Nassau.

He was an indefatigable and pesky spider whose web grew ever stickier, and once I had crossed the line, I was hopelessly entangled.

He was one of the most manipulative and deceptive individuals I ever met. If he owned a position in a company—any company—he tried to use me, and others, to help put that company into play. He might suggest, "I'll call Carl, you call Carl, let's get him from both sides." Such an attempt by an arb to influence Icahn, or any other raider, was patently unethical, and I tried not to get involved.

He was always interested in any fact or rumor concerning the market. "Is it a problem," he might ask, "for me to buy such-and-such? Is this something I could be comfortable with?"

Everything intensified when my superiors at Drexel asked me to handle Boesky's corporate finance business. Boesky was ready to take the next step on the ladder. Instead of merely speculating on takeovers, he wanted to become a takeover artist himself. He felt that he was in position to become the new entrepreneur on the block.

This was also in line with my own burgeoning fantasies. Gradually the concept was forming in my mind: When my bank account in Nassau grew large enough, I, too, could acquire a corporation and use that as a start to mold my very own, and very substantial, business empire. Why not? I was earning multi-millions of dollars for my clients. I knew how to create wealth and value. Why shouldn't I have a chance at the really big money?

When I began working with Boesky on this more intimate basis, I realized that he had a ridiculously tight-fisted view of the corporate raiding business. He was trapped by an inherent conflict. As an arb, he wanted to get the highest possible price for his stock. But as an acquirer, he wanted to pay the lowest possible price.

He wanted to buy the World Book Encyclopedia company. He wanted to buy Paramount Studios. He wanted to buy a vacuum cleaner manufacturer. He wanted to buy everything, but he was only willing to offer a bargain basement price. I concluded that he was deluding himself. The man was far too cheap to be a successful raider.

Nevertheless, our business relationship grew increasingly intense, and information was the stock that we traded on our personal, two-man exchange.

When he wore his arb cap, he was a man at the top of his profession, and he knew it. He surprised me one day with a copy of his book, *Merger Mania,* hot off the presses of Holt, Rinehart & Winston. It was inscribed:

> To one of the most creative investment bankers I know.
> I.B.

Late that night, unable to turn off the wheels of my mind, I picked up the book and perused. Here, Boesky described risk arbitrage as "Wall Street's best-kept money-making secret."

CHAPTER NINETEEN

THE BILLION-DOLLAR-PER-YEAR conglomerate Revlon Cosmetics was run by its President and CEO Michel C. Bergerac, an imperious, urbane businessman of French descent. Although Bergerac had been successful with the firm in its early years, many observers felt that Revlon had now stagnated. By making acquisitions and focusing its attention on subsidiary companies whose interests ran far afield, Revlon had lost dominance in its primary business. Profits in the consumer cosmetics arena had been flat for several years. Some analysts said that Bergerac did not crack the whip hard enough. Whatever the reason, the malaise had caused Revlon's stock to languish in the mid-thirties, considerably below its breakup value.

This fact, in the milieu of the 80s, was of considerable interest to anyone in the M&A business. To outside observers, Revlon appeared to be run by a wasteful bureaucracy. Bergerac's base salary was $1.3 million, and many wondered what he was doing to earn it. The most glaring abuse appeared to be the company-owned Boeing 727 that was outfitted to take Bergerac and his friends on hunting safaris to the far corners of the globe. It seemed obvious that a more prudent management team could trim expenses and fatten the bottom line.

The presence of the subsidiary businesses was equally intriguing; each was a distinct entity, likely to be of interest to another purchaser. They included Ethical Pharmaceuticals, Diagnostic, Vision Care, International Beauty, Noecliff Thayer, Technicon Data Systems and Rebeis.

Anyone who bought Revlon could probably sell off many of these subsidiaries rather easily in order to pay back all or most of the purchase price. The sum of Revlon's parts was greater than the whole. The situation was ripe for someone to step in and acquire Revlon through an LBO.

Drexel first identified Revlon as a takeover target for the Frates Group (named after its leader, Oklahoma investor Joseph Frates), but the deal fizzled. A similar probe by English investor Alan Clore also fell flat. Part of the problem was that Revlon had shark repellents in place. In the event that an outside entity took control, Bergerac was guaranteed a $20 million golden parachute. In addition, the board had systematically tightened its control by a variety of measures, including denying shareholders the right to call special meetings, dictating that directors could be removed only if 80 percent of shareholder votes approved (resulting board vacancies had to be filled by the remaining directors) and requiring advance notice of any proposal to be raised at a shareholders' meeting.

Bergerac himself had previously explored the idea of a management-led LBO, but concluded that a realistic stock price, in the low 40s, would not fly with the board.

All in all, Revlon had been shopped to death by us and others. Still, it had an unusual mix of businesses that would be attractive to just the right buyer.

David Kay came to me one day and suggested, "Why don't you go along with the team that's going to talk to Ron Perelman about Revlon?"

I had heard the name of Ronald Owen Perelman bandied about when I was with Lehman Brothers. I also knew that he had been at the Bond Conference, but I had not had the opportunity to meet him there. He was a forty-two-year-old raider, operating, perhaps, in the high minor leagues. His father, Raymond, had been a highly successful Philadelphia entrepreneur in his own right. Perelman had worked for a time in the family business, Belmont Industries; then, after earning an MBA from Wharton, had set out on his own in 1978. He parlayed a $2 million investment in the jewelry distribution firm of Cohen-Hatfield Industries into an ever-growing empire. Through Cohen-Hatfield he bought MacAndrews & Forbes Holdings, Inc., whose primary business was licorice. The company had fallen into difficulty because its main suppliers were based in the troubled countries of Iran and Afghanistan; Perelman found new sources of licorice and revitalized the company. Now, he was chairman of the board, CEO and, in fact, the sole shareholder of MacAndrews & Forbes, which, in turn, owned Consolidated Cigar Company, Video Corporation of America and the film processing firm Technicolor. Some of my associates at Lehman Brothers had become acquainted with him when they represented the Pantry Pride supermarket chain, Perelman's most recent acquisition.

Perelman claimed to be allergic to publicity, but this past January he had married Claudia Cohen, formerly the "Page Six" gossip columnist for the *New York Post,* then the "I, Claudia" columnist for the *New York Daily News* and now an entertainment reporter on Channel 7's "The Morning Show," as well as a regular guest on "Live with Regis and Kathie Lee." Perelman showed an affinity for show biz types; he was on friendly terms with Elizabeth Taylor (who attended his wedding) and Lew Wasserman, chairman of MCA.

Despite the glitz that filled his life, Perelman contended to a reporter for *The New York Times* that his idea of a good time was to be in bed by ten P.M.

Perhaps he dreamed of what he would do with the $750 million that Milken was in the process of raising for Pantry Pride through an issue of debt securities and preferred stock. The cash would constitute a "blind pool," a sort of pocket-money fund for the ambitious entreprenuer in search of a good deal.

I had only an hour or so to study the data prior to a scheduled meeting between Perelman's people and the Drexel crowd. The most difficult task was to get a handle on the values of the Revlon subsidiaries. We had to know how much ready cash they represented. Without knowing the tax bases of each division, it was difficult to calculate such important values in a short time, because a key tactic of our strategy would be to structure tax defenses. In other words, if the sale of a certain Revlon sub-unit would result in $50 million worth of capital gains, we would want to have a "mirrored" subsidiary in place that could minimize the tax consequence when divested.

Under the rush conditions, I conducted the analysis as best I could, making sure that if I erred, it was on the side of conservatism.

Perelman, I quickly discovered, held a particularly intriguing ace up his sleeve. His acquisition of Pantry Pride came complete with a Net Operating Loss of $340 million. In the convoluted world of high finance, an NOL can be a great asset, because it can be used to offset income from other sources and thereby reduce total tax liabilities.

In the company of others from Drexel who already knew him, I visited Perelman at his luxurious town house on East 63rd Street, between Park and Madison avenues. It was a multi-story building that housed both his offices and his home. We met in the second floor "war room," where a magnificent art collection gave notice that Perelman was already a man of means.

He greeted me with a firm right hand. His left hand held a cigar, which, I soon learned, was a constant companion. Perelman looked me directly in the eye and suggested that we get down to business. Save for the cigar smoke, I liked him immediately.

In the early stages of the discussion, I sat back, watching, listening, evaluating Perelman and his top aides, Bruce Slovin, president of both the holding company and Pantry Pride, and Howard Gittis, vice chairman of Pantry Pride (and Perelman's closest friend). Don Drapkin of the law firm of Skadden, Arps (and one of Joe Flom's principal lieutenants) was there, not merely as a legal adviser but also as another of Perelman's close friends. In fact, the Revlon attack was code-named "Nicole" in honor of Drapkin's beautiful one-year-old daughter.

Perelman seemed determined to move forward. I listened carefully to what everyone said. These were the men who had been tracking Revlon for some time. We moved excitedly between Perelman's and Slovin's offices in our efforts to gather all the available information.

The odds were very much against us; Pantry Pride was only one-eighth the size of Revlon. Even more intriguing was the potential personality clash. What we contemplated was a war, which, if we chose to declare it, would pit the upstart Perelman against the patrician Bergerac. It would be the anti-Establishment Drexel against the toughest traditional opponents that Revlon's money could buy, most likely Marty Lipton of Wachtell, Lipton and Felix Rohatyn of Lazard Frères.

This was a challenge not to be underestimated, and yet, as I sat in the lap of Perelman's luxury, all about me I heard the rosiest of predictions. If it was going to be easy to take over Revlon, I conjectured, someone would already have done so. Finally I opened my mouth, declaring, "I don't think that the type of transaction you are proposing works. Your breakup values are a little on the high side."

Several of the men in the room leveled stares at me, and the most scornful look came from Perelman himself, whose eyes asked, "Who the hell do you think you are?!"

I answered the unspoken question: "I'm the person who is going to fine-tune the numbers. I'm the person who will tell Milken whether this transaction makes any sense."

Everyone in the room tensed. Perelman, like anyone else—especially an entrepreneur—does not relish being told that he might be wrong.

The remainder of the meeting was strained and, as we left, I knew that my Drexel associates were wondering why I had been so quick to slow the process.

By the time I arrived back at my desk, a message awaited: Perelman wanted me to call. When I reached him, I attempted to be congenial, but firm. "Look," I said, "my job is to be very objective in all this. My first reaction is very negative. I don't think there is a strong command of the values, on the part of both your people and my people. I don't think enough thought has gone into the analysis. I think I want to get more comfortable with the numbers."

Perelman said nothing.

"What good does it do if you make an offer for Revlon and fall flat on your face?" I asked. "What good does it do you if you succeed in buying the company and then go bankrupt?" I repeated the theme that I had first broached with Milken. "We don't want to tee them up and lose," I said. "We have to win. And if we're going to win, we have to make a proper assessment ahead of time. We have to look at all the variables. Who are the other players? How are they likely to respond to our offer? How do we structure the deal? Most importantly, what is the right price to offer, the price that will work? You just can't decide all of that in an hour." I vowed to myself that this would not be a "Ready, Fire, Aim" deal. The stakes were far too high.

Perelman responded with a grudging agreement to give me time to study the numbers. He coveted Revlon, but he could not get past my argument. He knew that I was on a roll at Drexel, that I was the only executive there who had actually completed major M&A transactions. He had visions of glory, but he was not stupid.

I returned to my desk at Drexel, looking at the deal not from the perspective of what others thought they could get away with offering, but from a more realistic perspective.

The preposterous contention that an amalgam of a licorice company, cigar manufacturer and small-time supermarket chain should bid for a giant cosmetics company was evidence of how far the 80s had taken us. In the past, the vast majority of mergers and acquisitions were industry-driven deals, wherein complementary companies came together. Coastal and ANR—two pipeline companies—was a very recent successful example.

But here before me was evidence of the growing popularity of the financially driven transaction. This was a proposed marriage born in the minds of aggressive investors and their investment bankers, based solely upon balance sheet manipulations. Credit considerations were much more critical in these transactions. There was little, or no, room for error. I had to be sure.

The more I studied, the more I keyed in on the subsidiary companies. If you took a snapshot of the deal, it looked atrocious. Perelman would have to borrow so much money that, on Day One, it would appear that he could never hope to meet the interest payments on his gargantuan debt. But if you looked at it like a motion picture, you saw something different. *If* Perelman could sell off the subsidiaries, quickly and profitably, he could retire significant portions of the debt and eventually own a financially healthy cosmetics company. It was a big if.

We held a series of meetings with Perelman and conducted numerous conference calls with Milken, to determine how to handle the billion-dollar financing. Milken's first proposition was to offer the shareholders part cash, part paper, and this raised a red flag in my mind. I had argued against this approach months earlier on other deals. I did not ask Milken directly, but I assumed that he had tested the waters and realized that there was not enough capacity—or at least support—for this particular transaction among Drexel's financial sources. This told me that others, too, doubted whether Perelman could or should pull it off. In terms of cash versus value, this was one of the stickiest financing packages Milken had ever been called upon to create.

"What is Revlon going to do?" I kept muttering to myself. I needed a handle on Bergerac, as well as his board members.

A sudden idea came to me. I called Don Engel, a former managing director of Drexel, who now worked for us as a consultant, operating from a rented suite on the top floor of Perelman's town house/office. I knew that Engel was involved in a deal with Harold Geneen, the legendary former CEO of ITT. Bergerac had been Geneen's protégé, and had helped to negotiate numerous foreign acquisitions when Geneen was building ITT into the world's largest conglomerate. He had been considered Geneen's natural successor, until Charles Revson wooed Bergerac away to run the cosmetics firm. "Don," I requested, "see if hypothetically you can find out from Geneen how he thinks Bergerac will react."

Engel called back some time later and reported that, according to Geneen, "Bergerac will fight you to the death."

Okay, so be it, I thought. At least we knew what to expect.

I spent considerable time analyzing the board members. One of them was none other than Lew Glucksman, the man who had replaced Pete Peterson at Lehman Brothers and then sold out to Shearson/American Express. I knew my ex-boss as a careful man who would weigh all the issues thoroughly. I also knew that his primary concern would be the shareholders *and not Bergerac.* That was what the law dictated, and that, I was certain, was the role that Glucksman would assume, and he had the ability to persuade others to follow.

WE decided to start by proposing a friendly acquisition. Bergerac knew that Revlon was vulnerable, and perhaps he would surrender easily in order to cut the best terms for himself. After all, if anyone took over the company, he could float off into the sunset under his golden parachute. If a friendly offer worked, it would be the least expensive way to go and we could announce a nice clean deal. If he wished, Bergerac could stay on board as CEO of Revlon in its new incarnation as a subsidiary of MacAndrews & Forbes Holdings. This was a long shot at best. I could not imagine Bergerac agreeing to work *under* Perelman. The danger in the friendly offer, of course, was that it would alert Revlon to our interest, allowing Bergerac and his cronies the opportunity to take additional defensive measures. But we had to give it a try. Arthur Liman, who had worked as counsel for both Revlon and Perelman, set up a meeting.

On June 17 Perelman met with Bergerac in the latter's apartment and delivered the message that Revlon was one of a number of companies that MacAndrew & Forbes was looking at as acquisition candidates. The price, he said, would be somewhere in the 40s.

Bergerac responded that Revlon's investment adviser would only approve "a price which began with a 'five,' " meaning $50 or more per share. After an hour and a half of fruitless discussion, Bergerac suggested that the two men meet again the following week, over dinner, to continue. Although many on the team viewed Bergerac's willingness to have another meeting as a positive sign, neither Perelman nor I trusted him.

ON June 20, the day before Laurie's birthday, I surprised her with two tickets to Paris, via the Air France Concorde. We spent three days revisiting some of our favorite places. Then we flew to Nice, rented a two-seat Mercedes and drove to Antibes for a week's stay at the Hotel du Cap. Among the other guests there at the time were Kirk Douglas and his family, including his son Michael, who was in the midst of filming *The Jewel of the Nile.* In the mornings, before Michael set off for the shooting location on the other side of the Mediterranean, we sometimes encountered him, his wife Diandra, and their young son. They were a warm, down-to-earth family.

Throughout the week we dashed off on side trips along the shoreline from Monte Carlo to Cannes. For a few precious days I almost forgot about Wall Street. As the time passed, it was a delicious feeling to revel in the absence of a ringing telephone; Boesky was unable to harass me here.

One afternoon, as I lay next to Laurie on the sands of the French Riviera, listening to the waters of the Mediterranean lap against the shore, I wondered, does it get any better than this?

EVEN as I labored on the Revlon deal, Goldsmith continued to keep me busy. His relationship with the Crown Zellerbach board deteriorated steadily. The board persisted in its plans to split the company into three separate entities and called for the liquidation of its timberland partnership—the portion of the business that Goldsmith most coveted. Unable to persuade the board to accept his plans for the company, Goldsmith searched for a plan of action. We studied the fine print of Crown Zellerbach's poison pill provisions and discovered an interesting point. If Goldsmith's ownership level passed the 20 percent threshold, it would arm the first phase of the defense. Shareholders would receive the right to purchase half-price stock in any company that emerged as a survivor from a merger with Crown Zellerbach.

This set our minds working. During our discussions someone said, "What if Crown Zellerbach survives? Why do we have to buy 100 percent of the company and merge it into something else?"

We looked at one another, stunned. The answer was so simple. The pill was armed by 20 percent ownership, but it was not exercisable unless and until someone bought the entire company. If Goldsmith wanted control, he did not have to commence an offer for 100 percent of the stock. Any level of ownership from 51 percent to 99 percent would do just fine.

This was not a poison pill; it was a placebo!

Through multiple purchases, Goldsmith quietly increased his holdings. By mid-July the wisdom of his earlier decision to abandon his tender offer was apparent. He had acquired 52 percent of the outstanding shares at an average price somewhat below the $42.50 tender offer.

Most observers naturally assumed that Goldsmith now controlled the company, but Crown Zellerbach's board of directors obstinately raised another issue, resurrecting a provision of their corporate bylaws that allowed them to remain in control unless and until a single investor acquired two-thirds of the stock. Goldsmith took issue with that contention and threatened a lawsuit.

Crown Zellerbach filed its own suit, charging that Goldsmith's "start-and-stop" purchasing methods had caused instability in the market value of its stock and put pressure on shareholders to sell. *The Wall Street Journal* quoted my defense of Goldsmith: "All these purchases were done in the open market."

Despite their public objections, Creson and his board knew they were beaten. It is a basic rule of fair play that more than 50 percent ownership is ownership. Goldsmith could build a strong case in court, and/or before the SEC, that the bylaw provision defining ownership as a two-thirds majority was outrageous.

During a Sunday night telephone conversation, Goldsmith and Creson hammered out their differences, which is to say, Creson surrendered. The competing sides issued a joint announcement on July 23, declaring that they were "engaged in discussions to resolve matters between them." In short order Goldsmith was elected chairman of the board and his "people" assumed a majority of seats.

Goldsmith became known as the first raider to score a victory over a poison pill defense; Joe Flom, Finn Fogg and their team from Skadden, Arps received much-deserved glory for their legal triumph; and I became known, within the industry, as the investment banker who helped orchestrate it.

MEANWHILE, back at the Revlon ranch, Bergerac gave indications that, contrary to my expectations, he might accept Perelman's friendly approach. But at the last moment Bergerac canceled his scheduled dinner meeting with Perelman. When I learned that Marty Lipton had been retained by Revlon, I called him to find out what had happened. Lipton said cryptically, "Don't waste your time. Pantry Pride will *never* get Revlon." My biggest fear was that Revlon would now adopt Lipton's hallmark poison pill defense.

I told neither Wilkis nor Boesky about Revlon, yet something very interesting happened in the second week of August. The NYSE volume of trading in Revlon stock quadrupled from its long-term average of less than 300,000 shares per day up to 1.2 million shares. It was fresh evidence that other inside traders were at work. One arb after another phoned me, trying to unearth information. Some hinted that they had already heard of the deal from Drexel's Beverly Hills office, which was notorious for leaks.

We laid plans to announce a hostile takeover attempt, but I was dubious. Despite my continued objections, Milken and his boys were still considering a combination of cash and paper for the stockholders.

I argued, "Michael, you can't do anything less than an all-cash deal. It would be transaction suicide."

"We just can't," Milken replied.

"It has to be all cash, or it won't work," I repeated. "That's why Goldsmith worked. That's why Coastal worked."

Perelman decided to fly to Beverly Hills to thrash out the issue in person. The entire team piled onto his Gulfstream jet, with the exception of me. The financing was not my end of it, and I did not relish a cross-country flight in a small jet full of cigar smoke.

The more Milken argued that part of the deal had to be paper, the more I realized that he may be running scared. He had just finished raising $750 million for Pantry Pride and now was faced with the

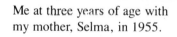

Me at three years of age with
my mother, Selma, in 1955.

My brother Robert and me on
a swing up in the Catskills,
around 1958. Simple times.

Robert M. Wilkis visiting my wife, Laurie, and me in Paris in 1979. It was on this trip that Wilkis and I decided to open Swiss bank accounts.

Working at home in 1980 as a Smith Barney associate. I could never leave my work at the office.

Laurie and me in Maui to celebrate her birthday in 1982. I had just made my first million at the age of twenty-nine.

Laurie and my young son, Adam, in our summer rental in Sands Point, Long Island.

On vacation at the Hotel du Cap in Cap d'Antibes, the French Riviera, June 1985. Success came so fast, it became a blur. I was unaware that half a world away the SEC was already investigating my trading activities.

Ronald Perelman and me celebrating his hotly contested takeover of Revlon, February 1986. My dual life was yet to be exposed. I thought the world held no limits. Little did I know . . .

The famous Ferarri Testarossa purchased to commemorate the Revlon victory. It would later be confiscated by the government as part of my settlement.

Rudolf Giuliani, who headed the U.S. Attorney's Office in the Southern District of New York. It was Giuliani who headed up the investigation of Wall Street abuses during the 1980s. (*Mark Vodofsky/* © New York Post)

Press coverage of the scandal. Not the way one wants to live life, believe me. (*©1986 Newsweek, Inc. All rights reserved. Reprinted by permission. From the* New York Post, *May 13, 1986. Reprinted by permission. © 1991 News America Publishing Incorporated. All rights reserved. Reprinted with the permission of* New York *magazine. © New York Newsday. Reprinted by permission. December 1, 1986 cover © 1986 U.S. News & World Report.*)

Leaving the U.S. District Court after being sentenced to two years in prison. It was without a doubt the most humbling day of my life. (*AP/Wide World Photos*)

Top left: Arthur L. Liman, my principal attorney. What he did for me and my family transcends the very best of what any client expects from a lawyer. (*Arthur L. Liman*)

Top right: Ivan Boesky leaving court in December 1987 after being sentenced to three years in prison for his role in the insider-trading scandal. (*UPI/Bettmann Newsphotos*)

Michael Milken shortly before his fall. (*UPI/Bettmann Newsphotos*)

Ivan Boesky soon after his release from prison. It changes people in a lot of different ways. It certainly changed me. (*Paul Adao*/© New York Post)

Addressing business students at New York University in 1989. It's my hope that I can steer them away from the mistakes I made. (*Barton Silverman*)

Dennis B. Levine today. A new job, a new life. Starting over . . .

proposition of generating another half billion. Was this one too big for Michael? I wondered. Were Drexel's private sources of cash finally tapping out?

Through Perelman's meetings in California, and conference calls back to New York, we struck a compromise. To raise the cash for Perelman to buy Revlon, we would offer junk bonds directly to the public. They had been marketed to the public before, but never for the express purpose of financing a hostile takeover. On top of this, Chemical Bank, which had never before participated in a hostile deal involving junk bonds, agreed to handle the senior financing; this development gave enormous credibility to Perelman's position.

Perelman made one last effort to pursue the friendly route. On Monday morning, August 12, he left a message, but Bergerac did not return the call.

Two days later, at nine A.M., after we learned that Revlon would spurn our offer, Perelman's board authorized a tender offer for the purpose of acquiring Revlon.

Before that offer was announced, the target company issued a press release, headlined: REVLON NOT FOR SALE. It revealed that Revlon had adopted a poison pill defense. The board had declared that, in the event that a single entity gained control of 20 percent or more of Revlon's common stock, each shareholder would have the right to exchange one share of common stock for a Revlon note with a face value of $65, paying 12 percent interest, maturing in one year. This would be voided if an outside entity consummated a tender offer for a minimum price of $65 per share. In plain English, Bergerac had just upped his asking price by 30 percent over his original demand for "a price which began with a 'five.'"

The directors also authorized Revlon to borrow $700 million in order to buy back between 5 million and 14 million shares of its own stock, which would put about 35 percent of the stock into the company's own hands.

At a press conference, Bergerac declared, "People have inquired. The message we have given to them is the company is not for sale. I am not soliciting offers. I don't want offers and we're not entertaining offers."

A tense, pressure-filled week followed. In New York, we talked over strategy and crunched the numbers again and again. In California,

Milken and Peter Ackerman worked to set up the financing. There was little time for sleep.

ON August 23 Perelman sent Bergerac a letter noting, "It appears that rhetoric and invective are taking over. . . . What we do not understand is why you are either unwilling to negotiate or let your shareholders decide for themselves." That same day Pantry Pride commenced a tender offer for Revlon at $47.50 per share. It was conditional upon the ability of Pantry Pride to raise $900 million in cash and on the removal of the poison pill provisions.

Now, of course, came the lawsuits. For me, this was the dull part of any battle, but the attorneys were in their glory. Perelman filed suit in a Delaware Chancery Court (where both MacAndrews & Forbes and Revlon—as well as many other U.S. firms—were officially incorporated), charging that Revlon's poison pill provisions "have transferred from the stockholders of Revlon to the board the power to consider any takeover proposals."

Revlon filed a countersuit in the same court, challenging the legality of Drexel's $750 junk-bond issue of the previous month. Revlon lawyers contended that the prospectus had been fraudulent, in that it did not identify the fact that more than a half billion of those dollars would be earmarked for the prospective purchase of Revlon. It also charged that a portion of the issue was a screen to enable Drexel to sell $200 million of its own junk-bond inventory back to Pantry Pride. The formal complaint also lodged a serious, but completely unverified, charge that Perelman's people were spreading false rumors. Unidentified individuals, the complaint charged, "have been selectively disseminating to arbitrageurs and market professionals certain information to the effect that defendants are about to attempt to acquire the Company through a formal tender offer" at a price as high as $55 per share.

I worked day and night on the Revlon deal, finding it to be the most exhilirating time of my career. Several times a day I shuttled between meetings at Perelman's town house and other meetings at Drexel. In between, I was on the phone with dozens of arbs who were all attempting to assess the pulse of the deal.

On top of this, it was the recruiting season and Drexel was determined to lure the best and brightest MBA graduates into its fold. Others had winnowed the candidates to the select few, and it was my job, as Drexel's young hotshot, to close the deal, to convince them to join the fastest-growing, most dynamic firm on Wall Street.

Drexel decided to bring them on board, literally, by renting an opulent yacht, giving them a sales pitch as they cruised around New York harbor in luxury.

As it happened, the day of the big bash found me back at Perelman's, in yet another strategy session. The meeting was engrossing, and when I happened to check my watch I realized that I was running very late. "I have to get out of here," I said. I told Perelman about the cruise. The yacht was due to sail within the hour.

"No problem," Perelman said. "Take my car."

A short time later Laurie and I arrived at the 23rd Street Marina, in a gargantuan, black, chauffeur-driven Rolls-Royce. I hopped out, stepped onto the yacht and addressed the job candidates, "Hi, I'm Dennis Levine. I'm a managing director at Drexel."

The eyes of my listeners told me that they were children of the 80s. Where else could you expect to earn a seven-figure salary so young? If this was what it was like to work at Drexel, they wanted in!

ONCE Perelman went public with his tender offer, I was able to do more precise work on evaluating the subsidiaries. Earnings, cash flow figures, book values and comparable sales prices are all meaningless compared to the simple fact: What is someone actually willing to pay for a given company? We opened quiet discussions with, among others, Bruce Wasserstein at First Boston to see what offers might surface. To our surprise, he reported considerable interest in some of the subsidiaries, at higher prices than we originally estimated. The deal was beginning to look better.

Now, instead of heading for the office, I often began my workday at Perelman's town house, arriving around eight A.M., just about the time that his wife, Claudia, left for the television studio. We talked business over breakfast, sometimes took a short break to watch Claudia on "Live with Regis and Kathie Lee," and then resumed our discussions. If the meetings continued past noon, we lunched at the ultra-fashionable

French restaurant, Le Cirque, two blocks away, which some of Perelman's men referred to as "our cafeteria." The diet-conscious Perelman loved pasta, but he made sure it had no oil on it.

Sometimes, during late-night meetings, Claudia popped in to ask, "How's it going?" She demonstrated not only interest and appreciation, but a keen knowledge of her husband's business. Beyond that, she was always the supportive wife.

We often worked on Sunday, but never on Friday night or Saturday, for Perelman was a practicing member of the Orthodox Fifth Avenue Synagogue.

Through it all, I developed an increasing appreciation of Perelman. He believed in what he was doing and never doubted for an instant that if he could gain control of Revlon, he could improve its operations. He was an aggressive businessman, but he tempered his style with the proper dash of caution. He weighed all of the variables before making any major decision, listening carefully to all of his advisers, including Milken, Flom, Drapkin and myself, then announcing his choice of options and sticking with it.

We craved information. We knew our position, of course, and we knew how much we were willing to modify it. But we did not know Revlon's position, nor the attitudes of the sideline players. One morning I suggested, "I'll call Ivan. He'll give us a sense of what's going on." Boesky, of course, held a large position in Revlon, for it was *the* deal of the moment.

Soon I had him on the line. I said, "Ivan, I'm here with Ronnie Perelman right now, and we're interested in your opinion. What do you think Revlon might do?" Perelman leaned toward the earpiece in anticipation, but he could not hear the answer. After a few moments I said, "That's very interesting, Ivan. Would you mind sharing that with my client? I'll put you on the speaker phone."

Boesky's voice filled the room. In a matter-of-fact tone, he reported, "I hear that there might be a leveraged buyout. You might want to raise your price." The words were predictable—an arb *always* advises a raider to raise his price—but Perelman was more interested in the tone. His expression was intense as he tried to discern the nuances.

After the call, Perelman asked, "What's Boesky like?"

I laughed and replied. "He's always asking me, 'What's Perelman like?'"

*   *   *

ON August 26 Revlon's board of directors unanimously determined that Perelman's tender offer was "grossly inadequate and not in the best interests of the Company and its stockholders."

Three days later Revlon commenced an offer to exchange 10 million shares of its common stock for a package of notes and preferred stock valued at $57.50—ten dollars per share higher than our offer. With that one stroke, Revlon turned 25 percent of its equity into debt, increased its long-term debt from $480 million to nearly $1 billion and reduced shareholders' equity from $1 billion to $460 million, making an acquisition, by anyone, far less attractive. In addition, the company's new paper included highly restrictive covenants prohibiting asset sales and additional debt, making it virtually impossible for anyone to take over the company without board approval.

Bergerac reportedly declared to his board, "We have just cut off Perelman's balls and nailed them to the wall."

CHAPTER TWENTY

ALTHOUGH I WAS NOT TO BECOME aware of it for several months, the trouble had begun back on May 22, the very day when I tipped Boesky to the Nabisco deal. On that day an anonymous source in Caracas, Venezuela, wrote a strange letter, full of errors in spelling and grammar, as well as typing mistakes, to the compliance unit at the headquarters offices of Merrill Lynch in New York. It arrived in a plain white envelope. The letter read:

> Dear Sir: pleased be informed that two of your executives from the Caracas office are trading with inside information. A copie with description of ther trades so far has been submitet to the S.E.C. by separate mail. As is mantion on that letter if us customers do not benefit from their knoleg, we wonder who surveils the trades done by account executives. Upon you investigating to the last consequencies we will provide with the names of the insider on their owne hand writing.

The letter identified the two suspected Merrill Lynch employees as Carlos Zubillaga and Max Hofer.

Even as Laurie and I were basking in the Caribbean sun, the letter had arrived on the desk of Richard Drew, second in command of Merrill Lynch's Compliance Division. Drew found the spelling and typing errors intriguing. If the letter writer was sophisticated enough to know that the brokerage firm would have a compliance unit, would not he or she also be better schooled in language skills? Drew concluded that the anonymous author was attempting to disguise his or her identity. He assigned Steve Snyder, a senior analyst, to look into the charges.

Snyder studied the files containing the trading records of Zubillaga and Hofer over the past year, and he came to attention when he read the names of some of their recent stock dealings: Textron, G. D. Searle, Sperry, Houston Natural Gas. Both men in Caracas exhibited the same curious pattern of buying takeover stocks immediately prior to public announcements. Zubillaga came from a prominent Venezuelan family and had once been in charge of the public debt for his nation, but how in the world, Snyder wondered, could he and Hofer have unearthed takeover information while operating in far-off Caracas?

He checked the records of their Merrill Lynch personal cash management accounts and learned that Zubillaga had written two checks, totaling $8,000, to a man named Brian S. Campbell, whom Snyder remembered as a young, blond-and-boyish Merrill Lynch broker right here in New York. A quick check disclosed that Campbell had left the firm a few months earlier to join Smith Barney. What was the connection? Snyder wondered. Why was a broker in Caracas sending money to another broker in New York? Digging into Campbell's personnel records, Snyder discovered that Campbell and Zubillaga had attended the same Merrill Lynch training class in 1982.

The next step was to look at Campbell's trading records. In deals for both his personal account and his client accounts, Campbell's activity showed the same pattern of successful investment in takeover stocks.

Snyder was on the scent now, working his way back up the trail. Where, he wondered, did Campbell's information come from?

Rather quickly, Snyder zeroed in on Campbell's biggest commercial customer, Bank Leu International, located in Nassau. The terms "offshore," "tax haven" and "bank secrecy" leaped into his mind.

The Bank Leu trading record sent a shiver of electricity up his spine. The Bahamian bank had traded in the same takeover stocks as Campbell, Zubillaga and Hofer, but on a far larger scale—5,000 or even 10,000 shares at a time. What's more, it had dealt in a far greater variety of takeover stocks, twenty-seven in all, by Snyder's count.

Snyder concluded logically that Campbell had spotted a pattern of success in the buy-and-sell orders coming from Bank Leu and had copied some of the transactions for his own account, and for several accounts that he managed. In addition, he must have passed on information to his friend Zubillaga in Caracas, who shared it with another friend, Hofer. As Snyder probed, he discovered that Campbell had also provided takeover tips to his girlfriend, his former college roommate and a business partner.

Unfortunately, as far as Snyder was concerned, the trail reached a dead end at Bank Leu. Given the tight-knit nature of the Bahamian bank secrecy laws, there was no way to obtain information from an offshore entity.

Snyder reported to Drew, and together they took their findings to Robert Romano, Merrill Lynch's expert on insider trading. Romano was a former enforcement attorney for the SEC who, in that capacity, had led the investigation into the insider trading activities of former Reagan administration official Paul Thayer. Romano looked at the paperwork trail and declared that someone at Bank Leu was "wired" into a very good source.

In mid-June, Zubillaga and Hofer were summoned to New York and questioned by the Merrill Lynch compliance officers. Both admitted that they had received their tips from Campbell, but they denied wrongdoing, claiming that, so far as they knew, Campbell was merely riding the coattails of a hot client.

Because Campbell was no longer a Merrill Lynch employee, Romano could not question him. So he called Gary Lynch, the SEC enforcement director. Lynch was a soft-spoken individual who had taken his post four months earlier, succeeding the flashy John Fedders, who had resigned in the face of accusations that he was a wife-beater. Lynch put together a team to begin a federal inquiry into the Bank Leu trades. The case was designated #HO-1743. Several high-level SEC officials were involved, but the principal day-to-day investigators were attorneys Leo Wang and Peter Sonnenthal.

It was early in July when the Compliance Department at Campbell's new firm, Smith Barney, informed him that he was under investigation by the SEC, on suspicion of insider trading.

For three days in August, Campbell was questioned by SEC investigators about his relationship with Bank Leu. He was asked, "Did it ever occur to you at any time that Mr. Meier had access to inside information?"

"No, I had no knowledge of that," Campbell replied. He acknowledged that he had piggybacked some of Meier's trades, but said he did
so only after he had checked out the given stock through Merrill
Lynch's research department. If Bank Leu was trading on inside information, he contended, he was merely an innocent bystander.

Investigators may have been unconvinced, but they knew they would
have a difficult time in prosecuting Campbell. Piggybacking is poorly
defined in the securities laws. Merely copying the trades of a successful
investor is not a crime—unless you know or ignore substantial evidence
indicating that the investor is trading on illegal information.

The government decided to train its investigative guns on the bank.
An SEC lawyer telephoned Bernhard Meier at Bank Leu on August 28
to ask him about the suspicious pattern of trading in twenty-seven
specific stocks. Meier, not knowing how to respond, said he would get
back to the caller shortly.

Somewhat shaken, Meier discussed the call with Bruno Pletscher. It
was an awkward situation, Meier said. Here was a U.S. agency attempting to obtain information from a bank operating in the Bahamas. They
should not have that right, Meier declared. Nevertheless, he acknowledged that the SEC would expect some sort of response, and so would
their own superiors at the parent firm in Zurich. It was the latter
consideration that particularly worried Meier. He did not see how the
SEC could hold them responsible for anything, since, he told Pletscher,
they never really had any confirmation that Mr. Diamond was an inside
trader. But problems with their superiors seemed more formidable,
because (as I would soon find out) they had violated certain bank
guidelines, and they knew it. Meier observed that they were in the
"shit." He moaned, "What are we going to do?"

Pletscher suggested that they see what I had to say about the situation. "Can you call him?" he asked.

"No," Meier said, noting that I had never provided them with a
telephone number. But I had been calling with frequent trading instructions. Meier said, "I am sure he will call within the next two or three
days."

Pletscher pronounced, "It does not look good. What do you think
we have to do? Do you think we have to give the SEC the information
they requested?" Pletscher suggested that they get legal advice from
their Zurich office.

Together the two men went to Meier's office and placed a call back to the SEC lawyer. Their message was that they would seek legal advice in order to respond appropriately to the SEC's request.

This must have dismayed the SEC man, for in fact he had only the most nebulous information. Campbell and his friends were clearly small eggs in a big basket. There was no evidence to indicate who was the real source of the information.

WHEN I placed a collect call to the Bahamas to make a routine check on the status of my account, Meier said, "There's a problem. We should get together soon."

"What kind of problem?" I asked.

He responded with the three letters I did not want to hear: "SEC."

"I'll be down on the weekend," I said immediately.

I hung up on Meier and called Wilkis. Within minutes we were together, out on the hot, summery streets of New York, and I answered the question in his eyes with the statement, "My people in Nassau have a problem with the SEC."

"Go down there," he suggested.

"I already told them I was coming." We chatted for a few moments and assessed the possibilities. Most likely, if SEC investigators were snooping around, my bankers needed some hand-holding, some reassurance that we were all fully insulated. Wilkis and I reminded one another that the Bahamian bank secrecy laws were strict. There was no way that my bank could release any information to the SEC without my prior approval. Whatever the problem, it was clearly manageable.

Despite its recent highly publicized cases, Wilkis and I still viewed the SEC as a paper tiger. "The feds have no idea what they are doing," Wilkis contended. "They can look at a whole list of stock sales, but there is no discernible pattern."

I went back to work, where the pace was hectic enough to keep my mind off of the SEC most of the time. Nevertheless, the image of U.S. government agents snooping around the Bahamas plagued me.

When the course of business took me to Boesky's office, I asked him a probing question. After all, he had been investigated—and cleared—by the SEC on numerous occasions. "Ivan," I said, "you get called down to the SEC all the time. What do you tell them?"

He took me into his file room and exhibited one thick folder after

another. Each contained substantial amounts of background information, such as press clippings and analysts' reports. He showed me how
it was possible to justify nearly any trade—in retrospect—on the basis
of publicly available information. You could go into the files of the
business press and always find a story or two that you could point to
as the source of your interest in a given stock. Searching back through
company literature, you could find some basis for optimism. And somewhere, there was always a brokerage house that had issued a buy
recommendation. How, Boesky asked, was anyone going to prove that
your source was private, rather than public? "I tell them that I buy
stocks in broad industry groups, and I have all this research to back
me up," he said. "The burden is on them. They can't prove otherwise,
so they buy it."

Boesky suggested that if I needed a lawyer, I might try his man in
Washington, Harvey Pitt. He was no Perry Mason, but he was the
former general counsel of the SEC, and thus had connections. He was
now in private practice with the firm of Fried, Frank, Harris, Shriver
& Jacobson. Pitt, Boesky said, "does all this crap for me."

I arrived at Bank Leu about one P.M. on the Saturday of Labor Day
weekend 1985, to meet with Meier and Pletscher. Jean-Pierre Fraysse
was at this meeting also, although Bank Leu would later deny it.

Fraysse explained that he was due to return to Switzerland at the end
of the year, and he re-introduced me to his replacement, Richard
Coulson. I had met Coulson years earlier when he was one of the bank's
lawyers. Fraysse reminded me that Coulson had been a director of Bank
Leu since 1982. He said that he had briefed Coulson fully on my
situation.

The bankers showed me the formal telex that had arrived from the
SEC, affirming the oral request for information and adding a twenty-
eighth stock to the list. The worst part of this, as far as they were
concerned, was that the SEC sent a copy of the telex to the bank's home
office in Zurich.

I told them flatly that under no circumstances could they provide any
information about my account to the SEC, or to anyone else for that
matter. Such an action, I said in a firm voice, would be a clear violation
of Bahamian law.

That was true, Meier acknowledged, but he noted that the situation was delicate, because the SEC had already identified so many of the trades.

"How?" I asked.

Somewhat sheepishly Meier said, "The SEC is investigating one of the brokers with whom we have been executing trades."

"What are you talking about?"

"We have executed a lot of our trades through one brokerage firm . . ."

"Stuff that I bought?"

"Yes."

"Weren't you instructed to always break up the orders, to trade through different firms?"

"Yes."

"Didn't you?"

"No. Not always." Meier explained that he did try to deal through several brokers, but he was concerned that a few of them had a tendency to talk too much, to pass tips on to their clients to show them that they had good information. Meier had tried to avoid these brokers, and had steered much of his business to Brian Campbell at Merrill Lynch. Campbell, he said, had a good sense of timing. He knew when it was acceptable and profitable to buy quickly, but he also knew when to slow the pace of his dealings, lest the SEC become suspicious. Furthermore, Campbell gave Bank Leu the best available break of brokerage commissions (which, I realized, Bank Leu had not bothered to pass on to me).

I still did not understand. "Why is this a problem?" I asked.

"Well," Meier replied evasively, "they questioned Campbell."

"Why would they question him?"

Meier was clearly uncomfortable as he explained, "It appears as though—this disappoints me a great deal—he was also buying the same stocks that you were."

I was frustrated, unable to see why they were dragging me into this. I said, "Unless you explain to me what is really going on here, I can't give you my instincts on how to handle the problem."

Slowly I coaxed the details out of Meier concerning the investigation into Campbell's trading activities.

Meier sought to reassure me that I was sufficiently insulated. "Everything is under control in New York," he said. "The guy has very good lawyers. But now the SEC wants to talk to us."

"What are you going to talk to them about? You're a Swiss citizen working in a Bahamian bank."

"We have no intention of talking to them. We cannot, under the law."

In frustration I asked, "Then what's the problem? You're telling me there is an SEC investigation. You're telling me that your brokers in New York were buying the stocks that I was buying—obviously they spotted a winning pattern. But you can't tell the SEC anything. *What's the problem?*"

Uncomfortable silence followed. Then Meier whispered, "There's another problem. We also bought the stocks here."

"Who?"

"I did," Fraysse admitted. Meier said he had, too. Of the bank's officers, he had plunged the most heavily, buying anywhere from 1,000 to 3,500 shares of each stock that I purchased. He had made a profit of more than $150,000 in his "Ascona" account at Bank Leu. Pletscher said he had at first expressed reluctance at risking his money, but finally he had invested also, under the code names "Yellow Bird" and "Grouper."

Pletscher and Meier indicated that they also maintained accounts at other banks, through which they also traded. This was a typical Swiss tactic of diffusion of assets. Meier, for example, had established a secret account at Banca della Svizzera Italiana in Nassau and had made a few trades through a small U.S. brokerage firm called Tucker, Anthony & R. L. Day.

After an uncomfortable silence, Meier added enigmatically, "Other clients of the bank." Meier was responsible for numerous managed investment accounts, and he had brought them into this busy arena, satisfying his customers by providing them with handsome trading profits and fattening his own commission and service-fee income.

"Let me get this straight," I said, feeling the level of my voice rise. "I place an order for stock. Now I am discovering that not only were my orders filled, but you bought the same stocks for your personal accounts and for other accounts here at the bank, and then your brokers in New York bought for themselves and other people." They had a cottage industry going here! They had piggybacked my trades and magnified the effects in markets around the world. I gulped and asked, "Well, how many of your so-called managed accounts did you make these trades in?"

"Twenty-five or thirty."

"Oh, my God! And you did most of this through one broker?"

Meier nodded.

"You know that it was in direct defiance of my specific orders?"

"I know," Fraysse said, "but we have to deal with this problem."

I repeated, "What's the problem? You can't talk to the SEC. You can't tell them anything or give them anything."

Fraysse finally admitted, "The problem is our home office. They are going to be made aware of all this, and if they find out we were piggybacking, well, it's going to be a very serious problem for us." I reasoned that it would also be difficult for them to explain why they had set up hidden accounts in other banks.

Typical middle-management bureaucratic mentality, I thought. There is no real problem here, because the simple fact of the matter is that they cannot give the SEC my records. But the first instinct, of course, is to cover your ass, and that was what each of these men was trying to do. I forced myself to control my emotions. I had always regarded the personal ties among myself, Bob Wilkis, Ilan Reich, Ira Sokolow, "Goldie" and Bob's "kid" to be the weakest links in the chain, and I had been careful to create no connection between them and my trading account. Conversely, my offshore bank dealings seemed safe. I could have shifted my account from one bank to another every year or so, but it had seemed more prudent to keep the business confined to one set of allies. The fewer people who knew, the better. But now their own profligate actions had landed them in trouble with their bosses back in Zurich.

The dimensions of the problem were staggering. The SEC was looking at possible insider trading profits in excess of $10 million. If it could prove the contention, the SEC could demand that the bank return the $10 million, plus pay treble damages. The resulting $40 million fine could be assessed by freezing the U.S. assets of the bank.

It's not my problem, I thought, with a mixture of relief and anger. It's their problem.

As the others went about their business, Meier privately suggested a solution. When he considered the options, he said, he thought about pointing out to his superiors that I had lost more than $2 million dollars throughout the five years that I had traded through Bank Leu. Why would he copycat someone who lost so much money in the stock market? Unfortunately, that would not wash. The amount of my losses was large, all right, but they only served to prove how difficult it was to be right, no matter how good your information was. Two million dollars in losses was negligible compared to more than $10 million in profits.

His operative suggestion, Meier said, was this: "We are proposing to say that yours was a managed account, just like all the others, that you played no role in the investment decisions. That way, your account will appear to be only one of the many that we managed successfully. I will say that I picked all these stocks." He added, "I would like you to come up with reasons."

"Reasons for what?" I asked.

"Reasons why I bought the stocks."

Meier told me that Campbell had "good stories" for each of his purchases and had already supplied Meier with data.

It was viable. As Boesky had learned long ago, in retrospect you can generally find much public material to support the contention that you were simply an astute market analyst, rather than a privileged insider. I was red with anger that I had to help these men cover for their stupidity; but I did not see any choice. I agreed to put together a package of information, including annual reports, newsletters, broker-age house analyses and press clippings, so that Meier could "prove" that he had an open and legal basis for making the investment decisions that were so lucrative for all of the "managed" accounts, including mine. Meier could argue that he was good, or simply lucky.

Fraysse rejoined us and suggested "that the files be updated to reflect the current situation." He placed a form in front of me, authorizing the Bank Leu officers to make investment decisions for my account at their own discretion. He asked me to sign it and backdate it. This was an old form, he explained. Recently the bank had updated the form, but he had scoured the files for an old copy, so that it would appear legitimate. I signed, and both Fraysse and Meier sighed with relief. The auditors were expected to arrive soon from Zurich to perform the annual check, and they wanted "proof" of the managed accounts.

Once more I emphasized that they were to provide no documents concerning my account to the U.S. government, or to counsel.

"Yes," Fraysse and Meier both agreed.

Meier muttered, "Files get lost all the time."

But my comment raised an issue in Fraysse's mind. He said, "We do not have any connection with counsel that would be appropriate to deal in SEC matters. Can you recommend somebody?"

I suggested that they hire a Bahamian lawyer to head up a legal team, but if they wanted a U.S.-based attorney, I offered the name of Harvey Pitt, the lawyer whom Boesky said handled the SEC "crap" for him. I told them that Pitt was formerly the general counsel for the SEC, and I was sure that he could use the authority of the Bahamian banking laws to quash the investigation on the U.S. end.

"What would it cost to do this?" Fraysse asked. "Twenty-five thousand dollars?"

"I'm sure it would cost a lot more."

Fraysse asked if I would help to defray the legal expenses.

Now, finally, I exploded. "This is not my problem!" I raged. "This is your problem. You deal with it. You guys have made millions on me, not only on commissions but, it appears, on trading. You have the nerve to ask me to pay for your lawyer? For a problem you created?"

Fraysse dropped the issue and gave me time to cool off. He ran off to instruct his secretary to try to call Pitt, then and there.

Stop it, Dennis, I told myself. Keep your wits about you. There is no reason to overreact. So what if these idiots have to answer to their superiors in Zurich? They still don't have to talk to the SEC. In a way, perhaps the scope of the piggyback trading could save me. They were right. My account was by far the biggest, but it was only one of many. How could any investigator sort out the real source?

Fraysse reported that Pitt was not in at the moment, so he began to draft an introductory letter to the lawyer, providing basic background information concerning Bank Leu International and its parent company, as well as Bahamian law.

"Look," I said to Meier, "give me a list of the stocks that the SEC is looking at, and the dates of the trades." Meier provided me with a copy of the SEC request. I scanned it quickly and saw that it covered many of my more lucrative trades. But I was somewhat relieved to see a few names of some stocks in which I had not traded, such as Colgate-Palmolive and Brunswick. "You should work on collecting information that could have led to the decisions from your side," I said. "See what Campbell comes up with, and I'll see what I can put together. As soon as I get back to my office I'll start working on that."

Fraysse said, "This seems to be the best way to deal with this problem."

At any rate, I volunteered, I would suspend my trading activities until this was all cleared up.

Pletscher was back in the room now, and he suggested that it might look suspicious to stop trading. If we traded, he contended, it would signal the SEC that we were unconcerned about its surveillance.

Meier had what he believed was a workable solution. He suggested that, for the time being, I trade through an entity called Oxford Financial Partners, based in New Jersey. We all looked at him strangely. This fellow's business ventures reached into unforeseen places.

"No trading," I decreed. "I don't want you to be distracted. It's important that you focus on your problem and get it out of the way."

BEFORE leaving the island nation, I picked up a tourist pamphlet entitled "Bank Secrecy: How It Works Here in the Bahamas." It reviewed the social and legislative history that had made the Bahamas one of the world's banking havens and concluded that Bahamian banking was in "a general upward trend."

CHAPTER TWENTY-ONE

WILKIS LISTENED TO MY STORY with controlled concern. He knew that we could handle the problem. Immediately he volunteered to help me assemble the necessary paperwork that would, in retrospect, justify my trades. After all, he was my friend. We were in this together.

We divvied up the list of stocks in which the SEC had expressed suspicion; fortunately, it encompassed only about 25 percent of all the trades I had made over the years.

Whenever I could steal a spare moment from the Revlon deal or one of the many other transactions competing for my attention, I punched instructions into a computer, calling up research materials that predated my transactions. It was a pleasant, calming surprise to realize that much justification existed. Here were publicly available stock analyses, company reports, brokerage studies and articles in *Barron's, The Wall Street Journal* and the financial pages of *The New York Times*— all of which could have persuaded an astute trader to invest. Only when I peered backward in time did I realize how much the financial press trades in speculation, educated guesses and outright rumors. And I only had to justify my buy orders. Rising price was reason enough to explain a sell order.

For each deal, I attempted to create a convincing paper trail, yet keep it simple, lest I load up the Bank Leu officials with details that were beyond their comprehension. I spent considerable time with long computer printout sheets, cutting them apart with scissors, making sure that any user code identification was removed before placing an item in my files. Many of the junior associates in the office were impressed with how much time I, as a managing director, devoted to research.

Wilkis met with me frequently, after work, to hand over his own sheaf of materials, and I collated this with my data. In retrospect, we were surprised to realize how easily we could have called some of our most lucrative deals without benefiting from any inside knowledge.

JEAN-PIERRE Fraysse traveled from Nassau to New York early in September and met with Harvey Pitt in Fried, Frank's office. He presented in person the letter he had begun to compose during our recent meeting. He also handed over a copy of the SEC's telex request for information concerning twenty-eight suspicious trades.

Pitt studied the material and, a few days later, he and his colleague Michael Rauch conducted a conference call with Meier and Coulson in the Bahamas.

WILKIS and I had a standing tennis date at seven P.M. on Monday nights at the Wall Street Racquet Club. Our play was now punctuated by quiet conversations and cryptic remarks concerning the SEC inquiry. One Monday evening, midway through our second set, Wilkis mentioned casually that he knew the identities of two other men in our network, Ilan Reich and Ira Sokolow. He had deduced Reich's involvement, he said, simply by studying the pattern of deals emanating from Wachtell, Lipton.

"How did you learn about Sokolow?" I asked.

He explained that once, when he, as "Alan Darby," called at my office, I had ended the conversation by saying, "I'm going to go talk to 'my kid.'" He then called back a few minutes later, and when my secretary said I was in a meeting in another office, he asked who I was with. The secretary replied, "Mr. Sokolow." Having told me this, Wilkis said that he had decided to distance himself from his "kid" at Lazard Frères and had, therefore, instructed him to open his own account in the Bahamas, so that he could trade securities for himself.

I thought this was a poor idea for two reasons. Number one, I pointed out, this took "the kid" outside of Wilkis's control. Why should he continue to feed Wilkis information if he could just trade on it himself? Number two, it increased the risk of exposure, because now we had to worry about SEC scrutiny of three accounts, rather than two. I asked, "Do you have any idea where he opened it?"

"Yes I do."

"Where?"

"A company called Bank Leu."

I dropped my tennis racket and muttered, "You dumb son of a bitch!"

His mouth fell open in amazement. "You're kidding?" he asked. "That's your bank?"

"Yes."

"Uh-oh."

We promptly ended our match so that Wilkis could call his "kid," to tell him to take his business elsewhere.

The more I thought about the episode, the more I was incensed by the behavior of the Bank Leu officials. They were already under scrutiny by the SEC and in hot water with their home office superiors, yet they had freely accepted the business of yet another Wall Street insider.

Only with difficulty did I keep my voice civil when I next spoke with Meier by phone. He informed me that the bank had followed up on my recommendation and hired Pitt to advise it on how to handle the SEC inquiry. Meier told me that he was coming to New York on September 18 to clean up his affairs with Brian Campbell and that Pitt was flying up from Washington to consult with him then.

I told Meier that I would contact him when he was here, to see how things were going. "Where are you staying?" I asked.

"The Waldorf-Astoria."

"I'll call."

EXHIBITING a "keep up with the Joneses" mentality, Philip Morris laid plans for a buyout of General Foods. I did not act upon this knowledge myself, although Wilkis did, and when I heard the scuttlebutt I called Boesky and advised, "I know that you have an enormous position in General Foods. On the basis of my information, I would increase that position." Soon, he pocketed more millions.

* * *

LAURIE'S father took a turn for the worse. Both of us were preoccupied with this personal pain. We spent much time on the phone with Laurie's mother in Florida.

On top of this, I labored as best I could to assemble the defense package for Bank Leu.

And amid everything else I found myself at the centerpoint of Perelman's epic battle. The new Revlon barriers seemed insurmountable, but Perelman was determined not to capitulate. I admired his tenacity. We all donned our thinking caps.

In analyzing the situation we realized that, in some ways, we were in a better position than before. Revlon's recent financial moves were designed to make it a less desirable acquisition. Thus, the Revlon board probably chased away other suitors; no white knight would consider an appearance now. At the same time, our own close scrutiny revealed a target that was more appealing than any of us had previously thought. Our soundings of the marketplace allowed us to estimate that the subsidiary sales, bringing in $1.675 billion to $1.9 billion, could more than offset the total debt required for the acquisition. Once they were sold, Perelman would be left with a cosmetics firm worth $800 million that he essentially acquired at little or no cost.

Perelman arranged for Morgan Stanley to take a subordinate slice of the deal. If and when he gained control of Revlon, it would be Morgan Stanley's job to turn those subsidiaries into cash as fast as possible—cash that Perelman could use to help retire his enormous debt before the interest payments squeezed him too tightly. My former boss at Lehman Brothers, Eric Gleacher, would handle that portion of the business. The Street was amazed to learn that Morgan Stanley had not only climbed into bed with Drexel, but also was willing to play a clearly subordinate role. Gleacher and his team came on board as valuable allies; it was a pleasure to work with him once more.

The most important point to emerge from our fresh analysis came as we pondered the implications of Revlon's move to dilute its stock value. Collectively, those of us who sat in Perelman's war room came to attention as a great truth dawned: We had offered $47.50 per share. In response, Revlon had found ways to cheapen the stock, reasoning that neither Perelman nor anyone else could persuade his lenders to fund him because the offer was now unrealistically complex.

Despite the uncertain atmosphere created by Revlon's new defensive measures, we continued to meet regularly. Often we discussed our options as we took walks along the hot summer sidewalks, leaving our suit jackets behind. To cool off, we would pounce upon a street vendor and dig into a supply of DoveBars.

The solution to our dilemma did not come when someone jumped up and screamed "Eureka!" Rather, the reality evolved from our discussions. Was the offer of $47.50 written in stone? Of course not. There were plenty of outs, written right into the thick tender offer.

If Revlon devalued the stock, why could we not devalue our offer?

We crunched the numbers one more time and decided that if we *lowered* our offer from $47.50 to $42 per share, we not only were paying a fair price to the shareholders, but we could move our junk bonds back to the private market and avoid the delay caused by SEC regulations of public issues.

Conventional market wisdom had never encountered the tenacity of Drexel. The investment world was flabbergasted when we rescinded our previous tender offer and commenced our lower offer on September 16. All the shareholders had to do was total up the values and see that we were still giving them a good deal—perhaps even better than before.

In the new offer, Pantry Pride detailed that it had $750 million in available cash (the bulk raised by Drexel in July), plus $340 million in bank credit. The remaining $500 million was to be raised in Pantry Pride notes marketed by Drexel, which was "highly confident" that it could do so. Pantry Pride paid Drexel a half million dollars for the use of those two simple words in the tender offer and agreed to other fees and commissions that would bring Drexel's total income to $60 million on this single transaction—if it closed.

On September 18 I located a pay phone in a restaurant at 95th Street and Third Avenue, a few blocks from my apartment. My paranoia was on the rise, and I made sure I found a phone I had never used before. The operator at the Waldorf-Astoria connected me with Meier, in Room 2341, and I asked, "How did it go?"

"Everything is fine," Meier reported. The relief that sounded in his voice buoyed my own spirits. He said that he had told the lawyer that the bank should take a tough stand and refuse to provide the SEC with any information, and in addition, he said, there was no case because he had picked all the stocks himself and executed the trades for managed accounts.

I was pleased. It sounded good to me, and I told Meier so.

"Excuse me," he said, "someone is at the door."

He returned to the phone in a few moments and announced in a shaky voice, "I have just been served with a subpoena." Actually, there were two: One demanded Bank Leu's business records from October 1, 1983, forward; the other sought access to Meier's personal records. He had until October 1 to deliver the package to SEC investigators.

"Call Pitt," I said. "This may be serious. Wait—look, I'm running out of quarters. Call me back at this number." I gave him the number of the pay phone and he returned the call immediately.

"How did they know I was here?" Meier asked.

"You had to fill out a form, right, when you came through customs? You had to list the hotel where you were staying?"

"Oh, yes."

"So they've been looking for you, waiting for you to enter the country."

"It's bullshit," he said, attempting a cavalier pose, but the tone of his voice betrayed tension. I heard the sound of him lighting a cigarette. "They have no right to do this to me. I'm a Swiss citizen."

I spoke very carefully, aware of the possibility that my words were being recorded. "I don't understand why you're having this problem, Bernie," I said. "You bought all these damn stocks. You picked them all. You asked me to help put all this information together. When you get my research, you'll see that it is all very legitimate. There is nothing to worry about."

Meier had calmed somewhat, and he agreed. With regard to the subpoenas, he declared flatly that the bank would not and could not provide any information. Furthermore, he added, he would "alter the files to protect the banks' interests."

After we hung up, Meier's final statement haunted me. If the bank was not going to turn over any records, I asked myself, why did it have to alter them?

* * *

"OH, shit!" Wilkis said when I reported to him. "You better make sure these guys stand up for you. This is still their problem. Make sure it stays their problem. There is no evidence of any wrongdoing whatsoever. The SEC has a list of stocks. They've spoken to a couple of brokers, who led them to your bank. But that's all they know. They do not have the slightest suspicion of who is behind it. There's nothing here but an enormous fishing expedition."

My head agreed, but my stomach was in turmoil.

IN front of me were pages of analyses: multiples of earnings, multiples of cash flow, mulitples of book values, for each of the Revlon subsidiaries. Revlon's management had made this information difficult to acquire by refusing to break down the statistics for each company, but we did the best we could with limited, publicly available data. I studied industry averages and the reports of other recent sales of similar companies, trying to come up with the most precise values possible.

I was busy at this task when an attorney called me from Drexel's Compliance Department and asked, "You worked on the Coastal/ANR deal?"

"Sure," I replied.

"Well, the SEC is doing an investigation on a whole bunch of deals, and they want to know who worked on them."

"Let me come over," I suggested. "I'll take a look at the whole list and see if I can help you out."

I walked across Broad Street to the Compliance Department. Inside I was dying.

The sight of the list staggered me, and I fought to hide my anxiety. It was identical to the list provided me by Bank Leu. The SEC was throwing out a net. I thought: There's more going on here than meets the eye. Somebody is not being straight with me. This may be a fishing expedition, but it is getting uncomfortably close to home.

Trying to keep my voice calm, I pointed out to the compliance officer that there were, indeed, several Drexel deals on the list in which I had some involvement. This was not unusual, and I knew that there was no way anyone could tie me, or anybody else, to a majority of these deals.

All the major players in the M&A business would show up at various points on the list. I said in what I hoped was an unconcerned tone, "Okay, I'll give you the names of all the people who worked on these deals with me. I'll get it over to you."

"Well, thanks, Dennis," the compliance officer replied. "I really appreciate your coming over here. Thanks for the help."

"Anytime," I said. "Anytime you get one of these things, just give me a buzz."

Shortly thereafter, Sokolow called me and asked for a quick meeting. As soon as we got together he reported, "I got the strangest request."

"What's the problem?"

"They showed me a list of stocks and wanted to know if I was involved in all these damn deals. Is this us?"

"Absolutely not," I lied, not wishing to alarm him. "It's nothing to be concerned about. Forget about it."

"Well, I got scared when I saw it."

I countered, "You think we're the only ones doing this?"

Through quiet inquiries I discovered that the list had been circulated to the major investment banking firms and all law offices specializing in the M&A business. The heat was on. In response, Wilkis and I expanded our research-in-retrospect.

ON September 22 Pitt and Rauch flew to Nassau and met with Meier at a hotel—bank management had instructed the U.S. lawyers not to come to the office, lest their presence alert employees to a potential problem.

The next day Pitt and Rauch met with Meier and Coulson, as well as Michael Barnette, the bank's Bahamian lawyer. Coulson took the lead in this meeting, declaring that the bank was extremely concerned about violating the secrecy laws, for such an action would surely have a dilatory effect upon their other accounts.

The U.S. lawyers asked the bankers to prepare details of their trading in managed accounts. Meier nodded his agreement, for he knew that both Campbell and I were already packaging the necessary research.

One day later Pitt phoned Zurich and spoke with Hans-Peter Schaad, the head of Bank Leu's legal department, apprising him of developments. Schaad said that he would discuss the situation with Hans

Knopfli, chairman of Bank Leu Zurich and the CEO of the Nassau
subsidiary. Clearly, Bank Leu had decided to deal with this issue at the
highest levels.

During this same week a team of inspectors from Bank Leu's parent
company in Zurich visited Nassau to conduct the routine annual audit.
Pletscher and Meier chose this opportunity to declare their concerns.
They informed the auditors that their trading activities were the subject
of an SEC inquiry that might involve insider trading. They noted that
they had hired an American lawyer and had also asked the Zurich office
to send the head of the legal department to assist them. But instead of
Bank Leu's chief lawyer, they said, Knopfli was coming over to look
into the situation personally. They noted that the amount in question
was about $10 million, and that the SEC had the authority to level
treble damages that could result in a total of $40 million in fines.

The auditors' main question was why they had retained a lawyer
from Fried, Frank, rather than using the bank's traditional U.S. firm,
Lord Day & Lord.

Pletscher admitted that the situation was so serious that they needed
counsel with SEC connections. He noted that the trading in question
was conducted through one major account, based on direct orders from
the client, but he admitted that they had conducted other trades based
on that client's activities, both for their personal accounts and for other
accounts that the bank managed. The bank's position had been compro-
mised.

The inspectors asked to see some of the trading records. Pletscher
and Meier complied, and Meier added that they might have to produce
some documents that did not reflect a true picture of how the transactions transpired. One of the inspectors replied that there are times, in
order to protect the bank's best interests, when certain documents must
be brought à jour—French for "up to date."

Pletscher and Meier took this as official approval of their strategy.

Following this conversation, the inspectors phoned Zurich to repeat
Pletscher and Meier's request that the bank's chief lawyer visit Nassau
to assess the situation. Pletscher learned the next day that the inspectors
were instructed to alter their travel plans so as to return to Zurich via
a connecting flight through London, rather than New York, presumably to guard against the danger of being slapped with subpoenas.
Clearly, Zurich was now calling the shots.

* * *

WILKIS and I were ready with an impressive package of research for Meier to use to write his own summaries for his superiors. It was a partial list; we would continue to work on other stocks.

I slipped away for a trip to the Bahamas on the last weekend of September to deliver the material. Upon my arrival at Bank Leu, I found, on a table in the conference room, the files from my Diamond Holdings account. Pletscher, Meier and Coulson, were waiting for me. Fraysse, busy with other matters, was able to attend only portions of the meeting.

Pletscher said that the bank was extremely concerned with the fall-off in its revenues since I had suspended my activities and explained that he had a plan that would allow us to resume trading. He suggested that we close the old account and open a new one, with no visible connecting links. The account balance would be transferred, via three unequal deposits, to a new bank account in Bermuda under the name of Midu Enterprises. For a few weeks, Pletscher said, the balance of my account would be invested in the Euro-money market. Meier and Pletscher would fashion an account statement in retrospect, phony documentation to "prove" that Midu Enterprises had been in business for years, conducting various stock trades that coincided with many of my activities. My true account record would be sequestered from the bank's normal files, covering my tracks.

The bankers had the necessary papers prepared, backdated to September 10. I signed.

Pletscher opened the folder of my Diamond Holdings account and removed my signature card and the photocopies of my father's and brother's passports. He said, "Since you now have a new corporate account, these documents are unnecessary."

Coulson took the documents from Pletscher. Here was the only hard evidence that linked me to the Diamond International account. Coulson indicated that I should follow him, and we went to his office. There, with deliberate movements, he placed the papers into the shredder adjacent to his desk and announced, "That should take care of this matter very nicely."

Huddling with Meier, I presented my research package. As I suspected, he was somewhat naive concerning investment strategies, and

I had to go over the material with him, piece by piece, to show him how to explain it all to his people in Zurich.

Meier said that, in the case of his personal account records, he might have to waive the secrecy requirements.

I advised against this strongly. I did not want him to provide any documents to the SEC. Giving the investigators a partial picture, I contended, would only set them on the trail more determinedly. They must be stopped now, while it was early.

Pletscher seemed not to hear this. He suggested that they might divide the records of my account into a series of subaccounts, so that each would appear to be one of the run-of-the-mill funds that Meier "managed." Instead of my transactions standing out as by far the largest of the managed accounts, they would disappear into the mix.

Referring to the bank inspectors, Meier said, "You see, they propose to produce documents that reflect what we are saying."

"It's not necessary," I said, "since you can't provide *any* information. It would only complicate matters."

At one point during the meeting, Meier remarked idly, "It's the strangest thing. Some time ago another Wall Streeter came down here and opened an account. Then, before doing anything with it, he decided to close it."

It was Wilkis's "kid," I knew, but I did not let on. I simply said, "It was probably somebody from the SEC. Be careful with new accounts."

Fraysse took some time to explain developments from the Nassau end. The bankers had told their attorneys, Pitt and Rauch, that the accounts in question were all managed and that Meier was in the process of assembling the documentation to show how he had made the astute investment calls.

Pletscher, Meier and Coulson all assured me that the "Bahamian secrecy defense" as well as the "managed accounts defense" had been approved by their superiors in Zurich. The auditors, I was told, had reviewed my account records and concluded that the files should reflect the official cover story, as supported by the research packages supplied by Campbell and myself.

But they were taking a new stance regarding the SEC. Zurich, it seemed, wanted them to share the research packages with SEC investigators.

I opened my mouth to protest.

"Don't worry," Fraysse said quickly. "We will not give them any information about the trading accounts. We will just give them the information about how these stocks were chosen."

SHORTLY after my departure, Hans Knopfli arrived for two days of meetings with his Bahamian employees, announcing to Pletscher that he was to be promoted to the post of managing director.

Pletscher and Meier told him they were surprised that the bank's chief lawyer was not in attendance as they had requested. Nevertheless, they wanted to tell Knopfli their story. At Knopfli's request, they showed him a breakdown of the trading in the twenty-eight stocks encompassed by the SEC inquiry. Meier noted that he had been subpoenaed to testify to the SEC.

The meeting was not recorded and, as events unfolded, divergent reports would surface. In my view, none of this should have been a surprise to Knopfli. After all, he was the CEO of Bank Leu International and had, early on, approved my request to trade on margin.

Pletscher claimed that, during this meeting, Knopfli stated succinctly, "Under no circumstances can you go to an authority and lie." But was that a statement with punch, or was it for show? Knopfli also declared that he wanted the men to do what was in the best interest of the bank. To Pletscher and Meier, this seemed to be a contradiction.

After the meeting, Meier purportedly said to Pletscher, "I think Mr. Knopfli does not understand the consequences."

Pletscher replied, "If he tells us to do what we think is the best for the bank, and this includes a lie, then we should do it."

CHAPTER TWENTY-TWO

THIS WAS ALL SO CRAZY! So much was happening on so many fronts that I could not keep track.

One day, for example, I found myself sitting in the office of Major League Baseball Commissioner Peter Ueberroth. I had been asked by Milken to meet with him and his friend Jerry Weinstein, the producer of *The Karate Kid*. Ueberroth knew he was on his way out as the commissioner and was laying his plans for future business. He and Weinstein were considering the purchase of a group of radio stations and had asked Drexel to evaluate the deal.

"Don't do it," I advised.

"Why?" Ueberroth asked.

I went over the numbers, explaining the economics of the broadcasting industry, as I had learned them from my own recent study. I concluded, "Your pockets aren't deep enough, even with Drexel's financing."

Ueberroth and Weinstein reluctantly agreed with the analysis.

ON another front, we were suddenly confronted by a pair of white knights who appeared on the horizon, riding headlong toward Revlon's rescue. The private investment partnership of Adler & Shaykin agreed to buy the cosmetics portion of Revlon's business and set to work negotiating a price. The LBO firm of Forstmann Little was prepared to purchase the remainder of the company in a sweetheart deal that would allow Bergerac and other members of Revlon's top management to come along for the ride.

The news of these developments confirmed the rumor that Boesky had passed on to us, that an LBO was in the offing. Meeting in Perelman's office, our team speculated on the source of Boesky's information.

We were aware of the negotiations but, of course, not privy to them, and we acted to head off the competition. Perelman, fighting mad, wanted to raise his tender offer from $42 to $50 per share. We agreed with this strategy, but had to analyze the financial variables before committing to it. Perelman drove his troops to rework the numbers, and at Drexel, I had others hard at work on the same task. Dozens of calls were placed between Perelman's office and Beverly Hills. Could we finance the deal at a historic level? The answer, after much consultation, appeared to be yes.

On October 1, we heard a rumor that the private deal between Revlon, Adler & Shaykin and Forstmann Little would result in a combined bid of $52 per share, topping us by two dollars. It was a world-class poker game now and Perelman refused to fold. He called the two dollars and raised another dollar, offering $53 per share. We knew that the Revlon board was meeting to consider the pending issues and we wanted to get this information to them quickly, so I rode off in a chauffeured Rolls-Royce to personally deliver this latest bid to Revlon's headquarters in the General Motors Building.

On that same day, Harvey Pitt met with members of the SEC staff and informed them that their subpoenas raised certain considerations regarding Bahamian law. He contended that the subpoenas, delivered to Meier, related only to Meier's activities and not to the bank's records as a whole.

They hashed out a compromise whereby Meier would provide his own trading records along with a copy of his background research records. He would also submit to a deposition. In addition, Bank Leu agreed to provide records of the managed accounts, but all materials that might identify the traders would be edited out.

When Meier advised me of these developments via the telephone, I wondered where the bank's Bahamian counsel was throughout this process. The bank apparently had set up a strategy whereby it was about to break Bahamian law.

Although I would have preferred a hard-line approach, there was nothing I could do to stop Meier from turning over his records, or from testifying. And, when I thought about it, I concluded that the SEC investigators would soon realize that they had encountered a stone wall. Under law, the bank could not supply the name or information about any depositor without that depositor's consent. Meier would argue his position as a premier stock market prognosticator, and if he was asked for details concerning the managed accounts, would stand firm behind the defense of the secrecy laws. The SEC, although undoubtedly dubious, would have to swallow his story.

BERGERAC, continuing to spurn Perelman and acting as if the public corporation was his own property, announced on October 3 that he would sell to his cronies. Adler & Shaykin was going to buy the cosmetics end of the business for $900 million and the rest of the conglomerate would be sold to Forstmann Little for $1.4 billion, with Bergerac as one of the principal new owners. Forstmann Little would sell off one of the subsidiaries to American Home Products and keep the rest. It was a carefully crafted LBO that, upon close inspection, contained some intriguing provisions The terms called for Bergerac to receive a $35 million golden parachute as compensation for losing his Revlon post. He, in turn, would be able to use that money to become a major player in the Forstmann Little buyout. In effect, Revlon was paying Bergerac the money he needed to buy back his own job and to increase, substantially, his own stake in the company, albeit without the cosmetics end of the business. It smelled very fishy, but it also smelled successful, because this new proposal would net the shareholders $56 per share. Outside observers now seemed confident that the pot was too rich for Perelman.

There was, however, a kicker here that we believed Revlon had overlooked. In order to make the company worth $56 per share, the board had voted to remove the restrictive covenants it had previously created. Just that suddenly, the poison pill defense had been abandoned.

What did that mean? In Perelman's office, we all knew the answer. Now, suddenly, the company was worth more than ever!

Again we crunched the numbers, calculating ways to minimize the tax consequences via creative accounting. Perelman finally offered $56.25 per share and Milken backed that with an announcement that we had already raised most of the necessary cash and were "highly confident" that we could place the remaining $350 million in junk bonds.

I held extensive conversations with the press to make sure that our position was reported accurately, and I kept Perelman up to date on market developments. He called me four or five times a day, just to ask, "What do you know? What do you hear?"

IT was Arthur Liman, the attorney who had first brought Bergerac and Perelman face to face, who now orchestrated a late-night meeting among the principals, this time adding Ted Forstmann to the mix.

Shortly before midnight, October 9, Perelman, Drapkin, Engel and I walked down Madison Avenue from 63rd Street, heading for Revlon's offices at 59th Street and Fifth Avenue. The night air was cool. Traffic was light. As we walked, we discussed possible scenarios. None of us knew what Revlon might propose, so we decided that we had no choice but to play the meeting by ear.

Revlon's offices were decorated with the stuffed heads of trophies from Bergerac's safaris. About fifteen of us, representing every side of the transaction, gathered there. Perelman, Drapkin, Engel and I sat on one side of the table. Forstmann and Fraidin were across from us. Bergerac was on the premises, but waiting off in another room with his advisers from Lazard Frères and Wachtell, Lipton. Liman attempted to mediate.

By four A.M. we had hammered out the parameters of what we hoped was an acceptable compromise. Perelman would get Revlon, except for one of the health-care subsidiaries, which would go to Forstmann Little and which Bergerac, floating off on a gigantic golden parachute, could run. Forstmann said it was okay if Bergerac agreed.

He did not. In fact, he was adamant in his declaration that he would never sell to Perelman. Bergerac's behavior was in line with all of our intelligence estimates, which painted him as arrogant and intractable.

Off to one side, our team huddled to consider the next move. Our greatest concern was the veracity of the numbers. Revlon, even at this meeting that was supposed to be more-or-less friendly, refused to supply us with a breakdown of the operating numbers of its all-important subsidiaries. This was especially frustrating. It was galling to know that, across the table from us, the Forstmann Little people had all the relevant information.

"We'll use Forstmann as a stalking horse," Perelman suggested. "If he is confident that he can go to a certain price on the basis of his bank financing, we know we can do better with your financing."

Perelman left the meeting with a promise: Whatever additional offer Forstmann Little made, he would top it by 25¢ per share.

We walked back uptown with brisk and confident strides, sensing that victory was ours.

But Bergerac would not back down. Within days, Forstmann Little raised its bid to $57.25 per share, and the Revlon board, succumbing to Forstmann's threat "to walk," announced plans to grant it a lockup option (the automatic right to buy two of the health-care subsidiaries, Vision Care and National Health Laboratories, at a cut-rate price of $525 million if anyone else acquired 40 percent of the stock). It was another, new "show-stopper," and it would effectively preclude any other bidder from coming in.

That's illegal, we responded. It was a Thursday when we asked Justice Joseph Walsh of the Delaware Chancery Court to grant a temporary injunction to stop the plan. Skadden, Arps' litigators, Stu Shapiro and Mike Mitchell, did an outstanding job of arguing that the sum total of Revlon's anti-takeover moves was, quite clearly, not in the best interests of the shareholders, because it had the effect of quashing a bidding war and thus preventing them from realizing the best available price. The judge scheduled hearings for the following week.

In the meantime, the Revlon board met on Saturday, blithely ignored the pending lawsuit and granted the lockup. Monday was a bank holiday, but Revlon managed to transfer certain cash assets of the two subsidiaries in question into an escrow account at Morgan Guaranty, stashing the money neatly away from Revlon's general fund.

That move angered Justice Walsh. One day later he enjoined Revlon from transferring any more assets prior to his ruling in the case.

Two weeks passed, and the waiting was excruciating, rather like the last few weeks of pregnancy. Finally, Justice Walsh formally declared that by granting the lockup option the Revlon board had "failed in its fiduciary duty to the stockholders." Once it became apparent that Revlon would be sold to somebody, the judge declared, the only proper role for a director was as "an auctioneer attempting to secure the highest price for the pieces of the Revlon enterprise." He directed the board to sell to the highest bidder.

Perelman's response was to raise his offer to $58 per share.

Revlon and Forstmann were unwilling or unable to top the bid. Instead, they appealed the judge's ruling, which kept everything in limbo.

The Street followed every nuance of the deal. Justice Walsh had enunciated a key principle that was critical to the future of the M&A business. If the appeals court upheld the ruling, it would place an official seal of approval on the principle that anyone could buy any company—so long as he could come up with the most money.

As we waited for the dust to settle, we learned of a fascinating development. Some of the Revlon board members had hired their own lawyers to guide them through the maze, to make sure they discharged their duties in a responsible manner, in the interests of the shareholders, rather than management. It was an unprecedented move, and it was certain to drive a wedge between the board and Bergerac, and it was further confirmation of the value of our psychological intelligence-gathering. This was exactly how we had expected certain directors to react.

We had them now. I knew it!

IN mid-October I attended a dinner at Lutece, considered by many to be New York's finest French restaurant. It was a typical "let's get to know you" function, designed to allow senior members of Drexel's M&A Department to mingle with their counterparts in the law firm of Fried, Frank. The dinner was attended by, among many others, Harvey Pitt, the attorney I had recommended to Bank Leu. He was a portly, bearded, curly-haired man full of self-assurance.

I was unimpressed. In my opinion Arthur Fleischer, the senior partner of the firm, overshadowed him.

Pitt, of course, did not know that I was the mysterious trader behind the Diamond Holdings account.

THE Delaware Supreme Court was scheduled to rule on Revlon's appeal on November 1, and everyone on the Street knew that this was the final battle. Billions of dollars were staked on the outcome.

The arbs were in up to their eyeballs, and the market had developed to the point where a single moment of time could make a huge difference in profit and loss figures. Every major arb in the country had a representative on the scene in Delaware. Hours before the court was due to convene, they commandeered every pay telephone in sight, keeping an open line to someone back at the office, determined to outrace even the Dow Jones ticker.

I knew that, once the ruling was announced, our own lawyers would be tied up in the courtroom, attending to the details, and we did not want to wait for the Dow ticker either. So, as we sat in Perelman's office, our stomachs rumbling in protest over the sumptuous breakfast that we were too nervous to digest, I kept a phone pressed to my ear. On the other end of the line was an arb from one of the major brokerage firms, doing me a favor.

Engel was there, having come down from his upstairs office.

Gleacher was there with his people from Morgan Stanley.

A team from Chemical Bank joined us.

Drapkin and an assault squad from Skadden, Arps and MacAndrews & Forbes were there.

Perelman's secretary Sue, anticipating victory, set exquisite goblets upon a silver tray. In her hand was an ice-cold bottle of Cristal, Perelman's favorite champagne.

Minutes passed in quiet, nervous small talk, but as the time dragged, the room grew silent.

Perelman puffed on a cigar. His eyes issued a silent scream: What do you hear?

"Yes?" I said into the phone.

The room came to attention.

I dropped the phone, turned to stare Perelman directly in the eye and said softly, "We won."

Suddenly everyone was on his feet, engulfed in a collective embrace. Sue popped the cork on the champagne bottle.

* * *

PERELMAN'S tender offer officially closed at midnight that night, and Revlon shareholders were enriched significantly. By November 5 we filed the final forms with the SEC, indicating that Pantry Pride, Inc., had acquired control of Revlon, Inc.

When I arrived at my office later that morning, I felt like a general returning home from a victorious battle. We had just won the most fiercely contested takeover in history. There were dozens of congratulatory phone messages awaiting me. Several magnums of champagne were sent over by arbs and even by competitors.

At its final meeting, the old Revlon board found Bergerac in tears. He likened the experience to a woman being raped. But it was difficult to feel too sorry for the man; when he resigned, he took with him $15 million in severance pay plus five years' worth of salary and bonuses as well as stock options; it all added up to about $35 million. The board elected Perelman to the posts of chairman and CEO.

Gleacher was ecstatic, for his Morgan Stanley team could earn up to $30 million for the divestitures. Drexel's $60 million in fees set a record as the highest investment banking commission in history, and I knew that my end-of-the-year bonus would make personal history, amounting to more than $1 million in cash. I treated my colleagues to a case of champagne.

Drexel rented out Le Club for a victory bash. Perelman brought along some of his new employees, Revlon's top fashion models, to add sparkle. After dinner, the evening's entertainment began with a performance by our hastily assembled team of dancing girls, the Drexelettes. Then, the bevy of Drexel advisers who had worked on the deal presented a skit. Dressed as a big-game hunter, with a toy gun and an ammo belt stretched across my torso, I played the role of Michael Bergerac on a hunting safari. My quarry was Perelman, of course, played by Don Engel, in a dark, custom-tailored Fiorentino suit and Gucci loafers, with a fat cigar hanging between his lips. In a satirical French accent, I informed Perelman that he was a low-life peasant. I offered him a bottle of Château Lafitte Rothschild, but he said he preferred vodka.

Finally we presented Perelman and the others with a bright-red sweatshirt emblazoned with white lettering. On the front it declared:

DREXEL HALL OF FAME
Ron Perelman
Pantry Pride, Inc.
has acquired
Revlon, Inc.
Drexel Burnham Lambert

Perelman read the inscription on the back, laughed, and displayed it for all to see:

"What do you hear?"
"What do you know?"
"Do you know anything?"
"What do you think this means?"
"Get me Engel!"
"Get me Levine!"
"Get me Flom!"
"Get me Drapkin!"
"Call Arthur!"

We all thought, that night, that Drexel was unstoppable.

ABOUT a week later I walked into a showroom just off First Avenue, and announced to a salesman, "I would like to buy a Ferrari Testarossa."

"There's a long wait," he replied.

"I would like the car tomorrow," I said. "And I realize that to do that, I'm going to have to pay above the list price. So let's not enter into any games here. You tell me the best deal you can make so that I can have the car tomorrow."

He quoted me a price $15,000 higher than the sticker.

"Now you're trying to be cute with me," I said. I listed the custom equipment I wanted on the car, and then I told him what the price *should* be: $125,000.

"You know what you're talking about."

"I've done my homework," I said. "Here's a check for ten thousand dollars. I want to finance half of the price. I'll pay you the balance."

Laurie and I were planning to take Adam out into the country for the weekend, so I left the office early on Friday to pick up the car. It was an awesome, fire-engine-red dream with a beige interior, and when I pulled it through the arched gateway of the entrance to my building and into the circular drive, the doormen went berserk.

"Mr. Levine," one of them said, "is that *yours?*"

"Yeah, I just bought it," I said. "Keep an eye on it, please."

"Yes, sir!"

I brought Laurie down to see my surprise. Her mouth dropped open in amazement at the incredible beauty of this machine. She said, "Dennis, I'm so happy for you. I know it's what you always wanted." She hesitated, then asked, "How much did it cost?"

When I told her she whistled. Despite all that we had been through over the years, the concept of big money still stunned her. I had to remind her that we were going to receive a bonus check soon worth more than one million dollars.

We headed over to pick up Adam from his school. Proudly I inched my new Ferrari into the midst of the line of black limos waiting for the children of New York's elite. Adam bounced out of school, saw us and squealed. He and his friends gathered around to take a closer look.

Then we were off for the weekend. I headed the Ferrari out of the city, dropped my foot heavily onto the accelerator and—convinced that my allies at Bank Leu were positioned to fend off the SEC, confident that the Revlon deal would solidify my position in the most compelling business Wall Street had ever invented—drove off into the sunset.

CHAPTER TWENTY-THREE

As THE AIRLINER MANEUVERED on its landing approach to Nassau, I pondered my peculiar set of problems.

Already the press was characterizing Revlon as, perhaps, the pivotal deal of the 80s. If Perelman's lowly Pantry Pride, aided and abetted by Drexel, financed by Milken's magic money, could prevail over one of America's entrenched corporate giants, then who among the Establishment was safe? No one, of course. The world had changed.

Reporters from the financial press dubbed me the new star of the M&A business, and, after the adrenaline faded, I found this surprisingly unsettling. I always envisioned a good investment banker as a sort of invisible man, working discreetly to accomplish his client's goals. Yet only a few days earlier, Tom Cassidy, a business reporter with Ted Turner's Cable News Network, had called me with a proposition. He wanted to profile a rising star in the M&A field. "We want to spend an entire day with you," he said. "We'll go all around Wall Street, see what your life is like."

"How could you do that?" I asked. "Everything I work on is confidential."

"Well, we would turn off the mikes whenever you're doing sensitive things. We just want to track a day in the life of a dealmaker, and you're the hottest new guy on the Street."

"I'm flattered," I said. "But no way."

In this business, I reasoned, publicity creates animosity among your peers. I did not need that. Nor did I need any kind of high profile at this moment.

Once on Bahamian soil, I hailed a taxi and headed for the all-too-familiar offices of Bank Leu, armed with additional paperwork that Wilkis and I had assembled. We had, thus far, succeeded in putting together a reasonably comprehensive portfolio to document Meier's supposed wisdom in selecting twenty-three of the twenty-eight stocks in which the SEC had expressed interest.

Meier was pleased to see the extra documents, for he knew that Pitt could not stall the SEC investigators much longer. It was already more than one month past the deadline in the SEC subpoena; Meier was going to have to give the investigators some sort of deposition, or face the wrath of his superiors in Zurich and, probably, the end of his career. I assured him that our documentation was thorough. All he had to do, I stressed, was remain cool throughout the interview and stick to his story that he was an astute trader.

Pletscher entered and asked, "How is it going?"

"The SEC is just on a fishing trip," I said. "You do not have to worry that they can prove anything." I explained that only a few of the trades were connected with my own work. "Continue with this plan, and, Bernie, you just go ahead and testify. You will not have a problem. You just have to go there relaxed and the whole thing will be over. Your own laws protect you. You cannot supply any account data to them. You can only give them generalized information. The SEC does not have a single bit of evidence to prove anything."

To my relief, Meier agreed with my assessment. He reported that Pitt's own research team in Washington had studied the trades carefully and had been unable to discern a pattern that might identify any one person or firm as the source of information.

Pletscher was more anxious than ever to see me resume stock trading, so much so that he suggested that I hire his fiancée, Sherrill Caso, a Bahamian citizen, to front for me. She could act as the nominal president of a new corporation and, on paper at least, conduct my trades.

I said no. I still thought it best not to begin trading again, although, in truth, I itched to do so.

*   *   *

WHAT I later learned shocked me. Some days after I returned home, on November 21, Meier, Pletscher, Fraysse and Coulson reviewed the situation and agreed with the grand strategy. Meier would stick to his story, and everything would be fine, but he wanted something in writing to prove that the others backed him in this decision. The others agreed. When the desired memo was ready, all four signed, reaffirming their intention to have Meier testify falsely to the SEC. Pletscher kept the original and each of the others was given a copy.

Meier now presented to Pletscher a set of documents detailing his "background research." For example, in regard to his purchases of stock in G. D. Searle for numerous managed accounts, it was a simple matter to point out the rosy prospects of the company due to the sales of its product Aspartame (NutraSweet). The report stated:

> G. D. Searle (drugs—ASPARTAME—)
> A cheap stock on fundamentals with good earnings growth potential. The latest earnings reported were outstanding (tremendous sales gains +53%, operating income +137%, Pretax profits +220%, and net income +97%).
> Everybody spoke about Aspartame and its bright future; earnings estimates were increased and the only problem the company had at the time was capacity to be able to ship enough Aspartame. New plant in Georgia to come on stream by the end of '84 to handle excess demand. Various brokers recommended this stock. Searle's Aspartame was viewed very positive, substantial earnings power and visibility of earnings were attributed to this product . . . to me this company was a most unlikely target since the family owned a large block and who wants to sell a star? It came as a great surprise to me that the founding family considered the possible sale of the company.

In other words, Meier claimed that he bought Searle stock strictly on the basis of solid fundamental research, and, by chance, reaped the benefits of a takeover deal.

Regarding the transactions in McGraw-Edison stock, Meier's report relied upon a combination of fundamental research and the good, old, nebulous Wall Street scuttlebutt:

> McGraw-Edison (electrical, energy-related products for industrial, commercial and utility use)

I heard rumors on the Street that somebody was acquiring the stock (Carl Icahn)—never loses money! . . .

I was especially encouraged by a research report of Smith Barney stating that the company was putting efforts into reducing costs and doing some restructuring programs . . .

The bid by Forstmann Little for a leveraged buyout came as a real surprise to me. I sold my position because I felt that the bid by Forstmann Little was more than adequate.

In hindsight I should have held on for another day or two to be able to participate in the higher bid by Cooper Industries.

When he had to, Meier used the ultimate argument:

Houston Natural Gas (natural gas pipeline)

A very interesting industry group with lots of rumors.

Various articles in the press about the whole group . . . All natural gas pipeline companies produce huge cash flows and have valuable assets . . .

Rumors were all over that Internorth would make a bid for Houston at $70 to $75 a share cash; Internorth completed earlier a $2.5 billion line of credit for so called "general purposes."

It was also mentioned to me that Ivan Boesky was a big buyer of the stock.

The package looked good to Pletscher, but Meier was now worried about another point concerning his own trading account, code-named Ascona. The SEC had zeroed in on twenty-eight of my deals, beginning on August 30, 1983, but, in fact, I had traded in about 100 stocks over the years. Meier wanted to eliminate from his personal account any record of his own dealings in all but the twenty-eight stocks that were under scrutiny. He asked Pletscher to make the necessary changes in the bank's computer.

Pletscher refused to tamper with the bank's master records in the mainframe computer, but he was in sympathy with Meier's objective and, in a conspiratorial move, he offered an alternate plan. He would copy Meier's account records onto a personal computer and allow Meier to play with them at will. Meier agreed and soon Pletscher produced a printout. Meier drew lines through those transactions that he wanted deleted. He first excised all trades prior to August 30, 1983, the starting point of the SEC inquiry. Then he removed any later trades that had not been identified as subjects of investigation. He also edited certain transactions that he told Pletscher were unrelated to the subject at hand, such as a $5,000 wire transfer to Delaware National Bank in Delhi, New York, on August 13, 1984, which he said involved a real estate deal. He changed this to the simple notation: "Withdrawal cash $5,000." To complete this phase of the coverup, the changes were punched into the personal computer and an expurgated version of Meier's own transactions was printed.

Meier noted that it was his intention to give this printout to the bank's American lawyers and to ask them to pass it on to the SEC. He said that he would place his original account statment into a sealed envelope and secure it in a place other than the regular files.

MEANWHILE, back home, I calculated our profits. In six years we had transformed an initial investment of $40,000 into an account balance of more than $10 million. Reich's share amounted to about $480,000 (although he had never taken a dime) and Sokolow's profits were approximately $540,000; Sokolow had taken several cash payments from the account and passed a portion of the money on to "Goldie." As I pondered, what struck me as the most amazing aspect of it all was that I had accumulated this fortune with very little time or effort. During the five years of my activities, I averaged less than two trades per month. I had spent far more of my time on the legitimate end of the business.

Perhaps it's enough, I thought. Maybe now I'll just deposit the money and let it amass interest.

FRED Joseph received a call from John Shad, Chairman of the SEC. Shad was planning a roundtable discussion to examine recent developments in the M&A field and to probe its enormous effects upon the securities markets in general. This would give the commissioners a chance to hear from the actual practitioners. The media would cover the event also. Shad asked Joseph to send one of Drexel's key men to participate, along with a dozen or so other investment bankers and attorneys. My boss, David Kay, was originally scheduled to go, but he had to back out at the last minute. "I'd like you to do it," Joseph said to me.

"I'd rather not," I demurred.

"You're our most knowledgeable M&A guy," he countered. "I'd like you to do it. You're going to be in distinguished company."

It seemed so bizarre. There I was in Washington on November 26, sitting at a large, U-shaped table with a nameplate in front of me, hobnobbing with SEC officials when, for all I knew, their colleagues were in Nassau snooping around Bank Leu. In addition to Shad, Commissioners Charles Cox and Aulana Peters were present. I shook their hands with a smile on my face and prayed that my palms were not unduly moist. Here, too, was Arthur Fleischer, Harvey Pitt's colleague. Here was Eric Gleacher, my former boss. Here was my old friend and worthy adversary in the Revlon deal, Marty Lipton of Wachtell, Lipton, who also happened to be Ilan Reich's boss.

My paranoia was acute. Every time I opened my mouth I worried that I was providing the SEC with a record of my voice. What if investigators had tapped the phone lines at Bank Leu, or had recorded my conversation with Meier at the Waldorf-Astoria, and could match the voiceprints?

The morning session evolved into a broad examination of whether the recent wave of takeovers was healthy for the economy. Lipton, champion of the Establishment, was on his soapbox as usual, orating against "junk-bond bust-ups" and "bootstrap takeovers."

I countered by pointing out that the fact that a deal was financed through high-yield securities should be of no concern to the shareholders. Cash is cash, I said. Beyond junk bonds there was always an element of traditional bank financing involved, and to zero in on one aspect of the lending seemed to me to be inappropriate and unfair.

I argued that the M&A trend was beneficial to the entire economy. "These activities create wealth," I said, not realizing the irony in my words. I argued that, at present, the free market was dictating that certain assets in corporate America were undervalued and underutilized by incumbent management. By producing more attractive incentives and more attractive capital structures for these corporations, Wall Street was managing to create significant wealth and operating efficiency in these companies, and the effects trickled down. "There is clearly a flow of funds into the hands of shareholders and institutions which by and large is reinvested in the secondary market and many times invested in consumption, thereby stimulating spending and production," I pointed out.

I agreed with the contention that a serious recession would produce business failures. Certain LBOs had proved perilously expensive and a measure of bankruptcies and restructurings was inevitable, but was not this the normal course of business, even for companies that were not the subjects of takeovers?

I conceded that an investment banker has a responsibility to assess the likelihood of a company surviving in a recession. Management's projections are always optimistic, and it is part of the job of an investment banker to discount them and place them in the context of a recessionary cycle. I always tried to stress to a corporate raider what might happen to his new company if times turned tough, and I hoped that other investment bankers did likewise, as well as the lawyers of commercial banks, insurance companies and other lenders who were involved. If a deal did not pass the recession test, I always recommended against it.

Everyone listened to my remarks with respect, for I was one of the emerging authorities.

I sat next to Shad at lunch. Over London broil, we continued the discussion.

The afternoon's program centered upon the possibility of stock manipulation in recent takeover attempts. Shad was concerned not only with indications of insider trading, but also with the suspicion that corporate raiders were banding together, quietly buying blocks of stock for one another in order to subvert the SEC's requirement of written notice of 5 percent ownership.

Lipton shared the concern, and declared, "I think it would be worth the commission's while to look at the trading in some of the more notorious takeovers of the past two years."

THREE days later, the day after Thanksgiving, I returned to Nassau to find that everyone at Bank Leu seemed confident that our defenses were strong. Pletscher again suggested that it was all right to resume trading. He was, in fact, anxious to do so.

Despite my previous resolve, I found the temptation irresistible.

Almost every day on the job there was a new tip floating around. There was money to be made.

We created a new company, called International Gold, and a new account in that name at Bank Leu. Over the next few weeks, Meier and Pletscher explained, they would redeposit the balance of my assets in increments, transferring them back from the Midu Enterprises account in Bermuda into my new International Gold account. From then on, it would be business as usual. A new managed account agreement was drafted, allowing the bank to trade in high-risk securities (takeover stocks). The account, for record-keeping purposes, now had a clean slate. Meier and Pletscher were the new signatories. My name no longer appeared on any bank records. The bankers were now very relaxed and eager to resume earning commissions.

This time, I assured them, I would be careful to assemble public domain justification for my trades before the fact.

We had to settle on a new telephone code name. Diamond Holdings was dead as a corporate identity, buried in the temporary entity of Midu Enterprises, so Mr. Diamond was no longer operative. I suggested the logical name, Mr. Gold, but Pletscher and Meier worried that someone might get my account confused with the bank's gold trading operations, so we decided to use the name of another commodity.

When I left the bank that day, Mr. Diamond was dead; Mr. Wheat had risen in his stead.

THE stock market is a mirror of the vicissitudes of life. In December 1984, a leak of poisonous gas from a Union Carbide plant in Bhopal, India, killed more than 2,000 people. Quite apart from the personal horrors, the event was a financial tragedy for the company. One year later, Union Carbide's stock was still severely depressed, leading GAF Corporation, less than one-tenth as large, to the decision that it could mount a successful takeover bid; it was another David v. Goliath deal. Sam Heyman, the CEO of GAF, hired Kidder Peabody to fashion the deal and Kidder put its best man, Marty Siegel, to the task. Siegel was well known on the Street for his successful role in helping Martin Marietta fend off the takeover bid of the Bendix Corporation back in 1982.

It had started when Bendix commenced a tender offer for the stock of Martin Marietta. Siegel, along with Marty Lipton, orchestrated Martin Marietta's defense, which was to turn the tables and issue a counter tender offer for Bendix' stock, a tactic quickly dubbed the "Pac-Man defense." The intent was for the prey to gobble up the would-be acquirer. The battle raged, and while it was tied up in court by means of suits and countersuits, United Technologies slipped in with a proposal to buy a controlling interest in Bendix and sell some of the assets to Martin Marietta. When those negotiations broke down, a new white knight appeared in the form of Allied Corporation. Allied arranged to buy a controlling interest in Bendix for $1.9 billion and swap with Martin Marietta the stock that each had already bought in the other. When the dust had cleared, the original target, Martin Marietta, survived as a separate, thriving entity, and Siegel became known as the first investment banker to successfully employ the Pac-Man defense.

He was a young-looking, handsome man with jet-black hair, a trim athletic build, and genuine star quality. He was smooth and well respected, principally for his ability to guard a company against a takeover, and there was one particularly interesting fact about him: He lived in a beautiful Manhattan co-op and also maintained a home on the Connecticut shore. Heyman and Siegel were neighbors in Connecticut, and occasionally commuted to Manhattan together, via helicopter. Siegel's country residence was referred to by some as "the House that Boesky Built." This speculation was based upon the fact that Boesky had taken a major ownership position—large enough to file a Schedule 13D—on many deals that Siegel handled for Kidder.

Now Siegel was on offense, hoping to capture a stricken chemical company, but he needed help in raising the money. Heyman came to Drexel to arrange $3.5 billion in financing and Milken prepared a "highly confident" letter, covering the largest amount of money to date.

It was a measure of the vicissitudes in my own life that I succumbed to this latest temptation. I had a whopping eight-figure account stashed in the Bahamas. I had a legitimate income nearing $2 million a year. I had a Park Avenue co-op, a BMW and a Ferrari Testarossa. And I had the SEC on my tail. Yet I could not pass up this deal. On December 3, I called Bank Leu and instructed Pletscher to buy 100,000 shares of Union Carbide. "It will not draw any attention to the account," I said. "There is enough public information that could lead a portfolio manager to a decision to buy Union Carbide."

"I'll do it," he said.

I checked back later in the day for a report. On my behalf, Pletscher had bought the stock at a cost of $6.3 million. What he did not tell me was that—even in the midst of his own set of problems created by his piggybacking activities—he had also bought 300 shares for his own account.

PITT visited the Bahamas the very next day to review the redacted records and to go over the testimony that Meier would give in his deposition. Still banned from the bank's offices, he met with Pletscher and Meier in a hotel room.

Pitt studied the explanations Meier had prepared to justify his trading and announced that they were acceptable. He also studied Meier's computer printout of his account transactions through his Anscona entity. Meier did not reveal his trading activities through his other, secret account.

Meier's position was that he would present the SEC with his Anscona records and also with the bank's omnibus trading records, but he would not break down the numbers to reveal activity in individual accounts.

Pletscher reiterated that it would violate Bahamian law to disclose the names on any of those private accounts or any details concerning them.

On the following day Bank Leu promptly violated that law by providing Pitt with the actual statements of approximately twenty-five managed accounts. Pitt made a rough total of the accounts, compared it to the omnibus records, and realized that a large gap remained. Rather quickly, he called the bankers' bluff.

Where, Pitt asked, were the missing records? Neither Pletscher nor Meier nor Coulson knew how to respond. The only records missing were mine. One of the bankers said, "There are certain sensitive accounts that we are unable to tell you about, without permission from the home office."

This was, perhaps, Pitt's first real indication that the trading activity had emanated from a single, well-informed source.

Back at their office, Pletscher and Coulson discussed this impasse and decided to call Zurich for advice. Coulson was informed by his superiors in Zurich that Hans-Peter Schaad, the bank's chief counsel, was scheduled to arrive on Sunday, December 8, to deal with bank business, and to discuss the situation with them.

Pitt returned to Washington to think things over. Tense days passed for the bankers.

SOKOLOW called me for a meeting. At our rendezvous he announced, "RCA is in merger discussions. Buy the stock. Big numbers."

Again I called Bank Leu and plunged, tying up nearly all of my remaining capital.

ON the eighth, Schaad met with Pletscher, Meier and Coulson in a room at the Royal Bahamian Hotel. Although the team from Nassau had repeatedly contacted Zurich for guidance, although the auditors were apprised of the situation and ordered home by a circuitous route, and although Schaad himself had originally objected to hiring the law firm of Fried, Frank instead of the bank's traditional U.S. counsel, Schaad played dumb at this meeting, as though he was hearing the story for the first time.

ON Monday morning, December 9, I learned that MidCon Corporation, a natural gas pipeline company, was the potential takeover target of a Wagner Brown partnership. I had relatively little money to invest; nevertheless, I called Bank Leu and put the remainder of my cash into MidCon stock. *I simply could not stop.*

Meier took the order happily; we both assumed that we were back to a posture of business as usual. At the time, neither of us knew that our carefully crafted plan was about to unravel.

Even as Meier placed the stock purchase orders, Pitt, having returned to the Bahamas, met with Schaad. The latter now confirmed what Pitt suspected, declaring that one account was responsible for the majority of the suspicious trading. Schaad asked for an opinion.

Pitt insisted that Bank Leu immediately stop trading in the account, and Schaad apparently agreed. Pitt also suggested that the assets of the account be frozen.

Pitt summoned Pletscher and Meier, questioning them into the night.

The bankers flinched, and in one instant everything fell apart. They disclosed that the customer was an investment banker in the New York office of Drexel Burnham Lambert. They referred to me as "Mister X."

Pitt considered the alternatives. He could still wage an all-out battle in the interests of the bank secrecy laws. Alternately, the bank could agree to identify "Mister X" to the SEC in return for a pledge of immunity from prosecution for the bank and its employees. He favored this latter, settlement strategy, although it was a very early stage in the course of the investigation, for it would shift the emphasis from the bank to its client, despite the fact that it constituted a flagrant and willful violation of both law and tradition. No wonder Pitt had done so well at the SEC.

ON the following day MidCon, by sheer coincidence, announced an increased dividend, news that drives up a stock's price as surely as merger rumors. I checked the Quotron in my office and calculated that I would earn more than $60,000 on the small, quick transaction, and I hustled out to a pay phone tucked away behind the bar of Delmonico's restaurant and called Meier.

I did not know it, of course, but he must have been exhausted from a long night of discussions with Pitt, and from his own turmoil.

Before I could issue the sell order, Meier moaned, "It's no good."

"What's no good?" I asked quickly.

"It's no good, it's no good," he said. "They know."

"They know?" I replied. "Do they know my identity?"

Meier would not, or could not, talk further.

I felt a sharp pain in my chest, as if a dagger had pierced my heart. I knew with certainty that someone else was in Meier's office in Nassau, listening to this conversation, perhaps recording it. My body went limp.

"Sell everything," I commanded. "Now! I'm coming down."

CHAPTER TWENTY-FOUR

"WE'VE GOT A MAJOR PROBLEM," I said to Wilkis over the phone. "We have to meet."

We linked up at the corner of Broad and Pearl streets, in front of Goldman Sachs, and we walked through the cold New York afternoon, talking. I detailed the phone call.

"You've got to get your ass down there," he advised. "Find out what's going on." He added, "If they get you, they're going to get me."

"That is absolutely not true," I vowed. "That is not going to happen."

I could not possibly get away until the weekend. Numerous times over the next several days I tried to call Meier back, to try to catch him at a moment when he could speak more freely. These were person-to-person calls, and when the operator asked for Meier, whoever answered the phone in the Bahamas simply said that he was not in the office. In desperation I tried his apartment number at the posh Lyford Cay Club and was told that the phone was disconnected. I called every hotel in Nassau, but none had a Bernhard Meier registered.

Nevertheless, Meier was still in town, still torn among his options. On the night of Friday the thirteenth, while driving out to dinner at the Lyford Cay Club, Pitt played a game with Meier. He knew that "Mister X" was in a high position at Drexel, and he tossed out various names, asking Meier, "Is it . . . ? Is it . . . ?" Finally, he asked, "Is it Dennis Levine?"

Meier responded quietly, "Yes."

Pitt surely remembered me from the dinner party at Lutece, two months earlier.

ON Saturday, December 14, I arrived at the Bank Leu offices with the documentation for the final five suspected stock trades, to discover that Meier was gone, his desk cleaned out. I knew that he had been due for rotation back to Zurich, but he had obviously departed in haste.

Pletscher and Coulson sat down with me in a conference room. They reported that I had sustained a net loss of about $50,000 by liquidating my final three stock holdings. I could have made a bundle on the RCA stock, and many others had; in the four days prior to the announcement of RCA's purchase by General Electric, the stock jumped in price by 33 percent, indicating that there was a significant number of other investors out there doing exactly what I was doing. The MidCon stock had exhibited a similar pattern of insider trading activity.

Pletscher and Coulson both spoke guardedly, and throughout the frustrating meeting, both scribbled notes on yellow legal pads. Coulson said, "Everything is still under control, but we have decided to delay Bernie's testimony to the SEC investigators. It would give us some serious exposure right now. He has taken a vacation. He is skiing with his wife, I believe."

"Uh-huh," I muttered skeptically. They waited for me to say something more. I tried to maintain my composure, but my mind raced with speculative scenarios. I wanted to scream, "You're full of shit!" But I asked politely, "Tell me what's going on."

Pletscher explained that they had turned over certain trading records to counsel and were considering authorizing him to submit them to the SEC. He held up a hand to stop me from jumping out of my chair. "Our lawyers will, uh, redact them."

This was a strange statement to hear from a banker to whom English was a second language. I knew, from my long association with teams of lawyers, that "to redact" means to edit something from a legal perspective. I also *knew* that the word must have been defined for Pletscher very recently. I demanded that they get the documents back from their U.S. lawyers immediately and reminded them that this action was a breach of Bahamian law. "You have very good lawyers,"

I pointed out. "But you have engaged these lawyers to prevent the SEC from obtaining information. You should control your lawyers and not let them control you." I suggested the obvious: that Bahamian counsel, not American attorneys, should be orchestrating this whole affair. I reminded them forcefully, as I had many times in the past, that they could not provide any information concerning my accounts. Even, I added, if it was "redacted."

"Your name will not appear on the documents," Coulson assured me.

At one point in the conversation, when Coulson and Pletscher excused themselves briefly, I checked under the table and behind a picture frame, searching for a microphone.

"THERE is something screwy going on here," I reported to Wilkis. "The conversation was all very controlled. They were taking notes. They told me that Meier had gone on a sudden, extended vacation. It was all very 'un-Swiss-like.' "

Wilkis considered this and declared, "The first thing you've got to do is get your money out of that bank. Why don't you just transfer it to my account?"

"Are you out of your mind?" I shrieked. "That would be a direct link between you and me."

"Yeah," he agreed. "Well, why don't you set up an account in the Caymans, like I have? I'll refer you to my lawyer and he'll take care of you."

That seemed plausible.

ON Tuesday, December 17, Pitt visited SEC headquarters in Washington and met with Gary Lynch, the SEC's enforcement chief. Several other staffers attended. At this point the SEC had no idea that the investigation might lead them to anything or anyone of significance. They were, indeed, on a fishing expedition keyed by the relatively small trades of Campbell and his Venezuelan friends. They knew they were up against the Bahamian secrecy laws, which they had never been able to penetrate before. Their only viable strategy was to seek information and see what happened. Lynch and his staff must have been ecstatic to realize that Pitt had come to cut a deal.

Pitt wanted an "off-the-record" conversation, so that what he said could never be attributed to him or his clients. There was good reason for this request, for in attempting to appease the SEC, Pitt had to violate Bahamian law. Once his listeners agreed to go off-the-record, Pitt then offered to facilitate the SEC's efforts to nab the bank's customer in exchange for immunity for the bank.

This must have been a sweet shock to Lynch's ears. Never before had the SEC been presented with such an attractive proposal to circumvent a foreign government's bank secrecy laws.

Pitt sweetened the pot, adding that the individual in question is "a status player on Wall Street." He hinted that the man was a "big fish," and, as a result, SEC investigators dubbed their prey "Moby Dick."

The bank's lawyer then initiated a similar discussion with the U.S. Attorney's Office in Manhattan, concerning immunity for possible criminal charges against Meier, Pletscher & Company.

It was about this time that Pitt had a sudden flash of doubt. What if the man whom Meier had known as Dennis Levine and, in turn, Mr. Diamond and Mr. Wheat, was *not* the Dennis Levine whom he had met at Lutece? What if "Mister X" or "Moby Dick" had been shrewd enough to use phony identification the very first time he visited the bank? What if he was a mere flunky who, perhaps, worked for the real Dennis Levine? Pitt had to find out before he proceeded further. He obtained a copy of Lehman Brothers' 1983 annual report and hired a photographer to make several copies of my picture. Then he placed a photo of me among a sampling of other snapshots, hopped a plane for Nassau, showed the photos to several Bank Leu employees and asked them to identify Mr. Diamond. To his relief, they all pointed to my image.

MEIER complained to his co-workers, "You have said you will follow through with this plan, and now you want to turn back and go in the opposite direction." Obviously he felt hung out to dry.

Meier now bolted. He determined not to be bullied into this new plan to violate the banking laws; it went against everything in which he believed. He decided to hire his own lawyer and go it alone.

*   *   *

Soon thereafter we concluded the necessary details to announce GAF's attempt to take over Union Carbide. We finished late one night in Arthur Liman's office. Sam Heyman, the CEO of GAF was there, along with Marty Siegel, his adviser from Kidder Peabody.

With the deal set, our Drexel team piled into cars and headed for the Corporate Finance Department Christmas party, held at the Palladium, an exclusive New York night spot. Others were there ahead of us, anticipating the celebration, but it looked more like a wake. Despite the booming disco music, dozens of Drexel associates, men in gray flannel suits and women in conservative dress, stood around the bar, quietly talking business. I was a jumble of emotions. I needed desperately to get my mind off of the developing drama in the Bahamas, and I tried to cultivate a festive spirit. After all, I had just helped put together yet another deal that would enhance my reputation. On an impulse I shouted, "Hey, let's get going here. It's a party!" I paired up some of the men and women and pushed them out toward the dance floor. "Liven it up," I ordered.

That night, we closed the Palladium in the wee hours. By the time I headed for home, I had managed to drown some of my fears.

As it turned out, our victory party was premature. Union Carbide's board authorized a financial restructuring, swapping half of its equity for a package of securities with a value higher than we were prepared to pay. GAF could not compete with the offer, and the acquisition attempt died. It was the first successful use of the financial restructuring defense.

But if we lost on the deal, we gained a major star. Working closely with Drexel made Marty Siegel a believer. He reopened negotiations with Fred Joseph, which had apparently been going on quietly for some time, and now seemed eager to join Wall Street's superstar firm.

On December 26 Pitt met again with Lynch's SEC team to continue negotiations. The sticking point was whether or not Bank Leu would merely have to turn over its account records, with the name of the investor redacted, or whether it would be forced to reveal my name—although either scenario would still constitute a Bahamian crime.

Pitt informed Lynch that copies of the redacted documents were being prepared for delivery to the SEC.

* * *

I knew nothing of the secret negotiations; nevertheless, I could feel the investigators getting closer.

The critical task was to remove my money from the Bahamas and deposit it in the Cayman Islands. If I managed to get it out of the hands of the Bahamian bankers, whom I now regarded with distrust, then, no matter what happened to me, the money would be safe. I could let it sit in the Caymans until I was ready to funnel it into some legitimate venture, sometime in the now uncertain future. I found a pay phone and placed a collect call to Nassau, from Mr. Wheat, to Mr. Coulson.

"Mr. Coulson is not in," a receptionist's voice informed the operator.

"I'll speak with Mr. Pletscher," I said.

"Mr. Pletscher is not in," the receptionist said.

THROUGHOUT this time, Drexel was involved in a variety of legal battles that threatened to undermine our business.

A bill was introduced into the U.S. Senate to deal with alleged abuses in the takeover industry. At Drexel, we read it with care. It appeared to be innocuous as far as we were concerned. It waffled on the junk-bond issue, suggesting that any legislative action be deferred until further study was conducted.

But now a new threat loomed, similar to the issue Revlon had raised in court. The governors of the Federal Reserve Board proposed that would-be acquirers be subject to the same margin requirements that govern the normal purchase of common stock, specifically, that they be allowed to use the target's assets to finance no more than 50 percent of the cost of an acquisition. If the proposal was accepted, it would bring the death of the LBO. It could spell an end to the corporate raider and, by extension, Drexel. Asked to comment on the idea, Fred Joseph declared, "As drafted, the rule could shut us down."

The Reagan Administration mounted a major public relations counterattack. Arguments against the proposal came from the Justice Department, the Treasury Department and the Office of Management and Budget. But we all knew that Fed Chairman Paul Volcker marched to the beat of his own drummer, and we worried about the outcome.

Milken asked for a personal audience with Volcker, but was rebuffed.

On January 8 the Federal Reserve Board, despite the active and forceful objections of the Reagan Administration (and the opposition of the two Reagan-appointed members of the board), formally adopted its new rule limiting takeover financing to 50 percent of the purchase price, but by now the rule was considerably weakened. The Fed decreed that it would apply only in instances where the potential acquirer was a shell company with no demonstrable assets. That was a provision that any good takeover attorney could get around.

So it was to be business as usual.

ONCE more, on January 16, Pitt met with the investigative team, including representatives from both the SEC and the U.S. Attorney's Office. This time, in return for immunity for his clients, Pitt offered the bank's full and speedy cooperation, as well as testimony that would not actually reveal "Moby Dick's" name but would probably lead the SEC to identify him.

The U.S. Attorney held his ground, declaring that he would grant immunity to Bank Leu and its employees only if they disclosed "Moby Dick's" name.

Pitt pledged that the bank would try to get the necessary permission from the Bahamian government, but he could not guarantee results.

Another hitch was the reluctance of Bernhard Meier, now back home in Switzerland, to testify against me.

That same day I spoke to Coulson by phone, once more cautioning the bank against providing any information to the investigators without my permission. When I suggested that Coulson might wish to discuss the issue with my Bahamian lawyer, Hartis Pinder of McKinny Bancroft & Hughes, he laughed at me.

But eleven days later, when I again spoke to Coulson by phone, he reassured me that Meier was proceeding with the "managed accounts" story. The bank's Bahamian lawyers, he said, were trying to decide on the best way to approach the Bahamian government to allow even this breach of law.

I stood at the desk in the bank lobby, wondering what to do. I looked once more at the check in my hand. It was my annual bonus from

Drexel, and it amounted to more than $1 million—after taxes. By now I was supposed to be sophisticated in the face of such numbers. I juggled billions of dollars for my clients. I juggled millions in the Bahamas. But this money was, somehow, more *real*. Do you just deposit a million-dollar check in your account, as if it was a normal event?

I filled out a deposit slip, endorsed the back of the check and stood in line like everyone else. When it was my turn, I approached the teller's window and slid the deposit toward her.

She grasped it with a routine, somewhat bored air. Then her eyes caught sight of the check and she did a double take. "Mr. Levine," she squealed, "you're rich!"

Yes, I thought. Yes, I am. This was the quantification of my legitimate success. No more trading, Dennis, I said to myself. No more.

IN 1985 the M&A business, as a whole, pulled off deals totaling a record $144 billion. Drexel's revenues amounted to $2.5 billion and its pre-tax profits were about $600 million. Drexel had now risen from the obscurity of the 70s to become a close second, to Salomon Brothers, in the investment banking field. Everyone at Drexel was determined to catch the front-runner during this new year, and we had a fresh weapon.

In early February, Marty Siegel came on board with a guaranteed annual salary of about $3 million a year for three years, plus bonuses and the chance to participate in Milken's network of investment partnerships. He moved into the office adjacent to mine and assumed management responsibilities for our M&A Department, sharing the duties with David Kay and Leon Black. He held the potential for adding a much-needed balance to our office for, unlike me, he had made his reputation as a defender of takeover targets. He had championed Marty Lipton's poison pill defense and had devised the Pac-Man defense. Together, we would make a formidable team, able to work either side of any potential deal.

Siegel was as enthusiastic as he could be, well aware that in January alone, Drexel had made more money than his old firm, Kidder, had earned during the entire previous year. Almost immediately he left for the West Coast to spend several days under Milken's tutelage. When he returned he set about contacting his old clients, especially those among the blue-chip firms. His goal was to sign them up for Drexel on huge retainers, guaranteeing that we would be ready to defend them in the event of a takeover attempt.

Siegel was retained by Lear Siegler because the Belzberg brothers, longtime Milken clients, were accumulating its stock. Acting as an intermediary, Drexel worked out a greenmail settlement that netted the Canadian raiders more than $7 million. At the very same time, Drexel represented the Belzberg brothers in their pursuit of Ashland Oil, which resulted in a greenmail payment reported to be in excess of $15 million. We were walking on both sides of the Street now, and everything was more complex and somewhat confusing.

I was intensely curious about the rumors that Siegel had a relationship with Boesky. At the first opportunity, I asked "Ivan, what is your relationship with Marty Siegel?"

"Marty is a very capable guy," Boesky replied, "somebody I talk to frequently, somebody I view as a very competent professional." He paused, then added, "Somebody not to be trusted."

CHAPTER TWENTY-FIVE

AT DREXEL it was business as usual, and I found it difficult to concentrate on any one of the incredible themes that ran through my life.

Fred Joseph assigned me a major role at the upcoming, 1986 version of Drexel's Bond Conference. I was now Drexel's major M&A spokesman, and I was to talk about the highlights of the Revlon deal and paint a glowing picture of future M&A possibilities.

As we laid plans for the Conference, Siegel and I double-teamed Joseph on a touchy subject: the perennial presence of female companions at the Bungalow 8 party. This was a long-standing Drexel tradition and an open secret that, Siegel and I both argued, had run its course. Joseph did not like to acknowledge its reality; both he and Milken always found convenient reasons for absenting themselves during the height of the Bungalow 8 festivities.

"It's not consistent with the image we're shooting for," I reasoned. "If we want to be truly respected, we've got to clean up our act."

Siegel added his agreement.

Clearly, Joseph would have preferred to dodge the issue. He knew, as well as we did, that certain of Drexel's clients would arrive at Bungalow 8 "rarin' to go." But he acknowledged the wisdom of our reasoning and promised to see what he could do.

In the meantime, I busied myself in early discussions with Perelman concerning another megadeal. I was also doing some developmental work for Gulf + Western as well as a general search for Warner Communications, seeking to identify takeover targets. Then there was a sweet, comparatively small, $262 million LBO for the Connecticut-based diversified company, Hart Industries, and a deal for Contel, a mid-Atlantic telecommunications firm. We worked with Ted Turner to finance his $1.6 billion acquisition of Metro-Goldwyn-Mayer from financier Kirk Kerkorian.

A half-dozen other transactions floated in and out of the picture. First City Financial, the Canadian holding company controlled by the Belzberg brothers, had its eyes on Dayco, an Ohio firm that manufactured automobile components. Along with Sam Belzberg, I met with Dayco's investment bankers, Salomon Brothers, to review the numbers. I kept my own counsel during the meeting, but afterward I said to Belzberg, "They're trying like hell to sell the business to anyone foolish enough to overbid." Back at the office, we took another long, hard look at the numbers. Belzberg agreed with me that the values just weren't there to justify Dayco's asking price.

Milken called me one day to discuss the Haft family of Washington, D.C. The father, Herbert, was known for his chain of discount Dart Drug Stores. A few years earlier he had sold Dart to its employees in a heavily leveraged deal that was proving too costly for the new employee-owners, but that was no longer his concern. The son, Robert, had developed the popular chain of Crown Bookstores, which were providing stiff competition for the Walden and B. Dalton chains.

In the past couple of years the Hafts had been on the prowl for acquisitions. They had made runs on the stocks of several companies and then backed off, garnering charges that they were simply out after greenmail. They were itching to consummate a deal, and Milken told me that one of his senior traders, prompted by a Drexel research report, had pitched the conglomerate of Kraft Foods, Inc., to them. The Hafts had already purchased a block of Kraft shares and now wanted to talk about a multi-billion-dollar takeover attempt.

The Hafts were out in Beverly Hills, Milken said, and he wanted me to hop a plane to discuss the deal face to face.

My immediate reaction was concern. Here was a throwback example of Drexel's "Ready, Fire, Aim" mentality. Why had Milken not contacted me or one of the other M&A specialists first, to research the deal before anybody sank any money into it?

Within hours one of my associates and I were on a jetliner headed for California, and we studied as we cruised. In fact, although the numbers were fresh to me, I already had a good handle on the target company. Kraft was a Lehman Brothers client and I had enjoyed working with some of the company's principals in the past. Kraft's CEO was a good leader, a strong personality who I knew would resist any attack. What's more, the current numbers confirmed my suspicion that Kraft was a healthy company with plenty of resources to fight off a hostile, highly leveraged offer.

In the Drexel conference room in Beverly Hills, we sat down with the Hafts, along with Milken and several of his team members. As usual, the Drexel food service department had provided an array of refreshments, coffee, tea and elegant canapés. During the early portion of the conversation, I munched on a snack to help keep my own mouth busy for a time as the others spoke their minds. Everyone around me was gung-ho and I knew that I had to give them opportunity to vent their enthusiasm. Milken's chief trading assistant, Jim Dahl, was a particularly loose cannon. I could see the wheels spinning in his mind, labeled: Sell, sell, sell. Commissions. Distribute. Sell.

Finally, when it was my turn to speak, I said, "This has been an interesting presentation. I've heard all the reasons why we should go ahead with a tender offer. I've heard all about how good the numbers look on paper. But what I haven't heard are the strategic considerations."

I sketched a personality profile of Kraft's management and made my case that the target would mount a fierce defense that would, rather easily, I thought, thwart an acquisition by just about any independent raider. Then I played my trump card. "What's going to happen," I prophesied, "is that you're going to put Kraft into play and lose out to a white knight, a major corporate acquirer such as RJR or Philip Morris—any of a number of well-capitalized players who could bail out Kraft."

The Hafts were visibly concerned with this prognostication, and I followed up by asking them if they knew who would head Kraft's defense. They shook their heads, no.

"Marty Lipton," I said. "Kraft was a client of ours when I was with Lehman Brothers. They had Marty on a retainer. So if you go after Kraft, you go after the chief takeover defender in America, the man who invented the poison pill. He's not only a genius in working out the financial defense, but he'll skewer you in the press."

Herbert Haft turned to Milken and said, "Well, Michael, I can clearly see that not everybody here at Drexel is a yes-man."

My arguments hit the father and son at the gut level. They were sensitive to the criticisms they had received after initiating numerous unsuccessful runs. They did not relish the idea of another P.R. debacle. They decided to sleep on the deal and ultimately abandoned it.

After the Hafts left, Milken bustled about cleaning up the conference room. He cupped a napkin in his hand and used another napkin to scrape crumbs off the table. I could not quite believe my eyes. Michael, I thought, you don't have to clean up. You have other people to do that.

But that was Milken, I realized. He was determined to clean up the mess. Everything in his world had to conform to his personal sense of order.

EARLY in March a Drexel compliance officer called and asked, "Hey, Dennis, do you remember that request I gave you several months ago?"

"Sure," I replied.

"Well, we got another one, on the same investigation."

"I'll come take a look," I said.

This expanded list contained about forty stocks, and I realized to my dismay that I had traded every one of them through my Bank Leu account! The cat, I knew, was out of the bag. Hoping that I hid my alarm sufficiently, I mumbled something about checking them out. Then I headed for the nearest pay phone and called Pletscher.

He assured me that everything was quiet and under control.

I told him that I was coming down on Friday, March 7.

Pletscher wrote a memo to preserve his record of the call. In it, he stated that he had lied to me and did not like doing so.

I showed Coulson and Pletscher the updated list of stocks from the SEC and cautioned them to push for an early end to the probe. All they had to do, I contended, was have Meier present his report based on the documentation we had compiled. "Is the bank still going along with the same strategy?" I asked.

Pletscher and Coulson told me that their plans had not changed.

I suggested that they arrange through counsel to have Meier give his deposition soon, so that we could bring an end to this entire episode.

WHAT I did not know at the time was that quiet negotiations between the bankers and the SEC had dragged through the winter months.

By the end of January, Bank Leu auditors had compiled a complete record of my transactions. These were collated into an eight-page document that listed the name of every stock that I bought, the amount of the purchase and subsequent sale, and the amount of profit or loss. The trades involved a total of 114 different transactions, from Dart Industries on June 5, 1980, to MidCon Corporation on December 9, 1985. The scorecard revealed seventy-one winning trades, generating a gross profit of $13,610,897.49 and forty-three losers cost me $2,052,300.52. It computed to a net profit of $11,558,596.97. The vast majority of that money was still on deposit at Bank Leu.

Now, apprised by Pletscher and Coulson that I appeared to be growing apprehensive, Pitt spoke to Lynch and both agreed to do their best to expedite the negotiations.

On March 19, Pitt and the SEC and Justice Department attorneys finally reached an accord. The U.S. lawyers pledged that Bank Leu would not be sued, nor would they seek to freeze any of its assets. No further subpoenas would be served and the bank's officers would receive immunity from prosecution if they produced, by April 7, the complete records associated with "Moby Dick's" trading activities. The documents would be redacted so as not to reveal the trader's identity. It was the first time in history that a Swiss or Bahamian bank had agreed to such a clear and willful violation of secrecy laws in order to protect itself.

Still, beyond the account records, the government felt that it needed a star witness. The logical choice was Meier, who had personally supervised my trading, but he was still reluctant. That snag was handled by the big boys in Zurich. For weeks Bank Leu's chief counsel, Hans-Peter Schaad, pounded away at Meier, to no avail, and Schaad finally settled upon a second choice. He told Pletscher that if he testified against me, his job would be secure—and the opposite course was obvious. Nervously Pletscher agreed to be a witness. From that moment on,

Pletscher was forbidden to speak with Meier, for fear that he would be dissuaded.

One week after the records were turned over, Pletscher would be required to give sworn testimony to SEC lawyers and would be under a stipulation to answer all questions truthfully, except those that would identify "Moby Dick." The only banker excluded from the immunity was Meier, who now achieved the status of a potential co-defendant. Bank Leu agreed to pay all of its piggybacking profits to the U.S. government, which, in return, pledged not to seek the treble damages that it could have demanded. Finally, the agreement specified that Bank Leu would have to reveal the identity of "Mister X"/"Moby Dick"— but none of the signatories of the other suspicious accounts—if a U.S. court ordered it to do so, or if it received permission from Bahamian authorities.

A rider attached to the agreement disclosed that the target of the probe was "an American customer who is presently a managing director of a major investment banking firm located in the United States. It is believed that the customer resides and works in the Southern District of New York." This was a reference to the jurisdiction of U.S. Attorney Rudolph Giuliani.

A key portion of the agreement called for Bank Leu to remain anonymous, so as to protect its reputation and avoid a rush of withdrawals from other, concerned customers. The SEC agreed, in any public document, to refer simply to a Bahamian "financial institution." In assuming that his client bank could prevent its name from disclosure, Pitt, in my opinion, revealed an enormous streak of naïveté.

THE phone rang, rousing both Laurie and me from sleep. As Laurie groped for the receiver, I opened one eye and checked the digital clock. It was six-thirty in the morning. Probably Ivan calling, I thought.

Laurie, holding one hand over the mouthpiece of the phone, whispered, "It's Michael."

Milken? At six-thirty in the morning? It's three-thirty in California. My God, I wondered, does the man ever sleep? It was only as I took the phone and said hello that I remembered that it was Saturday. Give me a break, I thought, but I said, "Good morning, Michael."

He asked how my family was, and I told him they were fine. Then he said, "We're about to get involved in Northwest Airlines' merger with Republic Airlines. We're going to represent Republic and I want you to handle it."

It was an $885 million transaction, the sort of routine business that Milken could relegate to three-thirty on a Saturday morning. During the week, he had much more to consider.

IT had begun about a year before I joined Drexel, about a year before I met Milken, about a year before I began to work with Boesky, and it came to a head on Friday, March 21. I would learn about it only in retrospect.

Government prosecutors would ultimately contend that Boesky and Milken had earlier conspired to violate securities laws in connection with transactions in the stocks of McGregor and Columbia Savings and Loan Association, but there is no question that the activities heated up early in 1984, when Victor Posner retained Drexel to arrange financing for his proposed acquisition of Fischbach. As Milken was working on the deal, he chanced to speak on the telephone with Boesky. In the scheme of things, Boesky was not an important Drexel client, but he held the potential to be. And Milken, perhaps seeking to ingratiate himself with the powerful arb or perhaps merely speaking injudiciously, suggested that Boesky buy a position in Fischbach. As I well knew, this is the sort of comment to which Boesky attends. But he was dubious of the prospect of this particular venture. The exact words of the conversation are lost to memory, but Milken indicated that Boesky would not lose money on the transaction. Another Drexel employee indicated later that he had virtually guaranteed Boesky a profit. Whether or not this was typical salesman's rhetoric, Boesky took it as assurance that Drexel would cover any losses. Boesky purchased blocks of stock in Fischbach until his holdings were just under 10 percent. Two memos in Boesky's files indicated that Milken's advice—or direction— was to hold the stock. On April 26 and July 9, Boesky purchased another 145,000-share block directly from Drexel.

Milken had every reason to believe in the prospects of the investment but, as luck would have it, Posner's takeover attempt was stalled in the courtroom, and Fischbach's stock dropped from more than $36 per share to about $25 per share. Boesky suffered heavy losses, which he expected Drexel to cover. Milken, of course, could not risk writing Boesky a check; rather, he attempted to steer Boesky into other, lucrative investments. The first was MCA, the second was Occidental Petroleum. Unfortunately the market again turned sour on both companies, and as Boesky's losses mounted, so did his hold over Milken. More trades followed: Carter Hawley Hale, Associated Dry Goods, Dayton Hudson, Federated, Macy's, May Department Stores and others.

On November 28, 1984, Boesky sent Milken a letter, which stated:

Dear Mike:

Enclosed you will find a self-explanatory list of information through and including November 27, 1984.

I think that it will be appropriate to resolve all of the enclosed . . .

Included with the letter were spread sheets showing losses of more than $8 million on the Fischbach trades and $96,600 on the MCA trades. In all, Boesky listed a dozen different securities transactions with losses amounting to more than $15 million. He, quite obviously, failed to include profitable trades on the spread sheets. The timing was interesting, for this was when Boesky was negotiating a restructuring deal with Drexel. He believed that the terms were too restrictive, and his spread sheets were an obvious message to Milken: You owe me.

For nearly a year, Boesky complained about the money that he claimed Drexel owed him as a result of the transactions. Early in 1985 Milken asked an employee to calculate the amount of the losses, which appeared to be far less than Boesky claimed. Nevertheless, Milken arranged for certain additional securities trades between Drexel and Boesky, which resulted in profits to the arb. On February 27, 1985, Boesky sold his Fischbach position substantially higher than the current market price.

Despite this, Boesky's accountant continued to call Drexel's Beverly Hills office to relay claims of losses resulting from Drexel-recommended investments. Boesky updated his spread sheet, deleting half of the claims but still clinging to six of them. One of the Drexel associates began to keep his own scorecard of the investments and Milken told him to make sure that he included those trades that were profitable to Boesky. Not surprisingly, the two sides encountered difficulty in reconciling their lists, and the rarely profane Milken, obviously growing tired of Boesky's incessant claims, referred to the claims and counterclaims as "a bunch of bullshit."

By March 21, 1986, Boesky and Milken were ready to finalize the details of their long-delayed restructuring deal, and they needed to clean the slate, to make a fresh start. They probably haggled over the price, but in the end, Boesky, obviously desperate to close the deal, wrote out a $5.3 million check for what was described as "consulting services," but what was more likely compensation covering a variety of proper and/or improper activities.

I was back in Nassau on March 24, to meet with Hartis Pinder, my Bahamian lawyer. I said, "Hypothetically, if I was trading securities through my Bahamian account and the SEC wanted to find out who was behind that trading, could I have a problem?"

"Absolutely not," he assured. "It would be a severe criminal violation of our laws. Don't concern yourself with that. It would undermine the workings of our entire industry."

"Will you put that in writing?"

"Sure."

He wrote a five-page opinion letter to Bank Leu entitled "Bank Secrecy Laws Bahamas" and detailed our position succinctly:

> It is understood that the Bank has no presence in the U.S.A. and there is therefore no basis on which a United States federal regulatory agency can even claim jurisdiction over the Bahamian bank.
>
> The English Common Law, which applies in the Bahamas, imports a very strict obligation of confidence in the relationship of a banker and his customer . . . it is an implied term of the contract between a banker and his customer that the banker will not divulge to third parties either the state of a customer's account or any of his transactions with the bank or any information relating to the customer acquired through the keeping of his account . . .
>
> Breach of any of the secrecy obligations would in addition to the criminal penalties . . . leave the banker open to a claim for an injunction and/or damages. There is, in our view, little doubt that a customer would be able to obtain an injunction to restrain the production of information regarding his affairs to an agency outside the jurisdiction of the Bahamas.

In the circumstances we must stress that the directors and other officers of the Bahamian bank owe a legal duty solely towards the Bahamian
bank and that any pressure from an associated Company or a regulatory
agency in the United States must be resisted to the full extent.

Armed with this document, I met with Coulson and Pletscher in the
boardroom at Bank Leu. They said they did not have much time—the
Easter holiday was coming up, they were short-staffed and were busy
closing their fiscal year records.

I told them I was going on a business trip to Europe within the next
two weeks and wanted to meet with Meier while I was there, but they
were unwilling or unable to give me either an address or phone number
for Meier.

Then I delivered Pinder's written, legal opinion. The letter pointed
out that if a bank disclosed details concerning an account, the depositor
could and probably would sue them.

I flew back to New York with a heart full of doubt.

CHAPTER TWENTY-SIX

WHEN I ARRIVED on the eve of the 1986 version of Drexel's Bond Conference and checked into the Beverly Hills Hotel, a bottle of expensive champagne awaited me, courtesy of the hotel owner, Ivan Boesky.

By six-thirty the next morning, April 2, as we assembled in the ballroom of the Beverly Hilton, I discerned a subtle but recognizable change in the structure of the audience. This year, no doubt thanks in part to our distinguished performance, more blue-chip companies were represented than last year.

Although it was still early in 1986, we projected that by the end of the year Drexel would be the most profitable securities firm in history. This week was to be our premature celebration.

Yet, the gut-wrenching and, paradoxically, glorious facet of that prediction was that, in the context of the 80s, this would be insufficient. Set a record for business volume in 1986, yes, but make sure you eclipse that record in 1987. There was no such thing as enough.

Ten minutes before seven A.M., Milken strode out onto a darkened platform and stepped into the spotlight, his image reproduced and magnified on giant screens that flanked the stage. He opened the conference with a genial, low-key speech predicting yet another record year for high-yield bonds—as much as $50 billion worth. The junk-bond market was pouring $4 billion into the American economy every month. By now, more companies were issuing high-yield bonds than were issuing the traditional kind.

The keynote speaker this year was Ronald Perelman, who detailed his successful fight to acquire Revlon. His presentation included a promotional film featuring models Kim Alexis and Lauren Hutton pushing Revlon cosmetics to a thumping disco beat.

Other presentations were given by principals of Beatrice Foods, Gulf+Western, Burroughs, Warner Communications and Lear Siegler. No less than four U.S. senators spoke: Bill Bradley and Frank Lautenberg of New Jersey, Alan Cranston of California and Howard Metzenbaum of Ohio.

Marty Siegel dazzled the audience by announcing his calculation that the personal wealth represented here was three times larger than the Gross National Product.

Nelson Peltz, who in one year had risen from obscurity to preside over a multi-billion-dollar network of corporations, gazed out from the speaker's podium and waved his hand at the assembled crowd and dubbed them "The Two Thousand." The men and women in this room were bound together through an intricate gridlock of bonds, warrants, debentures, stock certificates and other assorted financial instruments. To Peltz and all the others, the only possible route from here seemed to be upward, and if money was all that was needed to get there, everyone in this room was "highly confident" that it could be raised. Peltz's voice resounded: "Never have so few owed so much to so many!"

The prevailing theme of it all was presented in a big-screen film clip from the movie *Ghostbusters,* with dubbed voices singing:

> When it's money you need,
> And you gotta have it fast,
> Who ya gonna call? Call Drexel.

THIS was the gathering of the anointed. Only a handful of people in the entire world conducted business at our level. We were a small, tight community, able to work on a friendly basis as allies or adversaries, depending upon the needs of the moment. We knew one another's personality and style, and it was fun to mingle in a generalized setting and talk shop.

In the halls and hospitality suites, a chief topic of conversation was the latest chapter in the convoluted story of Norton Simon, Esmark and

Beatrice Foods. They were like predatory fish, each one larger than the next, that had swallowed their prey only to find themselves on the menu for the next dinner party.

It had begun back in 1983, when David J. Mahoney, chairman of Norton Simon, Inc., announced a plan for an LBO, wherein a group of company executives headed by him would repurchase outstanding stock from the shareholders in order to take the company private. There was a curious aspect to the plan. Mahoney's offer of $29 per share was only about 10 percent higher than the current market value of the stock, and this was generally regarded as too low to induce sufficient shareholders to sell. Some observers expressed suspicion that Mahoney was, in fact, simply putting his own company into play, seeking to induce someone else to pay more.

He did not have to wait long. A week after the announcement of the LBO offer, Kohlberg Kravis Roberts & Company jumped in with a bid of $33 per share. Shortly after that Esmark, Inc., the corporate successor to the meatpackers, Swift & Company, announced their own tender offer at the same price. A bidding war ensued, won by Esmark in September when Norton Simon accepted its offer of $35.50 per share. Perhaps the biggest winner was Mahoney, the chairman of Norton Simon, who received about $25 million for his personal holdings.

But in order to raise more than $1 billion to buy Norton Simon, Esmark was forced to stretch its own credit line to the limit. That set it up as a target in its own right. The following year Kohlberg Kravis commenced a $55-per-share tender offer for Esmark, but lost out in August to Beatrice Companies, Inc., the nation's largest food company, at $60 per share. The deal was worth $2.6 billion.

And with that, Beatrice had weakened its own defenses.

Now, Kohlberg was in the midst of a $50-per-share purchase of Beatrice. At a pricetag of $6.2 billion, it was the largest LBO ever, and Drexel was earning an incredible $86 million in commissions for selling junk bonds to help finance it all. In some ways we considered this the ultimate sequence of acquisitions and the fanciful question was, had it ended, or would it continue to the absurd conclusion when American business, or perhaps the world economy, was run by a single company?

Another major conversational theme was Carl Icahn's attack on TWA, which both he and Eastern Airlines' Frank Lorenzo had stalked for nearly a year. By the time Icahn's ownership position had reached

20.5 percent of TWA's stock, he had commenced a tender offer for the remaining stock at $18 per share. The key question had been whether Icahn really wanted the company, or if he was on another of his greenmail expeditions. Many were surprised to realize that he truly wanted the airline, even though it was losing $1 million a day on its current operations. Icahn's job now was to stop the bleeding.

As I circulated among the collection of CEOs, financial officers and corporate raiders, I jotted memos to myself on a pocket-sized notepad, trying to keep track of who was after what company. Sometimes I felt like a waiter, taking orders to sate the appetites of the voracious acquisitors.

BY Wednesday evening, many of the so-called heavy hitters had made their way to the Polo Lounge at the Beverly Hills Hotel, and they were naturally followed there by the variety of women who were "working" the Bond Conference.

I sat at a table, nursing a drink, making conversation with one of America's best-known raiders. Three tables away was one of his equally well-known competitors, who was openly fondling the woman on his lap.

"He's not going to have a very nice evening," my companion said. "I know. I had her last year."

I felt suddenly nauseous. As quickly and graciously as I could, I excused myself and headed off toward bed. As I trudged through the deep-carpeted halls of Boesky's hotel, I was struck by the changes of the past year. *Last* year I was also sickened by the booze and the party girls, but I would have toughed it out, not willing to give up a moment of valuable dealmaking time. This was the life, albeit without the sleazy details, that I had worked so diligently to obtain.

Dennis, I asked myself, isn't this what you always wanted?

And I answered, I don't know anymore.

A night's sleep refreshed me, and I woke resolved to get on with my business. I had a few details to clean up, but then it would be full speed ahead.

I stole a moment of time Thursday morning to call Coulson at Bank

Leu to see if there were any further developments. I suggested that we meet in his office a week from Friday to discuss things in person. Coulson replied that the lawyers had advised that we should not meet at this time, nor should we attempt to initiate anything new. Coulson called Pletscher in to listen to the remainder of the conversation.

Pletscher took the phone and reported that the lawyers had also advised that we should not conduct any large transactions that would further draw the SEC's attention.

"It sounds reasonable," I replied. "But I feel frustrated."

Pletscher reported that the bank's lawyers were still negotiating with the SEC, and that this was good. "They may talk forever," he said. "The whole case may die a natural death."

"No news is good news," I responded. "But do you expect any answer from the SEC in the near future?" I asked if any date had been set for Meier's deposition.

"No date has been set," Pletscher said. "I don't know when the lawyers spoke last with the SEC, but we will certainly contact the lawyers by the end of this week or early next week in order to find out where we stand, because we don't like this limbo situation. We will hopefully see clearer by that time."

Referring to Meier, I asked, "Is Bernie back to work?"

"Bernie is taking a long break and is probably enjoying his vacation," Pletscher said.

At the time, I had no way of knowing that nearly everything the Bank Leu officials said to me was a lie. Pletscher, at least, could not meet with me a week from Friday because he was scheduled to be in London to give a deposition to SEC investigators; he was afraid to do so in the U.S., lest he be arrested, or in the Bahamas, where he might also be arrested. And Meier was not on vacation—he was out of a job.

After the phone call, Pletscher hand-wrote a memo detailing the conversation for Pitt. In the memo, he complained, "Dick and I agreed, that this is very uncomfortable and it is entirely against our word to tell such a B.S. and to lie!"

IN Beverly Hills, it was business as usual. I spent much of Thursday with Nelson Peltz and his partner Peter May, to explore the possibility that their National Can might make an overture toward American Can.

With Jerry Tsai, the CEO of American Can, we enjoyed a poolside lunch in Boesky's cabana at the Beverly Hills Hotel. A few tables away, Perelman was working on a new ad campaign for Revlon. After lunch, we did a little chauffeured shopping up and down Rodeo Drive.

Later that afternoon Joseph, Milken and I triple-teamed Sandy Sigoloff, the chief executive officer of Wickes Companies, Inc., which owned a chain of home improvement stores and other retailing outlets. A former scientist who had been an expert in the field of atomic radiation effects, the genial and polished Sigoloff was now known for his ability to revitalize sick companies. In the 70s he had steered Daylin, a chain of retail stores, through bankruptcy and back into profitability; his stringent cost-cutting procedures earned him the nickname "Ming the Merciless." One month after he took over Wickes in 1982, the company filed the second-largest bankruptcy ever; Sigoloff sold off some subsidiaries, cut employment by 28,000 people and turned things around in less than three years. His hobby was to work out cash flow models on his home computer.

We went through a shopping list of companies that were ripe for the picking, including the California-based aerospace manufacturer Lear Siegler, Owens-Corning Fiberglas and Collins & Aikman, a New York textile firm. In addition, we laid plans to raise $1.2 billion for Sigoloff. (Within days of our meeting, Sigoloff was ready to commence an offer for National Gypsum Company, Inc.)

Numerous colleagues from Drexel buttonholed me for a few minutes of discussion with their particular clients on their particular deals. I spoke briefly with Linda Wachner concerning her investment group's possible purchase of Warnaco, the manufacturer of Arrow Shirts. I met with the Texan Charles Hurwitz, and discussed his Maxxam Group's, acquisition of Pacific Lumber Company.

That evening, inside Bungalow 8 of the Beverly Hills Hotel, the traditional contingent of women was in evidence, but in a decidedly less conspicuous manner than last year. This brought some grumbling from the more inebriated and raucous party-goers but it pleased me and Siegel as well. Others, like us, realized that it was time for Drexel to elevate its image. The vast majority of Bond Conference attendees had no interest in these extracurricular companions and applauded our efforts. We had not yet removed the ladies from the premises, but we had relegated them to the backrooms.

Outside, a picket line of TWA flight attendants marched around the two dozen stretch limos waiting to take everyone to Chasen's; they were protesting Icahn's takeover of their airline. Actually, Icahn was not here; he was on his way back to New York to deal with the aftermath created by a terrorist bomb that had exploded aboard a TWA flight from Rome to Athens.

There was considerable discussion concerning Drexel's plan to charter the Concorde to fly a select group of clients to England in July. Upon arrival, they would be ushered into a riverboat for a trip up the Thames to the Wimbledon tennis tournament. One man jokingly warned that it might be dangerous to put all the raiders into a single jet, making it an easy target for a corporate American terrorist.

At Chasen's, I was sitting at a table with Siegel and Henry Kravis when one of Drexel's richest clients crashed down into the chair alongside me. He was one of the men who had most forcefully bemoaned the atmospheric changes in Bungalow 8. He had persuaded several of the TWA flight attendants to fraternize with the enemy, but he was unsure of how to proceed. He leaned over and whispered to me in a thick, drunken tongue, "Dennis, how do I get to mount one of these-here little fillies?"

I replied with what I hoped was a firm but jocular tone, "We're a full-service firm, but I'd draw the line before providing that service."

Kravis and Siegel promptly moved off to another side of the room. I, too, found a different table and sat between T. Boone Pickens and Fred Joseph. Pickens and I struck up a conversation, but I did not pay much attention to the conversation. A morose mood settled upon me. I realized that I was nearer to a panic attack than I had ever been before. A debate brewed within me. One faction of my mind argued that everything was under control. Pletscher and Coulson were leveling with me; they were stonewalling the SEC. The opposition argued that my life was crumbling, that everything I had toiled for was about to go up in a brilliant flame.

I looked about and felt uneasy. Even without the excesses of Bungalow 8 this entire week was an orgiastic ritual of self-indulgence, a hymn to the human ego. And somehow, then and there, I *knew* that this week, this Bond Conference, was the apex of the 80s. It was the peak for me, for Drexel and for the M&A phenomenon. The trip to the top had been fast; I knew the descent would be faster.

Boesky appeared at my side and introduced his evening's companion, David Geffen. Geffen was dressed in a neat suit and tie, complimented by his trademark, sneakers. He was one of the most successful record producers in the country and his appearance was no surprise, for Boesky enjoyed associating with show-biz types.

Boesky leaned toward me and asked quiet, conspiratorial questions. Even now, he could not contain his thirst for market knowledge.

I parried with him this evening. I was, suddenly, disgusted with this unreal world that seemed to typify the decade. And I was afraid.

Perhaps more than anything, I was simply tired.

Suddenly Senator Alfonse D'Amato approached our table. He was working the room, greeting everyone effusively. He spoke briefly with Joseph and Bob Linton, then pumped my hand, slapped Pickens lightly on the back, said a warm "hello" to Boesky and moved on about his business.

Boesky, alluding to past contributions to the senator's election campaigns, muttered, "That bastard cost me five thousand dollars."

FRIDAY morning found me up early, preparing for my own moment onstage as the featured speaker at the Corporate Finance Breakfast. Senator Robert Dole was supposed to speak also, but he had to cancel at the last minute, and we were glad that we had kept his appearance a surprise.

I found myself standing alone on the stage of the Grand Ballroom of the Beverly Wilshire Hotel, the eyes of 2,000 executives trained upon me. They expected me to tell them about the Pantry Pride/Revlon deal, but I addressed that subject only briefly, since Perelman had already told the story on Wednesday.

Instead, I detailed what had transpired since the previous Bond Conference. I discussed several smaller acquisitions completed in 1986 and highlighted Nelson Peltz's successful acquisition of National Can. I continued with a recitation of what Peltz had accomplished in the nearly twelve months following the acquisition. He had moved through the company with just the proper amount of surgical precision, trimming overhead, reducing bureaucratic procedures, improving the morale of the line employees. To pay off the lion's share of his debt we refinanced many of the original bonds. What was the result?

Triangle Industries, Peltz's holding company, currently boasted the highest profit-in-relation-to-equity of any firm listed on the *Fortune* 500.

The audience applauded, and Peltz was aglow.

"This is how it should be done," I contended. "This is how it can be done. An acquisition should not take place merely in order to satisfy the ego. It should be done only if it makes good business sense.

"That's what Drexel can do for you. Sure, the biggest deals are exciting. But the good deals, whether large or small, are the most exciting."

When I was finished it seemed, somehow, extremely important for me to get back home, to Laurie and Adam. Thus I was more receptive than usual when a grateful Nelson Peltz and Peter May offered me a ride back to New York on their corporate jet, a Gulfstream. They were leaving Friday night, right after the show. My Drexel colleagues David Kay and Leon Black also accepted.

MILKEN, of course, led off the festivities at the Friday-night banquet, presenting a series of slides and film clips along with a deadpan line of patter. He spoke of how carefully Drexel groomed its executives as movie screens showed clips of the famous food-fight scene from *Animal House* and the equally famous flatulence scene from *Blazing Saddles*. He spoke of the potential of South America as a safe haven for investment capital as the audience viewed Butch Cassidy and the Sundance Kid shooting up banks in Bolivia.

Suddenly, there on the screens, was the image of actor Larry Hagman, playing his world-famous role of J. R. Ewing on "Dallas." He held up a "Drexel Express Titanium Card," flashed a toothy grin, announced that it had a $10 billion line of credit and proclaimed, "Don't go hunting without it."

Everyone, of course, was eager to discern the identity of the surprise headliner. Milken assured the audience that Drexel had spared no expense in this respect, and the film screens showed Imelda Marcos at a lavish party, singing off-key.

Then the stage lights came up. Dressed in glittering pink, Dolly Parton bounced onstage and declared, "This looks like the original cast of 'Lifestyles of the Rich and Famous.' "

* * *

THE moment that Dolly Parton finished singing, a limo whisked Kay, Black and me back to the Beverly Hills Hotel. We packed quickly and jumped into another limo for the trip to the general aviation terminal at Los Angeles International Airport.

Throughout the cross-country flight with Peltz and May, we discussed the possibilities inherent in the pending National Can/American Can transaction. Then, as we neared Westchester Airport, the ever-solicitous Peltz asked, "How are you guys getting back into the city?"

We told him that we were not sure; we'd grab a cab or something.

Peltz headed for a telephone.

After the jet landed, it taxied directly adjacent to Peltz's private helicopter. Peltz ushered us inside and the chopper took off for Manhattan. When it arrived at the 60th Street heliport, Peltz had a limo waiting to drive us to our homes.

SHORTLY after the Bond Conference, Boesky asked me if I would like an accounting of how much he owed me under our compensation agreement.

"Yes," I said. I gave him a list of the various deals we had discussed over the months.

He studied it and muttered, "Okay, this would be a five percent, that's a one, another one, let's forget about this one—we lost money on it—here's a five, a five, a one . . ."

He called in an associate and asked for an accounting of the trading results for each of the specific companies. We spoke of other things as we waited. When the list was prepared the associate left us alone once more. Boesky punched numbers into his hand-held calculator and announced that, in only a few months of acting upon my tips, he had profited more than $50 million. He declared, "I owe you $2.4 million dollars."

"Okay," I said, but I did not push for payment.

HERB Bachelor, the head of the Corporate Finance Department, stepped into my office and pointedly closed the door behind him. "What

I'm telling you, I'm telling you in confidence," he said. "Very few people are offered the type of investment I'm presenting to you." He explained that the Beverly Hills office had set up a partnership to invest in warrants for Beatrice Foods. It was one of the benefits that Drexel had negotiated from Kohlberg Kravis in exchange for financing the deal. Bachelor said that a decision had been made, "at the senior level," that I was to be allowed to buy into the deal.

I could invest as much as $250,000, Bachelor said. It was up to me.

It felt as if I had been knighted. This was not one of the run-of-the-mill partnerships sometimes thrown to the Corporate Finance people like crumbs. This was one of the big deals, with the potential for explosive growth. I knew now that I was one of the privileged few.

"It's your decision," Bachelor said. "You can buy what you want, but I would suggest that this is something you should own." Clearly, the "wink" was there.

I could have easily plunged in wholeheartedly. Most of my annual bonus check was still sitting in the bank. But I considered carefully. Given the track record of these private deals, I probably stood to make a great deal of money. Faces around here were still green with envy over a similar deal the Beverly Hills boys had swung on warrants for Harris Graphics. They bought in at a dollar per warrant and would sell out later at a significant profit. It was almost a no-lose proposition, because Drexel controlled so many of the variables that would dictate the success or failure of the venture. But it was not quite a sure thing. If Kohlberg Kravis fell on its face with Beatrice, the warrants and my investment could be worthless. When I announced that I had decided to invest only $100,000, Bachelor seemed to understand, for I was known for my conservative approach.

THE week of April 13, in a conference room at Fried, Frank's law office at 3 King's Arms Yard in London's financial district, Pletscher submitted to several days of informal questioning by a team of U.S. investigators. These included SEC attorneys Paul Fischer, Leo Wang and Peter Sonnenthal as well as Assistant U.S. Attorney Charles Carberry. A formal deposition was taken on April 15 and 16.

By now, Bank Leu had turned over thousands of documents to the investigative team. Much of it was a mishmash of data, difficult to collate. The investigators needed Pletscher to lead them through the maze of paperwork.

While under oath, Pletscher told a mixture of truth and fiction. For example, he indicated that, over the years, I had touted my information and actually encouraged the bank officers to piggyback my trades. Every witness in that conference room must have winced at these statements. It was an absurd contention, borne out by the facts—for it was the piggyback trades that spurred the entire investigation.

But Pletscher saved his most imaginative tales for a discussion of what the SEC investigators now called "the coverup." He said that, during our discussions of how to respond to the SEC inquiry, I had demanded that the bank destroy certain documents that would identify me, such as a personal signature card in the account file for my Panamanian company. I had never made that demand; perhaps the Bank Leu officers had decided to do this on their own. At any rate, Pletscher said that he and Meier had destroyed the documents. Pletscher stated that he had personally shredded a photocopy of my passport photograph, but this was, at best, a half-truth, for he never had a copy of it; what he had were passport photos of my father and brother. Furthermore, it was Coulson who had shredded the signature cards; he had done so in my presence.

Perhaps Pletscher was nervous or confused; perhaps his motivation was more sinister.

Pletscher was careful not to identify me by name, but he did drop a vital clue. He said that "Moby Dick," during one of their recent meetings in Nassau, had waved a letter from SEC Chairman John Shad, thanking him for his participation in a recent seminar. This information obviously narrowed the field of suspects.

Following the deposition, Pitt flew to Zurich to brief the officers of the parent company.

At this same time another SEC staffer, Edward Harrington, was laboring in Washington to piece together the government's formal accounting of the trades. From the redacted Bank Leu records, he culled the losing transactions and those that had only questionable links to takeover action, and was left with a laundry list of fifty-four trades. These would form the basis of the formal complaint against the still-mysterious "Moby Dick."

*   *   *

IT was one of those rare days when I left the office early. Laurie and I had a business dinner to attend this evening and I knew it would be a late night, yet I was already exhausted.

"I'm going to lie down for a while," I announced as I came through the doorway at four P.M. I headed directly to the bedroom, drew the curtains and turned off the lights. But I had barely closed my eyes before Laurie barged into the room and flipped on the overhead light. I glanced up in pain to see her standing over me, looking somewhat absurd with a headful of rollers in her blond hair.

"What are you doing?" I complained.

"I'll let you sleep in a minute, Dennis," she said, "but first, I want you to play a game of charades with me."

"What?"

"Charades," she repeated. "Just one."

The woman has lost it, I said to myself. She's gone 'round the bend. I'm tired and grumpy. Why do I need a game of charades?

Laurie held up three fingers and reluctantly I muttered, "Three words."

On the nose, she signaled.

First word, she pointed to herself.

"I . . ."

For the second word she inverted three fingers of her hand.

"M," I intoned. "I . . . M. I am."

On the nose.

Now she turned to one side, so that I viewed her in profile. Her hands outlined the silhouette of a bulging tummy.

I sat up in bed and screamed, "I am pregnant?!"

"Yes!" she squealed.

I leaped up and hugged her. A nap was out of the question now.

I floated through the evening. Now I knew that everything would be all right.

CHAPTER TWENTY-SEVEN

EVEN AS FRIED, FRANK'S HARVEY PITT was piecing together the defense for Bank Leu, another of the firm's partners, Steve Fraidin, was hard at work on a special deal involving Boesky and me. Fraidin, a round-faced gentleman who accentuated his features with large, oval-framed glasses, was a longtime Boesky adviser.

We met in Boesky's office one day to discuss, I thought, routine matters. Choosing his moment, Boesky walked out of the office on an "errand." It was then that Fraidin "happened" to mention that Boesky's number two man, Steve Conway, was leaving.

"Gee, that's interesting," I said. Fraidin remained silent, and the implication was obvious. I added, "I think Ivan would like me to take that job."

"It's a great job for you," Fraidin said excitedly. "It makes a lot of sense."

The prospect of actually working for Boesky was not so sweet, and I said as much. In the past, he was a deal-talker but not really a dealmaker. He tended to underestimate the value of his targets, and therefore was unwilling to bid realistically.

"Dennis, everything you are saying is true," Fraidin acknowledged. "However, you have to understand. *You* can handle him. You know how to do deals. You have access to Milken. You wouldn't take any shit from Ivan. It is a match made in heaven, because you can handle the man."

"If I come on board," I said, "I'll need an iron-clad contract. I've got a whole bunch of guys I'm bringing with me. It'll be big news."

"Great!"

Boesky returned, caught Fraidin's eye and suggested, "Let's resume this conversation over lunch."

Fraidin left us. Along with lunch, Boesky put his offer on the table.

He explained that, as usual, Milken's " 'druthers" had prevailed; it appeared that his long-delayed $660 million financial restructuring deal was about to close. Milken had silenced the more vocal members of Drexel's Underwriting Assistance Committee.

Now that the capital infusion appeared likely, Boesky had set up an entity, Hudson Funding Corporation, for the single purpose of marketing $660 million worth of notes. Drexel would act as the sales agent for the entire issue and Milken's group would also acquire $5 million worth of holdings in a limited partnership with Boesky's arbitrage operations. On his own, Boesky was also selling another $220 million worth of limited partnership interests.

Although I had nothing to do with the restructuring deal, it now appeared that I would become one of the chief beneficiaries. All told, Boesky was about to receive $900 million worth of fresh money, and he was ready to put me in charge of a large chunk of it, directing takeover operations. This new venture would be part of the Northview Corporation, the successor to Boesky's Vagabond Hotels subsidiary. "I'd like for you to come in and run it for me," he said. "You'll run the Beverly Hills Hotel, the Vagabond Hotels; you'll run my operation in London, everything here. But most importantly, I want to set up an LBO firm, which you will handle."

I had always dreamed of becoming a principal, and here was my chance. But I wanted to know the stakes. I countered, "How much money are you going to put into it?"

"One hundred million dollars."

"I want a carried interest. I want twenty percent."

He hesitated, then said, "All right."

All of a sudden my secret bank account almost seemed irrelevant. Boesky was offering me a $20 million personal stake in his LBO fund, just like that. "I want to bring in my own people," I said. "I can't do it alone."

"Yes." Then Boesky asked, "How do you think Michael would react to your departure?"

"I think Michael would understand, because I would explain to him why I'm doing it. I would explain that I would continue to be very close to Drexel and that everything we are going to do through this LBO company will be done through Drexel." Boesky nodded his approval of this; we could not afford to alienate Milken. Who could? I continued, "Marty Siegel is over there now and they're bringing up a lot of new talent. I'm not as critical to them as I was a year ago. We'll convince Michael that he's not losing an investment banker, so much as he's gaining a trusted, loyal client. Michael will understand that."

"Good," Boesky pronounced. That settled, he sweetened the pot. He offered what he called a "seven-figure" salary, plus bonuses that would bring my total annual income to more than $5 million. And on top of it all, he offered a signing bonus of $5 million.

When I told Laurie about Boesky's job offer, she was totally support- ive. She wanted me to do what I thought was best for my career. In my mind, I was through with investment banking as well as insider trading; I needed a new mountain to climb. My offshore money could sit for years—or forever—earning 7 or 8 percent interest. This, I theorized, is probably how lots of people started.

THE activities of our Corporate Finance Division were remote from those of the Trading Division, populated by "loose cannons." Much happened there that we did not know about.

For example, on April 23, Cary Maultasch, a trader in Drexel's New York office who had previously worked in Beverly Hills, was extremely active during the last nineteen minutes of the trading day. In that span of time, he placed repeated buy orders for purchases totalling 1.9 mil- lion shares of common stock in the Wickes Companies. The activity put upward pressure on the price of Wickes, which closed for the day at 6⅛.

That was a most significant price. Shareholders of Wickes preferred stock were due to receive a high dividend payment unless Wickes common stock closed at or above 6 ⅛ on twenty of thirty consecutive days and the closing price on this day happened to fulfill the require- ment to the letter. This negated the need for Wickes to make the dividend payments and, at the same time, activated a clause that re- sulted in the payment of a $2.3 million "standby" fee from Wickes to Drexel's High-Yield and Convertible Bond Department.

That same day in Beverly Hills, Milken's trading assistant Janet Chung noted that Wickes CEO Sandy Sigoloff had called to congratulate Milken.

ON April 24 I met Ilan Reich for lunch at the Water Club and told him that I had been approached by Boesky with an offer to become president of his company, controlling a $100 million LBO firm. "Would you be interested in coming in?" I asked.

"Absolutely," he replied. "I'd be very interested in that."

Sokolow, too, was ready to join the new team.

ON May 6 I headed for the Cayman Islands, changing planes in Miami for the short hop south of Cuba. I met with Wilkis's lawyer, who initiated the paperwork to set up a new corporation for me. Then, we walked over to the local office of Morgan Grenfell Ltd., where I was introduced to the bank's managing director, Brian Kieran, as "Robert Gold." I arranged to open an account under the name of my new business. I deposited $5,000 and informed Kieran that I would wire $10 million to the account within a matter of weeks, as soon as the necessary papers were filed.

This was a non-trading account. Once I got my money out of Bank Leu, I vowed, it was really, truly over.

FOR months my bankers had been terrified that I would attempt to withdraw my money. Their worst fears came true when I instructed them to transfer $10 million to the Cayman Islands. They immediately reported this development to Pitt, who relayed the news to the SEC investigators, and a horse race ensued. The bankers knew they could stall me for a time, but if I backed them into a corner, they would have to refuse to release any of my money. Then I would know that they were cooperating with the SEC. I could file suit in Bahamian court to enjoin them from any further violations of the banking laws, and I might also be able to rush a mandate through the Bahamian courts, forcing them to make the account transfer. If I succeeded in getting the cash to the Caymans, Bank Leu would have lost its leverage.

At three P.M. on Wednesday, May 7, the day after I opened my new account in the Caymans, Pitt, along with the American ambassador to the Bahamas and a team of men from the SEC, the U.S. Department of Justice and the U.S. State Department, descended upon the office of Paul Adderly, who, ever since the island nation gained independence from Great Britain in 1973, had held the posts of justice minister, public prosecutor and minister of education. The visitors disclosed to Adderly that they were on the trail of an American investor who had made what they suspected were illegal insider trades through a Bahamian bank account, and they wanted Adderly to grant extraordinary permission for the bank to disclose the customer's identity. Apparently, what they did not tell him was that the bank's senior management also had traded on the inside information and that the SEC's case was built *entirely* upon evidence that they had already provided in defiance of Bahamian law.

Since there are no securities laws in the Bahamas, I had violated no local provisions. Nonetheless, to almost everyone's surprise, Adderly consented. His rationale was that stock trading was separate from normal banking transactions; therefore, he could make the exception. He said he would formalize his approval in a letter to Bank Leu, to be delivered on Friday, two days hence, whereupon the bank would be free to disclose to the SEC the identity of "Moby Dick."

ON Thursday I slipped away from my desk and into a Drexel conference room. Using the phone there, I dialed the number for Bank Leu.

The receptionist informed me that Mr. Coulson and Mr. Pletscher were unavailable.

"I demand to speak to somebody who can make a decision!" I raged. "Get an officer on the phone. I maintain a significant account at your bank and I want some action."

Finally I reached Andrew Sweeting. I did not know who he was, but I identified myself as Mr. Wheat and told him I wanted all of my money transferred to my new account in the Cayman Islands. Sweeting responded that he could not accept a verbal order to do this; he would need the instructions in writing.

I called Hartis Pinder's office in Nassau and instructed him to hand-deliver the required letter.

*   *   *

ON Friday, May 9, I met with Boesky in his top-floor apartment at 56th Street and Second Avenue. It was surprisingly small and modestly furnished, but it did have a Quotron in the living room.

"I'm seriously considering your job offer," I said.

Boesky spoke for a moment about some of the companies he would like to go after. One was Lockheed, and that seemed possible. The other was Eastman Kodak, and when he mentioned it, I thought, This man's ego is out of control. Kodak is an American institution; it runs TV ads that make you cry. It is a mammoth corporation that might just be beyond the scope of *any* raider's reach, with or without Drexel's assistance.

I tabled that discussion and we resumed negotiations concerning the new job. One point in Boesky's offer stuck in my craw. Based upon our calculations, he owed me $2.4 million in cash for the investment advice I had provided, but he wanted to take that off the top of the $5 million signing bonus.

"One thing has nothing to do with the other," I argued. "If I'm leaving Drexel, I'm leaving significant future earning power. And if I'm going to do that, I've got to see some serious front money." My voice grew earnest. "I can do what you need done, Ivan. I have the people. I'm your man, but you've got to pay me."

Boesky responded, "We'll see."

That same day, Pitt, Pletscher and Adolph Brendle, an executive board member from Bank Leu Zurich, met with William Allan, head of the Bahamian Central Bank, to assure him that Bank Leu would remain a law-abiding citizen of the banking community. Since they were to be described in court papers merely as a "financial institution," they foresaw no upheaval in their ability to continue doing business.

At five-thirty P.M. that day, Justice Minister Adderly's letter arrived at Bank Leu. Pitt telephoned SEC enforcement director Gary Lynch and reported, "We got the letter. 'Moby Dick' is Dennis Levine, a managing director at Drexel Burnham Lambert."

A half hour later, the letter arrived from my attorney, Hartis Pinder, instructing Bank Leu to transfer my money to the Cayman Islands. It was too late.

Pletscher, with a sense of relief that it was over, looked forward to his wedding the very next day.

And I, unaware that my life was now out of control, went to the Gulf+Western building at Columbus Circle on Friday night for a buffet dinner and a private screening of their Paramount subsidiary's new release, *Top Gun.*

Boesky and I never had an opportunity to complete our negotiations, for, on the following Monday, I was arrested and tossed into jail.

And after that, I faced the formidable task of explaining everything to Laurie.

PART THREE
WITH-
DRAWAL

CHAPTER TWENTY-EIGHT

BOB WILKIS HAPPENED TO BE on a business trip to Omaha the day of my arrest, but he called me at home as soon as he could get through. He was arriving back in New York on Tuesday night, and he told me he would come straight over from the airport.

When we met each other at the door of my co-op, I reported the obvious: "Bob, they arrested me. I spent the night in jail."

"I know," he said softly, "they're gonna get me next."

"How could they do that? There's no way they could trace me to you, or vice versa. All of this is coming from the Bahamas. They don't know who my trading partners were, how this all worked up here."

We spoke briefly, and Wilkis's fears were allayed somewhat. We decided that, henceforth, we should meet only under controlled conditions. It seemed quite possible that I was under surveillance.

"Everything is going to be okay," I assured him.

"Everything is going to be okay," he agreed.

THE short-term effects were dramatic. One day soon after my arrest, Laurie and I stopped at a bank machine to get some cash, but the computer informed us that our account was empty; federal agents had seized it. Creditors called in our loans. It seemed as if every real estate broker in Manhattan phoned to see if we wanted to sell our co-op. I had to borrow cash to feed my family.

317

As the Street professed its shock, brokers, bankers, arbs, lawyers and financiers of every ilk searched frantically through their own closets, trying to clean out the skeletons. Everyone expected a flurry of subpoenas to descend. Government agents padlocked my office at Drexel and allowed access only to their own investigators, who poked and prodded through my personal effects, as well as my business files.

The worst pressure of all was that the government dragged in the rest of my family, issuing subpoenas to my father and my brothers.

Wall Street heaven was replaced by the hell of reality. Media crews camped around our building; my phone rang incessantly. Almost everyone wanted to talk with me, of course, but Laurie was not spared the unwanted attention. Diane Sawyer, Maria Shriver and Barbara Walters all called her, seeking interviews. Laurie agreed to speak with them in the privacy of her home, off camera.

For my part, I took Liman's advice to heart. "Cases are not won or lost in the media," he counseled. "They are won and lost in the courtroom." I refused all interview requests.

Whenever she stepped outside, Laurie was conscious of eyes watching her. We know who your husband is, they accused.

Laurie thought: At a time like this, you find out who your real friends are.

One afternoon just before Laurie was due to leave the building to pick up Adam, the doorman called and suggested, "Why don't you go out the back way? There are a whole bunch of reporters down here."

I did not know quite what to expect from my Drexel associates. It would be natural for them to distance themselves from me, and some did, but most offered their help. Several of my good friends at Drexel helped assemble the mountain of paperwork that we needed to verify what I did and—in some cases more important—did not do on various transactions.

Other, previous business associates were just as cordial, including many of my former Lehman associates.

Several days after my arrest, I encountered one of my elderly neighbors as we were both leaving the building. "I'm quite upset with you," he said. I expected an angry lecture, but he surprised me by smiling and commenting, "All these years we've been neighbors and I never knew you were in the market. How come you never gave me any stock tips?"

*　*　*

LIMAN'S partner Marty Flumenbaum, a Harvard Law School grad, was a veteran of the very same U.S. Attorney's Office[1] that was now preparing to present its evidence against me to a federal grand jury. Flumenbaum and the prosecutor, Charles Carberry, had known one another for years and their personal friendship deepened even as they sat on opposite sides of the table. Carberry was surprisingly congenial and cooperative, although firm in his commitment to exact punishment. Very quickly I gained respect for his professionalism. He treated me with dignity and fairness. He was a gentleman.

Flumenbaum's attention to detail overwhelmed me. One day, under court order, I was directed to provide the government with a sample of my handwriting. On the way over to the U.S. Attorney's Office, Flumenbaum asked, "Do you have a pen to write with?"

"Yes, I do," I replied.

"Let me see it." I handed over an ornate pen, inscribed with the Citibank logo. Flumenbaum examined it and asked, "How long have you had this?"

"Several years."

Slipping the pen into his pocket, he said, "I'm going to hang on to it for a while. I don't want them to have a sample of the ink you may have used on some document."

I was amazed and, at the same time, wondered if we were nearing paranoia. No, I decided, we cannot be too careful. I thanked Flumenbaum for his thoroughness.

IT took a hungry, enterprising press little more than a day to uncover the identity of what the SEC complaint had referred to as a Bahamian "financial institution." A researcher simply began wading through an international bank directory, until he found Bernhard Meier listed as an officer of Bank Leu International, Ltd., based in Nassau. The bank may have been immune from prosecution, but it was now vulnerable to an onslaught of adverse publicity.

MY attorneys' first priority was to gather information, since we were operating in the dark. A criminal complaint had been filed against me,

---

[1]His most celebrated case was the prosecution of the Reverend Sun Myung Moon.

but I was not indicted. By law, the U.S. Attorney's Office was not required to supply us with information concerning the evidence against me, unless and until I was indicted.

However, concerned that I might be able to transfer my account from the Bahamas, the SEC moved with unusual speed to file a civil action, and that left a door open for us. My attorneys settled upon the strategy of using the civil proceedings to "discover" the government's evidence against me—far earlier than we could have expected. An assault squad of attorneys and research associates scurried to dig up legal and press records regarding the fifty-four transactions that concerned the SEC. They enlisted various allies in Houston, Chicago, San Francisco, Los Angeles and anywhere else that I had done business. They went wild, issuing subpoenas to a variety of entities involved with Bank Leu, including major brokerage houses. Lew Clayton of Paul, Weiss did virtuoso work on this task. Within days they had copies of all of the evidence amassed by the SEC.

In response to our subpoena for Bank Leu records, we received an incredible reponse from the offices of Fried, Frank, declaring that "the request for information and production of documents from Bank Leu International is contrary to the laws of the Bahamas . . ."

"WHY don't you go into that office all by yourself," Flumenbaum said to me one morning as he handed over a loose-leaf binder. "Read this."

I had no idea what was in the binder, but I did as he suggested. In a quiet conference room, alone with my memories, I leafed carefully through the material. Flumenbaum, Karp and others had compiled the most damaging portions of the evidence and placed them here. It was beautifully organized, and even indexed.

Here was a copy of the SEC's telex of August 30, 1985, seeking information regarding trading in twenty-eight stocks. When I saw that the telex had been copied to Bank Leu's headquarters in Zurich, it confirmed my opinion that the top Swiss officials had been involved in the attempted coverup from day one.

I studied the printouts of Bank Leu's trading records, which depicted trade after trade occurring prior to a public announcement; it was an unmistakable paper trail leading back to my office at Drexel.

The bank had provided the U.S. government with copies of its bills from the Bahamas Telecommunications Corporation, indicating the collect calls that I had made. Almost all of these were from New York and the few that I had made from other locations were even more damning when correlated with my business travel records. The word REDACTED was stamped across the top of each phone bill, but they still identified my code names, first "Mr. Diamond," and then "Mr. Wheat." All of this seemed to go well beyond what the Bahamian Justice Minister had decreed that they could release. I grimaced when I read the ironic ad slogan printed at the bottom of each bill: "Use Direct Distance Dialing—It's Cheaper!"

Here was Pletscher's deposition, given in London in order to avoid Bahamian prosecution, describing how I had come to Bank Leu to trade securities through an offshore account, detailing how I had demanded stringent security procedures. Here was the list of other Bank Leu officers—with the notable exception of Meier—given immunity in return for a pledge to testify against me.

There were inconsistencies and obvious mistruths. Pletscher and the others from Bank Leu exhibited a natural tendency to cast their own actions in the most favorable light, as well as—now that they had immunity—succumbing to a natural temptation to tell the investigators what they assumed the feds wanted to know. For example, Pletscher belied Meier's contention in their conversation of August 28, 1985, that they had never received any confirmation that I was, in fact, an inside trader.

It was apparent that I had grossly underestimated the capabilities of the government investigators. They had carefully compared my business track record with the accounting of my trades. In some instances, it was clear that my inside knowledge had arisen from my own work, first at Smith Barney, then at Lehman Brothers and finally at Drexel. They eliminated those trades from the list and then correlated the remaining information, deducing that many of my other trades involved deals worked on either at Goldman Sachs or Lazard Frères. The noose felt tight.

There was evidence here that Fraysse, Pletscher and, above all, Meier had profited through their own piggyback trades, but I noted ruefully that they had only disclosed the trades they had conducted through Bank Leu. Pletscher and Meier had admitted to me that they had other accounts elsewhere and, presumably, were going to be able to shelter them from SEC scrutiny.

I sat up in anger when I saw an SEC allegation that Meier had a kickback scheme working with Merrill Lynch broker Brian Campbell. It seemed as if *everyone* was in on the take, and some of them, Meier especially, had found numerous ways to profit.

The bulk of the file, of course, was about me, and it was solemn, depressing reading. It was clear that I had few options. Dennis, I thought, all your life you've been a fighter. But this is a fight you can't win. You're guilty. You're caught.

I pushed the chair away from the table and stood up. My hands slapped against my forehead and remained there, trying to hold in the throbbing pain that had suddenly attacked. On wobbly feet I edged toward a window and glanced down upon Manhattan.

How high up am I? I wondered. Thirty-some floors. The people below were ants.

Which was worse, the pain in my head or the ache in my heart? Laurie's face appeared in front of me. My sweet, loving, innocent wife was carrying our child. And Adam, who looked to me as his guide for life. What had I done to them? How could I ever make it up?

Just jump, Dennis, I thought. They'll be better off without you. It'll be easy. Don't even think about it. Just pull open the window and dive through.

Many moments passed. I did not move.

Finally I said to myself, It's a long way down, Dennis. I reminded myself: You're not a quitter. Somehow, we'll get through.

When I finally stepped out of the conference room, my body still shook, and I knew my face was ghostly pale.

Liman tried to ease the tension with a quip. "The only thing I think we have a chance of winning," he declared, "is the parking ticket you got the night they arrested you."

We went over the evidence again, together, and it seemed to be just as damning upon a second reading. Liman issued an ironic chuckle when he referred to Richard Coulson. Coulson and Liman were fellow alumni, members of the same graduating class of Yale University Law School; Liman had graduated at the head of the class. In reading the evidence, there seemed to be plenty of reason to accuse Fraysse, Pletscher and Meier of impropriety, but Coulson came off clean as a whistle. This is ridiculous, I thought. Coulson had signed the papers incorporating Midu Enterprises, the shell company that Bank Leu designed to obliterate my trading record. Coulson was, in fact, the president of Midu Enterprises! If Ronald Reagan was the "Teflon president," then Coulson was the "Teflon banker." Nothing stuck to him.

Liman said that in all of his years as a lawyer he had never seen anyone delivered so completely to the government. Bank Leu, he said, had served me "on a silver platter."

My attorney saved his biggest shock for the end of the conversation, informing me solemnly that the government could use the Bank Leu evidence in an attempt to prove an organized criminal conspiracy and thus prosecute me under the harsh terms of RICO, the Racketeer-Influenced & Corrupt Organizations Act. That law was intended to be a tool for use against mobsters, but U.S. attorneys had discovered it to be a convenient pressurizing device to use against white-collar criminals. The potential penalty was pre-trial forfeiture of all my assets—down to the food in the refrigerator—and as many as twenty years in prison on each count. The "rubber hose" of RICO was a powerful weapon.

Liman spelled out the situation for me. This was America. I had freedom of choice. One, I could plead not guilty and stand trial. But, I had no chance of winning. The prosecutors would probably convict me under RICO and throw me into prison for a long time and, quite literally, confiscate all of my possessions and throw my family onto the street. Two, I could plead guilty and refuse to cooperate, but would have to plead to RICO. The consequences of choice number two, Liman said, were similar to those of choice number one. Three, I could agree to forfeiture of the proceeds of my trading and plead guilty to lesser charges, which the government would allow me to do *if* I agreed to cooperate; we could undoubtedly negotiate a similar settlement of the civil charges.

"You're going to do some time," Liman warned. But choice number three would result in a shorter sentence and—far more importantly—would allow my family to survive. He recommended that we enter into plea agreement negotiations with the government.

"I need time," I said to Liman. "I've got to think about it. I have to talk to Laurie."

My attorney nodded his understanding.

*   *   *

THROUGH the process of a preliminary hearing on the SEC charges, much of the evidence was placed on public record, and the press went wild, not only with me, but with Bank Leu.

Once the details began to appear in print, the Central Bank of the Bahamas, in a face-saving move, ordered the entire five-man board of Bank Leu International removed, and Justice Minister Adderly leaked word that his office was opening a criminal investigation into the bank's activities.

Pletscher, freshly returned from his honeymoon cruise, was fired.

Hans Knopfli, who lost his post as chairman of the Bahamian subsidiary but retained his position as chief executive of the parent company, attempted to distance himself. He declared that my trades were "executed exclusively by our subsidiary in the Bahamas and its management, without the knowledge of and in disregard of instructions from the parent in Switzerland."

This was the man who had personally approved my application to trade on a margin account. Over the years, several senior Bank Leu officers had written memos endorsing my trades.

I responded to all of this in characteristic fashion, by studying as much as I could concerning the phenomenon of white-collar crime. I studied statistics concerning criminal cases in the Southern District of New York. About 90 percent of all defendants pled guilty and agreed to cooperate. In the cases that went to trial, prosecutors enjoyed a conviction rate of more than 97 percent. Dennis, you should have done this research before you jumped in, I berated myself. Every book and magazine article I read carried the message: Do not fight a battle you cannot win.

An article in *The Wall Street Journal* reported that the government sleuths had tracked some of my sources to Goldman Sachs and Lazard Frères. At that point, Lazard hired Wachtell, Lipton to conduct an internal investigation. I theorized that it was one of Wachtell's probers who discovered that a former Lazard employee, Robert Wilkis, was a close friend of mine. At any rate, the investigators somehow identified Wilkis as a suspect, and I was not the one who told them.

*   *   *

I was in Flumenbaum's office one day in late May for another in the interminable round of strategy sessions, when someone said, "Dennis, the new issue of *Newsweek* is out, and you're the cover story."

"You've got to be kidding," I said.

"It's true."

I had never contemplated the notion that all of this would snowball into something so large.

Later that day Wilkis tracked me down by phone, to ask how things were going. I said, "I want to bring you up to speed. We should get together."

"Let's meet," he agreed immediately.

"Where?"

"Well, I'm at Fifty-second and Park. I park my car on West Fifty-first Street and Tenth Avenue. Meet me at the corner."

We met on the street and then walked into the parking facility, seeking privacy. It was a dark, dirty garage, crowded with cars, attended by one old man. We found a corner, near Wilkis's car. The smell of gasoline attacked.

Wilkis announced, "I've hired a lawyer."

"Why?"

"I've got to protect myself."

The gloomy cast in his eye gave me pause. "Bob, there's something you're not telling me," I accused. "What's going on?"

"I spoke to my cousin, who is an attorney in Washington, and she recommended that I hire a good criminal lawyer. I'm dealing with a guy in the New York office of Arnold & Porter."

This, I realized, did not answer my question. "Bob," I said, "you've got to come clean here. Our lives are in the balance. What did you tell your cousin?"

He wavered for a moment before he answered. Over the years, he explained, yes, he had taken all the precautions we had originally discussed. He had maintained various accounts at Crédit Suisse Ltd., in the Bahamas, and in the Cayman Islands at Bank of Nova Scotia Trust Company, Ltd., and Guiness Mahon Bank, Ltd. In one sense he had played more conservatively than I, for he had amassed a relatively low $3 million in profits. But in another sense he had been reckless, indeed. He now admitted in a morose, defeated voice, "Dennis, I bought and sold a good portion of the stocks here in the U.S."

"Through your mother's account?!"

"Through hers and others."

My jaw dropped. I thought, but did not say, You stupid son of a bitch. What I said was, "It's all over, Bob."

"How do you know?"

I told him that, once the investigators had my name, they had poked into the affairs of my entire family, to see if my wife, my father, my brothers or any other relative had any connection with my dealings. I had kept them out of it—a fact for which I was now extremely grateful. But now that they had learned Wilkis's name, I knew they would strike paydirt. He had left a paperwork trail that a blind man could follow, and I knew that it would lead to the others involved in our conspiracy. All of our care to use code names and pay telephones and cryptic messages was worthless. The government already had most of the puzzle pieces. "Bob, why? How could you do this?" I asked.

He met the question with stone-faced silence.

"It's all over," I repeated.

"I'm on my way to talk to my lawyer right now," Wilkis said.

More downtrodden than before, Wilkis trudged along West 51st Street toward his attorney's office. It took me a few minutes to hail a taxi. I directed the driver uptown, toward my home, and, as he sped the cab past Wilkis, I glanced back. My friend's face was pale and contorted with inner pain, as if he was heading off toward his execution. His first priority, like mine, would be to protect his family but, unlike me, he had involved them long ago. I knew at this instant that he was going to break.

When I returned to my attorneys' office, I detailed the story. One of my attorneys remarked, "I wouldn't be surprised if Wilkis was wearing a wire."

I do not believe he was, but the statement was an indication of the paranoia that beset us all.

Shortly after this, Wilkis retained Gary Naftalis to represent him. Naftalis, former chief of the criminal division of the U.S. Attorney's Office in New York, advised Wilkis to surrender to the government and tell investigators everything he knew.

"OKAY," I said to Liman. I took a deep breath. Through clenched teeth I said, "I'll plead."

"Okay," Liman agreed. His relief was obvious. He assured me that I was doing the right thing.

He drew Flumenbaum into the office and said to me, "Tell us what went on." They listened to my story carefully, taking notes, asking an occasional, pointed question. The words came out slowly. My mouth felt exceedingly dry.

Following this meeting, my attorneys briefed Carberry. Speaking in generic terms, they told him that my insider trading scheme had involved another investment banker who worked for a major firm, the vice president of another investment banking house and a partner in a leading M&A law firm. In addition, they said, I had conspired with "a major arbitrageur."

The attorneys hammered out a plea agreement that was acceptable to all parties. Carberry encouraged my lawyers to reach a rapid settlement with the SEC as well. The government was adamant on one particular: I had to answer the investigators' questions truthfully.

SPEAKING with the prosecutors would be tough, I knew, but not nearly as difficult as explaining all this to my family. Over time, Laurie's initial fury gave way to more deliberate anger. Night after night we stayed up until the wee hours, talking, sometimes arguing, often crying. She came to understand and even accept the fact that I had kept everything from her in order to protect her.

She did not condone my early deals, but she could understand the temptation. What was more difficult to comprehend was why I had pushed my luck so far, for so long. She simply could not fathom why I had persisted in jeopardizing everything for which we had worked so hard during the past decade. Why was the temptation so strong even after I had risen to prominence on the Street, when my legitimate income was far more than we needed?

I did not quite understand that myself.

"Dennis," Laurie asked during one of our extended talks, "do you realize how much you changed over the years when you were racing to the top? We—Adam and I—were always your top priority, but you became somewhat aloof. You were too busy and important to find time for people you considered beneath you."

This comment surprised and disturbed me. It stung. Had I been too blind to see it?

* * *

ON May 28 I was once again in Liman's office when I was summoned
to the phone for an emergency call. A nurse from the office of Dr.
Finklestein, Laurie's obstetrician, reported that the doctor could not
hear the heartbeat of our unborn child; he was very concerned.
"They're sending her over for a sonogram," the nurse said.

I copied down the address and rushed outside to flag a cab.

Laurie was still in the waiting room when I arrived. She looked
fearful. With tears streaming down her cheeks, she wailed, "I don't
want to lose my baby!"

We went into the examining room together and I felt my fists clench
as I watched a technician prepare Laurie for the test, applying a jelly-
like substance to her rounded belly. Many moments passed as the
technician scrutinized a video screen.

"Mr. Levine," he said, drawing me toward the screen. He pointed to
a thickening glow on the screen and announced, "That's the beat of
your baby's heart."

Laurie smiled and dried her tears. I squeezed her hand.

Life, indeed, goes on.

CHAPTER TWENTY-NINE

THE GOVERNMENT HAD ME in a box, from which there was no escape. I had seen the evidence and there was no denying its force. The Bank Leu officers, supposedly my friends and statutory allies, had turned against me. Wilkis had crashed. Liman had negotiated the best available deal for me. He had my interests at heart—of that I had no doubt—but he had pledged to the prosecution team that I would answer its questions truthfully. The idea revolted me. I had spent years guarding the interests of my friends, and I was determined to continue.

Still, I had to answer the questions, and I knew the process would be painful.

I felt numb. This was very real, but it did not seem so.

With Liman and his team busy preparing for the possibility of a trial and the certainty of several court appearances, I hired well-known criminal lawyer Mark Pomerantz of the firm of Fischetti & Pomerantz to help me through what I knew was going to be the arduous task of submitting to the government's debriefing. He was a scholarly lawyer, having clerked for the U.S. Supreme Court and having later worked as the head of the appeals division of the U.S. Attorney's Office in New York. What was far more important was that he proved to be a great friend.

* * *

329

LIMAN asked me to come over to his apartment on the afternoon of Sunday, June 1, the day before I was to meet with Carberry and his prosecution team. He lived close by and it only took me a few minutes to walk over. It was probably a pleasant, late spring day, but I did not notice.

When I arrived, Liman greeted me cordially and ushered me into his study, overlooking Fifth Avenue. He poured me a cup of tea and attempted to make small talk for a few minutes. He reported that Flumenbaum, down in Washington, had reached the final stages in his attempt to negotiate a civil settlement with the SEC. We wanted to be able to announce a civil and criminal settlement at the same time. Finally, recognizing my anxiety, Liman said: "I know this is going to be a difficult week for you. You are doing the right thing—the only thing you can do. You have no choice."

He leaned forward and continued, "Dennis, I want you to understand this. I know this is painful to you, and I know how difficult this is. I know you care a great deal about your friends. But when you agree to cooperate, we're not talking about eighty percent, we're not talking about ninety percent, we're not talking about ninety-five percent. We are talking about one hundred percent cooperation. You have no choice. You can't tell them half-truths. It's all or nothing. If you hold back, the deal is off."

I left Liman's apartment for the short walk home. Once more the spring weather was lost on me; I saw only the sidewalk. I searched my conscience and attempted to peer into the depths of my soul. Repeatedly I confronted the picture of tomorrow, when I would have to sit down with the government men and . . .

Talk.

Liman's words rang in my head:

"One hundred percent cooperation."

"You have no choice."

"All or nothing."

This was surrender, I thought. This isn't the way you do things, Dennis. You've lost everything. Do you have to lose your pride, too?

It took me two hours to walk home.

POMERANTZ and his associate Warren Feldman were there to figuratively hold my hand the next day.

Ensconced in Carberry's office, I had to give what is called a proffer, which was an overview of the scope of my improper activities. I explained that I had maintained a secret account at Bank Leu in Nassau and had attempted to keep the paperwork offshore.

"We know that," Carberry replied.

I explained that I had maintained, over the years, a relationship with another investment banker, and we had shared stock tips with one another.

"We know that," Carberry replied. "The guy who went from Lazard to Hutton?"

"Yes," I stammered.

Carberry said, "Robert Wilkis?"

"Yes." I was stunned, and I experienced a sudden, fleeting fear that Wilkis might be in the very next room, answering the prosecutors' questions.

Carberry asked, "Who else?"

I gulped at a glass of water in front of me. "An attorney," I stammered.

"What firm?"

"Wachtell, Lipton."

Carberry probed for the man's name, and finally I said, "Ilan Reich."

Minutes later Carberry had pulled Ira Sokolow's name from me, too. Then he asked, quickly and without preamble, "Who's the arb?"

Everyone in the room leaned forward. My world was very silent. I felt pressure in my temples, as if a vise was being clamped down. I said nothing.

Carberry waited me out.

I shifted in my chair, but this did not break the tension.

My eyes met Carberry's and I whispered, "Ivan Boesky."

Carberry could not hide his reaction. His eyes twitched and seemed brighter. He let out a deep sigh. I realized with sudden force what emotions were surging through him. A prosecutor spends his career dealing with the lower echelons of society, waiting in impatient anticipation for the big one to come along. Here was a major notch in Carberry's gun. It was his Revlon! With ill-concealed excitement, he asked for details.

"The relationship started at arm's length," I said. I felt my voice crack a few times as I detailed how Boesky had drawn me in, eventually proposing a commission scheme and how I had, ultimately, accepted.

Carberry wanted specifics on a few of the stock deals, and I provided them as best I could. "I never tipped him to any deal that Drexel was working on," I added.

The prosecution team pressed for more, but Pomerantz reminded them that this was only a proffer. It was exhausting, humbling and very, very painful.

I did not want to be here, and I told the others so. Several times during the torturous day, prosecutors indicated that they were unhappy with my reticence and indicated that they were ready to walk out and leave me facing a lengthy prison term. Several other times I was poised to leave and take the full dose of judicial medicine. Pomerantz and Feldman grew exhausted from their attempts to hold together Liman's deal.

"Have you had any contact with Boesky since your arrest?" Carberry asked.

"The last call I had was May twelfth," I said, "just before your men came to my office. He was calling to follow up on our previous meeting about the job offer."

"Right," Carberry acknowledged.

I felt weak, and I must have looked it.

"We appreciate your candor," Carberry said. "We know this has been very difficult for you and your family. We know it's a very hard thing for you to do."

They asked me if I knew of anyone else at Drexel who was involved in illegal activities.

"No," I said.

They pressed further, throwing names onto the table: Milken, Joseph, Icahn and others.

"No," I repeated. I stressed that my trading began long before I joined Drexel and pointed out that I had been very careful to keep those activities isolated. On the job, I asserted, I was known for my professional behavior, my conservatism.

It was already late in the evening when the government struck below the belt, first suggesting, then demanding, that I telephone my trading partners, seeking to elicit incriminating statements from them. I wondered, Is this how it works? Do I have to do this?

My mind was clouded and spent. I barely realized what was happening as they led me to a special room adjacent to Giuliani's office on the eighth floor, but my exhausted brain rebelled when I saw the equipment set up to record whatever was said on both ends of a telephone conversation.

"No way!" I shouted.

"The deal will be off," one of the investigators threatened.

"It won't work," I countered, desperate to find some argument that would make sense to everyone. I pointed out that it would be out of character, after years and years of subterfuge—using code names and all—for me, amid the glare of all the publicity, to call my friends—at their homes, no less—and try to get them to make damning admissions.

Pomerantz tried to keep me cool, but I was not a rational man at this moment. A bitter argument ensued for more than a half hour, punctuated by my screams of protest and shrieks of pain.

Finally, one of the government men decreed, "That's it. Make the calls or the deal's dead."

Silence followed for several full minutes.

Dennis, I thought, you have already hurt your family deeply. You have to do something to make it easier. Would it help them if you were sent away to prison for ten years or even longer?

It was clear that the system had taken control of my life. I no longer had the ability to make independent choices.

Did it really make any difference? I wondered. It was obvious that Wilkis was ready to talk, and he knew almost everything. By now it was clear that Giuliani and his crew had every intention of sending me to prison for an as-yet-unspecified period of time. Why were they being so harsh on me when they were allowing Bank Leu's management to walk away with immunity?

Pomerantz drew me aside and reminded me of the stakes. A manageable prison term—one year, perhaps two—seemed likely. But if I resisted, under RICO, the government could take me away from society and from my family for most of the rest of my life. He added, "Your friends might be walking in the door right now to cut their own deals. That's what I would advise them to do."

This was, I realized, the most painful, gut-crunching moment I had ever known. On the outside, I was sopping with perspiration. On the inside, I felt as if I were bleeding. The vise was closing . . .

Finally I returned to the investigators and announced quietly, "I'll make the calls if I can tell my friends the truth."

Someone asked derisively, "What's the truth?"

"The truth is quite simple," I replied. "I'll say, 'The government has an overwhelming case. It's all over. I'm pleading guilty, and I recommend that you get a lawyer and do the same.' " I felt my voice waver. Softly I said, "I'll tell them the truth. It's the only honorable thing I can do." What I would *not* do, I declared, was attempt to lure them into any self-condemning statements.

Another half-hour passed in negotiation before the feds agreed to the compromise plan.

By now it was eleven P.M. I was exhausted, hungry, too numb to even realize that I had, for the first time in memory, given up a fight. The activity around me was a dim cloud, obscuring reality.

As if from a distance I realized that someone was dialing Wilkis's number.

I recited my prearranged speech, and said no more. Wilkis wished me luck. Then a similar call was placed to Sokolow. He, too, wished me luck.

I prayed that they would minimize the consequences for themselves and their families.

When the ordeal was finally over, Pomerantz drove me home. During the ride, he told me that, throughout all his years of practicing criminal law, he had never seen a defendant react as emotionally as I did when I was asked to make those phone calls.

LAURIE was already asleep when I arrived home.

I lay my troubled head upon a pillow, but comfort eluded me. I felt my body twitch with involuntary spasms. I was making a mess of the bed covers, and I knew that I was disturbing Laurie. In frustration I rose and paced the living room floor.

How could it have come to all this? I wondered. It wasn't supposed to end this way. Was I really the mastermind that the government seemed to consider me? Or was I, more-or-less, a rather average man, blinded by unrelenting ambition, to be sure, but now facing consequences far beyond my calculations?

It was nearly four A.M. when I threw on some clothes and stepped out onto the nearly deserted Park Avenue sidewalk. I realized that my feet were heading toward the parking garage. I looked down and found the Ferrari keys in my hand.

"Don't drive the Ferrari!" These were Liman's words ringing in my memory as I slipped the protective blue cover off of my beautiful red baby. "Don't drive the Ferrari," he had warned. "The government is going to want it. It's a symbol. You must stay low-key. Don't touch that car!"

I drowned out the warning words with the explosive, satisfying roar of the 12-cylinder, 48-valve engine. Thunder reverberated through the parking garage and echoed inside my head.

I slipped the gear shift into position and heard the tires squeal on the pavement.

The machine glided along 96th Street to the FDR Drive. I threw a tape into the stereo and turned up the volume to its maximum level. I slid open the power windows and bathed my aching head in a rush of air. Only minutes later I was at the Triborough Bridge. I tossed coins into the toll hopper and squealed the tires once more.

With my foot to the floor, I headed for Long Island. I felt the satisfying smooth mesh of the gears as I upshifted. The car accelerated like a cannonball.

Suddenly a sharp turn appeared ahead of me, a full 90-degree angle. I downshifted and hit the brakes simultaneously, but still took the turn far too fast. G forces pushed my body against the door. I heard a shrill scream, louder than the radio, and realized that it emanated from my own throat.

A straightaway stretched in front of me and once more I shifted through the gears and floored the accelerator. Now my back was pressed hard against the seat. My breath came in deep draughts and my hands felt so slippery that I had to force myself to keep a tight grip on the steering wheel. I risked a quick glance at the speedometer and watched the needle shoot ahead.

One hundred ten. One hundred twenty. One hundred thirty. *One hundred forty!!!*

"Stop it, Dennis, stop it!" I screamed, or thought—I was not sure which.

I lifted my foot and felt the car slow gradually to a manageable pace. I forced myself to breath rhythmically. I felt the pounding in my chest recede in tandem with the speedometer.

I drove for hours, until the sun filtered into my consciousness and the highways were crowded. I looked with envy at the ordinary people driving their ordinary cars to their ordinary jobs.

* * *

LATER that day government investigators reviewed the tape recordings of the phone calls and expressed their outrage. They would be useless in court.

One of them growled, "You'll have to do it again."

As it turned out, this was not necessary.

I was allowed to clean out my desk. The task was to be accomplished on the evening of June 4, and Drexel bigwigs spread the word that all employees of the M&A Department were to be absent.

Liman's associate Brad Karp was with me. A Harvard-educated rising star in Paul, Weiss's litigation department, he had become my guardian angel. An IRS agent and a Drexel security guard accompanied us. When we stepped out of the elevator onto the eighth floor, I was surprised to see that one associate was still there, crunching his numbers late into the evening. He was a young man whom I had only recently helped to hire, partly because the eagerness in his eyes reminded me of myself, not many years ago. He did not glance up as our quiet procession made its way through the room.

We passed the office of Marty Siegel, Drexel's newest superstar in the M&A Department, and I reflected ruefully upon the news that someone at Drexel had yanked my picture from the 1985 annual report and replaced it with Siegel's image.

The security guard opened the padlock on my office door. Then, as the IRS agent watched carefully to make sure that I did not dip into the business files, I began the solemn task of cleaning off the walls, storing plaques in a cardboard box. There were numerous "tombstone ads" that had run in the financial press, announcing the successful culmination of deals. My associates had framed each of these and presented them to me. The most memorable was PANTRY PRIDE HAS ACQUIRED REVLON.

The IRS agent, fascinated by the Quotron next to my desk, asked how it worked. I punched a few buttons and showed him how we could, at this moment, get stock quotes from all over the world. He asked about a few particular stocks trading on the Vancouver Exchange, and I showed him how to access the information. "Thanks a lot," he said.

I went through the desk drawers, slowly, carefully, savoring each moment. Here were some letters, there were some photographs. After a time I had several boxes full of material.

There were no more drawers to explore, but still I sat at my desk for many minutes. No one spoke to me. Here was the symbolic end of the most exciting, fascinating portion of my life. I was thirty-three years old. I had been a managing director of the most upbeat, powerful investment banking house of the 80s. Around me was an array of phones and computer terminals and, of course, the Quotron. Just as real, although not visible, was an enormous sense of power. The current issue of *Barron's* quoted Michael Boylan, president of Macfadden Holdings, who proclaimed: "Drexel is like a god . . . and a god can do anything it wants."

This desk was a throne, and I had toppled from it.

I closed my eyes and wept inner tears.

Why? I asked myself. Why did I do it? With a start I realized that I was not asking myself, specifically, why I had crossed the legal line to become an inside trader. The larger question was why I had succumbed so completely to the lure of excess, whether gained legitimately or otherwise. It would be easy to blame it all on Wall Street, but the Street, at its most basic level, is simply the visible quantification of the current mood of American business. The Street pumps money into the business world, and it had done so in the 80s at a crazier pace, perhaps, than ever before. But the Street can only supply if there is a demand.

The demand of the 80s was incredible throughout the business world. Capital was available through pension funds, insurance companies, banks, S&Ls and international investors. And not only was the money available in enormous amounts, but the providers were willing to employ it in increasingly risky ventures. The political climate was receptive, willing to maintain deficit spending. Antitrust lawyers were looking for new careers as the Reagan Administration relaxed the standards. Shareholders demanded increased earnings, and the business world responded by producing the longest period of sustained growth in modern economic history. Factory utilization rates were high. Employment levels were high. All over the country people were earning money and spending it like never before.

So much happened and was still happening that it was easy to lose perspective, to forget that business in general and Wall Street in particular is cyclical. There are natural stages of expansion and contraction. One follows the other, like a sell order follows a buy order. If I had still been on the inside, if I had still been caught up in DrexelWorld, I might have missed the signals.

But now I was outside looking in, and I wondered why no one else seemed to realize that the markets were telling us: Enough is enough. It was, perhaps, understandable that the Baby Boomers, who came to the Street in the late 70s and early 80s, did not remember back to the mid 70s when interest rates were at 18 percent and the Dow languished in the 700s, but even the senior people on Wall Street did not seem to have a sense of history.

I wondered, where is it written that this fairy-tale growth is destined to continue forever?

There are no free rides. There is a tangible cost to everything. We pay it now, or we pay it later. Like nearly everyone else around me in this environment, I had grossly underestimated those costs. Too late, I totaled them up: My career had evaporated, my financial life lay in ruins, my self-esteem was zero.

My family was suffering intense anguish. I was going to jail.

Ahead was total uncertainty. The cumulative weight of the disgrace pressed down upon my shoulders, forcing me deep into the leather upholstery of the chair that I would never sit in again.

After a time, Karp approached the desk and gently broke into my reverie. "I'm very sorry," he whispered. "Let me help you carry this stuff out."

With my arms loaded down by a heavy cardboard box, I stepped out of my office for the last time. In the bullpen, the young associate was still busy. As I passed near his desk, he glanced up from his work and caught my eye. I stopped for a moment and returned his gaze.

His voice was low-pitched, soft and filled with warmth. He said simply: "Good luck."

CHAPTER THIRTY

IT WAS THE VERY NEXT DAY, June 5, less than a month after my arrest, when, without ever being indicted, testifying at a trial or appearing before a grand jury, I stood before Judge Gerard Goettel in federal court and declared, "To contest the charges against me on technical grounds would serve only to prolong the suffering of my family. It would also convey the wrong message. I have violated the law and I have remorse for my conduct, not excuses." Then I entered a plea of guilty to four felony charges. Sentencing was deferred until the judge could study all the issues; in the interim, I had to consider the sobering fact that I faced maximum penalties of twenty years in prison and $610,000 in fines.

That covered the criminal charges, but I still had to deal with the civil penalties. On the same day, I agreed to pay restitution to the SEC of the $11.6 million in alleged trading profits. The bulk of that was covered by the cash frozen in my Bank Leu account, but that still left about $1 million outstanding, and my assets were fair game.

Perhaps the worst of the civil penalties was that I had to agree to accept an injunction barring me from employment in the securities business for the rest of my life. The career that I loved, that was ingrained, was now forbidden to me.

Liman and I left the courthouse together. My lawyer instructed his driver to first drop him at the office, and then take me out to the

Marriott Hotel near LaGuardia Airport, where I had sequestered Laurie and Adam in order to isolate them from the press. Liman had to repeat the instructions carefully so that his driver, a recent Russian immigrant, could understand.

Some minutes later, as the car was in the middle of the Triborough Bridge, the driver cocked an ear to the all-news station 1010 WINS ("You give us twenty-two minutes and we'll give you the world"). The lead story was my guilty plea. The driver, listening intently, was less concerned about the possible prison term than he was with the nearly $12 million in fines. "Mr. Levine," he asked, "is dis you dey talk about on da radio?"

"Yes, it is."

"I can no unnerstan dis country," he said, shaking his head. "You make and dey take. It make no sense. You make and dey take."

LAURIE and I were allowed to keep the Park Avenue co-op, our personal effects, our 1983 BMW and personal savings that would allow my family to survive for a time, but the rest—real estate investments, my retirement account, my Drexel stock and my shares in various Drexel partnerships, including the $100,000 I had sunk into Beatrice warrants—vanished from our lives. It was called a "global settlement." This theme reached its peak the day the government demanded the Ferrari. Officials refused to pick up the car from the parking garage near our co-op because they were unsure they could handle such a high-performance vehicle on the streets of Manhattan. They insisted that I deliver it to a designated location.

The Ferrari had only 3,847 miles on the odometer and, thanks to its rising popularity, was now worth more than I had paid for it. Nevertheless, when the government tried to sell it, the only interested buyer was the dealer, who re-purchased it for less than the original price. My account was credited with that lower value.

Laurie and I traded in the BMW for a Ford.

THE very day I entered my guilty plea, Wilkis resigned his post at E. F. Hutton and officially turned himself in to the U.S. Attorney's Office. Very quickly he provided prosecutors with the identity of his "kid" at Lazard Frères. Investigators insisted that he make an incriminating phone call to the "kid," and he did so. He was Randall Cecola. He had been a junior financial analyst at Lazard from September 1983 to July 1985 and was currently a student at the Harvard Business School.

Meanwhile, investigators continued to probe into every nook and cranny of my affairs. I had to supply them with all of my personal telephone bills. From Drexel they received copies of my office long distance logs and my expense account vouchers. They demanded copies of all of my bank records, covering accounts of any kind. They wanted copies of all my canceled checks, front and back, from 1980 forward. They sought all of my credit card receipts; I supplied these, and they traced the records back through American Express and other companies, just to double-check. They examined all of my past and present business relationships, which, since I had been at Drexel, had burgeoned. They wanted copies of all of my correspondence, business and personal, as well as calendars and daily logs. They even demanded a detailed schematic of my family tree, dating back three generations. They hired the accounting firm of Touche, Ross & Co. to conduct a thorough audit of my financial records and to compare it to the data supplied by Bank Leu.

Hour after hour, day after day, they asked me questions, covering every detail contained in the mass of assembled paperwork.

The investigators concentrated their attention on two areas. They wanted to know all the machinations of my dealings with Bank Leu, and I realized that the information I was giving them probably differed in a few essential details from what the bankers were telling them. So be it; all I could do was tell them the truth.

The government's other major area of concern was Boesky.

It was June 25 when they asked me to make a monitored phone call to Boesky.

No, I thought, I don't want to do this. I argued, "I think with all this attention surrounding my case, it would be very unlikely that he would take my call."

"Well," someone responded, "we'd like you to try anyway."

Thomas Doonan, the investigator who had escorted me to the Metropolitan Correctional Center on the night of my arrest, came to my home the next day and took me to a very public place. I made the call, but was relieved to hear that Boesky was out of the country. "Please leave word that I called," I said.

After I hung up my mind raced. I could picture Boesky, flitting about between the Bahamas, the Caymans, Switzerland, Liechtenstein and elsewhere, shifting funds, shielding assets.

WE had to get away. We had to collect our thoughts. Our very dear friends Irwin and Dona Kruger, oblivious to the media circus surrounding our lives, invited Laurie, Adam and me to spend the July Fourth weekend with them at their home in East Hampton. We accepted the invitation immediately, eager for a chance to get away from the insanity of reality. The rest of the country was celebrating a great event, the centennial of the Statue of Liberty, which meant that, at least for a time, we could enjoy anonymity.

But over the weekend, Flumenbaum reached me by phone with a chilling report: NYPD headquarters had logged two phone tips from the same anonymous caller, who reported that he had overheard a conversation in a New Jersey bar, indicating that some "very serious" physical harm was going to befall Dennis Levine.

"The government is checking it out," Flumenbaum said. "But it may take some time in order to determine the credibility." He said that Doonan would call to brief me on appropriate precautions.

Within minutes Doonan was on the line. "President Reagan is in town," he explained. "The FBI, the Secret Service, all the NYPD agents who could investigate this threat—they're all busy."

Doonan issued instructions: For the time being, don't come home. Stay where you are or find some other place to stay; let us know how to reach you. Don't come into the city, but if you have to, stay away from your normal patterns. Don't go near your car. Even if you see that it has a flat tire, don't touch it.

I broke this news to Laurie as gently as possible, but, of course, she was as agitated as I was. We could not jeopardize our friends by remaining in their home, so we booked a room at an inn in Montauck, registering under an alias.

On the second day of our stay, we were surprised by a sudden knock on the door. My eyes checked to make sure the security bolt was in place. I peered through the peephole and saw a large, strange man. "Who's there?" I asked.

A heavy voice barked, "Security."

"What do you want?" I asked nervously.

"I'm checking the smoke detectors in all the rooms."

My ear heard a strong Brooklyn accent. Involuntarily I glanced around. Laurie was watching, nervous. Adam was glued to the TV set. "Uh," I stammered, "we're not dressed right now. I can't let you in."

"Look up at the smoke detector," he said. "See if the red light is on."

I reported that it was. This satisfied him, and I watched his distorted image through the lens of the peephole as he moved on to the next room.

I ran to the phone and called the front desk, inquiring whether there was, indeed, a security officer at the inn checking on the smoke detectors. After several agonizing minutes the bored clerk told me that, yes, there was.

I hung up the phone. My eyes met Laurie's and we wondered: What comes next?

THE paper trail led inexorably to others.

On July 8 the SEC served a subpoena on Wachtell, Lipton, demanding documents concerning numerous trades. At first, Ilan Reich was one of those assigned to compile the records, but Gary Lynch of the SEC disclosed to Herbert Wachtell that Reich was the target of the inquiry. Reich hired Robert Morvillo, the same attorney who had handled the case of Reich's former associate Carlo Florentino, years ago. Morvillo ran to the prosecutors, ready and willing to strike a deal.

As the heat increased, Ira Sokolow turned himself in and implicated "Goldie," who, I discovered, was David Brown, a vice president in the mortgage-securities department of Goldman Sachs. He and Sokolow had roomed together in college. I knew how difficult it must be for him to have to present evidence against his old friend. What particularly concerned the Street about Brown's involvement was that, in his job, he had no connection with M&A activities; he was either able to access confidential documents or he, in turn, had another source at Goldman Sachs.

The Justice Department theorized that Sokolow had been, perhaps, the single best source of my trades, with the Nabisco deal as the standout transaction. Investigators calculated that Sokolow had taken a total of $150,000 in cash from me and had passed on $27,500 of that to Brown.

The others reached a common decision. The cases were far too strong. There was no alternative but to plead guilty and cooperate.

Prosecutors pricked up their ears when Wilkis corroborated my account of my relationship with Boesky. He told them how I had tipped Boesky to the Houston Natural Gas and Nabisco deals. What he could not tell them about, since he was unaware of it, was the payment formula that Boesky had devised.

I was told that investigators subpoenaed my secretary, Marilyn, and asked her for a list of my frequent contacts. Boesky was at the top of the list.

But neither my lawyers nor I believed that the government could pin any real crimes on Boesky—not based upon the information elicited from me.

MORE than a week passed before Doonan said that he thought it was all right for us to come home, but he still advised extreme caution, especially in the use of our car.

He picked me up at our co-op on the morning of July 14, ostensibly for security reasons, but, I realized in retrospect, he also knew that it would be a particularly agitating day for me. He wanted me to once more attempt to reach Boesky by phone. "Don't you guys ever give up?" I asked in an effort to dissuade him. "There's no way he'll talk to me."

Doonan shrugged off my comments and drove me to 77th Street and Madison Avenue. He parked in an illegal spot and placed a placard on the dashboard, noting that he was a police officer working on a case. Then he took me into the Madison Hotel, located an isolated pay phone and produced a small cassette recorder and a suction cup microphone, which he placed near the mouthpiece of the phone.

Once more I felt ill. Once more I realized that I had no choice.

"Just try to speak to him," Doonan said. "We don't want you to try to draw him out. We just want to play on his mind. Try to set up a meeting with him."

Panic assailed me. "You want me to meet with him?" I asked. "You must be kidding!" I kept the volume of my voice low in this public place, but my words were forceful. After a week of hiding out on Long Island, I carried residual fear within me. Already I had developed the habit of constantly looking over my shoulder. "This is very serious," I raged. Doonan's eyes were steely. I continued more calmly, "Anyway, there is no way he is going to meet with me. He won't even take my call."

"I'm telling you what we would like to see happen," he said. "Don't try to draw him out in this conversation. Just try to set up a meeting with him."

Somehow, my fingers managed to punch in the numbers. When I asked for Boesky and his secretary said, "Please hold," I prayed that he would not answer. But, to my surprise and anguish, he took the call. It was ten A.M.

"How are you doing?" he asked in a warm tone. "How is your family?"

"My family is fine," I replied. "I'm not doing so well. The government is putting a lot of pressure on me. They want to know everything I did."

"Well," Boesky said, "I fully expected you'd tell them everything about our relationship. We've done nothing wrong. I want you to be aboveboard and forthright with the government."

My God! I thought, he knows this call is monitored! He's probably taping the call, too. I forced calmness into my voice as I said, "I'd like to get together with you."

"Why don't you call me later in the day, and we'll see what we can schedule," he suggested. Then he added, "Let me know if you need anything. Good luck."

As I hung up the phone Doonan said, "That was fine. This is now playing on his mind."

"I don't understand," I said. "What is it you are trying to accomplish here?"

"I'm gonna go back and play the tape for Charlie," he said, referring to Carberry. "I will call you and tell you what's required next." Clearly, whatever would be required next would not be a request; it would be an order. I hated this!

Doonan drove me back home. Shortly after noon he called and said, "We don't want you to meet with Boesky. It won't be necessary. Carberry says we should hold off on a meeting for right now."

I allowed myself a deep sigh.

"If he reaches out to you," Doonan said, "please let us know."

"What do you mean?"

"We think he's gonna contact you and offer you some money. Hush money."

SOON afterward, Boesky sought the advice of the man who, he had once told me, "does all this crap for me." It was none other than Harvey Pitt, who, in my opinion, had advised Bank Leu to negotiate a deal with the SEC when it could have rather easily hidden behind the veil of Bahamian law. Pitt's advice to Boesky had obviously been similar: Cut a deal as fast as you can.

Assistant U.S. Attorney John Carroll later contended that Boesky simply "walked in the door" and started talking. Another of Boesky's attorneys, Leon Silverman, agreed that Boesky himself "initiated contact with the United States Attorney."

Boesky told the government about his insider trading activities, not only with me, but with at least one other well-known investment banker. Beyond that, he detailed various schemes, concocted with those in the highest circles of power, to circumvent SEC regulations and tax laws. Said Carroll, "He has played fast and loose with the rules that govern our markets, with the effect of manipulating the outcome of financial transactions measured in the hundreds of millions of dollars."

At the request of the U.S. Attorney's Office, Boesky began to make and tape-record telephone calls to at least fourteen Wall Street high rollers, and to arrange face-to-face meetings with them, during which Boesky was fitted with a hidden microphone as he tried to induce incriminating statements. He submitted to the prosecutors more than a half million pages of documents, detailing his dealings with investment banks, particularly Drexel, and investment bankers, particularly Milken. Carroll said Boesky was "a model cooperator."

Prosecutors would later characterize Boesky's actions as "unprecedented," adding that his cooperation gave "the government a window on the rampant criminal conduct that has permeated the securities industry in the 1980s."

When I learned about all this, sometime after the fact, I knew that the government had given him no choice.

*   *   *

BOESKY flew to California to visit Milken at his home. As the two men sat about the pool, they discussed the effects that my arrest might have upon their own business dealings. They agreed that day that they should limit their transactions for a time, at least as long as there was increased scrutiny by law enforcement officials.

They discussed the need to substantiate the claim that the $5.3 million payment, made from the Boesky organization to Drexel on March 21, 1986, was for legitimate advisory services.

PLETSCHER, fired from his post at Bank Leu, returned to Zurich in August, along with his bride. Unable to find another job in banking, he took a sales position with a computer firm.

Meier, meanwhile, was charged by the SEC with eighteen counts of trading in stocks on the basis of confidential information. In his absence, a court entered a default judgment against him, leveling a fine of $427,808, which remained uncollected. He was reported to be living in Zollikon, Switzerland, near Zurich.

Foreboding developments occurred in the business world. As a result of information supplied by the Chicago Board Options Exchange, the SEC began focusing on the possibility of insider trading in options of CBS, Inc., during Marvin Davis's takeover attempt. News reports indicated that the SEC was looking at the activities of a dozen investors, as well as the role that First Boston played in the acquisition attempt, but no charges were ever filed.

LTV Corporation slipped into Chapter 11 bankruptcy and stopped payment on $2.1 billion worth of high-yield bonds. It was the largest junk-bond default yet and brought a fresh wave of criticism directed at Milken's financing tactics, despite the fact that it was a Lehman Brothers deal.

The new surge of M&A-bashing pushed its way into my consciousness, but I was, of course, too concerned about my own problems to dwell on the industry's situation. Late one night, after listening to a news report concerning the problems with LTV, I felt the now-familiar pain of my banishment and, yet, a new emotion surfaced. Was it relief? Or boredom?

Far more interesting was the cascade of what I could only think of as "fan mail" that poured in every day. Some of it was sent via Liman's office, but much of it came directly to my home, since the address was publicized widely. To be sure, there was a smattering of outrage, but my thumbnail count indicated that the letters ran about 10:1 in a favorable vein. Some expressed the foolish opinion that I was a political scapegoat; why, they wondered, should the government punish me for something that everyone on Wall Street did? Others unabashedly asked for investment advice.

IT felt as if I spent several lifetimes in my lawyers' offices. This time I was huddling with Liman when Karp ran in with a telephone message. One of Laurie's family members in Florida had called with the news that her father, after his long, valiant, painful struggle, had finally left us. Laurie was now seven months pregnant, and I had asked her family to tell me first, so that I could break the news to her as gently as possible.

"Go," Liman said. "Leave. Be with your wife."

Only a few minutes later, when I walked into our home, Laurie glanced up, alarmed to see me back so early. She read the message in my eyes. We clung to one another in sorrow, in desperation, in fear.

Liman spoke with Carberry, and the prosecutor responded in a gentlemanly fashion. He arranged to have my bail restrictions relaxed so that we could fly to Florida for the funeral.

At the cemetery, as the service neared an end, Laurie clutched at her stomach. I grasped her hand firmly. Then, as Leonard Skolnik went to his final rest, I felt his unborn grandchild shift and stretch.

IN October, Boesky asked for another meeting with Milken. One of Milken's close associates advised against this, for by now there were rumors that Boesky had been drawn into the whole affair and might be cooperating with the prosecutors. Milken said he would meet with Boesky, but assured his colleague that he would be "speaking for the record."

The suspicions were well grounded, for Boesky was, in fact, wearing a wire. The meeting was scheduled for poolside at the Beverly Hills

Hotel, but when Milken arrived Boesky insisted that they move indoors, to one of the rooms.

Again they discussed the $5.3 million payment. They assured one another that, in the event of a government investigation into their relationship, their subordinates would be reliable.

Some time after this meeting, Milken's associate asked if he had been "careful" with his words. Milken responded that he was not sure that he had been "careful enough."

CHAPTER THIRTY-ONE

ON OCTOBER 28 *The Wall Street Journal* reported an apparently significant decrease in price run-ups of takeover stocks prior to public announcements. They attributed this to an epidemic of paranoia on the Street in the wake of my arrest. The caution, the report declared, was particularly evidenced by the fact that Boesky, "probably the country's best-known takeover speculator, has reduced his market activity." The report added, "Mr. Boesky didn't return phone calls seeking comment."

DREXEL managed to slough off the negative publicity concerning my arrest, in large part by pointing out that my alleged insider trading activities had begun long before I joined the firm. I was cut loose, but Drexel soared ever higher.

Milken was at the very top of his game. *Institutional Investor* quoted an unnamed investment banker who dribbled praise: "Mike is the only person in the securities business today who can do it all. He is a master trader, salesman, deal structurer, credit analyst, merger tactician, securities venturer. And he does these things at the level of the best guy in each of these categories." Estimates of Milken's net worth ran as high as $1 billion. Some spoke openly of him as a candidate for Secretary of U.S. Treasury, but I was dubious; that would be a gigantic step down.

In a decade, Milken had taken the annual junk-bond market from $15 billion to $125 billion. Drexel now controlled more than 60 percent of the junk-bond market and was virtually the only firm that could amass multi-billions in capital overnight. Milken could negotiate fees almost at will. Increasingly, he demanded an equity stake in a venture, and as a result, Drexel was now partial owner of more than 150 other firms.

Milken was poised to export his messianic concepts to the Japanese business community, which was historically conservative in its outlook but was also accustomed to carrying a relatively high level of debt, since it could count on a friendly government to bail out any large company experiencing cash flow difficulties. On November 10, Milken held a version of Drexel's High-Yield Bond Conference in Tokyo. He brought in numerous associates to proclaim the wonders of the junk-bond revolution in America, and he was armed with the results of a new SEC study, which proclaimed that there was no "justification for new regulatory initiatives aimed at curbing the use of this kind of debt issuance . . ."

This was the first stage of a new thrust. Milken was looking beyond industrialized Japan. He now burned with a fervor to solve the debt problems of the Third World by using junk bonds to refinance existing shaky loans.

He was also busy with other activities. One of these was a humanitarian venture in cooperation with Monty Hall. On the surface it was ironic, for here was America's premier dealmaker in league with the legendary host of TV's "Let's Make a Deal." But, in fact, Milken's intent was extremely serious. The two men had become friends when Drexel had sponsored a benefit dinner for the neonatal center at Cedars-Sinai Hospital, and Hall had emceed.

Each was somewhat surprised by the level of the other's interest in charitable activities concerning youngsters. Hall helped to raise more than $20 million annually for various charities, principally Variety International, which aids sick, handicapped, abused and underprivileged children. He knew that Milken was a generous contributor to numerous charities, but did not realize that he was also a "hands-on" volunteer.

Milken plunged in, bringing other Drexel volunteers with him, shepherding children to picnics, baseball games, circuses and other outings.

One day, as they helped supervise the visit of hundreds of children to Universal Studios, Hall saw Milken give up his own cafeteria tray to a child who had not yet been fed.

"WHY all these delays?" I kept asking. "I'd like to get sentenced, get on with my punishment, get it over with, get started on my life once again. Why won't the government let this thing go forward?"

Several times over the past few months, Doonan had called to ask, "Is everything okay? Has Boesky tried to contact you?"

He had not, and I reported as much. There was, of course, no reason for Boesky to contact me now, for although I was unaware of it, he was already in government hands.

Doonan was apparently merely trying to keep me off the scent with his calls and his repeated assertion, "Let me know if we can do anything for you."

Thus I was kept in the dark, throughout the summer and into autumn.

I was necessarily preoccupied with my own affairs, but an occasional story from the outside world returned me to my Wall Street life. Perelman was ready to make his next move, and it was an audacious triple-play, indeed. He was considering simultaneous takeover attempts of Transworld (a hotel company), CPC International (a food processing firm) and Gillette. The Gillette deal alone would more than double the assets of his corporate empire. On November 14, with intense internal pain, I contemplated the news that Perelman had issued a tender offer, valued at $4.12 billion, for Gillette. I could have been there, I knew. I also knew that I would probably never be there again.

My phone rang shortly after the market closed, and I heard Flumenbaum ask, "Are you sitting down?"

"Yes." I took a deep breath, awaiting yet another blow.

"Ivan Boesky, today, is pleading guilty in a case related to yours. I don't have details, but I got a call from the U.S. Attorney's Office and they are announcing the deal. I wanted to let you know." I was in shock, like everyone else.

At that very moment Marty Siegel was in Marty Lipton's office at Wachtell, Lipton, stunned by the subpoena that a federal marshal had slapped into his hand.

Other subpoenas were served upon executives at Salomon Brothers,

Goldman Sachs and Prudential-Bache. Carl Icahn was handed a subpoena, and the word held that the SEC was looking into allegations that he and Boesky had cooperated in a plan to run up the price of Gulf+Western stock by spreading takeover rumors. Icahn swiftly denied the unfounded allegations (and they were never proved).

As these various Wall Street stars studied the details of the legal papers, the SEC went public with the announcement that Boesky was implicated in the insider trading scandal as well as other schemes to manipulate securities transactions, and had already pegged others.

Within minutes a cadre of federal marshals appeared with grand jury and SEC subpoenas for both Michael and Lowell Milken, as well as other employees of the "Drexel Bank."

Now it was announced that Boesky, through Pitt, had carved out an agreement with the U.S. Attorney's Office. The SEC agreement charged Boesky with profiting more than $50 million from non-public information that I had provided (*The Wall Street Journal* calculated the take at $203 million, but the SEC denied this assessment vigorously). Despite the fact that the government claimed evidence of an incredible array of crimes committed by Boesky, they agreed to allow him to plead guilty to a single count of conspiring to make a false filing with the SEC. That crime carried a maximum penalty of a five-year prison term and a $250,000 fine. In addition, Boesky consented to a civil injunction and an SEC order requiring him to pay a $50 million penalty and to place another $50 million into an escrow fund to settle claims against him and his companies. He resigned from the bar and agreed to accept a lifetime ban from employment in the securities market. It was interesting to note that the total amount of Boesky's penalty, $100 million, was only slightly less than the entire annual budget of the SEC.

Boesky was reported to have once said, "I can't predict my demise, but I suspect it will occur abruptly."

THE announcement of Boesky's fall was promulgated on a Friday, an obvious strategy to allow the market to digest the news over the weekend. Here was the confirmation of a widely held public suspicion that the market was a game rigged for insiders, and many investors decided they wanted out. Others exhibited the belief that the M&A onslaught was over. Everyone suffered a case of weekend jitters.

According to Jim Dahl, Milken called him on Sunday and asked him to come to the office to go over some things. Dahl arrived and busied himself at his desk for two hours as Milken sat at his desk. Growing impatient, Dahl finally said, "Mike, if there is something you want to talk to me about, let's do it because I am out of here soon." Milken drew Dahl off to the men's room, walked over to the sink, turned on the water and began washing his hands. Some would contend that this was a tactic to create a diversionary noise to thwart electronic eavesdropping; others would say that it was possible Milken merely wanted to clean his hands. At any rate, with the water running, Milken leaned over and purportedly said to Dahl, "Whatever you need to do, do it." He looked Dahl in the eye and awaited a response.

"Okay," Dahl replied. He left the men's room and went home. He interpreted Milken's statement as a suggestion to destroy any incriminating documents that the grand jury might seek, but he did not, in fact, comply with the request.

According to Terren Peizer, Milken's assistant, Milken came to him during the next week and asked whether Peizer still had a blue ledger book, containing records pertaining to various business agreements between Milken and David Solomon, whose Solomon Asset Management Company, Inc., managed mutual funds that specialized in high-yield securities. One was the offshore-based Finsbury Group Limited, which was underwritten by one of the affiliate companies in Drexel's complex web. The Drexel affiliate paid a 1 percent commission to agents who sold shares of the fund to foreign investors and, since those sales boosted the business of the Drexel Bank, the affiliate charged the commission to the High-Yield and Convertible Bond Department. Milken, Solomon and other Drexel officials had agreed on a plan to recoup those commissions by "adjusting" the fees paid to Solomon. In effect, the fund's customers paid the commission unwittingly. In addition to this arrangement, Milken had acceded to a tax-juggling scheme apparently proposed by Solomon in December 1985. Solomon had asked Drexel to conduct certain securities trades for one of his entities, Dina Partners, in order to generate short-term losses that would benefit his personal income tax status. Milken had assisted Solomon in various transactions, which resulted in a fast $1.6 million loss for Solomon and an equally quick profit for Drexel. The two men had an implicit understanding that Drexel would later provide Solomon with an investment opportunity to make up the losses.

According to Peizer, Milken told him to give the ledger book detailing these transactions to Lorraine Spurge, a trusted associate who was close to Milken. On the following day, Peizer reported, while standing with Spurge in the kitchenette adjacent to Drexel's trading floor, he turned on a water spigot to muffle the sound of the conversation, handed the ledger book to Spurge, and said, "Michael asked me to give this to you." (Spurge apparently disputed this story during her later grand jury testimony.)

THAT Monday the market did surprisingly well. The Dow Jones Industrial Average fell a modest 13.07 points and the Street breathed more easily—until rumors surfaced that Boesky had allowed government investigators to videotape his transactions with other high rollers. That word led to a continuing decline on Tuesday and by noon it was severe enough to trigger computerized trading programs into initiating further sales. By the end of the day the DJIA had toppled more than forty-three points.

Among the hardest hit were the stocks of companies rumored to be merger targets: Borg-Warner, Time Inc. USX (an Icahn target, formerly U.S. Steel), Stop & Shop and Lockheed. On Tuesday alone, Perelman's target Gillette dropped seven points to close at $60 per share. One listing of a dozen such takeover issues showed a loss of 8.7 percent of their value during the course of the following week. Analysts estimated that the arbitrage community took a $500 million bath that week.

Drexel chairman Robert Linton issued a statement declaring rumors that Milken was about to resign as "categorically untrue." Nevertheless, junk-bond prices plunged.

Sandy Sigoloff said that his Wickes Companies, finding the rug pulled out from under their financing arrangements, might have to back away from a $1.7 billion deal to purchase Lear Siegler.

"Ivan is still my friend," declared T. Boone Pickens, but not everyone responded with such grace.

Holt, Rinehart & Winston announced that it was withdrawing Boesky's book, *Merger Mania,* from circulation, declaring that it would be unethical to continue to promote the work.

Gillette used the Boesky affair as a basis to defend itself against Perelman's tender offer. Gillette filed suit, charging Perelman with violations of securities laws, and demanded access to Boesky's records concerning any dealings with Perelman. Perelman called the accusations "totally without merit and self-serving" and continued with his takeover campaign for a time. Gillette counter-punched by threatening to sell off 20 percent of its stock to an unnamed third party, rumored to be the Ralston Purina Company.

Eventually the principals reached a compromise. Gillette announced that it would pay the Revlon Group $558 million to end the takeover bid. The payment gave Perelman a profit of about $43 million, plus $9 million to cover his "expenses." It was sweet, but some analysts concluded that Perelman would rather have had the entire company and backed off as a result of the current controversy concerning takeovers. Daniel J. Meade of First Boston Corporation told *The New York Times,* "In the world post-Boesky, these things are coming under a lot of pressure."

As all of this filtered into the collective consciousness of the investment community, it caused tremors. While Boesky's fine was a whopper, it could have been at least twice as much, based on the treble damages provision of the law. Apparently, the government agreed not to garnish accounts in the names of his wife and children; in fact, fifteen days prior to the announcement of Boesky's fall, significant assets were transferred from Ivan Boesky to others, including his assets in the Beverly Hills Hotel. What's more, Boesky's lifetime ban from the securities markets would not take effect until April 1, 1988, giving him nearly one and one-half years to clean up his affairs.

The word soon leaked that, only days before the public disclosure of his fall, Boesky had sold off $440 million worth of his holdings in companies such as USX, TWA, Time Inc., Lockheed, GTE, Goodyear, Gillette and Borg-Warner. SEC Chairman John Shad, somewhat red-faced, explained to Congressional critics that Boesky had been permitted to sell out prior to the announcement in order to avoid panic in the markets. Rumor held that Boesky had liquidated as much as $1.6 billion worth of securities since his July agreement to begin cooperating with the government. Incredible! I thought. Here was the ultimate insider trade, aided and abetted by the Securities and Exchange Commission.

A joke circulated: Boesky would only have to pay $5 million of the $100 million fine because Drexel was "highly confident" that it could finance the remaining $95 million through junk bonds.

Why had the government allowed Boesky to get off fairly easily? It could only mean that he was cooperating with an ongoing investigation. It could only mean that others would fall. Press reports declared that attorneys known for their defense of white-collar criminals were besieged with phone calls.

These suspicions were summed up by Stanley Kon, a member of the finance faculty of the University of Michigan business school, who was quoted in *The Washington Post,* "Boesky had three hundred buttons on his telephone console. I wonder who else besides Levine he has been talking to."

THE U.S. Congress predictably jumped into the publicity fray. Only four days after the Boesky story broke, the House Subcommittee on Monopolies and Commercial Law heard testimony from Sir James Goldsmith on his current attempt to acquire Goodyear Tire & Rubber Co. Goldsmith had accumulated 11.5 percent of Goodyear's stock and offered $4.7 billion for the entire company. Committee member John Seiberling (D-OH), a member of Goodyear's founding family (which lost control of the company following a takeover fight in the 1930s), addressed Goldsmith curtly: "My question is: Who the hell are you?"

Undaunted, Goldsmith said he was part of the "rough, tough world of competition."

Two days later, Goldsmith backed off from the Goodyear deal, in part, he said, because of "this ghastly Boesky affair." More to the point, Goodyear's management bought him off for a greenmail payment that profited Goldsmith $93 million and raised a fresh outcry about perceived abuses by corporate raiders. Nonetheless, the mayor of Akron, where Goodyear was headquartered, reportedly gloated, "We kicked that slimy bastard out."

Various legislators introduced a total of nine bills directed at tightening the laws regarding securities transactions and corporate takeovers. The proposal that worried the Street most was Representative Dingell's campaign to stiffen the penalties against firms whose employees were found guilty of insider trading. But even as he lobbied for the bill, Dingell argued against writing a congressional definition of insider trading, claiming that it would create loopholes.

The executive branch acted also, directing the Office of Management and Budget, the Treasury Department and the Council of Economic

Advisers to activate a working group, which Treasury Secretary James A. Baker declared was assigned to perform a complete reappraisal of the Reagan Administration's policies on insider trading, takeovers, junk bonds and financial markets.

SPECULATION on the Street held that Drexel and Milken had been dealt mortal blows. Boesky was intimately associated with both, and it seemed most likely that Boesky had some sort of damaging information to report concerning the firm and Milken. The press seemed to assume guilt by association, and most observers theorized that if the feds really wanted to nail Drexel, they could find some way to do it.

Boesky now became one of the most closely watched men in America. He was singled out as the potential key witness against anyone who held a subpoena in his hands, and the targets of the government's probe were powerful, rich men, able to afford the best possible legal counsel. Milken, for example, hired Arthur Liman, as well as Edward Bennett Williams. Drexel added Peter Fleming, who already represented Sokolow, to its formidable legal team. The bevy of lawyers representing numerous clients regarded the possibilities and concluded quickly that, if Boesky loomed as the key witness, they would have to do their best to discredit him. Teams of the world's best private detectives, armed with the latest in surveillance devices, now monitored his every move. And now Boesky never went anywhere without his own crew of bodyguards. They were interested in more than business details. Any private quirk could be used on the witness stand to raise doubts about Boesky's credibility. They wanted to know if he had secret bank accounts in Switzerland or elsewhere. They wanted to know the details of his sex life.

Rival investment bankers began to make systematic calls to Drexel clients, seeking to lure them away. Across the nation, more and more CEOs began to take an unheard-of action—refusing to return Milken's phone calls.

Seventy-seven-year-old Tubby Burnham, Drexel's honorary chairman of the board, wrote a letter to the employees declaring that the "distortions" and "falsehoods" were so widespread that "one wonders if it isn't a plot" to put Drexel out of business.

On December 2, Drexel's Chairman Robert Linton announced that the firm was scrapping its $300 million plans to move its headquarters to the 47-story, 2-million-square-foot office tower at Seven World Trade Center. Drexel was to have received 49.9 percent ownership of the project in return for signing a 30-year lease at $100 million per year, but Linton explained that "with all the fallout" from the insider trading scandal, it was "not the most propitious time to go through this tremendous diversion" of energy and expenditures. He also cited changes in the tax laws that made the venture unfavorable.

Meanwhile, speaking at the annual conference of the Securities Industry Association in Boca Raton, Florida, Joseph came under fire for Drexel's use of the "sealed envelope" back in 1984 and 1985, wherein it submitted the names of target companies to potential financiers, with instructions not to open the envelopes prior to a public announcement. Joseph admitted that Drexel had stopped the practice because, he said, "We found the stock started to rise . . ."

It was Joseph's job, of course, to protect Drexel as best he could, and I could understand that concern. He repeatedly stated that Drexel never condoned illegal or improper activities and declared that the firm would cooperate fully with investigators. He pointed out that the majority of my insider trades occurred before I joined Drexel. My activities, he declared, were an aberration. I knew that he was practicing damage control, and I understood and appreciated that fact.

One day, after another extended session in my lawyers' offices, as I exited the elevator on the ground floor, I nearly smacked into Joseph. He was on his way up, also to huddle with lawyers. He looked as if he had aged a decade in six months.

But his haggard expression suddenly brightened. He extended his hand and asked, "How are you, Dennis?" His tone was extremely warm as he pumped my hand and said, "I wish you the best of luck."

"I wish you the same, Fred," I responded.

A *Business Week*/Harris Poll measured the public mood. Respondents were asked whether they believed that most people would purchase stock based on an inside tip. Eighty-two percent said yes.

And despite the surge of negative publicity, Wall Streeters fared well in the public's perception of their ethical standards. When asked to rate the morals of various professions, the public ranked investment personnel higher than doctors, corporate executives, reporters, lawyers and, most especially, politicians.

REPRESENTATIVE Dingell opened the December 11 hearing of the House Subcommittee on Oversight and Investigations with a lengthy statement regarding the highly touted electronic surveillance systems designed to identify insider trading on the nation's markets. "The surveillance systems identified numerous Boesky and Levine trades," he noted, "but these referrals to the SEC did not lead to any enforcement action. . . . Ironically, despite all the wonders of modern technology, hundreds of investigators at the firms, the exchanges and the SEC could not make a case. It took a twenty-six-year-old whiz kid to crack the code and piggyback on over twenty of Levine's insider trades . . .

"No one asked questions—not his employers . . . not the New York Stock Exchange, not the NASD and not the SEC. Only when the broker began sharing his 'tips' with a friend in Caracas did the scheme begin to unravel."

Dingell asked hard questions: Are the present surveillance systems effective in deterring, detecting and prosecuting illegal trading? What level of confidence can we have that individual investors are protected against major institutional insider trading and stock manipulation?

At the subcommittee's request, Assistant Comptroller General William J. Anderson had been studying the surveillance system and now attempted to answer. Detecting broad instances of insider trading is fairly easy, he contended. The hard part is to pin down a source. The vaunted electronic surveillance systems merely provide leads that SEC and Justice Department investigators must then analyze and investigate.

It all sounded very effective, but Anderson spelled out the parameters of the problem: "For the first eleven months of this year, the NYSE reported that over 9,000 alerts occurred." Obviously, manpower limitations snagged the surveillance procedures.

Computerized surveillance systems, Anderson concluded, "can provide an important and necessary part of the story. They can provide the initial leads indicating suspicious trading and produce a lot of circumstantial evidence. They can show, after the fact, who traded what stock, at what prices and when. But they do not produce irrefutable evidence showing who passed inside information to whom."

CHAPTER THIRTY-TWO

SARAH'S BIRTH ON DECEMBER 18, 1986, was so different from Adam's. Yes, there was unbelievable joy, but it was tempered with the realization that I would spend the first days, months, years—we still did not know how long—of her life in prison.

THE December issue of *The American Lawyer* carried a story based on an interview with Ilan Reich, depicting the fallen lawyer in a black-and-white photograph that accented his prematurely gray hair and his gloomy spirit. Here, I found myself cast as the seductive mastermind of a diabolical network, the man who preyed upon innocents. Reich, like others, was painting me as the heavy. I understood this, since it reduced his culpability, but it was disturbing to read.

The attack continued on December 22, when Wilkis pled guilty to four felony charges (securities fraud, mail fraud, tax evasion and failing to report that he brought $10,000 cash into the U.S. from the Cayman Islands) and declared to U.S. District Judge Peter K. Leisure, "I was recruited by Dennis Levine to reveal to him confidential information."

Fortune magazine named Boesky "Crook of the Year."

Two major U.S. corporations filed suit against Bank Leu, charging illegal trading activities.

Meanwhile, it was reported that Boesky's lawyer, Harvey Pitt, asked about casting for a possible movie about the entire affair, suggested that Boesky resembled Peter O'Toole. His own part, he said, should be played by Jack Nicholson.

THE Boesky story took on international proportions when SEC investigators passed the information on to British authorities that Boesky had played a secret, illegal role in the largest takeover in British business history.

In the early months of 1986, Guinness PLC, known for its Dewar's White Label whiskey, was in competition with Argyll Foods PLC, a supermarket chain, to finalize a $3.8 billion acquisition of the Distillers Company, producers of Johnnie Walker scotch and Gordon's gin. Guinness's chances of winning the takeover battle were enhanced, during the closing stages of the fight, due to a 25 percent upward movement in the price of its stock. Since Guinness had offered a combination of cash and stock for Distillers Co., the rise in its stock value equated with a rise in the amount of the offer. Ultimately the Guinness bid prevailed over the competition.

This was curious. In most takeover situations, the stock of the acquiring company falls, due to investor perception of increased debt, management problems and reduced pro-forma earnings.

Boesky provided one explanation as to the mysterious and uncharacteristic price run-up when he disclosed that he had purchased a large position of Guinness stock in the spring of 1986, during the midst of the takeover battle. His power to move markets was well known and the buying activity naturally boosted the price of the stock on the open exchanges. Two months later Guinness, in what seemed to be an obvious case of quid pro quo, invested $103 million in one of Boesky's ventures.

If, indeed, Guinness's investment was a commission for Boesky's stock purchases, it constituted a serious violation. Under British law, it is illegal for a company to purchase its own stock without shareholder approval, or to pay someone else to purchase it.

As a result of the SEC alert, the affair came under the scrutiny of Britain's Department of Trade and Industry, as well as of an ad hoc group known as the Takeover Panel and even of a police fraud squad.

Investigators learned that Guinness had orchestrated such stock purchases among a variety of other entities, forming a so-called "fan club" of investors whose actions drove up the price. About $300 million worth of stock purchases were involved.

I found diabolical pleasure in learning that Bank Leu AG of Switzerland was the major co-conspirator, involved in half of the purchases. Guinness disclosed that two of its directors had signed agreements that the company "could not lawfully have fulfilled" to induce Bank Leu to purchase its stock. Through two of its subsidiaries, in Zug and Lucerne, the bank had bought 41 million shares, or about $150 million worth of Guinness stock, after the firm secretly promised to redeem them later at cost, plus commissions. To cover that pledge, Guinness deposited $76 million in Bank Leu's Luxembourg subsidiary.

Bank Leu's initial response to the disclosures was that it could not comment, since the relationship was protected by Swiss bank secrecy laws. CEO Hans Knopfli said at a press conference, "All transactions consummated by our group were normal business activities in compliance with applicable Swiss laws." Nevertheless, the bank issued a statement declaring that it was seeking Guinness's permission "to cooperate with the DTI inspectors . . ."

Bank Leu contended that it acted in accordance with Swiss law, which does not forbid such share-buying and indemnity arrangements, but Kurt Hauri, director of the Swiss Federal Banking Commission, announced an investigation of Bank Leu's role in the scheme.

In all, Guinness's auditors, Price Waterhouse, discovered a total of $38 million in payments to eleven companies in at least six different countries, for which, the company admitted, there was "no satisfactory explanation."

The British probe became one of the largest business scandals in that country's history, resulting in the resignation of Guinness's chairman and CEO, Ernest Saunders, whom the tabloids dubbed the J. R. Ewing character in an "Alcoholic Dallas"; he was subsequently charged with approximately forty offenses, including theft, attempting to pervert the course of justice and destroying and falsifying documents. Having been convicted, Saunders is now serving a five-year sentence.

Bank Leu's supervisory board chairman, Arthur Furer, one of Saunders's closest advisers, was "invited" to resign from the Guinness board (Furer was also a director of Citicorp and Nestlé).

Many others fell by the wayside. Gerald Ronson, chairman of Heron International PLC and one of the country's wealthiest men, returned $9 million in payments made to him to guarantee any losses in his Guinness holdings; he claimed no wrongdoing, but he was subsequently arrested and charged with conspiring to make a false market. After his conviction, he was sentenced to one year in prison. The company's investment bank (and London's top merger bank), Morgan Grenfell & Company, was dealt a severe blow to its prestige when chief executive Christopher Reeves and Graham Walsh, head of the corporate finance department, resigned under pressure.

The politicians were incensed. Sir Anthony Grant, a Conservative Member of Parliament, declared that the British investment community seemed to be "long on cunning but short on morals." Robin Leigh-Pemberton, governor of the Bank of England, said that the affair posed a "threat to the entire basis of trust which still predominates in our business life." Former Prime Minister Edward Heath denounced the mess as an "orgy of insider dealing."

This was a huge story, and because of both the Boesky and Bank Leu connections, producers from the BBC as well as German and Swiss TV networks contacted me, seeking interviews.

As much as I longed to go on television and vent my wrath at the bankers, I declined. What good could it do? I wondered.

ON the home front, news sources reported that Oppenheim, Appel, Dixon & Company, the accounting firm hired by Boesky to restructure his investment corporation, had questioned the legitimacy of the $5.3 million payment from Boesky to Drexel. The invoice regarding that payment stated blandly: FOR CONSULTING SERVICES AS AGREED UPON ON MARCH 21, 1986. SEC investigators were reportedly digging for a more precise description of the reasons behind the payment and were also looking at another $3 million payment from Boesky to the "third market" brokerage house of Jefferies & Company. Additional reports indicated that government attorneys seemed to be interested in the relationship between Boesky and Marty Siegel.

All of this gained credibility on January 12 when SEC Chairman John Shad prophesied that there would be "more shoes to drop."

IRA Sokolow was the first to be sentenced, and we awaited the action nervously. Clearly, his term would serve as a benchmark. When he received a year and a day in prison, followed by three years' probation, I said to myself: Okay, Dennis, now you know. That's the minimum you can expect. Sokolow also agreed to pay the SEC $210,000 in illegal profits and fines. He began serving his time at the Federal Correctional Institution in Loretto, Pennsylvania. (His sentence was later shortened.)

David Brown received a thirty-day jail sentence, and the judge decreed that he could serve it on weekends in a Manhattan brownstone converted into a federal dormitory. He was also ordered to perform 300 hours of community service and was fined $10,000. He signed an SEC consent decree agreeing to surrender $145,790 in personal assets.

Ilan Reich pled guilty to one count of securities fraud and one count of mail fraud, which resulted in his automatic disbarment. Although the government said it believed us when he and I both asserted that he never took a penny of trading profits, he signed a consent agreement to pay the SEC $485,000 in assets, including his half interest in a home in East Quogue, Long Island. He was allowed to keep his home on West 94th Street, $10,000 in cash, $14,000 in an IRA account and a used Oldsmobile. He pled guilty to two criminal counts of insider trading and received a year and a day in prison, plus five years' probation. Implementation of the sentence was delayed for sixty days so that he could be present for the birth of his third child.

Randall Cecola neither admitted to nor denied the truth of the SEC charges against him, but he did agree to disgorge $21,800 in trading profits. He pled guilty to two charges of filing false tax returns and was sentenced to five years' probation.

Robert Wilkis received a year and a day in prison, plus five years' probation. He settled civil charges with the SEC by agreeing to turn over $3.3 million in assets, including the balance of his Cayman Islands account, as well as $50,000 in cash, which he had kept in a shoebox in his apartment.

Now, of our group, I was the only one awaiting sentencing.

* * *

I had always believed that I was not the only one supplying tips to Boesky. His information was too good.

Indeed, government investigators estimated that, between the years 1982 and 1986, Boesky made profits of more than $80 million by trading on inside information. If that was true, it was curious indeed. I never knew the man until the Drexel Bond Conference in March 1985.

The picture cleared on February 13, 1987, when Marty Siegel resigned from Drexel and pled guilty to charges of illegal stock trading and tax evasion. I was amazed to learn the details, which mimicked, but preceded, my own story. Back in August of 1982 Boesky had treated Siegel to lunch in the grill room of the Harvard Club and worked out a payment formula in return for stock tips. Siegel had succumbed to the temptation and began by tipping Boesky that Martin Marietta was going to employ the Pac-Man defense against Bendix. Over time, Boesky had paid out $800,000 for Siegel's tips, and Siegel had the audacity to accept the money via couriers who set up rendez-vous with him in various New York hotel lobbies, delivering suitcases full of cash.

The Siegel case continued the chain reaction. In his conversations with federal prosecutors, Siegel implicated Timothy Tabor, a former Kidder Peabody vice president; Richard Wigton, a current Kidder Peabody vice president; and Robert Freeman, a Goldman Sachs partner who served as the firm's chief arbitrageur. In a calculated public relations move, U.S. Attorney Giuliani authorized federal agents to descend upon these executives at their offices, during business hours, and haul them away in handcuffs. These were the most publicized arrests in the history of the investigation, and they were clearly designed to intimidate the growing array of defendants as well as those who lived in fear of further arrests.

However, the three vowed to fight the charges, rather than cooperate, and it appeared that the government's string of successes might end here.

Boyd Jefferies, whose Jefferies & Co. had created the "third market" that was so helpful to the arbs who wanted fast, twenty-four-hour-a-day action, was also caught in the web. Boesky had allowed the government to tape some of his conversations with Jefferies, proving that the two men were involved in various fraudulent market activities, many of them designed to hide assets and/or liabilities from public scrutiny. As a result, Boesky realized tax benefits and was able to avoid some of the SEC's regulatory requirements.[1]

---

[1]Marty Siegel was sentenced to two months' imprisonment plus five years' probation and 3,000 hours of community service. He agreed to pay $9 million to settle the civil charges against him.

Charges against Timothy Tabor and Richard Wigton were dropped. Robert Freeman pled guilty and received a relatively light sentence of four months.

Boyd Jefferies pled guilty to two securities law violations and received a probationary sentence. His cooperation and testimony led to the convictions of Paul Bilzarian, Salim (Sandy) Lewis, GAF Corporation and James Sherwin, but the GAF and Sherman convictions were reversed on appeal.

CHAPTER THIRTY-THREE

On February 20, 1987, Laurie and I were driven to the federal courthouse in White Plains, New York. The moment we arrived, the car was surrounded by a gaggle of reporters. They pounded on the windows and climbed on the hood. Between blinding flashes of light, all I could see was the word NIKON.

"Why are they doing this to us?" Laurie sobbed. "My God! Why are they doing this to us?"

The driver cursed at the media contingent for scratching the finish of his car.

The assault lasted a full fifteen minutes before mounted police officers could restore order and open the door. My brother Robert was so incensed at seeing this that he raced from the courthouse door and, like a linebacker with elbows flailing, helped clear a pathway for us. We ran a gauntlet through the freezing cold and into the temporary sanctuary of the tiny courthouse where Judge Goettel had recently been transferred. We entered an elevator and pushed the button for the third floor, where the courtroom was located.

I thought I was prepared for anything, but I was wrong. When the elevator door opened, Laurie and I hustled out and made a quick left turn, searching for the small office where I would be allowed a last-minute consultation with my lawyers. In our haste, we almost ran into Dad.

Our eyes met, and I saw within him the most excruciating pain I could imagine.

"Everything will be okay, Dad," I said.

He mumbled an incoherent response.

Dad took Laurie off toward the courtroom as I turned aside to huddle with counsel. I had a full contingent there: Liman, Flumenbaum, Pomerantz, Clayton, Karp, Feldman and many others. By now we all knew one another very well.

"Arthur," I warned Liman, "I'm going to probably be very emotional. I might have great difficulty speaking to the judge."

"Do the best you can," he said.

A standing-room-only crowd spilled into the hallways. Reporters and sketch artists were everywhere. When I entered the courtroom, Laurie was the first sight my eyes spotted. She appeared solemn and sad, but very pretty in a gray dress. She was seated in the spectators' section, flanked by Dad, my brother Robert, and our friends Irwin and Dona Kruger. I moved through the crowd toward the defendant's table, trying to stride rather than shuffle. The attorneys moved in concert to join me.

The judge had in front of him the results of a voluminous study that my attorneys and I had conducted. Just as I had done whenever I interviewed for a job, considered a stock purchase or analyzed a merger, I did my homework concerning the sentencing procedure. We provided the judge with a historical setting. In the majority of cases of insider trading, when the defendant pled guilty, the courts imposed probationary sentences, usually requiring a term of community service work. When jail sentences were imposed, the average term was less than one year. Even when a defendant pled not guilty and forced the government to conduct a trial, the sentences were often brief, generally ranging from three to six months. We knew, of course, that the scope of my insider trading activities was considerably higher than in most other cases, and we knew that the judge was under the glare of public spotlights, so we suspected he might be more harsh than judges before him; nevertheless, we wanted him to be able to place everything in perspective.

Liman issued an eloquent plea for leniency, pointing out that I had already endured a form of banishment.

Judge Goettel asked if I had anything to say. I certainly did, but as I rose to my feet, I did not know if I could say it. As a teenager I played keyboard in a rock band; we had performed before crowds much larger than this. Over the years I had made countless presentations to the richest and most powerful business executives in the world, and stage fright had never been a problem. Only ten months earlier, at Drexel's 1986 Bond Conference, I was the featured speaker at the Corporate Finance Breakfast for 2,000 CEOs and financial officers; the words had come easily. So why did I now feel as if someone had jammed a huge rock into my throat?

I heard my voice falter as I began. I struggled for breath and forced myself to recite the words that I had so carefully prepared. It was an out-of-body experience. This was not really happening.

"Last June," I said finally, "when I pleaded guilty before Your Honor, I was automatically sentenced to a life of disgrace and humiliation. I have disappointed my wife, my children, my father, my brothers, my family, my friends, my colleagues. I abused the system I believe in and I will never forgive myself. I'm truly sorry and ashamed, not only for my past criminal behavior, but for all the anguish and humiliation and embarrassment I caused my family, mostly because it's been their love and support that has sustained me throughout this very difficult period. Over the last ten months, Your Honor, I have been very hard on myself. I assure you that I have learned my lesson. I swear in this court that I will never violate the law again and I beg you to allow me, to give me a chance to put the pieces of my life back together, to help my family get through this, to try and become a contributing member of the community again. Thank you."

I remained standing alongside Liman as the Judge Goettel pronounced, "On count one, two years, fifty thousand dollars." The money did not concern me as much as the time.

I had the ratios memorized, and the calculator in my mind told me that minus good behavior time, the sentence was seventeen months and five days.

The judge said, "On count two, two years, fifty thousand dollars. On count three, two years, sixty-two thousand dollars. On count four, two years, two hundred thousand dollars."

The judge paused. The vital question now was whether the judge decreed that the terms run concurrently or consecutively.

I looked directly into his eyes. His gaze locked upon mine. What he said next would make the difference between seventeen months and five days and considerably larger multiple of that.

He said, "Sentences to run . . ."

I was sure that my heart had stopped.

". . . concurrently."

I turned to Laurie and heard her whisper, "What does that mean?"

I replied, "It means seventeen months and five days."

Although the sentence was twice as long as others in my case, I thought it was fair.

Then the judge announced that he would delay the imposition of the sentence for two months, so that I could spend time with baby Sarah.

Afterward, when I encountered Dad in the courthouse hallway, I saw anguish in his face. Here was his youngest son, of whom he had always been so proud, sentenced to prison. He wanted to cry, but his pain was beyond tears.

I repeated what I had told him earlier: "Everything will be okay, Dad."

Flumenbaum rode with us on the way back to New York. Shortly before we crossed over into Manhattan he exclaimed, "Oh!" He reached into his lapel pocket and extricated the pen he had confiscated from me before the government took samples of my handwriting. He returned it now with the comment, "I won't be needing this any longer."

ONE nagging question for both SEC and Justice Department investigators was: Why had Meier bolted? He knew he would have been covered by the immunity agreement. The logical conclusion was that Meier had something additional to hide. The sleuths had plunged into Meier's records and found themselves on a merry chase.

There was, for example, the $5,000 that Meier had transferred by wire to Delaware National Bank in Delhi, New York. He had disguised the transaction when he edited the personal computer printout of his records, but it remained in the mainframe accounts, and Pletscher's deposition alerted investigators to it.

Detectives headed for Delhi, a small college town in upstate New York, and tracked Meier's money to the account of a man named Mark Tuthill. Tuthill was questioned for five or six hours before SEC officials were satisfied that he was what he claimed to be, a simple carpenter. In the summer of 1984, he explained, he had been hired to repair two rental homes, and he demanded cash before he began work. The man who hired him, New York attorney Kevin P. Barry, said that the fastest way to get the cash was by wire and, within a short time, the money was there.

Barry, Tuthill said, had a partner in his real estate venture—none other than Merrill Lynch stockbroker Brian Campbell.

Backtracking, the investigators discovered that Barry had quit his job with the Manhattan law firm of Tenzer, Greenblatt, Fallon & Kaplan late in 1985 after reportedly boasting that he had been "amassing capital."

At least some of that capital was traced through an entity known as BCM Management, incorporated by Barry's law firm in September 1984. The initials were interesting. Some speculated that they stood for Barry, Campbell and *Meier*.

Meier's payment to the carpenter, made all the more suspicious by the banker's attempt to eradicate it from the records, held the promise of providing a critical connecting link in the SEC's case against Campbell. Here was evidence that he and Meier had more than a client/broker relationship, that Campbell knew he was trading on inside information, not merely copying the handiwork of a successful investor.

ONE of our biggest concerns was five-year-old Adam. Until now, we had tried to shelter him, making sure he was not around the television whenever a news report came on. But Laurie and I knew that we had to deal with the issue sooner or later. Adam needed to know why Daddy was going away.

I was supposed to be his role model. I was the one who was charged with the responsibility to impart wisdom to him, to help him set his personal standards, to teach him values. I had to admit to my son that I had broken some very important rules.

We were at my brother Robert's house, sitting in the den, when I tried to explain. I drew Adam onto my lap and began, "You know, when little people make mistakes, they have to be punished. Well, it's the same for big people. They get punished by a judge."

I had difficulty continuing, and Laurie picked up the theme. "Daddy made a mistake," she said. "He didn't hurt anybody, but he broke some business rules. He didn't realize it at first, but eventually he did know it was wrong, but he continued to do it. Now he has to be punished."

"I went to see a judge," I said. "A judge is a man who punishes big people."

Adam asked fearfully, "What did he do?"

My body went numb. I felt paralyzed.

Laurie tried to explain: "The biggest punishment that an adult can have, especially if he has children, is to be taken away from his family for a time. The judge is probably going to take Daddy away from us for a while."

Through tears Adam asked, "Daddy, did you know what you were doing was wrong?"

Through my own tears I replied, "Yes."

"So then why did you do it?"

The room reeled in front of my eyes. I still had no answer to this question.

CHAPTER THIRTY-FOUR

NEXT TO ME, Laurie turned restlessly, half-awake, as she had been all night. Down the hall I knew that Adam was awakening to a frightening and incomprehensible day. Only tiny, three-month-old Sarah had slept reasonably well, although I sensed that, somehow, she also knew that the world was awry. I knew that Dad and Robert were already on their way into the city, each probably lost in his own gray thoughts. This was the morning, April 6, 1987, that I was heading into the unknown.

A duffel bag stood out near the door, packed with supplies that I hoped I would be allowed to keep: several jogging suits, two pairs of sneakers, numerous books, writing materials, a stereo/cassette player, a calculator, toiletries.

I eased out of bed, and Laurie arose, too. We dressed wordlessly. I helped get Adam and Sarah ready for the day. Breakfast stuck in my throat.

Suddenly Dad and Robert were at the door. All too soon, it was time to go.

I cradled Sarah in my arms and caressed her soft, tiny cheek with my finger. Then I picked up Adam. He hugged me as tightly as he could and planted a slobbery kiss on my cheek. Laurie and I squeezed one another so hard that it hurt. Our tears mingled.

I followed Dad and Robert into the elevator and out the door of our building. We stepped into the courtyard, where my Ford waited. The garage man had left the engine idling. I turned to look back and up. They were there at the window, seven floors above, Laurie with Sarah in her arms and Adam at her side, waving good-bye.

I'm actually driving off to prison, I thought. It's really happening. It will be several weeks, at least, before Laurie and the kids can come to visit—and at least seventeen months and five days before I can come back home.

I waved back to my family and mouthed the words, "I love you." I stood there for many moments as the picture in front of my eyes blurred. I deserved this punishment, but they did not.

Then I felt the touch of Robert's hand on my arm and I let him guide me toward the car.

"I'll drive," I said. "It's going to be a long time before I can drive again."

"Are you sure you're up to it?" Robert asked.

"Yes."

I sat in the driver's seat and took a moment to compose myself. Then I headed the car out onto Park Avenue and guided it with deliberate slowness up FDR Drive, across the George Washington Bridge and out through New Jersey. We picked up I-80 and aimed west, toward Pennsylvania. Our destination was Lewisburg, a tiny town in the north central portion of the state. There are three federal prisons in the area. One is the Lewisburg Penitentiary, designated as a Level 5/6 facility (Level 6 is, in federal prison parlance, the highest echelon of security), probably best known as the place where Al Capone and later Jimmy Hoffa served some of their time. Up the road a few miles is the Allenwood prison camp, where several of the Watergate principals spent a few years. I was headed for the minimum-security federal prison camp adjacent to the penitentiary. It was about three hours away from home if you calculated the distance in driving time, but in fact, it was in an alien universe.

As I drove, Dad, after a few false starts, produced a letter that he had just received from Richard Dorfman, my cousin's husband and the lawyer who had handled the incorporation of my old, pre–Wall Street entity, Levine, Francis & Co. In the letter, my cousin-in-law, now a member of Shearson's mortgage finance unit, declared that he and his family would not attend the upcoming Passover seder because he did not feel he could risk "even the smallest relationship" with my family,

now or later. The family seder was a traditional ritual that extended
back at least three generations. It was a festive time that *always* included even the most distant relatives, including Dorfman's widowed
mother. By declaring that he would not attend, he was, effectively,
removing himself from the entire clan. He explained that the risks were
"terrifying" if anyone thought that he felt even a twinge of sympathy
for me. He complained of the personal embarrassment he felt and spoke
of the professional "disaster" that could befall him. In his letter he said
he could have no relationship with me, my wife and our children.

Never in my life had I seen Dad this angry. In our family, loyalty
is everything. Richard, he pronounced, was no longer a member of the
family.

This was probably the first time in my life that I ever drove the speed
limit, but we still arrived more than an hour prior to my one P.M.
reporting time. "Let's have some lunch," I suggested. "I want a last
meal." We spotted a diner in the center of the drab little town. I parked
the car and we got out, stretching after the drive.

As we walked toward the diner we passed a newsstand. I stopped to
buy a copy of *USA Today*.

We ordered sandwiches, and as we waited, I opened the newspaper.
There, inside, was a photograph of an inmate's cubicle at the Lewisburg
federal prison camp and a story about the place where Dennis Levine
would be serving his sentence.

The reality really hit after lunch, when I pulled the car down a long
tree-lined drive and stopped alongside a thirty-foot-high concrete wall
surrounding a foreboding complex of brick buildings. Atop the wall was
a system of sentry towers. In them, I could see armed guards watching
us. Then, as we neared the front gate, I saw a familiar crowd waiting.

"Even here," I grumbled.

It was an assault squad of reporters, photographers and videotape
crews.

My God! I thought. Will I ever have any privacy? "Drop me off,"
I said. "Get out of here."

Quickly I hugged my father and my brother, then I grabbed my duffel
bag and walked toward the prison entrance. I ignored the questions that
flew at me, concentrating on keeping dignity intact as best I could. Hold
your head high, Dennis, I said.

Elbowing my way past the media, not trying to be gentle and answering their questions with silence and a straightforward stare, I located a speaker box off to one side of the iron gate and punched the button.

A guttural voice asked for my name.

"Dennis Levine."

"We are expecting you. Please walk in through the door in front of you."

Immediately the gate slid open. Leaving the press behind, I scurried into what seemed, ironically, to be a haven. The door closed behind me quickly, and even as I heard it rumble shut, I felt the hands of a guard, patting me down.

I could still hear the click of cameras behind me. Reporters continued to shout questions through the open bars.

"What's in the bag?" the guard asked gruffly.

"I brought along some personal belongings."

"You won't be allowed to keep . . ."

He was interrupted by a phone call from the warden, instructing him to get me inside the main prison structure as quickly as possible, to bring an end to the media event.

The guards hustled me through a metal detector. They emptied out the contents of my duffel bag and studied each item. They said that I would be allowed to keep a few things, but not much.

Now the door on the far side of the entrance court slid open. "Follow me," a guard said. We stepped through the portal and strode along a thirty-foot walkway toward a mammoth red brick building. Still toting my duffel bag, I followed the guard in through the doorway, down a flight of stairs, through the guards' gymnasium and then through a series of barred doors that each seemed to shut behind me with an ever louder *clang.*

We negotiated a corridor deep in the cold, dank basement, marching to the accompaniment of hissing steam pipes, until we reached the processing room. I completed numerous registration forms and submitted to the obligatory fingerprinting and photo session, posing with the number 19484-054 under my chin; this was my new identity. An officer compared my photo with one sent by the courts, to make sure that I had not hired an impostor.

The Lewisburg camp, like nearby Allenwood, is reserved, supposedly, for non-violent, low-risk prisoners. But unlike Allenwood, it suffers the misfortune of being adjacent to the penitentiary and shares many of the same supervisory personnel. At the moment I was in dangerous territory, where an inmate murder was not considered to be a particularly extraordinary event and where, as in any other maximum-security facility, the match and the fuse were never far apart. I learned immediately that the guards exhibit a natural tendency to forget the distinctions between the penitentiary and the camp.

"Strip," a guard commanded.

Within moments I was buck naked.

"Run your fingers through your hair."

I did so.

"Bend over." Then, a gruff voice ordered, "Spread your cheeks."

Other commands were fired at me: "Stand up." "Lift your balls." "Wiggle your toes."

I weighed in at 241 pounds and was disgusted with the way I had let myself go.

Finally the guards handed me a set of surplus Army fatigues and a pair of blue sneakers. "Socks?" I asked.

"No socks."

As I dressed, the guards inventoried the contents of my duffel bag, shaking their heads. I filled out the necessary papers to ship most of my personal belongings back to Laurie.

A new man appeared and introduced himself as a "counselor," here to escort me to the camp. The absurdity of the concept almost brought a wry smile to my face.

"How do we get to the camp?" I asked. "How far is it from here?"

"Just down the road," he replied.

"Is the press still outside?"

"No, they left a little while ago. Don't worry. Normally we don't even escort inmates to the camp. They just walk down on their own. Minimum security, you know. But the warden wanted to put on a good show for the media. If any of them are still out there, they won't be able to get at you. We're going to drive you down."

The counselor took me back along the same route, through the foreboding series of steel-barred doors, up a staircase and out through the front entrance to a waiting station wagon, marked BUREAU OF PRISONS.

The ride was short and wordless.

The camp had no physical walls, but as we drove inside the compound I realized that the psychological barriers were formidable indeed. Here, just as surely as if I was behind the penitentiary's walls, I was separated from society, and from those I loved.

The counselor left me in the care of a dormitory officer.

"Find a bed," the officer said, not unkindly. "As a new inmate, you'll have to take what you can get, probably in the middle, near the TV room and the showers. It's noisier there. And don't count on finding a lower bunk."

If the camp had ever been a "country club prison," it sure was not now. The facility was built to hold 165 inmates, but there were about 240 of them in residence now, and about 90 percent of them were drug offenders. Two men had to share 4-by-7-foot sleeping cubicles that were designed originally for a single inmate.

The large dorm was relatively empty during the middle of the afternoon. I conducted what I thought was a thorough search, making my way through one cubicle after another, finding myself more and more disgusted by the filth that cluttered the place. Despite my efforts, I could not find a bunk that appeared unused.

Finally the dormitory officer assigned me a bed in a cubicle not quite in the center of the building. As he had predicted, it was an upper bunk. He issued me a pillow, sheets and a pillowcase, and left me alone.

I regarded the mattress with distaste. It was thin, lumpy and soiled. I made up the bed and, with nothing else to do, lay down and perused a seven-page package of orientation materials, which opened with a letter from Camp Administrator C. H. Crandell, who advised, "I encourage you to take advantage of the facilities and programs available at the Federal Prison Camp, to make this period of incarceration as constructive as possible. Your stay here is what you, as an individual, choose to make it. With a positive outlook, your time can be spent well and fast. GOOD LUCK!"

One full page of small type was devoted to a list of prohibited acts, ranging from "Killing" at the top of the list to "Conducting a business" at the bottom.

About four P.M. the inmates began to return from their various work assignments, which took them to the far corners of the 1,600-acre federal reservation. I kept my mouth shut, and my eyes and ears open. I felt a hint of a headache from the onslaught of cigarette smoke that accompanied the returning crews.

A burly Italian man entered the cubicle and grunted his disapproval at my presence. I sat up, wondering what to do. Do you introduce yourself to your cubicle-mate? Do you shake hands?

For a moment we stared into one another's eyes. To my astonishment, we each knew the other by reputation. He was a well-known organized-crime figure.

In a voice straight out of *The Godfather,* he said, "Mr. Wall Street, I ain't happy you're here."

"That makes two of us," I said.

"Count!" a voice cried from somewhere down the corridor. The other man assumed a stance somewhere between respectful attention and insolent slouch. He gazed toward the opening in our tiny living area that served as the door. I slid from my bunk and stood next to him.

After a few minutes, a guard poked his head inside, mumbled, "Thirty-three, thirty-four" and moved on. Soon after that a voice cried out, *"Count is clear!"*

The Italian turned to me and growled, "You're not allowed to sit on my bed," but he relented slightly, adding, "You can store some things under the bunk, if you want."

"Okay."

We regarded one another warily for a moment, before I ventured a question. I made a sweeping gesture with my arms and asked, "Do they ever clean this place?"

He found great delight in this, roaring with laughter, clutching his arms to his sides. He explained that for the past few days the inmates had been cleaning like crazy. The warden, knowing that the press was about to descend in concert with my arrival, had ordered a massive cleanup. Inmates were sent out to police the grounds for trash, to slap fresh paint on any wall visible from the outside and even to plant fresh flower beds in front of the main entrance. "They hate you," my cellmate said. "Everybody here hates you. You made them do all this extra work." He laughed even harder. "The hacks were on our case."

I stammered, "The hacks?"

"Guards," he explained.

I did not know what to say.

The mobster's face grew suddenly stern, and he declared, "I'm gonna see to it that you get moved outta this cube very quickly."

I shrugged.

He grinned once more and asked, "You got any hot stock tips for me?"

IT was an unseasonably cold night for April, and a brisk spring wind filtered through the poorly insulated dormitory. To combat the cold, inmates wore hats as they slept. I lay on my top bunk, wide awake, trying not to toss and turn, lest I disturb the man below. The view three feet above me was ceiling tile, yellowed from years of cigarette smoke. For a time I amused myself watching, in the dim glow of the night lights, my breath condense into vapor.

The night air was filled with sounds. Some men carried on late conversations. Some amused themselves with loud belches and artistic exhibitions of flatulence, occasioning guffaws. Some, oblivious to their milieu, snored contentedly. Others screamed in their sleep.

I was still awake when a guard peered in for the midnight count, but sometime in the wee hours I must have shivered myself to sleep, for I did not remember the three A.M. count.

THE next morning, after the six A.M. count and breakfast, I was put to work scrubbing toilets and urinals, then made to clean various nooks and crannies with a toothbrush. It was harassment, of course, and I simply shut up and swallowed it. I knew I was being tested. The hacks were as angry at me as the inmates were, and there was nothing I could do but accept the treatment and refuse to make waves.

In spite of a general air of animosity, almost no one, guard or prisoner, could resist the temptation that had overcome my cellmate. *Everyone* wanted some inside information on the market. "I don't know anything," I proclaimed.

The hazing subsided gradually. Soon I was placed on the basic maintenance crew, assigned to mop floors and mow lawns. For this, the prison system paid me eleven cents an hour. That worked out to an annual salary of $228.80, and I considered myself to be overpaid.

The social hubs were the two TV rooms, and I was educated on the viewing protocol one evening, shortly after seven P.M., when I wandered into one of the TV rooms and found it empty. The set was on, tuned to "Wheel of Fortune." I flicked the dial idly, settling upon CNN's "MoneyLine."

"Yo, mother!" boomed a voice behind me.

I turned to see a huge black man looming.

"What the hell do you think you're doing?" he raged. "You may have been running things on the outside, but you're not running shit on the inside."

Three or four of his cohorts appeared behind him.

I turned back to the TV and tuned in "Wheel of Fortune."

In fact, I soon realized, even a game show was an aberration. Most times the TVs were tuned to whatever action/adventure programs were on the air, and as I suppose was to be expected, everyone around me rooted openly for the bad guys.

It was no surprise to find myself in the midst of an antisocial crowd, but I was shocked to realize how many of the inmates exhibited symptoms of psychosis. Far too many of these men were strung out. The guards pretty much left them alone during the day, but every evening, shortly before the "lights out" call at eleven P.M., guards gathered together the more overt psychos and doled out what they called "hot medicine." Perhaps it was the powerful tranquilizer Thorazine. Whatever it was, the inmates craved it. They gulped the pills greedily and soon drifted into a chemical-induced euphoria, allowing the guards to relax and the rest of us to get some sleep.

Three phones were located in the middle of the dorm, and they were designed only for outgoing, collect calls. Long lines always stretched in front of them. Each call was limited to fifteen minutes in duration and was recorded for security purposes. We were not allowed to discuss business.

Recreational opportunities were limited. There was a gymnasium a short distance from the dorm, with a basketball court and other minimal exercise facilities, including a makeshift track and a baseball field. There was a tennis court here, but the surface was badly cracked and, when I asked, I was told that I was not allowed to have a tennis racket.

Sick call was a joke, conducted by a physician's assistant who routinely prescribed ibuprofen for any real or imagined malady. This was not a place to be seriously ill.

Here, as in the outside world, a market economy thrived. Some prisoners simply desired food to supplement the incredibly poor prison fare. Others wanted, and got, marijuana, cocaine and heroin. The unit of currency was the cigarette. In here, just as outside, everything appeared to be linked to supply and demand. If you were long on cigarettes, you could buy, for example, a plate of linguine with clam sauce, heated in an aluminum pie tin over an electric iron. After a time I discovered that the most coveted item, currently, was a cellular phone. Several inmates had them hidden at various points on the prison grounds.

Despite the accumulation of aggravations, I came to see that this physical prison could be a disguised blessing. For too many years I had raced through life, too busy to lift my head and either contemplate the past or gaze toward the future. Prison slowed the pace of my life long enough for me to see how I had trapped myself.

I had been at Lewisburg for little more than a month when I was visited by aides from the U.S. House of Representatives Energy Committee's Subcommittee on Oversight and Investigations, chaired by Representative Dingell. They grilled me on the subject of insider trading, and their special interest was whether or not such activity was encouraged, whether overtly or tacitly, by Wall Street employers. The men appeared very interested in what I had to say.

Soon after that I was served with a congressional subpoena and on June 1 found myself en route to Washington in the care of federal marshals. A day of debriefing with a few congressmen and several staffers was followed by a night in the Fairfax County (Virginia) Jail.

This was a maximum-security facility filled with hard-core felons. I doubted if many people here knew who I was, but I had a definite status as a federal prisoner. I heard the comment "Hey, we got us a fed" several times throughout the course of the evening.

After a cold, dismal dinner, I was placed into a tiny, one-man cell somewhere in the depths of this modern dungeon. It featured a toilet, a sink, and a slab of concrete that was supposed to serve as a bed. I asked a guard for a mattress, a toothbrush, a bar of soap, some toilet paper, but he refused me with a grunted obscenity.

I tried to ignore the fresh onslaught of smells and sounds and, still dressed in a business suit, eased onto the concrete slab and eventually fell into a troubled sleep.

Sometime later a nurse awakened me by clanging a metal cup against the bars of the door. "We have to do a medical profile on you," she announced in a husky baritone.

"What time is it?" I asked.

"Three-thirty in the morning."

"I'm leaving here at five or six. You don't have to do a medical profile on me."

"Procedure," she growled. "Ever had heart disease?"

I glowered at her through the bars. Finally, through clenched teeth, I responded, "No."

"Diabetes?"

"No."

"TB?"

"No."

Ten minutes of questions followed and I grew angrier by the moment. Finally she asked, "Have you ever attempted suicide or thought about it?"

"Yes!" I screamed in reply.

"When?"

"Right now!"

THREE or four hours later, I huddled in an anteroom of the Rayburn Building on Capitol Hill, discussing the parameters of my testimony with Flumenbaum and Karp, when we heard a commotion in the hallway. Karp looked out and reported the dismaying news that a slew of reporters had just been admitted into the hearing room.

"Can't they just leave me alone?" I moaned.

My lawyers sympathized, and they argued the point to Chairman Dingell. The congressman agreed that it was in the best interests of the committee to hear my testimony in executive session, with the press barred. The room was cleared.

I began by telling the congressmen that I felt honored to be asked to provide insights regarding the practices of the investment banking community, and I hoped that my testimony would assist them in crafting appropriate legislation. I tried to give them a realistic understanding of the securities industry from a practitioner's point of view, and explained some of the confusing terminology. The congressmen—wheelers and dealers themselves—were particularly interested in the personal dynamics of the M&A business.

At the request of several congressmen, I presented my views on possible corrective measures. My proposals ranged from improvements in market surveillance activities to enhanced supervisory policies within the firms.

In my view, I said, the best way to deter insider trading is not to increase the severity of the punishment, but to increase the chances of getting caught. Wall Streeters are risk evaluators by nature. When I began my insider trading activities, the risk of getting caught seemed so minuscule that I did not worry about the potential penalties. But today, I noted, the risk of getting caught is much more easily perceived, thanks, in large part, to my own bad example.

Consider jail terms and fines to be necessary, if you will, I declared. But beyond all that is the specter of two forms of punishment that are far more severe. The first is banishment from the industry you love, and that, to the Wall Street addict, is akin to capital punishment. Show him that illegal activities jeopardize his entire career, and you have instituted one of the most effective precautionary measures.

Finally, I noted in a choking voice, there is the punishment of public humiliation. I was ashamed of what I had done, and I knew not whether I could ever outlive that personal horror. I had seen the accusatory expressions in the eyes of my brother, my father, my wife and my son, and those gazes would haunt me forever. A jail term is finite; a fine is numerically definable. But for the rest of my life I would have to carry the painful knowledge that I put my family through a horrible ordeal and embarrassed the industry in which I was proud and privileged to work.

Afterward, I was whisked off in a white station wagon for dinner at McDonald's before I was returned to Lewisburg.

IN August, the U.S. Court of Appeals for the District of Columbia overturned a lower tribunal's contempt of court ruling against an international bank and one of its managers for refusing to consent to a U.S. grand jury subpoena to surrender account records. The unanimous decision was authored by former Supreme Court nominee Robert Bork. The case in question was no mere civil matter; it was a far more serious criminal investigation of a drug-running and money-laundering ring. Yet, the appeals court ruled that the bank and its officers could not be compelled to commit an action that would break the laws of their own country.

Had the precedent been set a few years earlier, in a drug and money-laundering case, perhaps Pitt and/or Bank Leu would not have settled so easily.

ON October 19, 1987, I sat in one of the TV room's at the prison dorm. My menial tasks were completed for the day, and most of the remainder of the inmates were out on various portions of the grounds, so I had the chance to watch CNN, and I was transfixed by the coverage of the stock market crash. The Dow Jones Industrial Average was in a free-fall, on its way to a record one-day plunge of more than 500 points.

Suddenly I became aware that two guards were standing behind me.

"Come with us?" one of them ordered.

"Why?"

They explained that one of the high-ranking prison officials wanted to see me.

I did not want to leave the news coverage but, of course, I had no choice. I followed the guards to the prison offices, where they ushered me in to see the official.

"Dennis," he said cordially, "please sit down. Cigarette?"

"No thanks," I replied. "I don't smoke."

He lit up, unconcerned whether or not the smoke bothered me. He took a drag and then, in a quiet voice that nonetheless belied tension, asked, "Are you aware of what's going on in the market?"

"Yes. I've been watching CNN."

He leaned forward. His eyes and the tone of his voice grew more intense. "Dennis," he asked, "can you give me some advice on what to do with my portfolio? Should I sell out and take my losses, or should I hold on?"

I countered in a lighthearted tone, "If I give you advice, is there any way I can go home sooner."

"Oh, no," he retorted. "No, I can't do anything like that."

"Then I can't help you," I said.

CHAPTER THIRTY-FIVE

PRIOR TO HIS sentencing, Ivan Boesky spent some of his time at the Cathedral of Saint John the Divine, working to help the homeless. He was accepted as a volunteer on the condition that he use an assumed name.

On December 18, 1987, when Judge Morris Lasker convened a sentencing hearing in the U.S. District Courthouse in Foley Square, Boesky's attorney, Leon Silverman, issued a plea for leniency. "Mr. Boesky was not caught," he pointed out. "He came in early, without compulsion, and in complete candor." Noting that his client had already been subjected to severe public scorn, Silverman said, "Mr. Boesky has been revealed as a stool pigeon, an informer, a turncoat and a traitor. He has become a leper in the financial community. . . . No one will take his calls; no one will be seen with him. He can't use a credit card without attracting unwelcome attention."

My own case was central to Silverman's argument that Boesky should receive a light prison sentence. "Surely," the attorney proclaimed, "Mr. Boesky should not receive as great a sentence as Dennis Levine." Silverman conceded that Boesky's financial crimes were greater, but, he said, Boesky's "cooperation, its timing and its value, more than outweigh the content of his criminality."

Judge Lasker delivered his own speech prior to imposing sentence. He acknowledged the truth of Silverman's words, but he also noted,

"Recent history has shown that the kind of erosion of morals and standards and obedience to the law involved in a case such as this is unhappily widespread in both business and government. The time has come when it is totally unacceptable for the courts to act as if prison is unthinkable for white-collar defendants but a matter of routine in other cases. Breaking the law is breaking the law . . .

"The signal must go out, loud and clear, to those attempting to skirt, fudge or deliberately break the law, that to preserve and to nourish moral values, to strengthen respect for the rule of law as governing society, so each of us has a fair and equal chance, and to preserve not only the actual integrity of the financial markets, criminal behavior such as Mr. Boesky's can not go unchecked."

That said, Judge Lasker sentenced Boesky to three years in prison.

He entered the minimum-security federal prison at Lompoc, California, in March 1988, where he was put to work in the dairy farm.

THE prison orientation material at Lewisburg had urged me to take advantage of the available educational opportunities, but these were limited to a GED course and drug rehabilitation counseling. Rather than take, therefore, I attempted to give. Repeatedly I requested the opportunity to help teach GED courses, but I was rebuffed. The authorities obviously wanted me to spend considerable time doing menial labor, specifically designed to humiliate the prisoner and make him docile, controllable.

Almost every day was the same, in a dreary way. Only a few incidents broke the drone. The major activity was to fight boredom.

I read many books, including Tom Wolfe's *Bonfire of the Vanities,* and was amazed at the strong parallels between my life and this fiction. I never saw myself as a "Master of the Universe," but like Wolfe's protagonist, Sherman McCoy, my life had spun out of control. We both learned very quickly that no one is bigger than the system.

One day I received a strange phone call from a Hollywood press agent, who said she had received permission from the Bureau of Prisons to show me a special screening of the movie *Wall Street.* When I realized that the star was Michael Douglas, the memory of our nodding acquaintance on the French Riviera was both amusing and painful. The press agent wanted me to write a review, but I declined.

After nearly a year, the administration relented and assigned me as a teacher for the inmates' high school equivalency program. Finally I was allowed to do something productive and uplifting.

I could not remember a time when I had time. At Smith Barney, at Lehman Brothers, and most of all at Drexel, there was never enough of the commodity. Here, the universal goal was to *do* time, to get it out of the way, to kill it. I discovered very quickly that one of the things you do with time is to think.

I took long, isolated walks on the prison grounds, and asked myself painful questions.

Why was I here? The answer was simple, but admitting it to myself was profoundly therapeutic: I was here because of my own actions. No one led me down the garden path. I was a big boy, and I made the decision to cross the line. *I was to blame.* There was a big part of me that wanted to take the easy emotional out and contend that everything would have been all right if my bankers had been more honorable; if they had played by Bank Leu's rules, they would not have piggybacked my trades; if they had played by Bahamian rules, they would never have sold me out. But this argument was a cop-out. I would have been caught, sooner or later. *I was to blame.*

There was simply no other explanation, and once I accepted this truth, other questions gnawed.

Why I had started? This was another easy question. In those early years I had regarded my offshore trading activities as just a method to make fast, easy money. Whether or not it was legal sometimes seemed to be a tough question, although, over the years, SEC Chairman John Shad and his investigators made the government's stance clear on this point. That was not enough to stop me. It doesn't hurt anybody, I rationalized. And besides, there was always that delicious delusion that everybody is doing it.

To be sure, it did not take me long to realize that, legal or illegal, insider trading was *wrong.* I tried to pinpoint the moment when I realized that I was stepping across moral boundaries set within me by my parents. The closest I could come was that first chemical company trade, while I was still at Citibank, but in truth, the process was more unstudied than immediate.

The difficult question was: *Why had I not stopped?* What was the answer to that nagging inquiry, voiced by Laurie and almost everyone else who spoke to me. Why did I continue trading on inside information well after my legitimate income was far greater than my needs? I was earning more than $2 million a year at Drexel. I had $10.6 million in my account at Bank Leu, and I did not need to touch it. So why did I continue? And why, when I already had a considerable bankroll and a comfortable, quiet system in place, did I make perhaps the single stupidest decision of all and agree to Boesky's deal? There was more at work here than simple greed. Indeed, the vast majority of my trading profits were still on deposit when I was arrested.

But if not greed, what was it?

I reconstructed my reasoning, although it had been vague at the time. It went something like this: So what if you have $10 million in the Bahamas, Dennis? You're helping your clients amass hundreds of millions of dollars. You negotiate billion-dollar deals every day, so where do you get off thinking that $10 million is big time?

Something deep inside forced me to try to catch up to the pack of wheeler-dealers who always raced in front of me. Whatever it was, placed in the context of workweeks that ranged from sixty to 100 hours, leaving little or no time for reflection, it had a narcotic effect.

But it was not money.

To those of us who raced along the Wall Street treadmill of the 80s, money assumed a mystical aura. Once you achieved a modest level of success, once you knew that you had your mortgage and your car payment covered, once you had a full belly, money simply became the way you gauged your level of success, compared to those about you. Competitive jealousy is normal in any workplace, but in this microcosm the numbers were so enormous that they threw everything out of scale.

In sum, money became the points on the scoreboard. If I checked the Quotron and discovered that I had just earned several hundred thousand dollars on an insider trade, I felt a rush of euphoria that had to be akin to a drug high. But the high always wore off, because I soon remembered that there were so many ahead of me on the scoreboard.

It was only in time that I came to view myself as an insider trading junkie. I was addicted to the excitement, the sense of victory. Some spouses use drugs, others have extramarital affairs; I secretly traded stocks.

I came to understand it all better when I compared my legitimate success to my illegitimate activities. In the beginning, perhaps, the insider trading was more intoxicating, but as my career progressed the excitement of "the deal" eclipsed, by far, the thrill of the private victory. Perelman v. Revlon was a much greater challenge than enhancing the value of my secret bank account. The adrenaline rush from the success of that one deal was an order of magnitude higher than any clandestine activity.

I spent a great deal of time thinking about this. Looking back, I could see that at each new level of my career, I had pushed my goals higher. When I was an associate, I wanted to be a vice president. When I became a vice president, I wanted to be a senior vice president. When I became a senior vice president, I wanted to be a partner or managing director. When I became a managing director, I wanted to become a client. When I was earning $20,000 a year, I thought, *I can make $100,000.* When I was earning $100,000 a year, I thought, *I can make $200,000.* When I was making a $1 million, I thought, *I can make $3 million.* There was always somebody one rung higher on the ladder, and I could never stop wondering: Is he really twice as good as I am?

Ambition eclipsed rationality. I was unable to find fulfillment in realistic limits. One frenetic meeting followed another. One deal was piled atop the next. The hours grew longer, the numbers grew bigger, the stakes grew more critical, the fire grew ever hotter.

By the time I became a managing director, I was out of control.

So was Boesky.

So was Milken.

So was Drexel.

As Americans, we were inherently competitive, taught to do the best we could—to go as far as we could. But at what cost?

I thought of Ronald Perelman, ranked number three on *Forbes* list of the 400 richest Americans. I wondered if he was content. Or was he obsessed with catching the two individuals above him? When does it stop?

Sometimes, with such thoughts spinning through my mind, I looked about in surprise at my environment. I might be out on an isolated portion of the facility. I might be in the TV room. I might be in the gym. No matter—here is where it stopped for me. I was in prison.

Dennis, I said to myself, this is a blessing in disguise. You need this withdrawal. You were hooked, just as surely as any junkie, alcoholic or compulsive gambler. That's the answer. You overdosed on deals. And you were not about to stop until someone caught you, or until the irresistible lure of the action on the Street killed you.

I burned with anger at my own blindness. I had to change my priorities. I had to regain control of my own life.

I looked down at my belly and vowed, Dennis, that's the first thing to go. Start making changes on the outside, and see if you can alter the inner man in the process.

WEEKENDS and holidays were visiting days. The visiting area was partially enclosed and partially opened up as a patio, furnished with chairs and picnic tables jammed on top of one another, precluding privacy. It was the outside area that held the potential for abuse, depending upon whether the assigned guard was lax or vigilant. Women visitors smuggled all manner of contraband in via their pocketbooks, which were rarely checked carefully. Drugs were rife, but another favorite was a hero sandwich; on weekends, Lewisburg's delis always did a booming business.

Overt demonstrations of affection were supposed to be confined to the beginning and end of the visit, but many of the couples were all over one another throughout the session. A favorite inmate trick was to slit a pants pocket so that your woman, sitting close at the picnic table, could slip her hand inside and relieve tension.

On one occasion I witnessed a couple move into the bushes adjacent to the picnic tables. They were out of sight for about a half-hour. Laurie was appalled. "How can they sneak off into the bushes like teenagers?" she asked.

This was the only environment where I could visit with my family. I will be haunted forever by the memory of Sarah taking her first toddling steps toward her daddy in a room crowded with convicted drug dealers and other felons.

Laurie dreaded these days. On the morning of a visit, she woke feeling disgusted and angry, wondering why she and her family had to suffer like this. After the exhausting three-hour drive she knew that guards would empty her purse and check Sarah's stroller for contraband. The degradation always rekindled her free-floating anger toward me, and she could not hide it, nor feign affection. She looked at the people around us and felt soiled. She came out of a sense of duty, but she did not want to be here and made sure that I knew it.

Once, Adam came in clutching a Mickey Mouse coloring book. The guard that day was a strict, humorless sort who grabbed the book out of my son's hand and growled, "You aren't allowed to bring that in here."

I was outraged. I could feel my face redden, but I held back my emotions as best I could. "Why can't he bring a coloring book into the visiting room?" I asked.

The guard sneered at me and answered, "We wouldn't want to stimulate the inmates' minds too much." He forced Adam to take the coloring book back to the car.

Near the end of that visit Adam asked the same question he always did: "Dad, when can you come home? I hate this stupid place."

I answered as I always did, through a parched throat, counting down the days.

Laurie, dazed and distressed, was too overwrought for tears. She only wanted to get home and jump into the shower.

It was no wonder to me that the wives of so many of my fellow prisoners filed for divorce.

THERE was an old piano in the education room, and sometimes I was granted the opportunity to spend an hour with it. Invariably, a few other inmates filtered in to sit and listen as I played.

Sometimes we sang together a song we called "The Lewisburg Blues."

CHAPTER THIRTY-SIX

AT AGE SIXTY, Hans Knopfli retired as president of Bank Leu, effective April 1, 1988. A bank spokeswoman declared that this had nothing to do with Bank Leu's role in the Guinness PLC scandal.

IN 1986 Drexel had, indeed, become the most profitable investment banking firm in history. This was the peak. Revenues continued high throughout 1987, but morale eroded. Following the crash of October 1987, Milken began to preach caution, urging his clients to "de-lever." He warned that it was time for a down-cycle.

As the realization dawned upon federal prosecutors that the road to Drexel and Milken led through Boesky, they fretted. An able defense attorney could tear Boesky's credibility to shreds, easily painting him as the manipulative devil who lured others into his own version of hell on Wall Street. That was an image that appeared real to me, as it surely would to any jury. The only choice for the prosecutors was to find other witnesses, how and where they could.

I heard that the federal attorneys had brought Jim Dahl before a grand jury and hit him with an offer he could not refuse. Apparently, Dahl was facing a string of charges arising from his trading practices and, obviously, he had every legal and moral right to avoid making any self-incriminating statements. However, when the government granted him immunity from any statements he made to the grand jury, they had him in a squeeze. If he refused to testify, he could be cited for contempt. If he lied, he could be convicted of perjury. He had no choice but to answer the questions truthfully.

I also heard that prosecutors used the same basic techniques on Cary Maultasch, who now worked in Drexel's New York office but was previously a close associate of Milken's in Beverly Hills.

A third key witness was Terren Peizer, who, after he was virtually compelled to testify to the grand jury, had to return to work in Drexel's trading room, where he sat at Milken's right hand.

Charles Thurnher, an accountant/administrator in the Beverly Hills office, was also said to be cooperating, as were three former Boesky employees, Setrag Mooradian, David Jackingyk and Michael Davidoff. Thurnher was believed to have confirmed that two different sets of books were kept for dealings between Boesky and Drexel. In all, eight of Drexel's staff members—and clients—were offered immunity.

The wagons were circling.

The information I could glean concerning the 1988 version of Drexel's Annual Bond Conference indicated that it was laced with unfamiliar overtones. For one thing, Dahl, Maultasch and Peizer were not welcome. No one knew what they had said to the grand jury, but everyone knew that they had testified.

Milken tried to maintain an upbeat image, revealing a "city of the future" display in the shape of a space station, augmented by a rock music video screaming, "We built this city on high-yield bonds." But the main question in the eyes of those in attendance was: Who in this room is about to be indicted?

Many worried that federal agents, choosing the moment for maximum publicity, might march right up onto the stage to arrest Milken.

ON the night of the Fourth of July, 1988, I watched fireworks in the distance, over the town of Lewisburg. It *is* a great country, I thought. You make a mistake, and it punishes you. But once you pay the price, it gives you another chance.

For me, however, Independence Day fell on July 5 that year. That was the day I was transferred to Manhattan House, a halfway facility located one block off Times Square on West 43rd Street, above the Café

43. I was allowed into the outside world during the day, but required to check in regularly through a special phone system. If all went well, before long the officials would allow me to spend a few nights with my family. And if I could land some sort of meaningful job and otherwise demonstrate my rehabilitative potential, I could be released by September.

IN one sense, I was a distant spectator of the securities industry, but in another I was more well informed than ever. My reading material was the same as before—*The Wall Street Journal, The New York Times, Barron's, Fortune, Forbes*—but I now had the leisure to think about what I was reading. I viewed the industry far more objectively than before.

When I assessed the general business climate, I concluded that we had accomplished much good. The Office of the Chief Economist of the SEC issued a report estimating that shareholders had cashed in big on the M&A trend and its resultant revaluing of common stock holdings. Analyzing the results of some 260 tender offers completed during the first half of the decade, the office declared that shareholders had reaped a windfall of $40 billion in profits.

Milken's new money had fostered competitive, hard-driving firms that changed the American scene. William McGowan's MCI helped topple the monopoly of AT&T and opened up the telecommunications field to vast new possibilities. In a mere six months Rupert Murdoch increased the value of his Metromedia television stations by $650 million; then he started a "fourth" television network. Ted Turner brought the nation twenty-four-hour-a-day news. Airline travel was now available to the masses. Scores of medium-sized corporations were poised for substantial growth.

There was no question that American industry now exhibited a more svelte profile, positioned to compete more efficiently with the growing threats from foreign businesses. A study of fifty recent LBOs, conducted by Professor Abbie Smith of the University of Chicago, concluded that the collective cash flow of the firms increased substantially and profit margins rose by 57 percent.

The Kohlberg Kravis Roberts & Co. LBO of the Beatrice Companies appeared to be a good example of a deal headed for a highly profitable bottom line. Kohlberg systematically sold off the subsidiaries—including Playtex International, Avis Rent-a-Car and International Foods—and was positioned to realize a substantial profit on its $6.2 billion investment.

But I also saw ominous developments. Frank Lorenzo seemed to have overextended himself with his acquisitions of Peoples Express and Frontier Airlines. His capital was tied up by long-term debt obligations and his flagship line, Continental, was under scrutiny by the FAA for major safety violations.

To meet his own debt payments, Ted Turner had to resell most of the MGM assets he had purchased the previous year; he was able to retain only the MGM film library.

In fact, the debt loads carried by many American businesses were astronomical, and increasing percentages of that were short term, meaning that corporations were, more than ever, vulnerable to recessionary pressures. I could not escape the conclusion that, in the seemingly forgotten words of President Truman, sooner or later it would add up to real money.

Other investment banking firms grew downright jealous of Drexel's success and sought a way to compete with its junk bonds and its "highly confident" letter but, in the process, pursuing ever larger fees, they proceeded with a decided lack of caution. Drexel, despite its freewheeling image, could boast that the default rate on its junk bonds was only 1.9 percent, compared to a 3.4 percent rate for the industry as a whole. The July 1986 bankruptcy of LTV Corporation, the largest ever, caused a default on junk bonds issued not by Drexel, but by Lehman Brothers. It was part of the evidence that the old-line investment banking firms had become careless in their frantic attempts to compete.

These firms attempted to counter Drexel's junk-bond financing power by, for the first time, putting up substantial sums of their own money, offering their clients bridge loans as short-term takeover capital, hoping, trusting—perhaps praying—that they could arrange the long-term financing without the help of the one man in the world who had a multi-billion-dollar ready-made market for junk bonds.

First Boston risked $1.8 billion of its own capital to back Canadian real estate developer Robert Campeau in his $3.6 billion hostile takeover of Allied Stores (whose retail operations included Brooks Brothers and Ann Taylor); Merrill Lynch was prepared to put up $1.9 billion of its own money to help finance Goldsmith's aborted raid on Goodyear Tire & Rubber Co. Goldman Sachs and Salomon Brothers together provided $600 million in temporary financing for a proposed $1.5 billion buyout of the Southland Corporation and its chain of 7-Eleven convenience stores, but the junk-bond market collapsed, and even though they offered a premium rate of 18 percent interest, the two investment banking houses could not underwrite the bonds and were left holding a $600 million bag.

Salomon Brothers ballyhooed its role in the LBO of Revco D.S., Inc., the drugstore chain, putting together $703.5 million in junk-bond financing. Having turned down the deal at Drexel, I was amazed that Salomon Brothers miscalculated so badly. Within sixteen months, Revco announced that its profits had dropped by 50 percent, forcing it to renege on a $46 million interest payment. To Salomon's deep embarrassment, Revco hired Drexel to help it restructure its debt.

I watched in dismay as the race for high fees eclipsed good judgment. Deals were executed at prices so high that it would be impossible for the new owners to service their debt. Campeau's acquisition of Allied Stores left him with a total debt of $4.5 billion—only $200 million less than his annual revenues. Despite his precarious balance sheet, Campeau then went after Federated Stores (including the fashionable subsidiaries of Bloomingdale's and A&S) with a tender offer that began at $47 per share but increased to $73.50 per share; the final purchase price of $6.6 billion was more than seven times higher than Federated's annual pre-tax cash flow.

These were acquisitions that had to appear dubious to anyone in a high-level position in the M&A field. For years both Allied and Federated were the subjects of numerous takeover rumors. We all had a strong sense of their actual value, and only Campeau seemed willing to pay far more than they were worth. The companies both had significant real estate holdings, and in an up market, they looked good. But everyone seemed to have forgotten that we were long overdue for a down cycle, and real estate would certainly be hard hit. I did not understand how Campeau expected to survive in the highly cyclical retailing industry during even mildly troubling times. He reached beyond his grasp, and I suspect that he acted on the basis of ego rather than analysis. To me, it was only a matter of time before both Allied and Federated filed for bankruptcy.

If we hit a recessionary cycle that caused a further collapse in the junk-bond market, it would be easy to pinpoint the problem areas. Drexel's largest junk-bond customers were insurance companies and mutual funds, which both represented 32 percent of the market. Congress may have missed the boat when, in an attempt to revive the flagging S&L industry, it decreed that the thrifts had to divest themselves of all junk bonds in their portfolios by 1994. In my opinion, junk bonds have taken a bum rap for the problems in the S&L industry. S&Ls represented only a small percentage of the market for Drexel's bonds; their collapse was keyed by the tightening of the real estate market, triggered in part by congressional attempts at tax reform, rather than the purchase of high-yield securities.

Junk bonds have also come under fire for their role in financing hostile takeovers when, in truth, only a small percentage of the public issues were used for this purpose. Twenty-three percent of the issues were used for friendly mergers or acquisitions, while the bulk of the money generated by this new instrument was simply used for the internal expansion of up-and-coming enterprises.

I paid special attention, of course, to reports concerning the SEC's attempts to stymie insider trading. The General Accounting Office issued a fascinating report, noting that, of the 609 instances of suspected insider trading referred by the exchanges to the SEC during the years 1986 and 1987, 226 involved "suspicious trades executed through foreign institutions." The SEC had pretty much ignored those cases, an SEC official explained to a congressional subcommittee, because the agency did not pursue suspicious trades emanating from certain countries, such as Panama, Luxembourg and Liechtenstein, because it had difficulty circumventing those nations' bank secrecy laws. Enforcement chief Gary Lynch disputed that statement and defended the agency's track record.

Numerous instances indicated to me that inside traders were conducting business as usual. *Business Week,* which had warned two years earlier that insider trading was rampant, conducted an updated study and concluded that, in the first year following my arrest and its resultant publicity, 70 percent of takeover target stocks continued to show mysterious, pre-announcement price rises (averaging 18 percent), calculated the odds of that occurring naturally at 392,000:1 and concluded, "Insider trading is as prevalent as ever."

The activity continued unabated. For example, on Thursday, March 31, 1988, the stock of MGM/UA Entertainment began a three-day run that took its price from $8.75 per share to $10.62. Only after a request from the New York Stock Exchange did the company's chairman, Lee Rich, announce that he had received "acquisition inquiries from several parties." Similar pre-announcement run-ups occurred in the stocks of Roper Corporation, Staley Continental, Koppers Company and Quaker State.

SIXTY-SEVEN pounds lighter than when I went off to prison, I was released from federal custody on September 8, 1988, pondering this question: After skyrocketing to the top of the world and crashing down even faster, what do you do next?

I realized that I would face each day with enormous uncertainty, feeling my way, trying to put together the scrambled pieces of the jigsaw puzzle of my life. I vowed to spend the bulk of my time with my family, to help heal their—our—emotional wounds.

One of the first things I did was take Adam to Disney World.

Then I had to come to grips with Laurie's pain.

"Do you know what I did the day you went to prison?" she asked.

"No."

"I went over to your once-sacred desk and began to reorganize it."

Ours had always been a traditional marriage. Laurie managed the children and the day-to-day running of the household. I went off to my business of juggling billions of dollars and, at home, took care of the family finances. Now someone else had to assume that task, and the only candidate was Laurie.

"I relabeled folders and arranged things the way I wanted them," Laurie recalled. In addition to the normal costs of running a household, there were extraordinary expenses. Every day brought a new stack of bills from the army of attorneys who had worked on my case, and each time she saw an envelope with an attorney's return address, her resentment grew. It increased further as our savings account dwindled.

In short order, Laurie had lost her father to cancer, given birth to Sarah and sent her husband off to prison. For seventeen months she was a single parent. She was the one who had to make the long drives to Lewisburg, with two kids squirming in the car. Socially she was a fifth wheel, a woman with two kids and no spouse. It was difficult for her to hold up her head with pride.

Nevertheless, throughout this time, she kept the pain inside, so as to minimize my own. After a time, she found herself enjoying her new independence, and as the months passed, she contemplated my return with a certain scary feeling of ambivalence.

The words cut deeply. There was no choice but to let her vent her accumulated rage. It was time to have it out, and we did so.

She was still angry that I had persisted in my trading long after my legitimate salary had increased exponentially. "How much money can one person spend?" she asked rhetorically. But she had come to understand the force of the addiction that had controlled me.

What bothered her most, now, was the nagging truth that I had been immoral. "My God!" she said. "It was like you were having an affair. There was a part of you I never saw."

Perhaps what kept us together was her growing understanding that, as sophisticated as I had seemed, I was, in reality, a victim of my own naïveté. She realized that I had been convinced, all along, that if I was involved in a crime, it was victimless. In my mind, I never hurt anybody.

Months passed before I began to see glimpses of the laughter that used to be endemic in our household. At that point, I knew that we could survive anything.

Nevertheless, she still cries whenever she discusses the year and a half when I was gone.

NEW charges continued to surface, and it seemed obvious that the government investigators would not stop until they reeled in as many targets as possible, including the largest. Without admitting or denying guilt, Kidder Peabody, Marty Siegel's former employer, had already agreed to pay $25 million to settle civil charges of insider trading and stock parking associated with Boesky's activities.

But it was my former firm that was, unquestionably, in the hottest water. Drexel, which contended that it had turned over more than one million documents in response to government subpoenas, issued a statement declaring that it "will not condone or tolerate any activities which violate the integrity of the markets."

This was not enough to stave off the assault. In an unprecedented action, the government applied the harsh provisions of the RICO statute against a financial institution, indicting a small trading firm, Princeton/Newport Partners, whose principal, Jay Regan, maintained a close association with Drexel and Milken. Throughout the late 70s and early 80s Milken and Regan were involved in several joint investment ventures. The government ultimately won the case, but the indictment itself was sufficient to put the firm out of business.

On the heels of that action, the government lodged numerous charges that Drexel had abused its position by such actions as parking stocks for other investors and pressuring entrepreneurs to initiate takeover actions against target companies in which Drexel quietly owned large positions. A Drexel spokesman declared, "A financial institution cannot stand up to a RICO indictment."

In January 1989, Drexel Burnham Lambert, Inc., and the Drexel Burnham Lambert Group, Inc., agreed to plead guilty to six felony counts involving securities fraud and market manipulation. The agreement called for Drexel to pay a total of $650 million in fines and penalties. Just as all of the individual defendants before, Drexel agreed to cooperate with the ongoing investigation. Although Milken had not been charged with any wrongdoing, part and parcel of the agreement was that Drexel "not be involved with Michael R. Milken directly or indirectly in any business transactions or activities." Drexel was forbidden to pay Milken any of the bonus compensation he had legitimately earned for 1988 or 1989.

I was astounded when I learned of Drexel's plea and the only conclusion I could reach was that the firm, also, was left with no other reasonable choice.

The action tore Drexel apart. Employees were told that speaking with Milken was now grounds for dismissal; they were told to advise their clients that if they talked to Milken, Drexel could no longer deal with them.

Milken's departure spelled the end for America's highest-flying investment bank. The day after Drexel agreed to plead guilty, when a supervisor made a job-related request to Terren Peizer, Peizer reportedly snapped, "Go to hell." He was told to take several days off.

Drexel financial analyst Glenn Boschetto said that the charges were "astonishing." Where once there was an environment encouraging "the open expression of ideas," he said, there was now only fear.

Fred McCarthy, one of my former partners in the Corporate Finance Department, commented that Drexel was frantic to prove that it "could sell securities without Mike Milken" even if it had to buy up portions of new junk-bond issues itself, financing the purchases with short-term funds. Drexel, McCarthy said, had "lost its soul," and subsequent events proved him correct.

At the very moment when Milken was forced out, Drexel, with net capital in excess of $1 billion, was still one of Wall Street's most viable firms. Only a few months later the Street gasped when Drexel exhibited a decidedly un-Milken-like behavior. One of its high-flying clients, Integrated Resources, Inc., suffered heavy losses, stemming from the 1986 Tax Reform Act. In the past, Milken would have armed-twisted throughout his network to find others who would assume the debt for the important client or—as a last resort—would have had Drexel swallow the loss. But now Drexel simply left the client hung out to dry. Integrated Resources defaulted on $1 billion worth of debt, leaving investors numb.

Nevertheless, Drexel persisted with its characteristic tenacity. One day I happened to encounter Leon Black on the streets of New York. He greeted me cordially and asked the obligatory questions. I brought him up to date and told him that I had just formed the ADASAR Group (named after Adam and Sarah), a financial advisory firm specializing in mergers and acquisitions and capital formation. I asked how he was doing.

"We're working on the Nabisco/RJR thing for Kravis," he said.

I said to myself, It's history-making, and I'm not involved.

"It's a very, very tough sell," Black remarked. "We've got everybody in the firm going on it. I think we'll pull it off."

And indeed they did. In the midst of a barrage of adverse publicity Drexel managed to place $4 billion worth of junk bonds to fund the LBO. It was the largest junk-bond issue ever.

Drexel earned fees of more than $200 million on the RJR deal, but it was the last great gasp. In the months that followed, trying desperately to maintain the image of a firm that was still dominant in its market, Drexel lowered its standards, financing marginal deals that Milken would never have approved. In several cases, such as junk-bond issues for West Point–Pepperell and Paramount Petroleum, the firm was forced to buy heavy positions in new securities issues because it could not sell them on the open market. This tied up its capital and made it difficult to meet short-term obligations.

For the first time, some Drexel clients filed for bankruptcy. The end was in sight.

THERE was, perhaps, only one fish bigger than Boesky, and the team of federal investigators pursued Milken relentlessly, declaring that a relationship between the two men "evolved as an exchange of mutually beneficial and unlawful accommodations." Prosecutors contended that Boesky and Milken initiated a "secret arrangement" in early 1984, calling for Boesky to buy and sell stocks at the direction of, and for the benefit of, Milken; this would allow Milken to make clandestine trades of stocks that were on Drexel's restricted list. At other times, the government said, Drexel bought or sold securities for Boesky, hiding the true identity of the dealer so that Boesky could reap certain tax benefits, or evade SEC reporting requirements.

On March 29, 1989, Milken was indicted by a federal grand jury on ninety-eight criminal counts. His brother Lowell was also indicted on a variety of complaints.

The charges alleged insider trading violations concerning securities of Caesars World, Viacom International, Inc., Republic Airlines, Lorimar, Inc., and other firms. For example, one immunized witness claimed that he overheard Milken tell someone else that Lorimar and Telepictures were going to merge; according to this witness, Milken wrote the numbers "2.2" onto a notepad, indicating the ratio of the stock swap. Anyone possessing this information would guess that Lorimar, the purchaser, would suffer a decline in its stock price. This witness claimed that Milken then instructed an associate to liquidate a hedge that Drexel held in Lorimar stock against a short position, in effect, betting on a downswing in price.

One of the accusations, in particular, seemed patently absurd to me. The government alleged that, sometime during the day of January 4, 1985, Milken instructed Boesky to buy stock in Diamond Shamrock Corporation and to sell short in Occidental Petroleum. According to the government, this advice was given on the basis of material, non-public information. But I was there when—the day I first met him in California—Milken heard the news that Occidental had announced, and I had seen the look of shocked surprise on his face. He was stunned by the news. What's more, the alleged trades occurred later in the day.

How could Milken have had inside information when, in fact, the news was broadcast over the Dow Jones tape? It would be the most natural thing in the world for an arb such as Boesky to buy Diamond Shamrock and sell short in Occidental on the day in question.

As the details surfaced, I was amazed to learn the astronomical total of Milken's Drexel income. The government said that in 1987 alone he was paid $550 million in salary and bonuses—and that did not count income from his various partnership arrangements; he was the highest-paid U.S. executive in history.

THE SEC tied up the loose ends of its investigation on August 7, 1989, when it filed a civil lawsuit in Manhattan federal court against former Merrill Lynch stockbroker Brian Campbell, his associate Kevin Barry and his Venezuelan trading partner, Carlos Zubillaga, for their roles in piggybacking on my investments. Campbell and Barry's investment entity, BCM Management, Inc., was also named as a defendant. The suit alleged fifteen instances of unlawful trading, from the period March 1984 through June 1985, but centered its attention on only five of the transactions, involving G. D. Searle & Co., Textron, Inc., McGraw-Edison Co., Nabisco Brands, Inc., and Houston Natural Gas Co. It alleged that the defendants, as well as their friends and family members, realized a total of $452,175 in illegal profits in those five instances and asked the court to award treble damages.[1]

MILKEN began spending his Saturday mornings at the library of the MacLaren Children's Center, a Los Angeles County shelter for abused, neglected and abandoned children. He instituted an informal class called Mike's Math Club. One Saturday he taught the children a simple exercise that enabled them to mentally multiply two-digit numbers ending in five (such as 65 x 85) faster than they could by using a calculator. On another Saturday he held a mock auction to teach the children how to save their money for important purposes.

In Mike's Math Club, no one was ever "wrong." If a child did not come up with the correct answer, he was "close."

---

[1] As of this writing, the case is pending.

Once, Milken took the children on a surprise outing. The children were amazed to arrive at Michael Jackson's ranch, where they were treated to a movie, a tour of the grounds and lunch with the famous singer himself.

SINCE the mid-80s the SEC had been probing the activities of the Zurich brokerage firm Ellis A. G. Their attention was keyed by a congressional study of fifty-four takeover situations that occurred in the first half of the 1980s. The researchers noted that Boesky had traded in seventeen of those stocks. I had traded in twenty-four of them. But Ellis A. G. traded in fifty-three of the fifty-four stocks!

It was late in 1989 when I learned that the SEC had turned its information over to Swiss authorities. The Swiss were reportedly reviewing the activities of Alfred Sarasin, former president of the Swiss Bankers Association and senior partner of a private bank in Basel, Sarasin & Cie. That bank owned Ellis A. G. in the early years of the decade, when the brokerage house conducted many of its trades. I was astounded to discover that Sarasin was still a director of Bank Leu AG in Zurich. And I remembered that Bernhard Meier had married into the family! It made me wonder whether the SEC and Justice Department investigators had missed, at least initially, the biggest piggybacker of them all. The investigation is still continuing.

IN December 1989, Drexel paid out its annual bonuses, amounting to tens of millions of dollars, for if the firm had reneged, employees would have staged a mass exodus. In many cases the senior people were also able to pocket lucrative profits from the Drexel partnerships. For example, the Beatrice warrants, by now, had appreciated by a whopping 5,000 percent. My investment of $100,000 would have been worth $5 million—if it had not been confiscated by the government.

The following month, Robert Campeau's Allied and Federated Department Stores filed for Chapter 11 bankruptcy protection, and the effects were felt economy-wide. The garment manufacturers were hit, as were the appliance manufacturers. In fact, any industry that sold products through these large department stores had difficulty collecting its accounts and the ripples washed on to their suppliers.

Left hung out to dry was a string of creditors who had funded Campeau's over-ambitious acquisitions. These included Citibank and numerous other U.S. banks; eleven Japanese banks; the investment banking houses of First Boston, PaineWebber and Dillon Read; Prudential Insurance; Equitable Life Assurance; the world's largest mutual fund company, Fidelity Investments; and the giant real estate developers Olympia & York and Edward J. DeBartolo Company.

The effect on the junk-bond market was chilling.

Drexel frantically sought bank financing to meet $100 million in obligations, due on February 13, 1990. The day before the deadline, Citibank led a group of lenders into a meeting to consider extending short-term credit. For collateral Drexel offered a portfolio of junk bonds, private placements and oil and gas limited partnerships. One banker called it "an eclectic collection of illiquid securities." Shortly before midnight, the bankers turned thumbs down.

The following day, at ten-thirty A.M., Eastern Standard Time, Drexel's 5,300 employees gathered in offices all over the world to listen to a statement from Fred Joseph. In a sober monotone Joseph announced that Drexel was filing for Chapter 11 bankruptcy reorganization.

CHAPTER THIRTY-SEVEN

"I WAS THE FOUNDER and head of the High-Yield and Convertible Securities Department at Drexel," Milken said, as he appeared in a Manhattan courtroom and began a lengthy statement before Judge Kimba M. Wood.

It was April 24, 1990. For years, now, Milken had been recognized as *the* force behind the junk-bond juggernaut and as Drexel's Midas-in-residence. Everyone wanted to know what made this man tick.

Still, he remained an enigma.

Part of the mystery surrounding Milken was undoubtedly due to his campaign to suppress personal publicity. But perhaps it was also a natural by-product of his frenetic life-style. No one outside of his immediate family really knew Milken, because no one ever spent more than a few moments with him—and those moments were devoted passionately to business.

The private bodyguards were gone, replaced by federal marshals and a phalanx of attorneys. Now he stood, symbolically naked, stripped by the government of his job and his glory. But even without those trappings, the mystique remained. The largest federal courtroom in Manhattan overflowed with spectators and hundreds more stood outside in Foley Square.

"I am here today because in connection with some transactions, I transgressed certain of the laws and regulations that govern our industry," Milken said. "I was wrong in doing so and knew that at the time, and I am pleading guilty to these offenses."

One by one, he addressed the six violations of securities laws to which he was admitting. In early 1984, he said, when Victor Posner had announced his intention to acquire Fischbach via Drexel financing, he encouraged Boesky to purchase Fischbach stock. Although Milken said he could not remember the exact words, he indicated that Drexel would cover any losses Boesky might incur on the transactions. Between April 26 and July 9, Boesky purchased more than 500,000 shares, or about 13.4 percent of Fischbach's outstanding stock.

The merger was delayed by legal machinations and Milken detailed, "Over the next months, he called me incessantly to complain that the price of the stock was dropping, that Drexel was responsible for his losses, that my comments to him were guarantees against loss and that he expected us to make good."

I could see it and hear it. Boesky was a hound. He never left you alone.

But it was wrong, and both men knew it. By not recording his agreement to make good on Boesky's losses, Milken assisted Boesky in the filing of a false Schedule 13D.

In August of that same year, Milken continued, a Drexel client, Golden Nugget, contracted with Drexel to sell a substantial position in MCA. Milken wanted to conceal the identity of the seller so as not to affect the price adversely. "So I turned to Boesky," he said, "whose business it was to buy and sell large amounts of stock," and who, Milken knew, had long been interested in entertainment industry stocks. Boesky bought a large block of stock, but complained to Milken when the value dropped. This put Milken into a bind, for he now had more MCA stock to sell. He now promised Boesky that Drexel would make up any losses encountered on future purchases of MCA stock. On the basis of this promise, Boesky bought each block of stock as it became available and then, armed with Milken's guarantee, dumped the shares quickly onto the open market, incurring losses that he intended to transfer to Drexel. The criminal violation was similar to the Fischbach episode. The arrangements were not necessarily illegal; but concealing them was.

The hidden sales worked two ways. Early in 1985 Boesky acquired a substantial position in Helmerich & Payne, an oil company. By July,

Boesky knew that he could realize a $4 million tax loss if he sold the shares; the problem was, he was considering a takeover bid and did not want to sell. He approached a Drexel trader and asked him to buy his position of one million shares and hold them until he, Boesky, was ready to repurchase them. This time, Boesky guaranteed Drexel against losses. Milken said he did not know of the deal at the time, but approved it in retrospect. It was a third instance of wheeling-and-dealing behind the scenes, where the actions of the privileged few were screened from the general scrutiny of the markets.

"There were other accommodations of a similar nature between the Boesky organization and Drexel," Milken admitted, "some of which were wrong." Early in 1985, as a result of Boesky's incessant complaints of losses incurred via the hidden trades, Milken instructed an employee to determine the extent of the losses. Then, he said, "I caused Drexel to execute certain bond trades which resulted in profits" to Boesky.

The two final charges to which Milken pled guilty involved transactions between Drexel and David Solomon, and related to the payment of commissions hidden to investors in the Finsbury mutual funds. Since the official paperwork did not disclose this arrangement, it constituted a violation of securities laws.

Finally, Milken admitted that in December 1985, he had assisted Solomon in conducting securities trades for the express purpose of benefiting Solomon's personal income tax status. He said he did so because Solomon was an important client. It was a tax evasion scheme, pure and simple.

With his voice breaking, Milken concluded, "I realize that by my acts I have hurt those who are closest to me. I am truly sorry."

Repeatedly Judge Kimba M. Wood asked Milken to assure her that he was, in fact, guilty of the crimes. Repeatedly Milken said yes, he was guilty. In my view, further evidence was unnecessary. Yes, it was true that an important part of Milken's plea agreement called for the government to drop all charges against his brother Lowell. Yes, it was true that the drama this day would bring an end to four years of hounding by government prosecutors. But—and I knew this fact well—no one pleads guilty to criminal charges unless he is, in fact, guilty.

The judge warned that the six crimes carried a maximum prison term of twenty-eight years.

Both Liman and chief prosecutor John Carroll indicated that Milken would cooperate fully in the government's continuing investigation. The written plea agreement declared that such cooperation would begin only after Milken was sentenced. Milken would then be required to speak with federal agents whenever he was asked and would be bound to "fully and truthfully disclose all information with respect to Drexel-related activities." The judge asked Carroll if the government would, in fact, induce Milken to talk.

"We certainly hope so, Your Honor," Carroll replied. "If he's not fully truthful and accurate with us, we can prosecute him for additional crimes. I think the incentives are there . . ."

The judge deferred sentencing until she could study pre-sentencing reports.

After the hearing, Lowell Milken distributed a prepared statement declaring, "I can take no satisfaction that the charges against me are being dropped. They never should have been brought in the first place, because I have done nothing wrong."

Nevertheless, he joined his brother in another room of the courthouse, where Michael settled the SEC's civil charges by agreeing to pay a fine of $200 million and further agreeing to place an additional $400 million into a restitution fund. It was the largest individual settlement figure in SEC history, exceeded only by Drexel's $650 million fine. Milken's remaining assets, which, by all estimates, were still considerable, would remain subject to perhaps dozens of civil lawsuits. Both of the Milkens signed consent decrees in which they neither admitted nor denied SEC charges, and both accepted a permanent ban from participation in the securities industry.

REELING from the revelations of its role in my activities and its apparent violation of Bahamian and Swiss laws, coupled with the scandal of its central role in the Guinness affair, Bank Leu sold out to Crédit Suisse in May 1990.

Shortly after the deal closed in September, Crédit Suisse realized that it had purchased additional infamy, when Bank Leu disclosed that it had been swindled out of 63 million Swiss francs (about $50 million) by the credit officer of its Duebendorf branch office, who allegedly concocted a scheme to make fake loans in the names of legitimate clients, and then share the proceeds with his partners in what was described as "the Zurich financial underworld."

THROUGHOUT the spring and summer, Judge Wood was bombarded with letters attempting to influence her course of action as she considered the appropriate sentence for Milken. The letters provided evidence that the public had difficulty viewing Milken as a human being, subject to the normal spectrum of impulses. The letters tended to polarize his personality, either on the side of good or evil. The same divergence of opinion surfaced among the lawyers.

In an attempt to sort through what she called "a stark contrast" between the defense and government versions of Milken's conduct, the judge announced on September 27 that she would convene what is known as a "Fatico" hearing (from *United States v. Fatico,* a 1979 2nd Circuit Court ruling), to consider evidence supporting claims of Milken's wrongdoing beyond the six counts of the guilty plea. The hearing, she explained, was not a formal trial, but "a way to educate the judge about the defendant's character." Her decisions in the hearings would be based upon a "preponderance of the evidence," rather than the more stringent "beyond a reasonable doubt" of the criminal trial.

Over a period of weeks, prosecutors called numerous witnesses, including immunized Drexel employees and clients, who were forced, under oath, to testify against the man who, in most cases, had played the key role in building their careers. There were notable exceptions. A number of Milken's former associates refused to testify. Milken himself exercised his rights under the Fifth Amendment and did not take the stand. But perhaps the most noteworthy absentee was Ivan Boesky, despite the fact that prosecutors called him "the most useful cooperator in the history of the securities laws."

Cary Maultasch testified that, on April 23, 1986, he manipulated the stock price of Wickes Companies at the direction of Drexel trader Peter Gardiner. Gardiner testified that Milken was behind the plan and said that, late in the day, Milken directed him to call Maultasch to find out "how many Wickes we had bought." But Gardiner did not provide the judge with sufficient credibility to pin the affair directly onto Milken. In particular, the judge noted that Gardiner, by his own admission, had lied under oath on two previous occasions.

Jim Dahl testified that Milken ordered him to buy bonds in Caesars World shortly after Milken had attended a meeting with Caesars World officials to discuss a proposal that might have increased the value of those bonds. But the judge determined that the government had provided insufficient evidence to prove that Milken, in this instance, had traded on inside information or violated laws, securities industry regulations or company policies.

Under subpoena, Fred Joseph took the stand to discuss the allegation that Milken offered warrants of Storer Communications, Inc., as an illegal gratuity to some favored clients. Joseph, forced to protect his company's interests, declared that Milken had violated Drexel policies and otherwise misled him on details concerning the Storer warrants.

Although the government concentrated its efforts on various deals, another serious issue surfaced. Peizer, for example, testified that he was directed by Milken to turn over the ledger, detailing Drexel's deals with David Solomon, to Lorraine Spurge—presumably so that it could be sequestered or destroyed. Peizer characterized Milken's words as "something to the effect that if you don't have them you can't provide them." The defense, in rebuttal, pointed to inconsistencies in Peizer's testimony, such as the fact that he claimed to have seen Michael and Lowell Milken conferring at a time when Lowell was actually at a doctor's appointment. Furthermore, when one of the defense attorneys asked Peizer, "Did you construe anything that Michael Milken said to you when you were going through your drawer as meaning you ought to throw out the documents?" he replied, "I don't think one can necessarily make that assumption."

The judge noted the inconsistencies in Peizer's testimony but was impressed by his demeanor on the witness stand, observing that he appeared to be "deeply reluctant" to testify against Milken, his former "mentor and benefactor" and, in sum, found him to be credible. "It can reasonably be inferred," she declared, from "the ledger's subsequent disappearance that the purpose of Michael Milken's giving that direction to Peizer was to keep the ledger out of the government's hands."

The judge also found Dahl's testimony "highly credible" as it pertained to Milken's purported attempts to obstruct justice. The defense argued that Dahl's story of Milken delivering instructions over the sound of running water in the men's room could be interpreted as Milken's attempt to advise Dahl to do what he could to retain customer confidence in Drexel. The judge discounted that scenario, based in part upon the secretive circumstances surrounding the event. "I conclude," she said, "that Michael Milken directed Dahl to come into the office that Sunday [following the announcement of Boesky's plea agreement] for the sole purpose of signaling to him, clandestinely, the advisability of removing or destroying documents . . ." The fact that Dahl did not destroy any documents, in the judge's opinion, did not lessen Milken's culpability.

Gardiner said that he was told pointedly, by a Milken aide, to "clean out your desk"; he said that he took certain papers home.

It was this theme of attempts to thwart the intent of the grand jury subpoenas that appeared to distress Judge Wood the most. She declared, "Michael Milken's pattern of wrongdoing, as shown in the crimes to which he pled guilty, is to step just over the line into unlawful conduct, and to do so in a way that preserves his 'deniability' and minimizes the risk of detection. His clandestine and subtle message to Dahl, and his slightly veiled message to Peizer, are characteristic of this way of operating. The court will not conclude that because Michael Milken chose to be subtle rather than blatant, no wrongdoing occurred."

ON the evening before he was to be sentenced, Milken was in tears as he greeted friends who stopped by to visit him in his suite at the Carlyle Hotel in Manhattan.

In court the next morning, November 21, Liman had the chance to speak first, and he admitted that the judge had seen two very different pictures of Milken. He said, "The government, which has not spent much time with him, tries to cast him in the Boesky mode, but I would say to Your Honor that that template does not fit. He's just not cut from the same cloth as Ivan Boesky . . .

"Michael's crimes cannot be condoned," Liman admitted, "but one crime that Michael is not guilty of is the crime of indifference. . . . His philanthrophy and community activities began long before this case, and they reached epic proportions. He's a young man still, but he's given away $360 million, and that's a staggering figure. More important to me, and I think to the court, he gave it away quietly, without fanfare, they way the scriptures teach is the most sacred way to give."

Now Liman turned his attention to the question that was on everyone's lips. Why did Milken commit his crimes? "I am not a psychiatrist," Liman said. "I have worked very closely with Michael, and I can't offer Your Honor an explanation as to how Michael slipped. . . . To say he is filled with remorse is to understate it. It's on his face. His family sees it. His lawyers see it. Everybody who knows him sees it. The court can see it. . . . Michael has been crushed. He's been crushed by the shame that he feels for his offenses, he has been crushed by four years of punishing publicity. He has been crushed by the realization of what he has done to his family, his children, his friends, his clients, to everyone. . . . He has been crushed by the knowledge that his name has been taken from him and has become sort of a by-word or symbol of a generation that he was never part of and whose values he doesn't stand for."

Liman concluded his presentation with a proposal that Milken be sentenced to work, under the supervision of the Los Angeles Police Department, in community programs dealing with inner-city children.

Milken spoke briefly in his own behalf and said, "What I did violated not just the law but all of my principles and values, and I will regret it for the rest of my life. I am truly sorry."

Assistant U.S. Attorney Jess Fardella, in a statement far shorter than Liman's, acknowledged that many good things could be said about Milken. Nevertheless, he pointed out, Milken's "profit motive was simple and evident." Beyond that, he declared, the judge must bear in mind the very serious evidence that Milken conspired to obstruct justice once the investigation began. "This is a case," he said, "in which an appropriate sentence can make a difference . . . it must convince the public at large that individuals of great wealth and power do not receive special treatment at the bar of justice."

Now it was Judge Wood's turn to speak and the courtroom was hushed as she declared that the evidence offered at the "Fatico" hearing was inconclusive as it pertained to many of the alleged offenses. But what that evidence showed, she said, was "that defendant engaged in the additional misconduct of attempting to obstruct justice . . ."

The judge took a moment to reflect upon the volume of poison pen letters she had received concerning Milken. "The letters," she said, "reflect a perception that we as a society must find those responsible for the alleged abuses of the 1980s, economic harm caused savings and loan associations, takeover targets and those allegedly injured by the issuance of junk bonds as well as by insider trading and other alleged abuses, and punish these criminals in proportion to the losses believed to have been suffered. These writers ask for a verdict on a decade of greed." Conversely, she said, she would not consider pleas for leniency based upon those who pointed to the jobs and business opportunities created by Milken's work. Rather, she would merely institute a sentence appropriate to the six crimes encompassed by Milken's guilty plea.

She lectured, "When a man of your power in the financial world at the head of the most important department of one of the most important investment banking houses in this country repeatedly conspires to violate and violates securities and tax laws in order to achieve more power and wealth for himself and his wealthy clients and commits financial crimes that are particularly hard to detect, a significant prison term is required in order to deter others."

She noted that part of Milken's plea agreement called for him to cooperate in the government's ongoing investigation, but only after sentencing, and she pointed out, "If you cooperate, and if the government moves for a reduction in your sentence based on your cooperation, the court can adjust your sentence accordingly."

After a few more qualifying remarks, she said, "Mr. Milken, please rise."

He stood, flanked by his attorneys, for the moment of judgment.

"You are unquestionably a man of talent," Judge Wood said, "and you have consistently shown a dedication to those less fortunate than you. It is my hope that the rest of your life will fulfill the promise shown early in your career.

"However, for the reasons stated earlier, I sentence you to a total of ten years in prison consisting of two years each on counts two through six to be served consecutively, and I also sentence you to three years of probation on count one. A special condition of your probation is that you serve full-time community service, 1,800 hours per year for each of the three years, in a program to be determined by the court."

THE week before Milken was due to report to prison, Judge Wood announced an extraordinary finding. Prosecutors still contended that Milken's six crimes bilked the investing public of $4.7 million. Another legion of lawyers backed lawsuits claiming billions of dollars in damages. Based upon all she had learned from the volumes of evidence she had reviewed and the hours of testimony she had witnessed, Judge Wood concluded that her best estimate of total investor losses from Milken's crimes was $318,082.

The judge indicated that she was surprised by the relatively low figure, and she further indicated that she now believed that Milken (pending his cooperation) would serve thirty-six to forty months of his ten-year sentence.

I felt a stab of empathy on Monday, March 4, 1991. This was the day that Milken was to report to the federal minimum-security facility in the ironically named town of Pleasanton, California.

The question of his motivation remained, as Milken was probably a billionaire by the time he allied himself with Boesky and other conspirators. Clearly, he did not have to break the law.

When I considered the available facts, I was left with only partial answers. In the weeks and months following my downfall, countless psychiatric "authorities" propounded various theories as to my motivation. Many of them attempted to peer into my childhood from a necessary distance. They proclaimed that my incessant drive for money and success was undoubtedly rooted in my relationship with my parents or siblings or school friends. To me it appeared to be so much hokum. My childhood was as normal as they come. And how could I, in turn, attempt to explain Milken's motivation?

Perhaps Milken's success was simply too great to hold. Perhaps he would have fallen, eventually, under any circumstances. But as far as his criminal conspiracy with Boesky is concerned, I suspect that—like Siegel and me before him—Milken was enticed into the web. Boesky was a serpent in the garden, whispering, "I can do certain things for you. I can be very helpful to you. I can show you how to cut some corners. You want control? I can help you control everything."

Milken spoke with arbs every day, dozens of them, calling back and forth from corners of the globe. Yet not a single charge of impropriety was raised concerning Milken and any other arb. I had to conclude that Boesky sucked him in.

And now, on this day, I could feel Milken's personal pain perhaps better than anyone else in America.

Getting your comeuppance hurts.

The ache lodges in your throat and remains there for a long, long time.

ALTHOUGH the investigation continues, for me, in a real sense, it is over. Laurie and I are extremely grateful for the positive reactions displayed by so many of our friends and business associates. To my surprise, upon my return to society, many companies sought out my advice. The luckiest aspect for me was that I was still relatively young, able to start over. This time I will do it right.

My goal, through the ADASAR Group, has been to go back into the business community and apply whatever skills I have with enthusiasm, and it is working. It is an uplifting feeling to realize that there are many fine men and women in the business world who believe that a man should be given a second chance.

INDEX